The History of Migration in Europe

The History of Migration in Europe belies several myths by arguing, for example, that immobility has not been the "normal" condition of people before the modern era. Migration (far from being an income-maximizing choice taken by lone individuals) is often a household strategy, and local wages benefit from migration. This book shows how successes arise when governments liberalize and accompany the international movements of people with appropriate legislation, while failures take place when the legislation enacted is insufficient, belated or ill shaped.

Part I of this book addresses mainly methodological issues. Past and present migration is basically defined as a cross-cultural movement; cultural boundaries need prolonged residence and active integrationist policies to allow the cross-fertilization of cultures among migrants and non-migrants. Part II collects chapters that examine the role of public bodies with reference to migratory movements, depicting a series of successes and failures in the migration policies through examples drawn from the European Union or single countries. Part III deals with the challenges that immigrants face once they have settled in their new countries: Do immigrants seek "integration" in their host culture? Through which channels is such integration achieved, and what roles are played by citizenship and political participation? What is the "identity" of migrants and their children born in the host countries?

This text's originality stems from the fact that it explains the complex nature of migratory movements by incorporating a variety of perspectives and using a multi-disciplinary approach, including economic, political and sociological contributions.

Francesca Fauri is Assistant Professor and Jean Monnet Chair in Economic and Migration History at the University of Bologna, Italy. Her research centres on Italian and European economic history, with a specific interest in the economic causes and impact of migration movements. In 2013 she won a Basic Research University Funding award to broaden her studies to the use of remittances and the history of immigrant business in Europe. She has co-edited *Novel Outlooks on the Marshall Plan* (Lang, 2011).

Routledge explorations in economic history
Edited by Lars Magnusson
Uppsala University, Sweden

The History of Migration in Europe

Perspectives from economics, politics and sociology

Edited by Francesca Fauri

Routledge
Taylor & Francis Group

LONDON AND NEW YORK

First published 2015 by Routledge

2 Park Square, Milton Park, Abingdon, Oxfordshire OX14 4RN
52 Vanderbilt Avenue, New York, NY 10017

Routledge is an imprint of the Taylor & Francis Group, an informa business

First issued in paperback 2019

British Library Cataloguing in Publication Data
A catalogue record for this book is available from the British Library

Library of Congress Cataloging in Publication Data
The history of migration in Europe: perspectives from economics, politics and sociology / edited by Francesca Angela Fauri.
    1. Europe–Emigration and immigration–History. 2. Migration, Internal–
    Ireland–History. 3. Europe–Emigration and immigration–Social aspects.
    4. Europe–Emigration and immigration–Economic aspects. I. Fauri,
    Francesca.
    JV7590.H59 2014
    304.8094–dc23   2014017617

ISBN: 978-1-138-77783-5 (hbk)
ISBN: 978-0-367-87009-6 (pbk)

Typeset in Times New Roman
by Wearset Ltd, Boldon, Tyne and Wear

Contents

Plates and figures

Plates

Figures

Tables

Contributors

Paola Corti is Professor of Contemporary History at the University of Turin. She has contributed to and collaborated with various Italian and foreign journals and cultural institutions. She is the author of many books and articles on contemporary society and Italian and international migration history. Her more recent publications include: *Storia d'Italia: Annali 24.Migrazioni*, Torino, Einaudi, 2009 (edited with M. Sanfilippo); *Emigranti e immigrati nelle rappresentazioni di fotografi e fotogiornalisti*, Foligno, Editoriale umbra, 2010; *Storia delle migrazioni internazionali*, Bari-Roma, Laterza 2010; *L'Italia e le migrazioni*, Bari-Roma, Laterza, 2012 (with M. Sanfilippo); *Temi e problemi di storia delle migrazioni*, Viterbo, Sette città, 2013.

Alessandra De Rose is Professor of Demography with courses in the PhD school in Demography. She is the Director of the Department of Methods and Models for Economics, Territory and Finance at the University La Sapienza in Rome and President of the Italian Association for Population Studies. Her main research interests are in the fields of family demography, marriage and union dissolution, gender studies, analysis of the relationship between population dynamics and social and economic trends.

Thomas Faist is Professor for the Sociology of Transnationalization, Development and Migration at the Faculty of Sociology at Bielefeld University, Dean of the Faculty and Deputy Director of the Collaborative Research Centre 882 "From Heterogeneities to Inequalities". His fields of interest are transnational relations, citizenship, social policy, development and migration. He held visiting professorships at Malmö University and the University of Toronto. Thomas Faist is a member of the editorial boards of *Ethnic and Racial Studies*, *South Asian Diaspora*, *Social Inclusion*, *Migration and Development* and the *Pakistan Journal of Social Issues*. Books he recently co-published include *Beyond Methodological Nationalism: Social Science Research Methodologies in Transition* (2012), *Transnational Migration* (2013) and *Disentangling Migration and Climate Change* (2013). His current research focuses on the transnational social question.

Francesca Fauri is Assistant Professor of Economic History at the University of Bologna, where she teaches Economic History at the School of Economics in Bologna and European Economic History at the School of Political Science in Forlì. She has published extensively on Italian and European economic history. She is vice-president of Forlì's Europe Direct Centre which in 2014 was nominated by the European Commission "Jean Monnet Centre of Excellence". She has won a Jean Monnet Chair in 2011 and Basic Research University Funding (FARB) in 2013, thanks to which she has concentrated her current main research interests on Italian and European emigration history, the use of remittances and the history of immigrant business in Europe.

Harlan Koff is Professor of Social Sciences at the University of Luxembourg. He is the President of the Consortium for Comparative Research on Regional Integration and Social Cohesion (RISC) as well as co-editor of the journal *Regions and Cohesion* (Berghahn Journals). His research focuses on migration, border politics and international development.

Jan Lucassen is Emeritus Professor of Social History of the Free University in Amsterdam, and research fellow attached to the International Institute of Social History. His research focuses on labour migration and the history of work.

Leo Lucassen is Director of Research of the International Institute of Social History (IISH) in Amsterdam and Professor of Global Migration and Labour History at the Institute for History in Leiden.

Debora Mantovani is Assistant Professor of Sociology at the Department of Political and Social Sciences of the University of Bologna. Her main research interests are in the fields of immigration and educational inequalities.

Gloria Naranjo Giraldo is Associate Professor at the University of Antioquia, Colombia with teaching experience in the fields of political science and anthropology. Her emphases on research are: migration, borders, citizenship and public policy. She is currently a PhD student co-supervised at the University of Granada, Spain and the University of Luxembourg.

Cormac Ó Gráda is Professor Emeritus, School of Economics, University College Dublin. His earliest publications were on the economic history of Ireland. His books on Ireland include *Ireland: A New Economic History 1780–1939* (Oxford, 1994), *Black '47 and Beyond* (Princeton, 1999) and *Jewish Ireland since the Age of Joyce: A Socioeconomic History* (Princeton, 2006). More recently he has focused on the global history of famines, and he is the author of *Famine: A Short History* (Princeton, 2009). In 2011 he was awarded the Gold Medal of the Royal Irish Academy for his work.

Gianmarco I. P. Ottaviano is Professor of Economics at the London School of Economics and Political Science and at the University of Bologna; Director of the Globalisation Programme at the Centre for Economic Performance, London; Research Fellow of the Centre for Economic Policy Research, London; Research Fellow of the Center for Financial Studies, Frankfurt; and

Non-resident Senior Fellow of Bruegel, Brussels. He is the co-author of many works in international trade, urban economics and economic geography. His recent publications focus on the competitiveness of European firms in the global economy as well as the economic effects of immigration and offshoring on employment and wages.

Sandro Rinauro is Assistant Professor at the Department of International, Legal, Historical and Political Studies, University of Milan, where he teaches Political and Economic Geography. His publications and research interests focus on Italy's emigration and immigration movements since the Second World War, on Italy's illegal emigration and on the history of social and statistical research since the nineteenth century.

Cristina Blanco Sío-López has earned a PhD in EU History and Policies at the European University Institute (EUI) and is currently a researcher at CVCE – *Centre Virtuel de la Connaissance sur l'Europe* – in Luxembourg. Her research interests focus on the history of European integration and European institutions, with particular attention to the European Parliament. She is currently in charge of two projects: "Spain and the construction of Europe" and the Action Jean Monnet project entitled "Initiative and constraint in the mapping of evolving European borders".

Donatella Strangio is Associate Professor of Economic History in the Department of Methods and Models for Economics, Territory and Finance at University La Sapienza in Rome, with courses in *European Integration Policies* – Master EuroSapienza *European and International Policies and Crisis Management.* Her main research interests focus on Italian migration, finance history, the economics of European Integration and Italian colonial history.

Paolo Tedeschi is Assistant Professor of Economic History at the University of Milan-Bicocca DEMS, where he teaches Economic History and European Integration History. He is also Assistant Professor at the University of Luxembourg, where he teaches European Integration History. His recent research and publications concern, in particular: the history of European integration, the economic history of Lombardy (eighteenth–twentieth centuries), and the history of Lombard business organizations, trade unions and friendly societies.

Pierre Tilly is Lecturer and Research Fellow at the Université catholique of Louvain, where he chairs the Centre for the Study of Contemporary European History. His fields of research are namely the economic and social history of the European integration, the colonial history and the dynamics of frontiers.

M. Elisabetta Tonizzi teaches contemporary history at the School of Social Science of the University of Genoa. Her research interests include the economic and social aspects of maritime history. She is a member of the editorial board of the *International Journal of Maritime History* and *Italia Contemporanea*.

Vera Zamagni is Professor of Economic History at the University of Bologna. She has published more than 20 books and 80 articles in Italian, English and Spanish on Italy's economic development since unification. Her research interests focus on regional disequilibria, income distribution and standard of living, and on business history themes such as the role of state intervention in the economy and the development of the cooperative movement.

Preface

Francesca Fauri

When, in 2011, I was awarded an EU Jean Monnet Chair with a project on Italian and European migratory movements, my research on the subject had just begun. As my effort went deeper I realized that a full understanding of past and contemporary migratory processes cannot be achieved by relying on the tools of one discipline alone or by focusing on single-level analyses: we need to broaden the investigation and rely on a multi-disciplinary approach. That's why I conceptualized this book, which embodies the contributions of top level authors in different disciplines and using different perspectives.

As an economic historian I can say that the theoretical approach to immigration that has prevailed for the past 50 years among economists does not come to terms with the complexities of the current reality nor, for that matter, with the migration flows of the past. It is quite clear that migrants do not merely respond to economic disparities between countries. Although migration is clearly related to differentials in wages and employment, economic disparities alone are not enough to explain international movements. Traditional explanations need to be modified to give more weight to non-pecuniary factors: when, for instance, the costs of leaving one's home country are high, they may predominate over expected gains from immigration. Similarly, migration cannot be considered an income-maximizing choice taken by an individual alone, but, as historians underline, it is often a household strategy, a decision taken within the family context to support and improve life conditions at home. Remittances may thus be considered as one of the most fundamental objectives of the decision to migrate, a choice which is made collectively for the well-being of the entire family group. Thus, the relationship with the family in the home country represents the core element of many migratory processes.

The complex nature of migratory movements requires a sophisticated theory that incorporates a variety of perspectives and a multidisciplinary approach. This is what this book aims at: to focus on the history of migration past and the present impact on Europe, through a multi-disciplinary approach that includes economic, political and sociological contributions.

I would like to bear witness to the great interest to which this cross-cultural multi-disciplinary adventure gave rise and that has made this book not only intellectually rewarding but also extremely fertile for stimulating intellectual confrontation and developing mutual understanding among an international community of scholars. A large part of the contributions included here originated, to some degree, in a conference on "Emigration from and to Europe: A Multidisciplinary Long-term View", held in Forlì, Italy in December 2013; in that venue some of the texts, in a preliminary version, were presented and discussed by their authors. The fertility of the perspectives and the findings of those papers suggested the opportunity to develop those works for this volume.

Finally, I should like to thank the members of the scientific committee – Paolo Tedeschi, Elisabetta Tonizzi and Vera Zamagni – as well as Fabio Casini and the Forlì Jean Monnet Centre of Excellence, for their assistance throughout the project. Without the funding of the above-mentioned EU Jean Monnet Chair my research and the gathering of such a prestigious group of scholars would not have been possible.

Abbreviations

AIRE	Registry of Italians Living Abroad
CCMR	Cross-cultural migration rate
CDLR	Committee on Local and Regional Democracy
CGE	Commissariato Generale per l'Emigrazione
CLOTI	Comité de liaison des organisations des travailleurs immigrés
EC	European Council
ECSC	European Coal and Steel Community
EDC	European Defence Community
EEC	European Economic Community
EIB	European Investment Bank
ESC	Economic and Social Committee
ESF	European Social Fund
ESS	European Social Survey
HAEU	Historical Archives of the EU
HDI	Human Development Index
ICEM	Intergovernmental Committee for European Migration
ICLE	Istituto per il credito del lavoro italiano all'estero
ILO	International Labour Organization
INES	Irish National Election Study
IOM	International Organization for Migration
IRO	International Refugee Organisation
OEEC	Organisation for European Economic Co-operation
PICMME	Provisional Intergovernmental Committee for the Movement of Migrants from Europe
PRO	Public Record Office
UN	United Nations

Introduction

Vera Zamagni

This book can claim a special originality, because it defeats several myths, among which are the following: (1) that sedentariness has been the "normal" way of life of people before the modern era; (2) that migrations only started in modern times and have constantly increased their numbers; (3) that the migrants are people who individually decide to improve their lives by migrating; (4) that politics has only a negative role in migrations, keeping certain areas backward or closing borders. None of these themes can be exhausted here, but each of the chapters raises questions and provides answers that often defeat conventional wisdom.

I would like to start a brief overview of the book chapters with a discussion of the idea of sedentariness, which was considered the normal way of living since the agrarian age, started some ten millennia ago. In the preceding forest-pastoral age, people were continuously mobile, wandering about to collect food, chase animals and find better places in which to spend their short lives. As Fisher has rightly stated: "We are all descendants of migrants."[1] Such migrations were generally *collective* and not individual, for reasons of defence and generation. When the agricultural age started independently in some parts of the world, not all people were involved in the new civilization and many remained nomadic. This gave rise for many millennia to a clash between nomadic and settled communities, which mixed up people and altered societies. Nomadic communities were in general better equipped of strong and cruel warriors than settled communities, which had to rely on farming and had a large population of peasants and slaves (or serfs) devoted to cultivation, the domestication of animals and the building and maintenance of larger and larger cities. Settled communities were in general richer and better organized, but fragile in their large land areas that were difficult to protect.

Nomadic communities were often capable of winning major agrarian empires, sometimes displacing them entirely for a long period, at other times substituting the local elites with their own, while adopting their culture and their civilization. The most well-known example of the former case is the defeat of the Roman Empire, which had been able for many centuries to protect itself, though not easily, from the "barbarian" attacks, but ultimately collapsed. An example of the latter case is the fall of the Ming dynasty in China. In spite of having tried to constrict central Asian nomadic raiders by settling military and farming colonies on their borders and by rebuilding and extending the Great Wall over 13,000 miles, the Ming dynasty could not resist the Manchu people, who by the middle of the seventeenth century invaded China and conquered power, ruling for many centuries. We can conclude therefore that not even in the agrarian age sedentariness prevailed, as a result of the many migrations produced by wars of conquest, colonization and defence. The prevailing motivations of the aggressions by nomadic people were generically economic – to get hold of the wealth of farming communities – but the conquest was achieved not by economic, but by military means.

Around AD 600, other types of migrations were added to the existing ones, mostly within the Mediterranean area: "holy" wars of conquest by Muslims and Christians, as well as pilgrimages towards the "holy" places. To these movements of people, a new class of merchants added the first important *individual* economic motive for migrating: opening up markets and enlarging the size of their business. The enlargement of commercial cities induced migrations from the countryside, which became more substantial when industrialization started in the eighteenth century and more cities came into existence. The vast geographical explorations that took place since the middle of the fifteenth century by the Europeans were led by the merchants and their large commercial companies and were supported by the European states, giving rise to migration waves of all types: forced migrations (mostly slaves, but also displaced people), settlement of nearly empty areas (North America, Australia), colonization of the least organized people around the world (central and South America, India, Africa). The motivations of these migrations were again economic and the means employed were partly economic, but largely supported by military power. The largest empire that ever existed in the world, the British Empire, was conquered by merchants, privateers and companies, and only later defended and governed by state power.

The age of the industrial revolution largely activated migrations from the countryside to the cities, but cities could well be outside the "nation" of residence. All along the nineteenth century the nation state strengthened its diffusion with a number of processes of "unification" in Europe and elsewhere and the migratory movements within the boundaries of nations were no longer considered of interest, so that the definition of "migrant" was reserved to those who chose to settle in another nation. Statistics were then collected to highlight this "inter-national" phenomenon, which started to be considered as a relatively recent one, while recent in true fact it was not.

This book starts here, with five chapters that address mainly *methodological issues*. The first chapter by Leo and Jan Lucassen aims at identifying a broader definition of migration than the one commonly used of inter-national migration, at the same time avoiding the trap of including all types of *mobility*. After considering the many definitions of migrants produced by the literature, the authors build their own, based on a sociocultural paradigm: migration can be basically defined as a *cross-cultural movement*. What the migrant crosses is a *cultural boundary*, encompassing important differences in values, technologies, religions, political systems and social rules; only in some cases this entails a crossing of political borders and the coverage of long geographical distances. A prolonged residence, that does not necessarily encompass the entire life of migrants, is needed to allow the cross-fertilization of cultures between migrants and non-migrants. Leo and Jan Lucassen have then to come to terms with statistical problems and they include in their definition movements of people that one way or the other can be measured: immigration and emigration as they are usually defined, plus movements of people to cities or the inverse movement to colonize the countryside, plus seasonal movements and temporal multiannual movements (soldiers, sailors, artisans and possibly other categories like domestics and journeymen).

Their extensive collection of data for Europe (European Russia included) starts as far back as the sixteenth century and reaches the twentieth century. There is much to be learned from these results. First, that the temporal multi-annual migrants and the migrants to cities were by far the most important components of the migration aggregate. Second, that emigration out of Europe was of massive importance between the middle of the nineteenth and the middle of the twentieth centuries, but did not constitute the majority of migrants even in this century. Third, that immigration into Europe started as an important phenomenon only in the second half of the twentieth century. Fourth, percentage-wise on the adjusted population there wasn't much change in the impact of migrations until the end of the eighteenth century; in the nineteenth century there was a substantial increase, but the real exploit was in the first half of the twentieth century, when as much as two-thirds of the European population was made up of migrants. Also rather surprizing is the diminished rate in the second half of the twentieth century, the reason being the important decrease of the temporary multiannual migration and of emigration.

The chapter by Leo and Jan Lucassen ends with two additional points: (a) a possible alternative in the use of data, i.e. the exclusion of migrants to cities within European states, on the grounds that such movements do not really cross cultures. This produces lower levels of migrations, but much the same pattern over time; (b) the extension of this work to cover Asia, something that the authors of the chapter are engaged in doing and that appears from preliminary results to lend support to the definition of migrations proposed by them.

The second chapter, by Paola Corti, deals with similar methodological issues from a sociological point of view, discussing the prevailing approach of considering migrations only a recent phenomenon. She reminds us that mobility was already employed by the household as a "normal" way of earning a living in the *Ancien Régime* (early modern times), by sending some of the members elsewhere to learn a craft, to serve in aristocratic milieus, to build churches and palaces, to paint portraits and decorate public and private buildings, to attend universities, to serve in armies, and to practice the "profession" of pedlar. Mountainous areas would send most of their people away for considerable spans of their lives. What this author specifically stresses are two aspects of this phenomenon: (a) migrations start and are more widespread in more developed areas (the Italian case being a good example of this); (b) it is the family that decides the migratory strategy and not the single individual. The chapter also addresses the issue of continuity or breaks in the migratory processes. The author is of the view that the big spurt in emigration achieved across the nineteenth and the twentieth century was produced by much the same old patterns within a new environment. Indeed, from Lucassen's data it appears that there is no break in the "quality" of migration patterns until the second half of the twentieth century, while there is certainly a break in quantities of migrations in the first half of the twentieth century.

The work by the economic historian Maria Elisabetta Tonizzi that is reported in Chapter 3 deals with the main reason for the explosion of migrations in Europe in the first half of the twentieth century: better and more rapid means of transport. She concentrates on steam ships, which allowed the transoceanic flows of migrations to grow as never before. The description she offers of the "age of sail" is appalling, with people amassed on old and unsafe ships, lack of food and water, the diffusion of all sorts of diseases, so that those ships were labelled "floating hells" or "coffin-ships". In the age of steam and steel, ships were enlarged and improved, the time needed to cross the Atlantic was shortened and regularly operated services were introduced. It was a true revolution in sea transportation, but a similar revolution took place in land transportation through the introduction of the steam locomotive. The chapter by Tonizzi continues by analysing the role of steamship companies, which became major businesses and deployed important organizational skills.

The fourth chapter, by the sociologist Thomas Faist, addresses another methodological question: if migration is mostly connected to the need of persons and families to improve their material conditions, does transnationality help in this? The author first tries to define transnationality as including all the cross-border transactions (financial, political, social, cultural). The meaning of border is defined generally as a physical border between nations, but the author agrees that this could be an unnecessary limitation of the concept. Next, he focuses on *inequalities* as a measure useful to judge the impact of migrations, and for the purpose of analysing this impact he proposes the building up of a transnational social space encompassing more than one state, so as to capture the effects of migrations on the sending and receiving countries. When this is done, it is possible to build a graph with two variables: *transnationality* (horizontal axis) and *capital* (including all forms of convertible resources, vertical axis). All four fields of the graph are to be used to locate people with reference to inequality, each space representing a continuum that can accommodate various degrees of the presence of the two variables, namely a heterogeneity of endowments and a propensity to move. If this approach can allow a more realistic analysis of the impact of migration, which can benefit some more than others and can even be a failure, one problem left is the definition of inequality selected for comparison, which tends to be differently defined in various societies. The author claims that his approach necessitates the analysis of the concept of inequality used, by at least comparing the different perceptions of inequality in existence. Whatever the equity concept employed, the answer to the question raised on whether transnationality helps in improving material conditions cannot be univocal. Inequalities between countries might be increased rather than diminished if migrations entail the movement of skilled workers, but inequalities within countries too might be increased by migrations if the unskilled workers received by an advanced country are not helped in integrating and enlarge the lower classes of that country.

The first section of the book ends with another methodological chapter, this time by the economist Gianmarco Ottaviano, who discusses the possible explanations of an empirical phenomenon that goes against the conventional wisdom of orthodox economic models, namely the observed improvement of wages and employment opportunities for native workers after immigration in at least a number of cases. He supports the view that orthodox models forecast that native workers will see their wages decrease, because they assume that the quality of native workers and immigrants is the same. If the quality is not equal, then the impact of immigration on the wages of the locals can be positive, as indeed it has been found in some empirical works. He also supports the view that it is indeed highly probable that the quality of native and immigrant workers is different, as a result of different education and experience. So, to identify the impact of immigration, there are more variables that need to be taken into consideration beside wages: employment and other "instrumental" variables that help in deciding the direction of causation.

In the light of the five chapters of Part I, we can say that the migratory movements encompass more components than simple inter-national flows, are often the result of collective choices (not always of individual ones), do not present major breaks in quality up until the second half of the twentieth century, while quantities are boosted in the second half of the nineteenth century by more rapid means of transport, and have impacts that are often different from what has been maintained until recently in terms of inequalities and the behaviour of native wages.

Part II of the book collects chapters that address one way or another the *role of public bodies* with reference to migratory movements, producing examples applied to single countries that mostly cover the latter half of the twentieth century. The chapter by the economic historian Francesca Fauri is concerned with the reactivation in Europe of the emigration flows that had been dying out in the 1930s as a result of the 1929 crisis. On top of the voluntary emigration of those who wanted to improve their lot, there were also flows of displaced people and refugees. An international agency connected with the UN started to lend legal protection to the refugees, while Europe only succeeded in putting in place an agency in 1952 with the aim of supplying transport and other services to those who wished to emigrate. The agency was also active in facilitating emigration. The author has gathered new archival materials to reconstruct the activity of the European agency from its foundation to the 1980s. She then moves to highlight what the Italian government did in the field of emigration immediately after the end of the Second World War, a relevant issue, given that most of the European emigrants at the time were Italians. When the steps towards European economic integration commenced, Italy supported the proposal of free movement of workers inside the community and in the end she was successful, though the complete liberalization of the labour market inside the EEC was achieved only in 1969.

But soon the European Union (EU) had to face the reverse flow, that of immigration from countries outside the Union. This, as noted before, is a real break with the past. Immigration into Europe by non-Europeans had always been a marginal phenomenon, after the invasions by Muslims and Ottomans. The data gathered by Lucassen and Lucassen too show that this immigration represents an absolute novelty. The chapter by Cristina Blanco Sío-López and Paolo Tedeschi gives an account first of the steps taken by the EU in the field of provisions for migrants and unemployed people, with the birth of the European Social Fund (ESF) mostly devoted to European Migrants. When Greece, Spain and Portugal entered the Union, the migrants from these countries too were considered "internal" migrants, but soon the immigration of people from outside the Union started. The chapter mostly deals with this new issue in relation with Spain, but it does quote EU decisions that apply generally. Among these, the 1985 Schengen agreement for free circulation of EU citizens is important, as well as the establishment of Frontex in 2006, to patrol the EU borders. Also the 2008 European Pact on Immigration and Asylum is of interest, although it actually legislated asylum, not general immigration. The well-known fact is that the present situation of the EU immigration policies is still very unsatisfactory, as the Lampedusa's events have repeatedly shown.

The next chapter is an interesting story of Irish immigration and legislation. The author, Cormac Ó Gráda, is well known as a historian of Irish emigration, and this time he wanted to deal with a little known chapter of the Irish history of immigration at the beginning of the twentieth century, before dealing with the present day issues of immigration into Ireland. The episode analysed tells of an alleged discrimination of foreigners in Ireland following the 1905 British Aliens Act. The author documents the "accidentality" of the tiny immigration of Jews and Italians before the First World War and their petty or strange activities that attracted negative reactions by the natives, although nothing that prevented the immigrants from continuing to live there. Then he moves on to the last decade, giving illustration of the anti-immigration feelings of the Irish, who pressed for a more restrictive immigration policy, particularly in the years of the very rapid inflow of immigrants, rising from 15 per cent of the population in 2002 to 25 per cent in 2005. Last, he touches upon the hot problem of the links between immigration and the welfare state, focusing on the story of "citizenship tourism", namely the habit of having a child in Ireland as an illegal immigrant, because the legislation allowed both the child and his/her mother to become Irish citizens, a practice dismissed by the 2004 referendum.

The next chapter, by Sandro Rinauro, deals with the widespread phenomenon of illegal immigration, which is so difficult to document. He sets out to sketch it for the Italian case, in a comprehensive and original way, by covering first Italian illegal emigration since the nineteenth century and next illegal immigration into Italy, a much more recent phenomenon. It is interesting to read in his chapter that illegal emigration was banned before the First World War by the Italian legislation and not by the legislation of the countries of destination, which were quite liberal. From the 1920s, the countries of immigration progressively enacted restrictive legislation, with the result of increasing the percentage of illegal immigrants, within totals that were much smaller. His example of Italian emigration into France between 1920 and 1933 is paradigmatic: illegal flows reached two-thirds of the total. After the Second World War, illegal flows of Italian migrants peaked again, the estimate being that illegal migrants doubled legal ones. Often this illegality was accepted, if not encouraged, by the receiving countries for a host of reasons. The decisions about free mobility of labour within the Common Market discontinued this flow of illegal Italian migrants, but promoted similar flows from other nations, like Portugal and Spain. The conclusion of the author are twofold: on the one side, official statistics underplay the actual migration flows, while present day illegal immigration from Africa into the EU is not a new phenomenon, although the conditions that bring migrants into Italy are worse even with reference to those prevailing at the time of sail ships. Rinauro shows that the extent of the Italian underground economy is the main cause of this illegality, pretty much as it was for the Italian illegal emigrants in many European nations after the Second World War. Legislation remains the main factor responsible in shaping the modes of migrations.

On another issue, which has become relevant above all after the Second World War – that of the so called "brain-drain" – we have Italy as an example. Donatella Strangio and Alessandra De Rose provide an illustration of this issue in the case of Italian emigration into Australia. This recent phenomenon is placed in the contest of the long term flows of Italian migrants to Australia, that reveals an important post-Second World War peak, then a remarkable slowdown in the period of general decrease of Italian emigration, followed by an unexpected increase in the first decade of the twenty-first century, which can be explained precisely in terms of skilled migration. This type of migration peaks when the crisis in the sending countries like Italy deepens and is a sign of the failure by the public authorities of the sending countries to develop appropriate incentives to employ skilled labour at home.

On the whole, Part II of the book depicts a series of successes and failures in migration policies. Successes arise when governments liberalize and accompany the international movements of people with appropriate legislation, while failures take place when the legislation enacted is insufficient, belated or ill shaped. But what clearly emerges is also that the movements of people can sometime overwhelm any legislation, when they are too large and temporally concentrated.

Part III of this book addresses some of the problems immigrants have to face not in the process of migrating, but once they have settled. This field of research is huge and has so far attracted mostly the interest of sociologists and political scientists, but it might be an interesting topic for historians of the future as well.

Do the immigrants want to "integrate" into the culture of the host countries? Which are the channels of integration – citizenship, political participation? Which is the "identity" of migrants and of their children born in the host countries? The chapter by Pierre Tilly gives an account of the belated opening of Belgium to voting in local elections by immigrants who are citizens of other EU countries (and later also to citizens of third countries) after the pronunciation of the EU in 1998. He puts this in a historical context, reminding us that the initial forms of participation by immigrants were in voluntary associations and trade unions and in local work and consultative councils, while it was only in the last decade that the step forward was made, with the EU having to send an "ultimatum" before the Belgian constitution would be amended. The author concludes that the acquisition of nationality remains the most important channel to acquire full political rights.

The chapter by Harlan Koff and Gloria Naranjo Giraldo discusses the position of EU areas that border with "non-European" areas and experience at the same time political division and efforts at cooperation, with places that only stress the former and other places that open up to the latter. The chapter produces two examples: Melilla–Nador and Bari–Durres. Melilla is a Spanish enclave in Moroccan territory and is surrounded by walls, but informally economic, social and cultural relations are entertained with the neighbouring town of Nador. This border has been a focal point of migration into Europe, with very active local NGOs, but it remains incapable of forging a really inclusive strategy. Bari too has been an important migration transit first for Albanians and later for nationals of other countries, mostly arriving through Albania. Bari stands out as a place where civil society cooperation has been important, often overcoming informality and building up official programmes to increase cross-border trade and investments, with the help of the EU. In their conclusions, the authors contrast the two examples and conclude that cross-border relations could be interpreted in a positive and constructive sense.

The final chapter, by the sociologist Debora Mantovani, reports the results of an extensive survey conducted in 15 secondary schools of Bologna among students, some of whom were foreigners or children of mixed nationality couples. The purpose was that of ascertaining the concept of "identity" these students declared to have with reference to the "communities" to which they reported being members of. The results are very interesting, both for Italians and non-Italians, because they reveal a widespread tendency to open up the concept of "citizenship" to encompass more than one nation, combining cultural elements and producing "multifaceted national identities". These complex identities sometime produce individual or family conflicts, but most of the time are seen as capable of reaching a superior synthesis.

In general, the final part of this book shows how outdated are the policies that today face, in Europe, the challenges of migrants coming from areas that do not share the basic cultural pillars of Western societies. The migrants themselves are engaged in finding practical solutions to bridge the differences, but open conflicts do exist.

There is one final contribution that the book as a whole makes. Migrations have predominantly been considered by the political, economic and sociological literature as a special topic, of interest to those directly concerned, but irrelevant for the general issues dealt with by those disciplines. This book shows that such a vision is totally inadequate, because it prevents a more appropriate analysis of social phenomena, in which migrations are intertwined with the other social factors. The relevance of migrations for the shaping of societies is an old story, but today more so than ever. If in fact we employ Leo and Jan Lucassen's definition of migration as a cross-cultural movement, we can easily admit that the more distant the cultures that come into contact are, the more impressive the impact of migrations on societies will be. In the past, there are numerous examples of migrations that entail a great "distance" of cultures, the insertion of African slaves into America being perhaps the most prominent one, but in general most migrants belonged to the same basic European culture, although interpreted in a variety of ways. Today, as a result of the fact that most migrants come from outside Europe, the "distance" among cultures of origin and cultures of destination is quite generalized, and the impact of migrations therefore much more substantial. It is time for the social scientists to face this new challenge.

Note

1 M. H. Fisher, *Migration. A World History*, Oxford, Oxford University Press, 2014, p. xii.

Part I

Who are the migrants and what is their impact?

1 Quantifying and qualifying cross-cultural migrations in Europe since 1500

A plea for a broader view[1]

Leo Lucassen and Jan Lucassen

Introduction

Although migration is the talk of the town, both in the public sphere and in academia, so far historians and social scientists have failed to come up with generally accepted definitions and typologies to measure and qualify migration in the long run. Whereas some (e.g. national statistical agencies) concentrate on people who cross international borders, others – guided by the concerns of politicians and policy makers – limit themselves to 'problematic' groups, either socially, culturally or a mix of both. In Europe this has led to a myopic view that privileges migrants from Muslim countries, whereas in the United States Hispanics attract the most attention (Zolberg and Woon, 1999). That conspicuous migrants need not always come from afar is shown by the problematization of Zimbabwean workers in South Africa (Wentzel *et al.*, 2006; Crush and Tavera, 2010), or internal migrants who have flocked in great numbers to large cities within large empires such as Russia and China (Siegelbaum and Moch, 2014; Whyte, 2010; Shen, 2014).

These diverging and partial definitions of what migration is make structured comparisons through space and time extremely difficult, if not impossible. We therefore have great trouble in assessing the rate of migration in different societies and time periods. As a consequence, questions as to whether some societies are more mobile than others, or whether in the current world we have indeed reached the zenith of spatial mobility, as many assume, cannot be answered satisfactorily. Scholars are even divided about such fundamental questions as to what constitutes a migratory step, let alone what impact such steps have on both migrants and the societies where they settle. As a result there is no agreement on key questions such as whether early modern societies were indeed less mobile than modern ones; whether we can compare current illegal African migrants in Spain to Bretons moving to Paris in the nineteenth century; and whether the mass migrations to Manchuria after 1860 are principally different from the Atlantic mass migrations to North America (Moch, 2012; McKeown, 2004. For North America, see Taylor, 2002).

This messy state of affairs, at least in analytical terms, explains partially why migration does not play a key role in larger debates on the long term determinants of economic growth, labour relations, inequality and social and cultural changes of human societies (Van Zanden, 2009; Morris, 2013; Putterman and Weil, 2010; Manning, 2013). Instead the phenomenon is largely reduced to a "problem" of low skilled and culturally alien newcomers who have to be assimilated or integrated by nation states. This leaves out the high skilled, temporary organizational migrants (those working for internationally operating organizations such as churches, states, NGOs and companies) and internal migrants. It is this myopic migration-as-a-problem framework produced by states and societies that dominates migration studies and severely limits our possibilities to study and understand the causes and effects of human migrations.

Although many students have suggested definitions, typologies and methods, historians and social scientists cherish their own idiosyncrasies and approaches or simply reproduce prevailing policy categories. This is partly explained by different research agendas and questions,[2] levels of analysis, and various forms of methodological nationalism and presentism (Wimmer and Glick Schiller, 2003), but it is also nourished by an unwillingness and an understandable but unjustified fear regarding too broad generalizations. These objections, however, have not restrained migration historians from publishing all kinds of wide-ranging and even global overviews, with mostly implicit (but mutually inconsistent) definitions of migration.

We think that many of the fears of, and aversion to, a uniform definition of migration are unwarranted and that they need not necessarily lead to reductionism and meaningless levels of aggregation. Instead of harking back to a naive and outdated form of structuralism, following Nancy Green we propose a 'poststructural structuralism' (Green, 1997), which combines explicit research designs and definitions with nuanced, layered, contextual, and culturally embedded historical research.

In this chapter we propose a method and typology that uses a much broader definition of human mobility and that helps us to make sense of the varied historical experience by allowing us to compare migrations on a global and historical scale. The model has been developed on the basis of migrations in Europe between 1500 and 2000, but is also applicable on a global scale (Lucassen and Lucassen, 2014b). The aim of this approach is not only to contribute to discussions about levels of migration and mobility in different parts of the world before and after the industrial revolution, but more importantly to better understand the effect different forms of migration have on social, cultural, and economic change.

Migration and mobility: definitions and concepts

The main reason for the wide range of migration definitions is the reliance on sources produced by states, which stem from their interest in certain types of migration. Thus France in the early nineteenth century created an administrative system that enabled bureaucrats to follow the residential moves of draftees until their mid-forties, so that they could be mobilized if necessary (Farcy and Faure,

2003; Lucassen, 1987). Empires like Russia (before and after 1917), Tokugawa Japan, and Maoist China or apartheid South Africa, also monitored internal migrations, for both economic and political reasons.[3] With the rise of the nation state, crossing national boundaries and the wish to distinguish between citizens and aliens became by far the most dominant criteria relating to migration (Torpey, 2000; Caplan and Torpey, 2001; Fahrmeir, 2007; McKeown, 2008). The idea that one's own citizens should enjoy preferential social, economic and political rights, but also that citizens abroad should be protected against unfair treatment (Gabaccia, 2012; Green and Weil, 2007), explains the rise of what Gerard Noiriel so succinctly called "la tyrannie du national" (Noiriel, 1991).

The gaze of the state has proved hugely influential in the way scholars have studied migration and this has privileged some definitions over others. States defined "migration", subsequently counted "migrants", and the resulting statistical data have determined the categories used by historians and social scientists. At the same time scholars were lured away from basic questions regarding the *distance* travelled, the *type of borders* people crossed, the *intention of the move*, and the *time spent* away from home. Because state definitions loom heavily, "real" migration is often juxtaposed to "only" spatial mobility, assuming that "real" migrants travel over long distances, cross international (or even intercontinental) boundaries, and have the aim to take root at destination, or at least stay away for many years, leading to standard distinctions as shown in Table 1.1.

Although within the field of migration history there is no *communis opinio* about these binary oppositions, most scholars abide by the conventional definition of "real migrants". When it comes to distance, for example, most migration

Table 1.1 Conventional binary oppositions between migrants and movers

	Real migrants (migration)	Other movers (mobility)
Distance (geographical)	Long	Short
Border crossing	International/intercontinental	Internal (municipal, regional, provincial, federal state)
Intention	Final stay at destination	Return to origin in short or long run (sojourners)
Time	Long term	Short term (seasonal, multi-annual labour migrants)
New social ties	High (at least in the long run)	Low (social and cultural isolation in gated communities)
Class	Low	High (e.g. expats) and low (e.g. Gypsies)
Power	Migrants who *join* and *follow the rules*	Migrants who come as *invaders* and *set the rules*
Agency	Free	Coerced (slaves) or prescribed (expats)

Source: Lucassen *et al.*, 2014a.

scholars prefer national (or even continental) boundaries over local ones. And this explains the neglect of most internal migrations, both in Europe and Asia, as is demonstrated by the invisibility of tens of millions of intra-Asian migrants in studies on the eighteenth and nineteenth centuries (McKeown, 2004).   Second, little attention is paid to temporary movements, such as seasonal labour, the migration of domestics from villages to cities, or that of tramping artisans (Lucassen, 1987; Moch, 1992, 2007; Ehmer, 2011). Consequently, in most mainstream overviews of migration, temporary and small-scale moves are conspicuously lacking and often left to geographers and (historical) demographers (Lee, 1966; Lawton, 1968; Zelinsky, 1971; Grigg, 1977; Oshiro, 1984; Chang, 1996; Fan and Huang, 1998; Pooley and Turnbull, 1998; Rosental, 1999; Van Poppel *et al.*, 2004; Kok, 2007). The underlying assumption is that "real" migrants move with the aim to settle somewhere else for good, preferably in a faraway country. Such assumptions are in line with the nation state paradigm that assumes a fixed membership and views migration as an exemption to the sedentary rule. In the case that people do move, this would involve a painful process of uprooting and subsequently rerooting.[4]

The often implicit assumption seems to be that migration, in contrast to mobility, has a much larger cultural impact on both the migrants and the societies in which they settle, leading to conflicts, integration problems, or, more positively, to social and cultural change. This explains why nowadays in Western Europe, many scholars study the migration and settlement process of Moroccans, Turks, Algerians and other postcolonial migrants, but ignore people coming from neighbouring countries or with high skills (such as Japanese) (see, e.g. Crul and Mollenkopf, 2012). Germans in the Netherlands or French in the United Kingdom in our current era are normally not considered as "real" migrants, because their culture is assumed to be more or less similar to that of the natives. Added to these considerations are policy definitions that tend to privilege lower class migrants who would cause social problems over highly educated ones, defined as "expats" (Hanerz, 1990; Sassen, 1991; Salt, 1992; Smith and Favell, 2006; Favell, 2008; Green, 2009; Bickers, 2010; Blower, 2011; Bade *et al.*, 2011; Fechter and Walsh, 2012; Van Bochove, 2012).

Next, there is a strong tendency to overlook involuntary migrations, which has resulted in the exclusion of the forced shipment of 12 million African slaves across the New World from the mainstream Atlantic migration story.[5] Furthermore, Asian migrants – if noticed at all – (in the past as well as in the present) are often assumed to move in some form of bondage, whether as labourers or through trafficking. The same is true for prisoners of war and inmates of concentration camps. There is an implicit assumption that migrants have less power than the people they join and therefore have to adapt or assimilate. This explains why Europeans who ventured into Asia and Africa from the fifteenth century onwards, or the Spaniards who conquered Latin America, are often not considered as migrants.

Finally, it is remarkable that migrants who display extremely mobile behaviour, not with the aim of staying but as a consequence of their profession, such as travelling artisans, seasonal workers, sailors and soldiers, are also frequently excluded from migration histories, as they do not fit the "from A to B and then stay" format. However, their geographical mobility often had a great impact on the migrants themselves, those they (temporarily) joined and those to whom they eventually returned (Sanborn, 2005; Zürcher, 2013). Take the example of John Smith from Lincolnshire. Born at the end of the sixteenth century, he first fought in the Netherlands, after which he joined the Austrian forces fighting in Hungary against the armies of the Ottoman Empire. When he was taken prisoner in Romania he made it to Austria, after which he left for Virginia in the autumn of 1607 (Acemoglu and Robinson, 2012, p. 21). However, few historians, including those from whom we borrowed this *petite histoire*, would class John Smith as a migrant. This mix of state preoccupations and other culturally and ideologically determined associations with the term "migrant" has divided and fragmented the field dramatically and stands in the way of a more fundamental understanding of human migrations.

The opposition between "real" migration and mobility is the result of highly stylized post hoc and teleological constructions of much more intricate human spatial and social behaviour. Two major difficulties stand out. First, the difference between intention and result: migrants may have the intention to leave for good, but for all kinds of reasons return after shorter or longer periods. The opposite is also true; some move multiple times and finally return after decades (Brettell, 1986; Cinel, 1991; Morawska, 1991; Wyman, 1993, 2001; Reeder, 2003; Alexander, 2005). And in the case of sojourners it may even take generations.[6] A good example of the often considerable disparity between intention and result is that of migrants who moved within colonial circuits, such as the Dutch or English empires (Bosma, 2007a, 2007b; Feldman, 2007; Harper and Constantine, 2010; Bickers, 2010), but also informal empires such as the American since the late nineteenth and the Japanese empire in the first half of the twentieth century (Gabaccia, 2012; Young, 1998; Uchida, 2011; see also Lucassen, Osamu and Shimada, 2014). Migrants in colonial circuits travelled thousands of miles, but mostly with the ultimate aim to return home. While many died en route, and others stayed away for good, a substantial number did indeed return, but only after having been exposed to very different cultures and ways of life. Europeans who stayed in the colonies often married indigenous partners, whereas their descendants at some point in time returned from the (ex-) colonies to their "fatherland". Although these "retornados" exercised a considerable economic, social, cultural and political impact on the communities they returned to, this has attracted only limited attention (Smith, 2003; Bosma *et al.*, 2012).

Second, with respect to geographical distance, it is important to note that short distance moves may also bring migrants into culturally and socially very distinct worlds, and force them to build new social ties. As Leslie Page Moch and others have convincingly argued (Moch, 1992, 2012), the temporary move of young French girls in the nineteenth century to a nearby town or city where they found employment as domestics in bourgeois family houses, would probably have had more influence on their lives than travelling from one expat community to another had on a highly skilled migrant. Or, as the geographer Wilbur Zelinsky put it:

> Genuine migration obviously means a perceptible and simultaneous shift in both spatial and social locus, so that the student cannot realistically measure one kind of movement while he ignores the other. Which family is more migratory, the one transferred 3,000 miles across the continent by an employer to be plugged into a suburb almost duplicating its former neighbourhood, or the black family that moves a city block into a previously white district? Ideally, we should observe shifts in both varieties of space in tandem, but given the dearth of techniques and data for handling purely social movement, we are forced to rely almost solely on territorial movements as a clumsy surrogate for total mobility.
>
> (Zelinsky, 1971, p. 224)

This means that three conceptual units of analysis that are basic to migration history have to be questioned seriously before we can start making meaningful comparisons between different parts of Eurasia: the state, the household and cultural units.

(Nation) states and their subsections

Since the nineteenth century national states have produced a wealth of statistics on "immigration" and "emigration".[7] As a result, most historians, for both practical and substantive reasons, define migration as a permanent move over national boundaries, notwithstanding the arbitrariness of such a choice. It means, for example, that Belgians in the French-speaking southern provinces who choose to settle on the other side of the border in France, moving 10–20 km, are considered international migrants, whereas the pre-revolutionary Russian trader who left Vladivostok to build a new life in Kiev, travelling almost 7,000 km, is considered an internal migrant. Within the nation state paradigm he will remain below the radar of the mainstream migration historian.

Another well-known example is the often temporary and circulatory migration of skilled British workers who crossed the Atlantic from the 1870s onward to earn higher wages on the east coast of the United States. Through such urban to urban moves an integrated North Atlantic migration field emerged in which a move from Birmingham to Liverpool was not fundamentally different from an ocean crossing to Pittsburgh (Berthoff, 1953; Thomas, 1954; Baines, 1985; Blewett, 2011). Nevertheless most studies ignore the Birmingham–Liverpool type labour migrations and cherish the Liverpool–Pittsburgh variant and thus stick to a fundamental distinction between internal and international migrations.

Our myopic view on migration is not only explained by implicit ideas on what constitutes a "real" spatial move, but also by the available national sources, which fail to register most local and temporary migrations. Such limitations, however, need not be an insoluble problem. Alongside the *nation state*

paradigm, demographers already in the late nineteenth century developed sophisticated methods to measure and map local and internal migrations by using
local registers and genealogical data.[8] At the aggregate level, national censuses
often provide information about international as well as internal migrations that
have been used to detect patterns and regularities. The most famous contribution
in this respect was made by Ernst Georg Ravenstein, a German-born fellow of
the Royal Geographical Society in London,[9] who in 1885 published his "Laws of
migration", based on the British 1871 and 1881 censuses, with additional
information about the birthplaces of those counted (Ravenstein, 1876, 1885,
1889; see also Grigg, 1977). This enabled him to measure flows at the county
level in the British Isles (including Ireland) on the basis of which he formulated
seven "laws" of migration. The most important of these were that short distance
migrations were much more common than long distance moves, that each current
of migration produces a compensating counter-current, and that women are more
migratory than men (Tobler, 1995).

Individuals and households

Many scholars, including Ravenstein, who have studied migration through the
lens of censuses, paid little attention to the social embededness of individual
migrants and either analysed migration in terms of anonymous "push" and "pull"
forces, or implicitly assumed migrants to be heroic males who dared to break
away from tradition and ventured into an unknown promised land (Handlin,
1951). With the rise of social and economic history in the 1960s, influenced by
new trends in anthropology and sociology, this methodological (and gendered)
individualism has been abandoned by most scholars. Their focus on individuals
as members of larger social units (families and households) made visible a pleth-
ora of moves that had considerable consequences for people's lives, and showed
how family strategies had an important influence on who was to move and how.

When we look at how family members decided who was to leave and who
was to stay, we can go beyond abstract macro push and pull models and understand much better the reasons behind human migrations at the micro (individual)
and meso (household) level. This approach has generated a wealth of detailed
studies that show how mobile people have been long before the Industrial
Revolution (Lucassen, 1987; Lourens and Lucassen, 1999; Kok, 2010). But it
also opened new windows of opportunity with respect to structured (and often
unexpected) comparisons over time. A good example are the Italian seasonal
migrants from the Apennines and the Abruzzi mountains. From the early modern
period onward they worked year in, year out in large numbers in the central
Italian coastal plains to harvest grain (Lucassen, 1987, pp. 117–118). From the
mid-nineteenth century onward, with the introduction of steamships, many of
them decided to trade the Campagna Romana for the Argentine Pampas, which
from a nation state perspective immediately made them not only international
but even intercontinental labour migrants (Frid de Silberstein, 2001). Notwithstanding the spectacular increase in the distance travelled, however, the primary

reason for moving, and the function of their migrations for the family economy, did not fundamentally change. In both cases men left their wives and children behind on the small (peasant) family plot with the aim of earning high wages, overseas or (until the mid-nineteenth century) in the plains in central Italy. In both instances they hoped to prevent the forced sale of their land and thereby full-scale proletarianization (Lucassen, 1987). From this and many other examples we can conclude that migration can be studied more fruitfully from the perspective of household members who cross temporary or permanent borders, irrespective of whether they are national, regional, or local. At the least, this is the case when we want to understand the impact of migration on labour markets and economic development, as well as on household dynamics and individual life cycle developments.

Another most instructive example that shows both similarities and differences in the migration mechanisms of household members is that between internal migrants in European states in the nineteenth century and present day (West) African young (often) male migrants who take huge risks to enter Europe. At first sight the differences appear stark. Young men from Senegal or Mali, for example, pay considerable sums to traffickers who promise to take them to Italy or other destinations within the EU. The ultimate aim is to find work as an illegal worker and then transfer money to the family members who stayed behind and who invested in his adventure. If we compare this with the internal moves of male and female Europeans in the nineteenth century (or earlier), it is clear that the risks have increased considerably over time. In contrast with the earlier migrations, the determination of states to protect national (or supranational) borders against unwanted migrants from outside its territory has created a profitable market for traffickers and smugglers who often reap huge profits. The very visible and spectacular attempts to reach European soil and the sometimes dramatic and lethal consequences of such migrations, and not in the least the sensationalist press coverage, have obscured the systemic similarities with earlier intra-European migrations. Just like French or German internal migrants before the First World War, African migrants who try to enter Europe are primarily motivated to contribute to the household economy and their agency should be primarily seen in the light of household economics. Such comparisons between two apparently very different historical contexts, using the household as the unit of analysis, show the great advantage of moving beyond the conceptual and ideological straitjacket of nation states.

Studying migration from a household perspective means a great leap forward in historical migration research, but it also has its disadvantages because it focuses predominantly on free migrations. Forced migrations, by the state or other third parties, and therefore not primarily resulting from family strategies, are almost always ignored. This is unjustified, however, because coerced forms of migration can also be determined by family decisions, at least to some extent. Think for example of households (in debt) that sold children or other family members to outsiders in order to survive, as was the case during the Ming dynasty in China in the sixteenth century (Hofmeester and Moll-Murata, 2011), or Christian families in the Ottoman Empire who had to hand over one of their (young) sons to be enlisted in the (elite) Janissary corps (Ágoston, 2005). Furthermore, there are other readily available examples involving indentured labour and selective refugee migrations (often primarily young men, much more so than the elderly or children) (Jordan and Walsh, 2007; Morgan, 2001).

The freedom that families have to decide who is to move, however, is reduced to near insignificance in the case of slave migrations, forced removals of entire populations, and genocidal forms of replacement to sites of mass murder, as in the case of Jews and kulaks (and other 'enemies' of the Soviet state) in Europe between 1933 and 1945, especially in Poland and the Ukraine (Snyder, 2010), or the Armenians in Turkey. But even in these atrocious cases, agency was not entirely lacking. Some families anticipated persecutions and left, or sent certain family members (e.g. children) ahead. Others, who had this option, could decide to hide, or choose some of their members, again often children, to go into hiding.

Cross-cultural boundaries

A major advantage of the household approach is the framework it offers to compare permanent and temporal, local, international and intercontinental migrants over time and space. However, it tells us little about the *nature of the boundaries* that migrants cross and thereby about the social, political and cultural effects of their moves, both on themselves and on the society they enter. Some may travel far, but stay within a well-known ambience, linguistically and culturally, whereas others travel over short distances, but nevertheless plunge into a new world with different values, technologies, religions and political systems or rules about social behaviour.

To overcome the manifold unproductive binary oppositions between migration and mobility (Table 1.1), we propose a paradigm – inspired by Patrick Manning – that in principle includes all moves, but that distinguishes between migrations within a similar cultural space ("home community migration") and migrations that cross a cultural boundary (Manning, 2005, 2013). The core assumption behind this *sociocultural paradigm* is that, unlike people moving *within* their relatively culturally homogeneous "community" (which may be a language group, a region, but also a state), "cross-community migrations" have different and more far-reaching transformative effects, for better or worse.[10] The peaceful or violent confrontation of people with different cultural baggage has the potential for cultural and social change, at the personal, organizational, and societal level. As migrants and non-migrants learn from each other, this may generate new ideas, which in turn can lead to all kinds of innovation. In cases where migrants are invaders (Vikings, colonial expansion, Chinese troops in Tibet), it obviously may also culminate in massive violence and the wiping out or marginalization of the "natives", as the aboriginal population of the Americas and Oceania experienced from the sixteenth century onward. But even in these cases of extreme asymmetric power relations there are ample indications that cultural encounters, violent and one-sided as they often were, not only had an impact on the receiving society, but also changed the migrants themselves. Moreover, we should realize that in most cases cross-cultural migrations were less destructive and resulted in more peaceful and extensive sociocultural changes (Hoerder, 2002).

The transformative power of cross-cultural migrations is a good starting point for a new and global method that enables us to measure and compare in a rigorous and systematic way the rate (and different manifestations) of cross-cultural migrations within a given territory. The added value of such a standardized method is not only that it produces standardized benchmarks for the *extent* of migrations, but also for their *impact*, both on the sending and receiving areas, and of course on the migrants themselves. Differences in the share of cross-cultural migrants in the total population (the *migration rate*) between areas raises important questions about the vitality and dynamics of a society and its potential for economic growth.

The CCMR method

These considerations have led us to develop the cross-cultural migration rate (CCMR) method, which calculates the chance an individual has of experiencing at least one cross-cultural migration in his or her life, and which can be expressed as the share of the population in a certain territory (which can be a city, a region, a nation state, an empire or a continent). Because this model should be applicable to different time periods and parts of the world, we have moved beyond conventional boundaries, such as nationality, religion or race. Instead we have chosen cultural boundaries that are common to most human societies in at least the last millennium and which transcend political boundaries.

The first is people who move from rural settings to cities. Until very recently, cities required other cultural skills and other types of human capital than those available in the countryside. Without completely reproducing the Weberian modernization language of ascription-achievement and collective-individualism, city air had a number of specific features that were lacking or less developed in villages. Strong (family) ties were less pervasive, public institutions and civil society initiatives more widespread, cultural subcultures more viable, labour markets more diverse, possibilities for upward social mobility and the development of human capital more accessible and commercial stimuli stronger. This made the stay in cities, for long or short periods, for country folk a significant experience and forced them to adapt to different cultural and social norms and codes. With the homogenization of nation states, in terms of language, skills, identity, education and communication, the cultural boundary between the countryside and cities largely evaporated, especially in Western Europe after the First World War, but in large parts of the world until this very day, think of Russia, China, India or sub-Sahara Africa, the migration to cities should still be considered a major cross-cultural migration.

Less numerous, at least in Europe, but involving considerable numbers in empires such as China and Russia, are migrants who change one ecological setting for another and who move within the countryside to new frontiers. There they encounter not only different climatological conditions, but also people with different languages, religions and cultural practices. We therefore decided to distinguish this second type of cross-cultural migration and labelled it "colonization", because such moves are often stimulated by (imperial) states with the explicit aim of colonizing scarcely populated marginal territories at the frontiers.

A third type of cross-cultural migration is that of seasonal workers who combine their own small family plot in semi-autarchic regions, often mountainous areas, with wage labour in highly commercialized regions with large scale farms that produce for external markets. This type of migration is, in contrast to the first two, largely male dominated (although not exclusively), brings migrants into contact with a much more monetized economy with different labour relations and often leads to the formation of organized work teams with appointed leaders and systems of internal remuneration. Moreover, the money earned by wage labour in 'farmer' regions is often ploughed back into the home community, which transforms existing status differences, consumption patterns and worldviews.

Whereas seasonal migrants normally return within a year, the fourth category we have distinguished are temporary migrants who stay away longer, and – depending on their luck and agency – may never return. The bulk of these temporal multi-annual labour migrants voluntarily join organizations that force them to serve at least a few years in order to make the investment in training worthwhile or simply because the work cycle is longer than one year. By far the most important labour market for these cross-cultural migrants is the military, especially before the advent of national (draft) armies, followed at great distance by the maritime labour market for sailors. A third category are tramping artisans and migrating domestics. As in the case of seasonal migrants, this segment was heavily male dominated and until the twentieth century almost exclusively male (domestics being the most important exception). The cultural boundary was not only, or primarily, constituted by the predominance of wage labour, but by the norms and values of the organization they entered: discipline, mutual (male) solidarity, work ethic, which together produced an in-group feeling that drew a firm line with the outside world. Moreover, these micro societies (a regiment, a ship) consisted often of people with different linguistic and religious backgrounds, which also led to cross-cultural encounters. As with seasonal migrants the transformative effects of temporal multi-annual migrations are not only felt by the migrants themselves, but also by the people they encounter (in violent or peaceful exchanges) and the people they return to, infusing them with new ideas from far away countries and the institutions they were part of. A good example are the African-American GIs who served two years on German bases in the 1950s where they discovered, for the first time, that racial segregation was not the normal state of affairs and which upon their return played an important role in the American Civil Rights Movement (Höhn and Klimke, 2010).

To these four basic categories we added two other ones, which are necessary to arrive at a complete quantitative picture of the total number of individuals who experienced at least one cross-cultural migration in their lives: people who entered and left a given territory, defined as "Immigration" and "Emigration". For a full understanding of the nature of the cross-cultural moves these two categories have to be unpacked and subsumed in the four basic variants we distinguish in our typology. Only then do we know how many of the immigrants or emigrants went to (or came from) cities or rural areas, and moved as soldiers, sailors, or seasonal workers. These considerations lead to the following six categories that encompass all cross-cultural movements within a given territory (T) (irrespective of scale), measured in 50-year periods (Lucassen and Lucassen, 2009):

1   Immigration (people moving into T);
2   Emigration (people moving out of T);
3   To cities (generally from rural areas, within T);
4   Colonization (moving to rural areas often with a different ecological character, within T);
5   Seasonal (generally between peasant and farmer regions, within T);
6   Temporal multi-annual (soldiers, sailors and artisans, within T).

The relationships between the six categories is visualized in Figure 1.1:

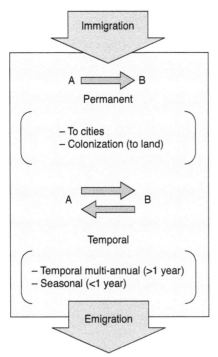

Figure 1.1 Cross-cultural migration rate (CCMR) method for a given territory and time period.

In relation to the population size of a given territory in a given time period, the total impact of geographical migration may be expressed in the following formula: (Lucassen and Lucassen, 2009)

$$P_i(p) = \frac{\Sigma p (M_i^{\text{perm}} + M_i^{\text{mult}} + M_i^{\text{seas}} + M_i^{\text{imm}} + M_i^{\text{emi}})}{N_i(p)} \cdot \frac{E_i(p)}{L_p}$$

Note: $P_i(p)$ denotes the probability of a person living in period p and geographical unit i migrating in a lifetime. M_i^{perm}, M_i^{mult}, and M_i^{seas} denote permanent (to *cities* and to *rural areas*), multi-annual (*labour migration*), and *seasonal* cross-community, often long-distance, movements inside unit i, respectively. M_i^{imm} is the number of *immigrants* to unit i from outside, and M_i^{emi} the number of *emigrants* from unit i to elsewhere. The notation Σ_p indicates that these migration numbers are summed over period p. $N_i(p)$ is the average population in geographical unit i in period p. To compensate for over counting in the migration numbers, the expression needs to be corrected by the second factor, in which $E_i(p)$ denotes the average life expectancy in period p and L_p is the length of the period.

A different picture: applying the CCMR method to Europe since 1500

Most mainstream overviews of migrations stress the unprecedented levels of migration in our own time. The twentieth century, and especially the latter half, is considered "The age of migration", to reiterate the title of the widely cited reference work by Stephen Castles and Mark J. Miller (2003). Defining migration as international movements, they state that never before have so many people migrated. In their own words:

> Migrations have been part of human history from the earliest times. However, international migration has grown in volume and significance since 1945 and most particularly since the mid-1980s. Migration ranks as one of the most important factors in global change.
>
> (Castles and Miller, 2003, p. 4)

Adam McKeown and others have shown, however, that Castles and Miller ignored large scale labour migrations between Asian countries, but due to their limitation to international migrations also overlooked large-scale cross-cultural and often long distance migrations *within* states such as China, India, Indonesia and Russia since the mid-nineteenth century (McKeown, 2004; Bosma, 2009). Finally, Gozzini (2006) argued that even when we stick to the nation state definition of migration, the share of international migrations at the end of the nineteenth century (1870–1914) was probably higher than a century later (1965–2000).[11] In other words, the implicit assumption that migration is directly linked to the process of modernization in the nineteenth and twentieth centuries, leading to a linear increase in international migrations, should be rejected.

When we apply the CCMR method to Europe (without Russia) since 1500 the "modernization paradigm" that supposedly gave way to a "mobility transition" with very low levels of migration before 1800 and very high levels thereafter, becomes even more doubtful (Figure 1.2). Instead, our results show that although the CCMR rose significantly after 1750, levels were already substantive from the sixteenth century onward.[12] Moreover, an important increase is visible already in the first half of the nineteenth century – before the advent of railways and steamships. Furthermore our calculations for the twentieth century show a remarkable and unexpected result: an all-time high in the first half of the century and a considerable decrease after the Second World War.

Although the migration rate in the post-war period is considerably higher than a century earlier, the difference is caused not so much by immigrants from other continents (for example, Turks, Moroccans, Algerians, refugees from the Middle East and colonial migrants from the Americas, Africa and Asia), but by the continuing (partly internal) drift to cities. The dominant idea that we now live in an unprecedented migratory age should therefore not only be nuanced, but also qualified.

For the first half of the twentieth century, apart from millions of internal and intra-European city dwellers, the all-time high was to a large extent caused by the two world wars that generated an unprecedented number of cross-cultural migrations by soldiers, predominantly within Europe but also from other continents (troops from America, Canada, Australia and furthermore from French and British colonies). Apart from soldiers, the wars caused enormous flows of refugees, such as the 14 million Germans who were resettled immediately after the armistice in 1945, constituting, according to R. M. Douglas (2012, p. 1), the "largest forced population transfer – and perhaps the greatest single movement

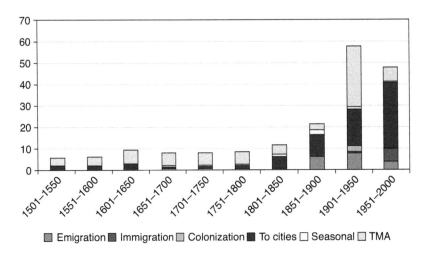

Figure 1.2 Total net CCMRs per category for Europe without Russia, including internal migrations, 1501–2000 (%).

of peoples – in human history".[13] Most of them had initially moved to the new 'Lebensraum' in the East (especially Poland) from 1939 onward, whereas others had lived for generations in various countries such as Hungary and Czechoslovakia, Yugoslavia and Romania. In the CCMR method, most of them are counted as people moving "to cities", in the same trend that saw many other war-induced refugees remaining in Europe.[14] Other refugees left the old continent as emigrants for overseas destinations, including Israel. Among these emigrants were also 10,000 Nazis, for example Adolf Eichmann, who took refuge in countries such as Paraguay, Argentina, Brazil and Chile (Cesarini, 2006).

In the second half of the twentieth century, army-related migrations decreased considerably but remained an important phenomenon. This is explained first of all by the huge numbers of American (15 million) and Russian (10 million) soldiers and their families who were stationed at bases in West and East Germany during the Cold War (Müller, 2012; Höhn, 2002; Höhne and Moon, 2010). Furthermore, there were smaller numbers of Europeans fighting colonial wars in Indonesia (Dutch), Vietnam (French), Algeria (French),[15] and various African countries (Portuguese, French and Belgians). These soldiers, however, did not counterbalance the unprecedented mobilization of armies in the period 1940–1945, which largely explains the decline in the overall migration rate.

After the Second World War, people moving to cities (both internally and intra-European) remained by far the most important form of cross-community migration and eclipsed "immigration", which is often privileged in standard migration overviews (Castles and Miller, 2003; Goldin *et al.*, 2011). The share of migrants from other continents, guest workers from Northern Africa and Turkey, intercontinental refugees, or former colonial subjects, did indeed soar, but on the whole constituted at 11 per cent only a small part of the total CCMR.[16] The bulk of the cross-cultural migrations, as in the first half of the century, are the result of the ongoing urbanization process that drew people to large cities, as Table 1.2 shows.

Table 1.2 Migration to cities in Europe (without Russia), 1901–2000 (millions)

	1901–1950	*1951–2000*
Increase urban population	108	281
X 2/3 (1901–1950) and X 1/2 (1951–2000)	65	140
Minus intercontinental immigrants	3.1	24.7
Total European rural migrants to cities	61.9	115.3
Average population Europe	395	512
Migration ratio (%)	15.7	22.5

Source: Lucassen *et al.*, 2014 (from table 148).

Note
We applied the same method as in our calculations for the period 1501–1900, taking urban growth as point of departure. The only difference being that we estimated that in the first half of the twentieth century two-thirds, and in the second half only 50 percent, of the increase was caused by migrants. Finally we subtracted immigrants from other continents in order to avoid double counting.

At this point some readers might object to the decision to continue to regard people who move from the countryside to cities *within* Europe as cross-cultural migrants. As we argued in the beginning of this chapter, given the increasing (national) homogenization of states in the twentieth century, one could argue that since 1850, or at least since 1900, internal migrants in national states by definition no longer crossed cultural boundaries. This is in contrast to internal migrants in (former) multicultural and vast empires, such as Russia and China. On the other hand, also in (new) nation states the evolution of peasants into national citizens was far from uniform and straightforward, as the example of Italy shows. More importantly, however, is that including internal migrants in the twentieth century allows us to make structural comparisons through time (and space) of cityward migrations. Finally, it highlights how national borders have monopolized public, political and academic debates on what migration means. Nevertheless, suppose we would exclude internal moves to cities, and revise our results in line with conventional ways of measuring migration, the picture remains basically the same until 1950. The era of world wars resulted in a record high percentage CCMR of almost 50 per cent of the population; however, the picture in that case shows a much sharper decrease after 1950.

Figure 1.3 illustrates very well the most significant difference between conventional (international, or even intercontinental) definitions of migration and the CCMR method. Whereas the intercontinental part of the former highlights our "Immigration" category, the CCM rate considers people from other continents who settle in Europe as only one of six possible expressions of cross-cultural experiences and thus offers a very different picture.[17]

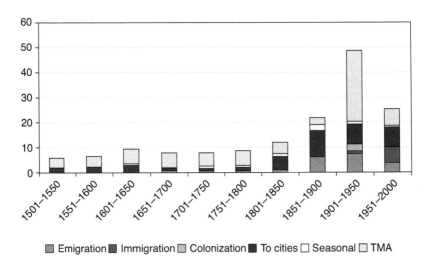

Figure 1.3 Total net CCMRs per category for Europe without Russia, excluding internal migrations, 1501–2000 (%) (source: Lucassen *et al.*, 2014).

Those who, for whatever reason, are not convinced by our argument that soldiers who fight in other countries should be considered as migrants at an equal level with the other cross-cultural migrants, can simply leave them out. And these same goes for Europeans who migrated to cities within nation states (see Figure 1.4). But even if both categories are excluded, our conclusion that migration rates in the first half of the twentieth century reached an all-time high still holds.

Conclusion

After implementing the proposed methodology to quantify and qualify cross-cultural migrations, as presented in this chapter, and thus diverging fundamentally from the (nation) state driven obsession with international and socially and culturally "problematic" migrants, a lot of questions still remain to be answered. To start with, what relative weight should we assign to the different kinds of cross-cultural migration in relation to their causal effect on social and cultural changes, in societies of origin and destination? By "weight" we mean the propensity of migrants to interact with inhabitants of the region of destination and vice versa, as well as the chance this offers for cross-cultural (ex)change. One could, for example, assume that migration to cities has a much greater transformative effect than migration to the countryside (colonization), because of the much greater social and spatial density and intensity of interpersonal contacts. And on the other hand one could argue that the impact of migrants very much depends on the specific historical context. The cross-cultural influence of sailors, for example, who remained most of the time aboard their ships and in foreign harbours only visited bars and prostitutes, was limited. To the contrary, soldiers,

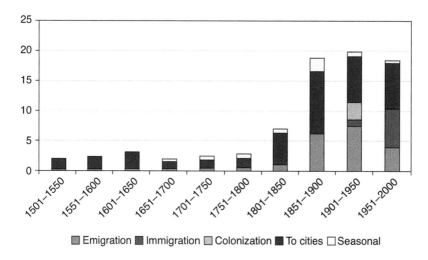

Figure 1.4 Total net CCMRs per category for Europe without Russia, excluding migrations to cities within nation states and excluding temporal multi-annual migrations, 1501–2000 (%).

such as the black American GIs in Germany, who were confronted with a very different institutional setting, or who were regarded by the native population as agents of a higher (consumption) culture, could cause crucial changes, upon return and/or at destination.

Although contingency certainly is key to understanding the specific influence of a certain type of cross-cultural migration, this does not release us from the obligation to specify more structural determinants, of which we would like to highlight the two most obvious candidates. First of all, the specific composition of the migrants, in terms of size, status (Van Lottum, 2011), gender composition, human capital, beliefs and migration motives, and, second, the extent of "open access" of the prevailing membership regime in the societies of destination. Pertaining to the human and cultural capital of migrants, this largely determines what segments of the population migrants come into contact with, in terms of class, but also religion and subculture. Zones of interaction can thus be quite specific and largely restricted to, for example, certain scientific disciplines or industries. And small groups with a high status (in whatever respect), such as missionaries, can sometimes forge much more change than large groups with a low status. Gender matters in many respects: at present second generation migrant girls perform better in schools than boys (Lucassen and Lucassen, 2014c). And finally groups may choose, for religious and cultural reasons, to keep a certain distance from the new society in terms of marriages and social contacts, and thus reduce interaction themselves.

These various kinds of agency, however, always interact with the structure of the receiving society. It seems not far-fetched, for example, to assume that cities or states that are characterized by an "open access order", (North *et al.*, 2009; Bosma *et al.*, 2013) created many more chances for cross-cultural interactions and thus social change than polities that restricted the membership of newcomers. Here we can think of a continuum with at one extreme zero interaction, as exemplified by the Nazi death camps, through chattel slavery, indentured migrants, guest worker and Bracero systems to polities that actively recruit migrants and immediately grant them full membership, as in the case of former colonists who return to their fatherland (Smith, 2003).

Another dimension that should be kept in mind is the time perspective. The cross-cultural interactions that take place between migrants and natives, and that may be "weighed" or measured, extends over many years, if not over many generations. At least three time horizons may be distinguished: the initial propensity of migrants at their arrival to interact with inhabitants of the region of destination and vice versa; the development of this propensity during the migration process and the life of the migrant him- or herself; and this development over generations. Let us give one example that actually dominates the public debate in Western Europe: the interaction between "guest workers" from the Mediterranean and the receiving societies of Western Europe. Initially both migrants and society at large supposed that the interaction would be only temporal and encounters mostly superficial, but not unfriendly. After the oil crisis and the ensuing "family reunification", guest workers themselves fell victim to unemployment in large numbers and relations deteriorated. This had a negative impact on the willingness and possibility of both first and second generation migrants to integrate into Western European societies. The "integration pessimism" that subsequently has gained popularity in Europe received an extra stimulus over the past decade, which has led, it seems, to the outright rejection of "Western values" by some of the second or even third generation youngsters. This is certainly also a form of cultural interaction, but definitely of a completely different nature from that of the start of the process in the 1960s (Lucassen and Lucassen, 2014c).

This is not to say that cross-cultural exchange is absent here. As this example demonstrates, the experience of exclusion by migrants and their descendants, as well as the experience of feeling excluded, in itself is a highly transformative cross-cultural experience for all those involved. In other words, cross-cultural exchanges can have very different outcomes and the nature of the process can vary widely. If we strip Manning's argument to the bare bone, we might say that without cross-community migration there is far less chance of cross-cultural exchange, but cross-cultural exchange as such certainly is not always to the advantage of all those who take part in the process.

Notes

1 This chapter is an adapted and updated version of Lucassen and Lucassen, 2014a. We thank Irial Glynn for his critical comments.
2 Postcolonial migrants for example, such as the 6.5 million *hikiagesha* who returned to Japan after the Second World War (Cohen, 2012), are often not considered as migrants, but as expats. Furthermore, forced migrants, especially slaves or expats (Green, 2009; Smith and Favell, 2006), are often excluded.
3 Light, 2012. The United States did not systematically monitor internal migration. There are presumably ways to quantify these migration waves, however. Historians have analysed ship manifests and slave traders' records to quantify domestic slave migration from 1790–1860, for example. US census records allow us to track migration into the western territories (although we don't always know where these migrants originated from). Migration to cities is also mostly tracked through census records.
4 As in the classic study of Oscar Handlin (1951), which was fundamentally criticized by Bodnar (1985).
5 See for example Klein, 2000. Some American historians are starting to combine research on African-Americans' international forced migrations with research on their internal migrations within America. See for example Berlin, 2010.
6 The term "sojourner" was initially reserved for Chinese outside China (Siu, 1952), but has become a general category (Manning, 2005), and is also applied to American artists in Paris for example (Blower, 2011) or colonial expats (Bickers, 2010).
7 Well known and famous examples are the two-volume study by Imre Ferenczi (of the International Labour Office in Geneva) and Walter F. Willcox (of the National Bureau of Economic Research) (Ferenczi and Willcox, 1929; Willcox, 1931). See also DeWind, 2003, p. 74. For the more recent period, see Foner and Lucassen, 2012.
8 See, for France, Moch, 1983 and Sewell, 1985; for Germany, Hochstadt, 1999; for the Netherlands, Kok, 2004; for the United Kingdom, Pooley and Turnbull, 1998; and for Sweden, Dribe and Lund, 2005. In East Asia, Japan (Wilkinson, 1965; White, 1978; Hayami, 1993) and Taiwan (Wolf and Engelen, 2008) developed similar administrative systems, and thus opened possibilities for historians to study small-scale migrations.

9 Born in 1834 in Frankfurt am Main, he moved to London in 1852, where he became a naturalized British subject. He subsequently worked for the topographical department of the War Office (1855–1872) before joining the Royal Statistical Society (Baigent, 2013).

10 Be it as invaders, sojourners, settlers or itinerants, with "settlers" defined as people who "join" another community and follow the prevailing rules. Invaders on the other hand set the rules and force natives to abide and adapt (Manning, 2005). See also Bosma *et al.*, 2013.

11 Nevertheless the idea that international migration flows have continued at historically unprecedented levels is reproduced time and again (see for example the – otherwise highly stimulating – book by Hampshire (2013, p. 156).

12 This time period represents the starting point for our observations. It is very well possible that this also holds true for the (late) Middle Ages, but this awaits new historical research (Jaritz and Müller, 1988; Postel, 2004).

13 A serious "competitor" would be the "Partition" between India and Pakistan (estimated at 12 million forced migrants): Khan, 2007, p. 6.

14 See for the First World War: Tucker and Wood, 1996, pp. 86, 258, 294, 313, 373, 525, 610; Aldrich and Hilliard, 2010, pp. 525–526; Busch, 2003, p. x; Brooking, 2004, p. 103; Rutherford Young, 2005, p. 508; Pati, 1996, p. 37; Marshall, 2001, pp. vii–viii; Sharp *et al.*, 2002, p. 285. See for the Second World War: Vego, 2009, pp. iii–37; and Kennet, 1997, p. 4.

15 In Algeria two million French soldiers have been active (Aldrich, 1996, p. 297).

16 "Immigration" was good for a migration rate of 4.1 per cent in the second half of the twentieth century and thus constituted 11 per cent of the total rate (37.7 per cent).

17 Our CCMR method aims to quantify individuals who experienced at least one crosscultural move in their life. They may have more experiences, but these are not included here in principle. Nevertheless, because we treat the different migration types separately, all kinds of double counts are possible, such as emigrants from Europe who, for various reasons, returned. Most of these overlaps, however, have been avoided in our calculations (Lucassen, Lucassen, De Jong and van de Water, 2014).

References

Acemoglu, D. and J. A. Robinson (2012). *Why Nations Fail. The Origins of Power, Prosperity and Poverty*. London, Profile Books.

Ágoston, G. (2005). *Guns for the Sultan. Military Power and the Weapons Industry in the Ottoman Empire*. Cambridge: Cambridge University Press.

Aldrich, R. (1996). Greater France: a history of French overseas expansion. Houndmills, Palgrave.

Aldrich, R. and C. Hilliard (2010). The French and the British empires, in: J. Horne (ed.), *A Companion to the First World War*. Oxford: Wiley Blackwell, 524–540.

Alexander, J. Trent. (2005). "They're never here more than a year": return migration in the southern exodus, 1940–1970, *Journal of Social History*, 38 (3), 653–672.

Bade, K. J., P. C. Emmer, L. Lucassen and J. Oltmer (eds) (2011). *The Encyclopedia of Migration and Minorities in Europe: From the 17th Century to the Present*. New York: Cambridge University Press.

Baigent, E. (2013). Ravenstein, Ernst Georg, *Oxford Dictionary of National Biography*. Oxford: Oxford University Press.

Baines, D. (1985). *Migration in a Mature Economy: Emigration and Internal Migration in England and Wales 1861–1900*. Cambridge: Cambridge University Press.

Berlin, I. (2010). *The Making of African America: the Four Great Migrations*. New York, Viking.

Berthoff, R. T. (1953). *British Immigrants in Industrial America, 1790–1950*. Cambridge, MA: Harvard University Press.

Bickers, R. (ed.) (2010). *Settlers and Expatriates: Britons over the Seas* Oxford: Oxford University Press.

Blewett, M. H. (2011). The dynamics of labor migration and raw material acquisition in the Transatlantic worsted trade, 1830–1930, in: D. Gabaccia and D. Hoerder (eds), *Connecting Seas and Connected Ocean Rims*. Leiden and Boston: Brill, 338–370.

Blower, B. L. (2011). *Becoming Americans in Paris: Transatlantic Politics and Culture between the World Wars*. Oxford: Oxford University Press.

Bodnar, J. (1985). *The Transplanted: A History of Immigrants in Urban America*. Bloomington: Indiana University Press.

Bosma, U. (2007a). Sailing through Suez from the South: the emergence of an Indies-Dutch migration circuit, 1815–1940, *International Migration Review*, 41 (2), 511–536.

Bosma, U. (2007b). Beyond the Atlantic: connecting migration and world history in the age of imperialism, 1840–1940, *International Review of Social History*, 52 (1): 116–123.

Bosma, U. (2009). European colonial soldiers in the nineteenth century: their role in white global migration and patterns of colonial settlement, *Journal of Global History* 4 (2): 317–336.

Bosma, U., J. Lucassen, G. Oostindie (2012). Introduction. Postcolonial migrations and identity politics: towards a comparative perspective, in: U. Bosma, J. Lucassen and G. Oostindie (eds), *Postcolonial Migrants and Identity Politics: Europe, Russia, Japan and the United States in Comparison*. New York and Oxford: Berghahn, 1–22.

Bosma, U., G. Kessler and L. Lucassen (eds) (2013). *Migration and Membership Regimes in Global and Historical Perspective*. Leiden and Boston: Brill.

Brettell, C. (1986). *Men who Migrate, Women who Wait: Population and History in a Northern Portuguese Parish*. Princeton: Princeton University Press.

Brooking, T. (2004). *The History of New Zealand*. Westport: Greenwood Press.

Busch, B. C. (ed.) (2003). *Canada and the Great War: Western Front Association Papers*. Québec: McGill-Queen's University Press.

Caplan, J. and J. Torpey (eds) (2001). *Documenting Individual Identity: The Development of State Practices in the Modern World*. Princeton: Princeton University Press.

Castles, S. and M. J. Miller (2003). *The Age of Migration: International Population Movements in the Modern World*. New York: The Guildford Press.

Cesarini, D. (2006). *Becoming Eichmann: Rethinking the Life, Crimes, and Trial of a Desk Murderer*. Cambridge, MA: Da Capo Press.

Chang, S. (1996). The floating population: an informal process of urbanization in China, *International Journal of Population Geography*, (2): 197–214.

Cinel, D. (1991). *The National Integration of Italian Return Migration 1870–1929*. Cambridge: Cambridge University Press.

Cohen, N. L. (2012). Return of the natives? Children of empire in post-imperial Japan, in: U. Bosma, Jan Lucassen and Gert Oostindie (eds), *Postcolonial Migrants and Identity Politics: Europe, Russia, Japan and the United States in Comparison*. New York and Oxford: Berghahn: 155–180.

Crul, M. and J. Mollenkopf (eds) (2012). *The Changing Face of World Cities. Young Adult Children of Immigrants in Europe and the United States*. New York: Russell Sage.

Crush, J. and D. Tavera (eds) (2010). *Zimbabwe's Exodus: Crisis, Migration, Survival.* Cape Town, Unity Press.

DeWind, J. (2003). Immigration studies and the social science research council, in: N. Foner, R. G. Rumbaut and S. J. Gold (eds), *Immigration Research for A New Century: Multidisciplinary Perspectives.* New York: Russell Sage, 69–75.

Douglas, R. M. (2012). *Orderly and Humane: the Expulsion of the Germans after the Second World War.* New Haven and London: Yale University Press.

Dribe, M. and C. Lund (2005). Determinants of servant migration in nineteenth-century Sweden, *Continuity and Change,* 20 (1), 53–91.

Ehmer, J. (2011). Quantifying mobility in early modern Europe: the challenge of concepts and data, *Journal of Global History* 6 (2): 327–338.

Fahrmeir, A. (2007). *Citizenship: the Rise and Fall of a Modern Concept.* New Haven: Yale University Press.

Fan, C. C. and Y. Huang (1998). Waves of rural brides: female marriage migration in China, *Annals of the Association of American Geographers,* 88 (2): 227–251.

Farcy, J. C. and A. Faure (2003). *La mobilité d'une génération de Français: recherche sur les migrations et les déménagements vers et dans Paris à la fin du XIXe siècle.* Paris: Institut National d'Études Démographiques.

Favell, A. (2008). *Eurostars and Eurocities: Free Movement and Mobility in an Integrating Europe.* Malden, MA: Blackwell Publishing.

Fechter, A.-M. and K. Walsh (eds) (2012). *The New Expatriates: Postcolonial Approaches to Mobile Professionals.* London: Routledge.

Feldman, D. (2007). The politics of internal migration, *International Review of Social History,* 52 (1), 105–109.

Ferenczi, I. and W. F. Willcox (1929). *International Migrations* (Vol. I). New York: National Bureau of Economic Research.

Foner, N. and L. Lucassen (2012). Legacies of the past, in: M. Crul and J. Mollenkopf (eds), *The Changing Face of World Cities: Young Adult Children of Immigrants in Europe and the United States.* New York: Russell Sage, 26–43.

Frid de Silberstein, C. (2001). Migrants, farmers and workers: Italians in the land of Ceres, in: D. Gabaccia and F. Ottanelli (eds), *Italian Workers of the World. Labor Migration and the Formation of Multiethnic States.* Chicago and Urbana: University of Illinois Press, 79–101.

Gabaccia, D. (2012). *Foreign Relations: American Immigration in Global Perspective.* Princeton: Princeton University Press.

Goldin, I., G. Cameron and M. Balarajan (2011). *Exceptional People. How Migration Shaped our World and will Define our Future.* Princeton and Oxford: Princeton University Press.

Gozzini, G. (2006). The global system of international migrations, 1900 and 2000: a comparative approach, *Journal of Global History,* 1 (1): 321–341.

Green, N. L. (1997). The comparative method and poststructural structuralism: new perspectives for migration studies, in: J. Lucassen and L. Lucassen (eds), *Migration, Migration History, History: Old Perspectives and New Paradigms.* Bern etc.: Peter Lang: 57–72.

Green, N. L. (2009). Expatriation, expatriates, and expats: the American transformation of a concept, *American Historical Review,* 114 (2): 307–328.

Green, N. L. and F. Weil (eds) (2007). *Citizenship and those who Leave: The Politics of Emigration and Expatriation.* Urbana and Chicago: Illinois University Press.

Grigg, D. (1977). E. G. Ravenstein and the laws of migration, *Journal of Historical Geography,* 3 (1): 41–54.

Hampshire, J. (2013). *The Politics of Immigration. Contradictions of the Liberal State.* Cambridge: Polity.

Handlin, O. (1951). *The Uprooted: the Epic Story of the Great Migrations that made the American People.* New York: Grosset, Dunlap.

Hanerz, U. (1990). Cosmopolitans and locals in world culture, in: M. Featherstone (ed.), *Global Culture: Nationalism, Globalization and Modernity.* London: Sage, 237–250.

Harper, M. and S. Constantine (eds) (2010). *Migration and Empire.* Oxford: Oxford University Press.

Hayami, A. (1993). Jinkōshi (Demography). In A. Naohiro (ed.), *Nihon Tsūshi* (The Japanese History), Vol. 1. Tokyo: Iwanami Shoten, 115–147.

Hochstadt, S. (1999). *Mobility and Modernity: Migration in Germany, 1820–1989.* Ann Arbor: University of Michigan Press.

Hoerder, D. (2002). *Cultures in Contact: World Migrations in the Second Millennium.* Durham and London: Duke University Press.

Hofmeester, K. and C. Moll-Murata (2011). The joy and pain of work: global attitudes and valuations, 1500–1650, Introduction, *International Review of Social History*, 56 (special issue), 1–23.

Höhn, M. (2002). *GIs and fräuleins: the German-American Encounter in 1950s West Germany.* Chapel Hill and London: The University of North Carolina Press.

Höhn, M. and M. Klimke (2010). *A Breath of Freedom: the Civil Rights Struggle, African American GIs, and Germany.* New York: Palgrave Macmillan.

Höhn, M. and S. Moon (eds) (2010). *Over there: Living with the US Military Empire from World War Two to the Present.* Durham: Duke University Press.

Jaritz, G. and A. Müller (eds) (1988). *Migration in der Feudalgesellschaft.* Frankfurt: Campus.

Jordan, D. and M. Walsh (2007). *White Cargo: the Forgotten History of Britain's White Slaves in America.* New York: NYU Press.

Kennet, L. (1997). *GI: the American Soldier in World War II*, Norman: University of Oklahoma Press.

Khan, Y. (2007). *The Great Partition: the Making of India and Pakistan.* New Haven and London: Yale University Press.

Klein, H. (2000). *The Atlantic Slave Trade.* Cambridge: Cambridge University Press.

Kok, J. (2004). Choices and constraints in the migration of families: Central Netherlands 1850–1940, *History of the Family: an International Quarterly*, 9 (2), 137–158.

Kok, J. (2007). Principles and prospects of the life course paradigm, *Annales de Démographie Historique*, (1), 203–230.

Kok, J. (2010). The family factor in migration decisions, in: J. Lucassen, L. Lucassen and P. Manning (eds), *Migration History in World History. Multidisciplinary Approaches.* Leiden and Boston: Brill: 215–250.

Lawton, R. (1968). Population changes in England and Wales in the later nineteenth century: an analysis of trends by registration district, *Transactions of the Institute of British Geographers*, 44: 55–74.

Lee, E. S. (1966). A theory of migration, *Demography*, 3: 47–57.

Light, M. (2012). What does it mean to control migration? Soviet mobility policies in comparative perspective, *Law and Social Inquiry*, 37 (2): 395–429.

Lourens, P. and J. Lucassen (1999). *Arbeitswanderung und berufliche Spezialisierung. Die lippischen Ziegler im 18. und 19. Jahrhundert.* Osnabrück: Rasch.

Lucassen, J. (1987). *Migrant Labour in Europe: the Drift to the North Sea.* London: Croom Helm.

Lucassen, J. and L. Lucassen (2009). The mobility transition revisited, 1500–1900: what the case of Europe can offer to global history, *Journal of Global History*, 4 (4): 347–377.

Lucassen, J. and L. Lucassen (2011a). From mobility transition to comparative global migration history, *Journal of Global History*, 6 (2), 299–307.

Lucassen, J. and L. Lucassen (eds) (2014a). Measuring and quantifying cross-cultural migrations: an introduction, in: idem (ed.), *Globalising Migration History: the Eurasian Experience (16th–21st Centuries)*. Leiden and Boston: Brill.

Lucassen, J. and L. Lucassen (eds) (2014b). *Globalising Migration History. The Eurasian experience (16th–21st centuries)*. Leiden and Boston: Brill.

Lucassen, L. and J. Lucassen (2014c). *Gewinner und Verlierer. Fünf Jahrhunderten Immigration. Eine Nüchterne Bilanz*. Münster: Waxmann.

Lucassen, L. (2013). Population and migration, in: P. Clark (ed.), *The Oxford Handbook of Cities in World History*. Oxford, Oxford University Press: 664–682.

Lucassen, L. J. Lucassen, R. de Jong and M. van de Water (2014). *Cross-cultural Migration in Europe 1901–2000: a Preliminary Estimate*. IISH Research Papers. Amsterdam: International Institute of Social History.

Lucassen, L., O. Saito and R. Shimada (2014). Cross-cultural migrations in Japan in a comparative perspective, 1600–2000, in: J. Lucassen and L. Lucassen (eds), *Globalising Migration History: the Eurasian Experience (16th–21st Centuries)*. Leiden and Boston: Brill: 362–411.

McKeown, A. (2004). Global migration 1846–1940, *Journal of World History*, 15 (2): 155–189.

McKeown, A. (2008). *Melancholy Order: Asian Migration and the Globalization of Borders*. New York: Columbia University Press.

Manning, P. (2005). *Migration in World History*. New York and London: Routledge.

Manning, P. (2013). *Migration in World History. Second edition*. Abingdon and New York: Routledge.

Marshall, S. L. A. (2001). *World War I*. New York: Mariner Books.

Moch, L. P. (1983). *Paths to the City: Regional Migration in Nineteenth-Century France*. Beverly Hills: Sage.

Moch, L. P. (1992). *Moving Europeans. Migration in Western Europe since 1650*. Bloomington: Indiana University Press.

Moch, L. P. (2007). Connecting migration and world history: demographic patterns, family systems and gender, *International Review of Social History*, 52 (1): 97–104.

Moch, L. P. (2012). *The Pariahs of Yesterday: Breton Migrants in Paris*. Durham: Duke University Press.

Morgan, K. (2001). *Slavery and Servitude in Colonial North America*. New York: NYU Press.

Morris, I. (2013). *The Measure of Civilization: How Social Development Decides the Fate of Nations*. Princeton: Princeton University Press.

Müller, C. T. (2012). *US-Truppen und Sowjetarmee in Deutschland Erfahrungen, Beziehungen, Konflikte im Vergleich*. Paderborn: Ferdinand Schöningh Verlag.

Morawska, E. (1991). Return migrations: theoretical and research agenda, in: R. J. Vecoli and S. M. Sinke (eds). *A Century of European Migrations, 1830–1930*. Urbana: University of Illinois Press, 277–292.

Noiriel, G. (1991). *La tyrannie du national: le droit d'asile en Europe (1793–1993)*. Paris: Calmann-Lévy.

North, D. C., John Joseph Wallis and Barry R. Weingas (2009). *Violence and Social Orders. A Conceptual Framework for Interpreting Recorded Human History*. Cambridge: Cambridge University Press.

Oshiro, K. K. (1984). Postwar seasonal migration from rural Japan, *Geographical Review*, 74 (2): 145–156.

Pati, B. (1996). *India and the First World War*. New Delhi: Atlantic publishers.

Pooley, C. G. and J. Turnbull (1998). *Migration and Mobility in Britain since the Eighteenth Century*. London: UCL Press.

Postel, V. (2004). *Die Ursprünge Europas. Migration und Integration im frühen Mittelalter*. Stuttgart: Kohlhammer.

Putterman, L. and D. N. Weil (2010). Post-1500 population flows and the long run determinants of economic growth and inequality, *Quarterly Journal of Economics*, (November): 1627–1682.

Ravenstein, E. G. (1876). The birthplace of the people and the laws of migration, *Geographical Magazine*, 3: 173–177, 201–206, 229–233.

Ravenstein, E. G. (1885). The laws of migration, *Journal of the Royal Statistical Society*, 48: 167–235.

Ravenstein, E. G. (1889). The laws of migration: second paper, *Journal of the Royal Statistical Society*, 52: 241–305.

Reeder, L. (2003). *Widows in White: Migration and the Transformation of Rural Italian Women, Sicily, 1880–1920*. Toronto: Toronto University Press.

Rosental, P.-A. (1999), *Les sentiers invisibles: espaces, familles et migrations dans la France du 19e siècle*. Paris: Éditions de l'École des Hautes Études en Sciences Sociales.

Rutherford Young, D. (2005). Great Britain colonies, in: S. C. Tucker (ed.), *The Encyclopedia of World War I*. Santa Barbara: ABC Clio, 508–509.

Sanborn, J. A. (2005). Unsettling the empire: violent migrations and social disaster in Russia during World War I, *Journal of Modern History*, 77 (2), 290–324.

Sassen, S. (1991). *The Global City: New York, London, Tokyo*. Princeton: Princeton University Press.

Salt, J. (1992). The future of international labour migration, *International Labour Migration*, 26 (4), 1077–1111.

Sewell, W. H. (1985). *Structure and Mobility: the Men and Women of Marseille, 1820–1870*. Cambridge: Cambridge University Press.

Siegelbaum, L. and L. P. Moch (2014). *Broad is My Native Land. Repertoires and Regimes of Migration in the Twentieth Century*. Ithaca and London: Cornell University Press.

Sharp, M., I. Westwell and J. Westwood (2002). *History of World War I*. New York: Marshall Cavendish Corporation.

Shen, J. (2014). From Mao to the present: migration in China since the Second World War, in: J. Lucassen, L. Lucassen (eds), *Globalising Migration History: the Eurasian Experience (16th–21st Centuries)*. Leiden and Boston: Brill: 335–361.

Siu, P. C. P. (1952). The sojourner, *American Journal of Sociology* 58 (1): 34–44.

Smith, A. L. (ed.) (2003). *Europe's Invisible Migrants: Consequences of the Colonists' Return*. Amsterdam: Amsterdam University Press.

Smith, M. P. and A. Favell (eds) (2006). *The Human Face of Global Mobility: International Highly Skilled Migration in Europe, North America and the Asia-Pacific*. New Brunswick, NJ, Transaction Publishers.

Snyder, T. (2010). *Bloodlands: Europe between Hitler and Stalin*. New York: Basic Books.

Taylor, A. (2002). *American Colonies: the Settling of North America*. London: Penguin Books.

Thomas, B. (1954). *Migration and Economic Growth: a Study of Great Britain and the Atlantic Economy*. Cambridge: Cambridge University Press.

Tobler, W. (1995). Migration: Ravenstein, Thorntwaite, and beyond, *Urban Geography*, 16 (4), 327–343.

Torpey, J. (2000). *The Invention of the Passport: Surveillance, Citizenship and the State*. Cambridge: Cambridge University Press.

Tucker, S. C. and L. M. Wood (1996). *The European Powers in the First World War: an Encyclopedia*. New York: Garland.

Uchida, J. (2011). *Brokers of Empire: Japanese Settler Colonialism in Korea, 1876–1945*. Cambridge, MA: Harvard University Press.

Van Bochove, M. (2012). *Geographies of Belonging: the Transnational and Local Involvement of Economically Successful Migrants*. Rotterdam University: PhD thesis.

Van Lottum, J. (2011). Labour migration and economic performance: London and the Randstad, *c.*1600–1800, *Economic History Review*, 64 (1), 1–20.

Van Poppel, F., M. Orris and J. Lee (eds) (2004). *The Road to Independence: Leaving Home in Western and Eastern Societies, 16th–19th centuries*. Bern: Peter Lang.

Van Zanden, J. L. (2009). *The Long Road to the Industrial Revolution: the European Economy in a Global Perspective 1000–1800*. Leiden and Boston: Brill.

Vego, M. N. (2009). *Joint Operational Warfare. Theory and Practice*. Newport: United States Naval War College.

Wentzel, M., Marie Wentzel, Johan Viljoen and Pieter Kok (2006). Contemporary South African migration patterns and intentions, in: P. Kok, D. Gelderblom, J. O. Oucho and J. v. Zyl (eds), *Migration in South and Southern Africa: Dynamics and Determinants*. Cape Town: Human Sciences Research Council: 171–204.

White, J. W. (1978). Internal migration in prewar Japan, *Journal of Japanese Studies*, 4 (1), 81–123.

Whyte, M. K. (ed.) (2010). *One Country, Two Societies: Rural Urban Inequality in Contemporary China*. Cambridge, MA: Harvard University Press.

Wilkinson, T. O. (1965). *The Urbanization of Japanese Labor, 1886–1955*. Worcester: University of Massachusetts Press.

Willcox, W. F. (1931). *International Migrations. Volume II Interpretations*. New York: National Bureau of Economic Research.

Wimmer, A. and N. Glick Schiller (2003). Methodological nationalism, the social sciences, and the study of migration: an essay in historical epistemology, *International Migration Review*, 37(3): 576–610.

Wolf, A. P. and T. Engelen (2008). Fertility and fertility control in pre-revolutionary China, *Journal of Interdisciplinary History*, (38), 3, 345–375.

Wyman, M. (1993). *Round-trip America: the Immigrants Return to Europe, 1880–1930*. Ithaca and London: Cornell University Press.

Wyman, M. (2001). Return migration: old story, new story. *Immigrants and Minorities*, 20 (1), 1–18.

Young, L. (1998). *Japan's Total Empire: Manchuria and the Culture of Wartime Imperialism*. Berkeley: University of California Press.

Zelinsky, W. (1971). The hypothesis of the mobility transition, *Geographical Review*, 61 (2): 219–249.

Zolberg, A. and L. L. Woon (1999). Why Islam is like Spanish: cultural incorporation in Europe and the United States, *Politics and Society*, 27 (5): 5–38.

Zürcher, E.-J. (ed.) (2013). *Fighting for a Living: a Comparative History of Military Labour in Europe and Asia, 1500–2000*. Amsterdam: Amsterdam University Press.

2 Migrations as a historical issue

Paola Corti

Paradigms and stereotypes on mobility

In this chapter, I will try to show how the historical interpretation of territorial mobility in Europe and in Italy has been of crucial importance in the achievement of new interpretative models on the study of migrations. Before entering the merit of the matter, however, it is necessary to bring into focus which have been those *idols* that, in different disciplines, have long prevented mobility from being seen as a historical issue. First, I refer to those who, in the same historiographical analyses, have delayed the estimation of such a variable as an essential element of the historical process. I then refer to the stereotypes, which, in sociological investigations, have prevented the acceptance, in their own interpretations, of a historical perspective, limiting, in fact, migrations to the present.

Let us start with historiographical analyses. Summarizing the way in which mobility has indeed been alien to many historical reconstructions, the anthropologist Dionigi Albera coined, at the time, an effective expression: the paradigm of sedentariness (Albera, 1995). According to this interpretation, in many studies men had been considered sedentary, and the history of humanity has been read in its diachronic temporal movement, but not in its spatial movement. This amnesia is not merely by chance. It should be ascribed, instead, to the way in which human mobility has been perceived at times and within the different socio-political organizations. The exclusion of mobility, however, should be considered relative to the negative connotation of foreigners in many societies and in different historical phases. Let us think of how the nomadic populations have been treated within the various European realities, both in medieval times and in the modern age. In particular, let us think of the rules and regulations, based on defence and punishment, dispensed by every established community towards strangers, or to the even stricter juridical exclusion of foreigners from these same communities. Such normative hostilities have then assumed an even more focused codification during the nineteenth century, when – with the development of the nation-state, and with the introduction of the citizenship laws, the principles of legitimacy and the issues of defence – a more explicit exclusion of the foreigner from civic life was introduced in various countries (Odmalm, 2005; Rosental, 2005; Green and Weil, 2007). It is a matter of customs and legislative practices that, on the operational level, have kept the nomadic population outside civic society, while, on the theoretical-interpretative level, it has fuelled the interpretation of mobility as an unusual phenomenon, so delaying the analysis of many important aspects of migrations linked to everyday life, to domestic organization, and to the economy of many communities.

Some established sociological interpretations have, in turn, contributed to the solely contemporary interpretation of migrations and to the evaluation of them as mainly mass phenomena. Some demographic theories take their cue from Malthus, such as the one that considers migratory movements as effects of a mechanical opposition between overpopulation and the lack of it. These theories, on the one hand, have reinforced the theory that emphasizes the exceptional nature of migratory movements – considered as dependent from clear and circumscribed demographic cycles – and on the other hand, they have brought about a reduction of these phenomena to a purely collective dimension, rebuilding it through cyclic trends of natural movements of the population. While the economic theories of *push–pull*, – not very different from the previous ones in their fundamental mechanical setting – have mainly sustained statistic and demographic approaches, they link the development of territorial migration to the expulsion induced by the economic deficiencies of certain territorial areas and to the attraction of richer, more productive geographical areas. The attractive elements, which differ in nature according to the different interpretations, have been identified mainly in the economic and demographic structure of the areas of confluence of the migration (pull areas). Among these factors, the emphasis is above all on the demographic deficiency and the correlated need of manpower, on the dynamic nature of the markets, the presence of infrastructures, the energetic and/or technological resources that are absent in the areas of origin (push areas), on the earnings gap between the areas of origin and the areas of arrival and on the positive contractual conditions of pull areas. Ultimately, according to this interpretative model, migration not only depends on international economic and demographic laws, but also responds to a specific difference from one country to another, or from different regional areas of the same country.

Other stereotypes can be linked to this kind of interpretation, no less relevant for their consequences on the basic interpretations: the identification of economic migrations; the singling out of territorial areas that are considered only as points of emigration (push areas), and of other areas considered, on the other hand, of exclusive immigration (pull areas). Such interpretations, applied to different countries and different realities to explain the origins of migration (Scidà, 2006), have identified the ideal type of territorial mobility in the process of urbanization that has characterized industrialization in its different stages, from the first English Industrial Revolution to the later continental phenomena of the nineteenth century, until the more recent processes of urbanization linked to the European post-war economic boom. Furthermore, these interpretations have underestimated other relevant aspects, such as the political dimension and the non-economic motivations of migration; individual and domestic choices; players of migration projects and the social networks built by these players.

The long duration of migrations: beyond the stereotypes

Migrations became a historical issue from the development of investigations founded on events preceding the industrial expansion; this issue has been subjected to significant interpretative transformations. In fact, we must not forget that although research on the *Ancien Régime* has mainly fostered the paradigm of sedentariness, it was precisely those investigations carried out in different European realities during that period that have allowed significant elements to be identified, questioning this as well as other paradigms on migrations (Brettel and Hollifield, 2007). Such analyses, mainly referring to local demographic sources, have first highlighted the protagonists of a movement that certainly lacked the exceptionality conferred to the territorial movements of the population. A particularly relevant example of this kind of mobility is described in the model of the *life-servant-cycle*. According to this famous reconstruction, boys that left their families not only had the task of supplementing the home's income by working for wages outside their home and their community, but from that same work they also had to save enough for their own wedding. As a matter of fact, the *life–servant–cycle* not only was linked to age, marriage and bachelorhood – imposed on youths by specific domestic systems – but also to the organization of the farmer's properties, with its relative forms of inheritance (Laslett, 1983). It was an educational experience for both sexes; for young men, migration was often undertaken in order to learn a craft. Besides, once the technical experience had been acquired, periodic migration also became a way of life to earn the new domestic income; no different to what was happening regarding agricultural jobs, representing the other constant incentive for migration within the societies of the *Ancien Régime*. The separation of members from their family in many rural and manufacturing realities of old Europe, therefore, belonged to the sphere of domestic strategies for earning an income for the family. This migration included that of the *élite classes* of architects, artists and technicians – people who, even then, were working in a precociously transnational dimension – as well as that of officials, clergymen and soldiers who travelled to capital cities and other urban centres, to the headquarters of administrations, universities, religious institutions and military districts (Page Moch, 1995).

The most relevant result of these studies on the pre-industrial age – studies not only methodologically focused on places, subjects and specific social actors, but also on the dynamics present in local micro-realities – can be summarized by the fact that migration appears mostly as one of the variables "normally" used by families for their survival. Not only this, but also the non-exceptional nature of the movements in these analyses is linked to the survey of other relevant aspects. First of all, the fact that mobility affected all social classes; second, that migration was characterized by the temporary nature of the departures, by consistent returns and the cyclic nature of the returns; last, that their economic result was particularly important for the life of the communities of origin (Corti, 2003, p. 3). Regarding this last aspect, what has been discovered in the studies carried out in mountain areas seems particularly paradigmatic. These places – which according to the historian Braudel's interpretation represented a "factory of men for the use of others" – have long been considered the perfect area dominated by push factors, as they are considered poor, overpopulated, alien to contact and static in their traditional repetitiveness (Braudel, 1966). In fact, the development of many demographic and anthropological studies focused mainly on the Alpine area on its different sides – the so called "Alpine laboratory" – and then extended to the mountains of the various Mediterranean realities, have highlighted the fact that many mountain communities of various European areas were the centre of the spread of big migratory movements throughout the pre-industrial age. Furthermore, these communities connected the commercial and artisan networks that were scattered throughout Europe. These networks facilitated the cyclic return of craftsmen and merchants, allowing a concentration of domestic wealth in the same mountain communities (Viazzo, 1989; Albera and Corti, 2000). In conclusion, research carried out for many years has allowed new relevant points to be added to the analysis of the Alpine laboratory, working towards a non-reductive interpretation of territorial mobility. It has, above all, shown the inconsistency of the long considered theory that migration originates solely from poverty and need.

The Dutch historian Lucassen, starting from a Napoleonic inquiry, gathered information that enables us to focus on other aspects of the matter. These aspects, in their complex articulation and territorial distribution, not only return the territorial movements of the *Ancien Régime*, but also provide new knowledge regarding the mechanisms of formation and development of the migrations (Lucassen, 1987). The identification of out-and-out migratory systems, passing through various Western European realities, and annually involving thousands of workers, has definitely been the most tangible rebuttal of the paradigm of sedentariness. In the systems rebuilt by Lucassen, in fact, certain fixed geographical paths can be observed that are repeated over time, and that cross Western Europe in a constant way. In addition, areas were developed along these routes as rest and refreshment stops and hotels, accommodating craftsmen, merchants, seasonal workers and farmers. In a reality that was considered static, such as pre-industrial Europe, a whole economy linked to migration was created (Bade, 2001). Since then, in the same migratory dynamics, some of the most important mechanisms of social aggregation came into being: migratory chains based on work and family relations and territorial links.

Historical analysis of the pre-industrial age, the various and articulate historic and anthropological contributions on alpine and mountain mobility and the identification of consolidated European migratory systems have ultimately allowed us, first, to broaden Marc Bloch's famous definition of history as "a science of men in time" because, besides the diachronic temporal movement, the dynamics of mobility in the *Ancien Régime* also reveal the geographical spatial movement (Bloch, 1949). Second, all these studies clarified the multiple motivations for migrating, and finally they have showed that mobility was assuming organizational forms based on social relationships, which in turn often changed in the construction of the same territorial paths (Page Moch, 1995). Resorting to local and qualitative sources rather than statistic and quantitative collections of data, said investigations reached relevant theoretic and methodological results, and, overall, allowed further stimulus vital for migrations to be collected, in the projects and in the strategies of single persons and families.

The tangle of periodization: continuity or breakage?

Starting from the long duration of territorial mobility observed in different studies, Dick Hoerder, among others, proposed a periodicity of European migrations between the Middle Ages and 1914, where he identified some significant phases. A first period between the Middle Ages and the Thirty Years War (1648), is characterized by the predominance of infra-European migrations; the second, between 1650 and 1800 – though it includes the transoceanic exodus – is still characterized by the predominance of rural and original industrial movements; the third, between 1800 and 1815, includes, on the other hand, minor movements put in motion by the Napoleonic Wars and mainly supported by man. Since 1815, a first substantial increase in transatlantic movements can be observed; while it was only with the most well-known phase of the "Great Migration", and at least until the Second World War, that the United States of America became a privileged migratory destination (Hoerder, 1985).

Dealing with the periodicity proposed by Hoerder, as well as with other diachronic combination studies (Castles and Miller, 1998), the necessary question concerns the issue of continuity or breakage in the long duration of migratory movements. In other words, starting from the European experience, the question is, where does this "traditional" mobility become the mass migrations of the nineteenth century? We should not ignore the fact that the alleged immobility of the *Ancien Régime* was also based on the fact that, in this phase, any migration that occurred was not of the mass dimension or the definitive character of the great transoceanic migration of the nineteenth century, nor did they cause the uprooting and relinquishing of farmland, which was typical of urbanization processes brought about by industrialization. All the stereotypes described in the first pages of this work have been, in fact, built up starting from collective phenomena observed during these most well-known migratory processes. The Great Migration has indeed been the most analysed of this phenomena. The large volume of studies on this period plays a part in considering the transoceanic migration as the first form of exodus or, in any case, in emphasizing its character of deep division compared to the previous forms of migration. In fact, its development has been linked to a series of events that are crucial for the acceleration, increase and standardization of migratory movements: the great demographic transition of the late eighteenth century; the transformations of the economy and ship transport linked to the effects of the Industrial Revolution; political changes brought on by the American and French Revolutions; the change caused by the birth of nation-states, by revolutions against liberalism, with the resulting affirmation of liberal migratory policies; and the attraction of American markets, in particular the United States (Baines, 1991).

However, as Leslie Page Moch pointed out at the time, the transoceanic exodus followed a series of transformations that, at the beginning of the nineteenth century, had already hit the big European migratory systems. Let us think of the sturdy development of infrastructures that in Europe was of great assistance for internal migrations, causing significant quantitative and qualitative changes: an increase in number and specialized construction work of the migrants and with it, due to the prolonged times and rhythms of great infrastructural activities, the higher duration of seasonal and circular migration. The results of such changes were, inside Europe itself, (a) a progressive reduction in the circularity of migrations that followed the seasonal rhythms of agriculture, as well as those of the productive discontinuity of pre-industrial manufacture, (b) the standardization of influx that had previously involved just a few thousand workers within each migratory system and (c) the territorial extension of the paths, which in the past were no more than 350 km per year.

This temporal, numerical and geographical extension of migratory flows that, with the transoceanic exodus, would later reach even greater dimensions, was therefore the product of internal changes within pre-existing migration, rather than a new migration clearly separated from the past. In fact, if we analyse the internal mechanisms of migration – and the strategies enacted by the various actors during the nineteenth century – we can observe interesting common behaviour between previous and present migrants. The analysis carried out in various migratory regional and national European realities has indeed highlighted how, in transoceanic migrations, the first to depart were those with professions and expertise that had followed the paths of migratory chains inside the regional, national and international areas of pre-industrial Europe (Glazier, 1996; Bade, 2001, p. 162). In Italy, for example (Corti and Sanfilippo, 2009, 2012), the migrants of the past crossed the oceans when migration started travelling regularly by ship, both in the southern areas later affected by the Great Migration, where travellers and musicians had always followed internal and infra-European paths (De Clementi, 1999), and in the alpine and manufacturing areas of the centre and north, which had for a long time been affected by the exportation of expertise and professional skills. In fact, it was precisely the experience of some of these manufacturing areas that gave such importance to the "mobility culture" common amongst migrant workers during well-established migratory traditions. It was cultures like this that, thanks to the "continuity" of migration of certain professional categories such as builders, encouraged passage towards the transoceanic mass exodus (Ramella, 1984; Castronovo, 1986–2000). The increase and acceleration of migration, encouraged by social networks within the migratory flows – and by news passed along by the emigrants (the pioneers, who helped in the boom of American destinations) – resulted in the propaganda used by big sailing companies in various urban and rural realities of old Europe (Glazier, 1996).

To conclude, the promotion of American destinations in migration was significantly assisted by the organizational characteristics of the oldest infra-European migration. Therefore, rather than the Great Migration to America symbolizing a break with the past, as mentioned above, the quantitative, geographic and temporal dimension of the flows was expanded: however, these migrations often revealed themselves as inconclusive even in the first transoceanic routes (Lorenzetti and Granet-Abisset, 2009).

The Italian example: the circularity of migratory processes and early transnationalism

The Italian example is particularly relevant because, already in the national trend of the Great Migration we can see the emigrants' widespread inclination return, not only during the big nineteenth century exodus, but also along the various migratory waves from the country. Indeed, the number of repatriations has been evaluated only after 1900 and, in any case, until 1921 such evaluations are limited to those from America (Cerase, 2001; Corti, 2006b; Audenino, 2009). On the whole, however, from the years of the Great Migration to the post-war period, return migration has been estimated at about half that of departure. In itself, this already seems relevant in as much as it shows how these same transoceanic movements have preserved one of the particular features of the previous forms of mobility: the circular trend (Corti, 2013, pp. 15–40). In fact – although return migration has not been proportionately calculated because of the difficulty in quantifying it compared to the exit flows (Bonifazi and Heins, 1996, p. 284) – clues and behaviours seen from a series of concentrated investigations, show how widespread return migration was.

Also in this case, there have been anthropological and sociological studies – starting from the 1980s with an increase in, often long-term, local and regional research (Corti, 1995; AaVv, 2006, 2007) – which have contributed to rebuilding, in a more significant qualitative way, both the above mentioned migratory attitudes as well as others, adding their own contribution to the theoretical redefinition of migrations, and, as we will see, to the blasting of the most well-established stereotypes on the subject. Regarding the involvement of the core families' income in migration, we were able to highlight how the close relationship with the land, the possession of small land holdings and the widespread multiple activity that existed in large Italian geographic areas impelled emigrants not to cut all connections with their countries of origin. Furthermore, from the same studies, it emerged that, since the pre-industrial age, domestic income through paid work – as well as by the migratory contribution of men and women – has been crucial in the agricultural and manufacturing realities of the country's economy (Albera *et al.*, 1991). Nevertheless, this relationship was relevant during the late nineteenth century's changes and the start of a mass exodus: work and mobility customs, tested in the *Ancien Régime*'s migrations, were changed by the families according to the times and rhythms of the new migration towards America (Reeder, 2003; Salvetti, 2013). Analyses on different Italian localities, from the Alps to Sicily, have provided evidence on the development of a domestic economy in which part of the domestic income – the men's – was earned abroad, sending their salary from the various European and transoceanic locations, while the other half of the domestic earnings, together with the above mentioned half, was managed by the women living in Italy (Merzario, 1989). Through the long-distance correspondence and information exchanged between members of the same family, it was possible to form domestic transnational *ménages*, no different from those that can be observed today among immigrants crossing Europe (Corti, 2009; Brycelson and Vuorela, 2002; Kofman, 2004).

It is well known that the paradigm of transnationalism – one of the most used during the last 20 years – in its most common reading and in its various declinations, has been exclusively applied to the age of globalization, and it has been considered a direct product of the acceleration of transport and communication, typical of the present age (Levitt and Glick Schiller, 2004; Vertovec, 2004; Portes *et al.*, 2007). The research carried out on single professional migratory and territorial chains in Italy during the Great Migration, as already said, has instead shown how the emigrants of various Italian places already acted in the same way. As a matter of fact, certain studies not only defined the families related to these emigrants as "multi-locals" or "transnational" (Baily, 2005; Albera *et al.*, 2005), but also the paradigm of internationalism was conferred to the entire phenomenon of Italian emigration in the study on Italian exodus conducted by the American historian Donna Gabaccia (Gabaccia, 2000). This conclusion, besides restoring a historical perspective to the same transnational reading of the migrations, has also been useful in highlighting the central role played by women in building a transnational domestic model, in restoring the focus on one of the main subjects of the migrant economy, thereby showing the importance of gender issues in the general interpretation of migration (Gabaccia and Iacovetta, 2000).

Other significant theoretical and methodological contributions of the Italian studies on the interpretation of migrations can be found in other research results. The attention focused both on the departure and arrival areas, and the choice of analysing agricultural and manufacturing realities with a long migratory tradition have allowed us, among other factors, to detect behaviour useful in reshaping some of the theoretical consequences of the economic and demographic interpretations discussed at the beginning of this work. I refer, in particular, to those aspects mentioned already that represent a sort of corollary of the push–pull paradigm: the identification of the migratory areas with the most economically underdeveloped zones, the identification of migrations for reasons of employment or survival, the juxtaposition between those areas considered "expulsive" and that considered "attractive".

As regards the identification of migratory areas and the reasons for departure, the Italian case (no different from that of countries with a long tradition of emigration, such as Great Britain) shows how the economically more developed regions have contributed first to the mass exodus. The geographical dynamics of the departures show, in fact, that the first migratory areas were not the poorer and underdeveloped areas of the South, but those of the North, in which capitalistic transformations had caused distress in the previous economic and social balance, pushing a lot of people towards new forms of emigration. Furthermore, as was already the case in the Great Britain of the *Old Migration*, in these areas, besides the departures of small landowners and representatives of the rural class, the migration of craftsmen and skilled manufacturing workers were just as common. Cottage workers of the old textile system, in fact, rather than working in factories as industrial workers – and in so doing, losing their status as independent workers – preferred to migrate elsewhere (Ramella, 1984). The choice of abandoning their country, therefore, was not always imposed by the absence of employment or by the expulsion of less qualified persons, but also by the choice to export the craftsmen's skills and work independence elsewhere.

Nevertheless, what results from analyses on the Italian case calls into question the juxtaposition of the migratory areas hypothesized by the push–pull paradigm. This dichotomy has been called into question by some of the previously mentioned studies on the Alpine area, amongst others, which revealed how certain areas, such as Piedmont and Valle d'Aosta, despite their pride in having old manufacturing and mining industries, also had a deep-rooted and enduring migratory vocation. In these areas, in fact, rather than the exclusive employment attraction typical of the pull areas, emigration, internal migrations and immigration were all observed, both during the Great Migration and over the following years (Corti, 2006a). Italy, on the whole (or rather, the country of the *New Migration* with the highest presence of emigrants) has proved to be, after a very long and more attentive analysis on the various forms of migration – even during the Great Migration years – a place of constant interconnection between migratory phenomena that is considered to be unconventional (Corti and Sanfilippo, 2012, pp. v–xvi).

To conclude, as seen from literature on migrations in Europe and, specifically, the Italian case, historical analyses have mainly focused on the continuity of territorial mobility, the well-structured composition of the subjects involved and the motivations and social relationships that encouraged the mobility, hence restoring the diachronic dimension and complexity that had been ignored for so long in the evaluation of migratory movements. Besides, such studies have helped to restore a longer lasting dimension to customs such as those defined as "transnational", showing that the territorial dispersion of members of the same family and the endurance of supranational bonds were already present in the domestic strategies of certain ancient Italian migratory areas. Thanks also to these research contributions, we have been able to redefine the same theoretical meaning ascribed to transnationalism. In fact, from a wider diachronic overview on migratory behaviours, rather than from a new paradigm, such interpretation proves more to be one that "enriches and develops the numerous approaches variously used in studying international migrations" (Ceschi, 2007, p. 125). Similarly, the historiographical approach that focused on the social relationships of migrants has also helped to reshape the stereotypes built on the mechanical interpretation of demographic and economic paradigms, revealing the existence of situations in which the dichotomic lecture of the push–pull – and the subsequent miserable vision of individual choices – are contested both by the presence of immigration and emigration dynamics in the same geographic area, and by the prematurity of departures in the economically more advanced areas, by the presence, in the first waves of exodus, of people with skills and resources that could be used outside their territorial borders. These are the results and new theoretical and methodological elaborations that have been processed thanks to the relocation of the heuristic perspective of migration studies from the strict Euclidean spheres of territorial spaces to the wider spheres of relationships of the migrants' "social spaces" (Gribaudi, 1997).

References

AaVv (2006). Modelli di emigrazione regionale dall'Italia centro settentrionale. *Archivio storico dell'emigrazione italiana*. 2 (1): 5–142.

AaVv (2007). Modelli di emigrazione regionale dall'Italia centro meridionale. *Archivio storico dell'emigrazione italiana*. 3 (1): 5–98.

Albera, D. (1995). Dalla mobilità all'emigrazione. Il caso del Piemonte sudoccidentale In Corti, P. and Schor, R. (eds) *L'émigration transfrontalière: les italiens dans la France méridionale, Recherches régionales*. 3ème trimestre: 25–61.

Albera, D. and Corti, P. (eds) (2000). *La montagna mediterranea. Una fabbrica d'uomini? Mobilità e migrazioni in una prospettiva comparata (ss. XV–XX)*, Cavallermaggiore: Gribaudo.

Albera D., Audenino, P. and Corti, P. (1991). I percorsi dell'identità maschile nell'emigrazione. Dinamiche collettive e ciclo di vita individuale. *Rivista di Storia contemporanea*, xx (1): 69–87.

Albera, D., Audenino, P. and Corti, P. (2005). L'emigrazione da un distretto alpino: diaspora o plurilocalismo? In Tirabassi, M. (ed.) *Itinera. Paradigmi delle migrazioni italiane*, Torino: Edizioni della Fondazione Agnelli: 185–209.

Audenino, P. (2009). Quale ritorno? Tempi, significati e forme del ritorno nelle Alpi italiane dall'Otto al Novecento In Lorenzetti, L. and Granet-Abisset, A. M. (eds) *Les migrations de retour. Rückwanderungen. Histoires des Alpes, Storia delle Alpi, Geschichte der Alpen*, 14: 57–74.

Bade, K. (2001). *L'Europa in movimento. Le migrazioni dal Settecento ad oggi*, Bari-Roma: Laterza.

Baily, L. (2005). Transnazionalismo e diaspora italiana in America Latina In Tirabassi, M. (ed.) *Itinera. Paradigmi delle migrazioni italiane*, Torino: Fondazione Agnelli: 43–69.

Baines, D. (1991). *Emigration from Europe, 1815–1930*, London: Macmillan.

Bloch, M. (1949). *Apologia della storia o mestiere di storico*, Torino: Einaudi.

Bonifazi, C. and Heins, F. (1996). Le migrazioni di ritorno nel sistema emigratorio italiano: un riesame. *Studi Emigrazione*, xxx (122): 273–303.

Braudel, F. (1966). *La Méditerranée et le monde méditerranéen à l'époque de Philippe II*, Paris: Colin 2nd edition.

Brettel, C. B. and Hollifield, J. F. (eds) (2007). *Migration Theory: Talking Across Disciplines*, New York, London: Routledge, 2nd edition.

Brycelson, C. and Vuorela, C. (eds) (2002). *The Transnational Family: New European Frontiers and Global Networks*, Oxford: Berg.

Castles, S. and Miller, M. J. (1998). *The Age of Migration: International Population Movements in the Modern World*, New York: The Guildford Press.

Castronovo, V. (ed.) (1986–2000). *Biellesi nel mondo*, series Banca-Sella Fondazione Sella, Milan: Electa.

Cerase, P. (2001). *L'onda di ritorno: i rimpatri*, In Bevilacqua, P., De Clementi, A., Franzina, E. (eds) *Storia dell'emigrazione italiana. Partenze* Rome: Donzelli editore: 113–125.

Ceschi, S. (2007). Esistenze multisituate. Lavoro, condizione transnazionale e traiettorie di vita migrante. *Mondi Migranti*, 2, 2007.

Corti, P. (1995). Les recherches sur l'émigration italienne: historiographie, anthropologie et recherche comparatiste. *Revue Européenne des Migrations Internationales*. 11 (3): 5–18.

Corti, P. (2006a). Mobilità, emigrazione all'estero e migrazioni interne in Piemonte e Val d'Aosta. *Archivio storico dell'emigrazione italiana*. 2 (1): 7–18.

Corti, P. (2006b). Dal ritorno alle visits home. Le tendenze di studio nell'ultimo trentennio. *Studi Emigrazione*, XLIII (164): 927–946.

Corti, P. (2009). Famiglie transnazionali In Corti, P., Sanfilippo, M. (eds) *Migrazioni, Storia d'Italia, Annali 24*, Torino: Einaudi, pp. 303–316.

Corti, P. (2003) *Storia delle migrazioni internazionali*, Bari-Rome: Laterza 1st edition.

Corti, P. (2013). *Temi e problemi di storia delle migrazioni italiane*, Viterbo: Sette città.

Corti, P. and Sanfilippo, M. (eds) (2009). *Migrazioni, Storia d'Italia, Annali 24*, Torino: Einaudi.

Corti, P. and Sanfilippo, M. (2012). *L'Italia e le migrazioni*, Bari-Roma: Laterza.

De Clementi, A. (1999), *Di qua e di là dall'oceano. Emigrazione e mercati del lavoro nel meridione (1860–1930)* Rome: Carocci.

Gabaccia, D. (2000). *Italy's Many Diasporas*, Seattle: University of Washington Press.

Gabaccia, D., Jacovetta, F. (eds) (2002). *Women, Gender and Transnational Lives: Italian Workers in the World*, Toronto, Buffalo, London: University of Toronto Press.

Glazier, I. (1996). L'emigrazione dal XIX secolo alla metà del XX In Bairoch, P. and Hobsbawm, E. J. (eds) *Storia d'Europa*, vol. V, *L'età contemporanea*, Torino: Einaudi.

Green, N. L. and Weil, F. (eds) (2007). *Citizenship and Those Who Leave: the Politics of Emigration and Expatriation*, Urbana: University of Illinois Press.

Gribaudi, M. (1997). Movimenti migratori e mobilità sociale, In Societa' Italiana Di Demografia Storica, *Disgualianze: stratificazione e mobilità sociale nelle popolazioni italiane (secc. xiv. xx)*, vol. I. Bologna: Clueb: 171–176.

Hoerder, D. (ed.) (1985). *Labor Migration in the Atlantic Economies: the European and North American Working Classes during the Period of Industrialisation*, Westport: Greenwood Press.

Kofman, E. (2004). Family-related migration: a critical review of European studies. *Journal of Ethnic and Migration Studies*. 2: 243–262.

Laslett, P. (1983). Family and household as work group and kin group: areas of traditional Europe compared. Wall, R., Robin, J. and Laslett, P. (eds) *Family Forms in Historic Europe*, Cambridge: Cambridge University Press.

Levitt, P. and Glick Schiller, N. (2004). Conceptualizing simultaneity: a transnational social field perspective on society. *International Migration Review*, 38 (3): 1002–1039.

Lorenzetti, L. and Granet-Abisset, A. M. (2009). Les Migrations de retour. Jalons d'un chapitre méconnu de l'histoire alpine In Lorenzetti, L. and Granet-Abisset, A. M. (eds) *Les migrations de retour. Rückwanderungen. Histoires des Alpes, Storia delle Alpi, Geschichte der Alpen*, 14: 13–24.

Lucassen, J. (1987). *Migrant Labour in Europe: the Drift to the North Sea, 1600–1900*, London and Wolfeboro, NH: Croon Helm.

Merzario, R. (1989). *Il capitalismo nelle montagne. Strategie famigliari nella prima fase di industrializzazione nel comasco*, Bologna: Il Mulino.

Odmalm, P. (2005). *Migration Policies and Political Participation: Inclusion or Intrusion in Western Europe?* New York and Basingstoke: Palgrave Macmillan and Houndmills.

Page Moch, L. (1995). *Moving Europeans. Migrations in Western Europe since 1650.* Bloomington-Indianapolis: Indiana University Press.

Portes. A., Escobar, C. and Radford, A. W. (2007). Immigrant transnational organizations and development: a comparative study. *International Migration Review* 41 (1): 242–281.

Ramella, F. (1984). *Terra e telai. Sistemi di parentela e manifattura nel biellese dell'Ottocento*, Torino: Einaudi.

Reeder, L. (2003). *Widows in White: Migration and Transformation of Rural Italian Women Sicily, 1880–1920*, Toronto: University of Toronto Press.

Rosental, P. A. (2005). Migrations, souveraineté, droits sociaux. Protéger et expulser les étrangers en Europe du XIXe siècle à nos jours. *Annales.* 66 (2): 335–373.

Salvetti, P. (2013). Tra miracolo economico e crisi petrolifera. Vedove bianche: una storia da scrivere In Pisa, B. and Boscato, S. (eds) *Donne negli anni Settanta. Voci, esperienze, lotte*, Milano: Angeli: 93–114.

Scidà, G. (2006). Nonna Maria e i paradigmi dell'azione migratoria: un'esercitazione. *Altreitalie*, 31: 52–73.

Vertovec, S. (2004). Migrant transnationalism and modes of transformation. *International Migration Review*. 38 (3): 970–1001.

Viazzo, P. P. (1989). *Comunità alpine. Ambiente, popolazione, struttura sociale nelle Alpi dal XVI secolo ad oggi*, Bologna: Il Mulino.

3 Maritime history and history of migration

Combined perspectives

M. Elisabetta Tonizzi

Introduction

From the 1820s to 1880 some 11–12 million Europeans migrated and about 30 million did the same from 1881 to 1915: it was the well-known Great Migration, by any reckoning one of greatest non-colonial voluntary mass migrations of all times. The Americas (in descending order the United States, Argentina, Canada and Brazil) received more than 85 per cent of that unprecedented overseas relocation.[1] Starting from the 1880s the outflow shifted from northwestern to south-eastern Europe; poorly qualified agricultural workers became predominant and single males, migrated on a temporary basis, replaced family groups in search of a permanent settlement in the New World. Return and repeated emigration became a distinguishing feature of New emigrants, as they were famously dubbed. The major point of origin of that huge flow was Italy (where southern regions, Calabria, Campania, Sicilia, etc. substituted northern ones as Liguria, Piedmont[2] and Veneto), closely followed by the multinational Russian and Austro-Hungarian empires.

The Great Migration, especially thanks to in-depth studies by economists, sociologists and political scientists, has been scholarly explained as the result of combined reasons such as the economic growth and industrialization of the New World and its scarcity of labour forces corresponding to the overpopulation of Europe; international free trade and open-border migration policies (until the US Congress passed the "country-quotas" regulations in the mid-1920s that severely cut the number of European immigrants allowed in America),[3] within the so-called "first wave of globalization" (Hatton and Williamson, 1998). The "transport revolution" (steam navigation[4] and railways connecting ever larger parts of European population and zones, which were as much significant for overseas migrants because they facilitated links to and from port cities) along with the "revolution of information" (land and submarine telegraph and later on radio-telegraph) permitted and eased the transcontinental circulation of people and goods (Scholl, 1998).

Besides this mix of well-identified "push and pull" factors, the basic import-ance of "migration chains" has also been argued. According to this bottom-up analytic model, emigration was a personal decision taken by individuals selected by the family circle and acting within a transnational system of kinship and community networks extended on both shores of the Atlantic. Migration chains, the most widespread pattern of emigration there has ever been, were built up on epistolary information and constituted a form of social capital that helped to minimize fears and economic costs and risks, assisted after arrival, and so increased the expected net returns of migration. Help comprised psychological (encouragement to take the plunge and move overseas and primary adjustment in the country of destination) and financial (money, pre-paid tickets and an immediate access to the labour market) assistance. Relatives, friends and also "friends of friends" provided both of these. The relevance of the latter, that is migration networks extended to distant acquaintances, had been argued by sociology since the 1970s and recently reasserted by historians on the basis of maritime primary sources.[5]

In addition to economic-directed "push and pull" factors and personal-family choice taken by individuals within the framework of migration chains, State regulations of migrant seaborne transport were as much important. The historical literature on the Great Migration, and the New emigration within its framework, is well-known, easily available and too broad to attempt to discuss or even to make reference to in these pages. Consequently, and not least for brevity, it will be taken for granted.

Nowadays, scholars have shifted their attention to "global" migrations, both of the 1800s and the 1900s, and stressed the importance of long-distance migration circuits different from the Euro-Atlantic one throughout the "long nineteenth century" and beyond.[6] Nevertheless, some aspects of the latter are still worthy of consideration and other weighty "factors" must be added to the preceding list.

It is a glaring obviousness, and actually so much self-evident as to become "invisible", that emigrants could neither cross the Atlantic by train nor on foot but had to voyage on a ship (unlike today, there were not other travel modes), a steamship from the 1870s onwards, and that to board on it they had to buy the ticket sold by a shipping company's agent, go to a port and spend a certain amount of time there.

To put it in other terms, "how" Europeans moved, and the wide-ranging network of actors involved in the overseas relocation, matters as much as "why" they emigrated (and why most of them did not).

It is now (and starting from the late 1980s) of common knowledge among historians (Lucassen, 1987; Moch, 1992; Lucassen, 1997) that well before the "discovery" of America (i.e. the nineteenth–early-twentieth-century transatlantic migration) the Europeans were all but immobile. Perpetually in search of better employment opportunities, since the early modern age they were acquainted with long distance journeys within intra- and trans-regional networks. Prior to the turn of the nineteenth century, intercontinental migrations had become an extended phenomenon. Nevertheless, for the multitude of New emigrants the transatlantic voyage was a totally alien and fearsome experience, never confronted by previous generations. Poor and illiterate peasants living in tiny and remote rural villages, they had never seen the sea or, if they had, were used to perceiving it as a threat more than a resource. Thus, they had to make up a completely new, seaborne migration skill.

The ocean passage was very often carefully described in emigrants' letters home and deeply rooted in their personal written and oral memories. In addition, it was the only common denominator of the throng of people coming from very heterogeneous countries and ethno-linguistic groups. Conversely, in almost all studies on the Great Migration, transatlantic liners are mentioned but mostly as simple "vehicles" to transfer flows, and the historical narrative evokes the crossing hastily and anecdotally as if it was not a decisive "segment" of emigrants' patterns but an annoying parenthesis, separating the "old" from the promising "new" life they were impatient to begin.

In sum, it is a matter of fact that without fast, regular, safe and affordable passenger steamship services of high carrying capacity and their related maritime networks (shipping agencies and agents, port facilities dedicated to emigrants, etc.) there would have been no mass migration (Hoste and Fischer, 2007, pp. 2–3) and that the history of migration cannot be written "independently of that of seaborne business and maritime infrastructures" (Miller, 2012, p. 3). Moreover, migrations are an integral part of the multifaceted interaction between mankind and the sea that is the professed scope of maritime history (Broeze, 1995; Harlaftis and Vassallo, 2004). Notwithstanding, migration and maritime historians have tackled their respective issues as if they were independent topics. Their research paths have been compared to two ships passing in the sea at night without seeing each other (Miller, 2007, p. 275).

Only recently, at a conference held in Florence in November 2005, have scholars explicitly attempted to bridge the disciplinary divide so to enhance the understanding of the interactions between maritime and migration networks in order to integrate the role of maritime-related institutions and actors (shipping companies, agents, port facilities, etc.) in the decision-making process of migration.

To be sure, it was not the first attempt to find a mutually convenient collaboration, a common ground for the two historical sub-disciplines. In August 1985 the International Commission of Maritime History held a conference in Stuttgart aiming at a scrutiny of "Maritime Aspects of Migration", the proceedings of which, including some essays regarding the epoch of the Great Migration, were published in 1989 (Friedland, 1989). During the roughly 20 years that passed in between, some progress has occurred, but not so substantial as to keep the Editors of Florence conference's proceedings, issued in 2007 (Feys *et al.*, 2007) to wish further developments of the interdisciplinary dialogue (Hoste and Fischer, 2007, p. 7).

They have not written in vain and since then the "state of the art" has improved: some noteworthy works on the maritime implications of the transatlantic Great Migration have been published. This chapter focuses on our current historiographical knowledge of the "maritime ring", as I like to call it, of migration chains.

Prior to proceeding, two points must be stressed. First, the body of literature is very unbalanced indeed, and not only from a linguistic point of view. As the United States were the "great magnet" for the European mass migration, so, and fully understandably, they have "magnetized" the attention of contemporary historians. Therefore, the majority of studies I will refer to are concerned with North American (US) destinations and/or written in English but also some South America-related and Latin-language-written researches will be taken into account. Second, all this is mentioned with the full awareness that I will not provide a complete review on the selected topic.

The multifaceted "maritime ring" of migration chains: an overview

"Floating hells": migration "under sail"

The demand for labour and the difference in real wages between donor and recipient countries were major factors in determining the volume of the nineteenth–early-twentieth-century transatlantic migrations. To connect supply with demand, an adequate transport system was necessary. As Nicholas Canny wrote about 20 years ago: "emigration occurs only … where transport is in place to convey prospective emigrants to their new home" (Canny, 1994, p. 278).

It was right in the heyday of the Great Migration that sailing ships were forced out of the passenger trade and steamship companies became dominant in that kind of transport: at that time railroads linked ports to the far reaches of Europe. Before the "steam revolution", begun on the transatlantic routes in the 1850s and definitely established in the late 1870s, migration occurred on sail ships.

At the "age of sail" (Cohn, 2009) (hereafter meant as the early 1800s up to the 1870s), finding a ship was not easy and departures were not scheduled but rather decided at the captain's discretion. Vessels remained in the harbour until they had filled their cargo hold, an operation that usually took weeks, during which emigrants waited camped on the dockside or along the neighbouring roads (Veraghtert, 1989; Rössler, 2010).

Despite that migrants were very profitable substitutes of ballast on westbound routes, they had no dedicated accommodations aboard. They travelled on freight ships and were lodged on the same and all but clean deck where cargos were stored. Neither the captain nor the crew were skilled in dealing with passengers; drinkable water was rationed and provisions were not supplied.

The trip from England to North America lasted a good 45 days: to the same destination but leaving from continental Europe, Bremen was the most distant port, it was a week longer. On the route to south America, from Lisbon to Rio de Janeiro as an example, over two months were necessary (Costa Leite, 1991). Therefore, even if transatlantic fares were costly and disproportionate to the quality of services, other expenses had a much higher incidence, about 65 per cent of the total cost of one move from Europe to the United States.[7] Including the overland journey and lodging costs waiting for embarkation, the period of time when the migrant did not earn but had to run through his saving or live off his family was extremely long. But, besides "time", the ocean passage had another type of additional cost.

Shipwrecks were a catastrophe, always extensively press-covered and so terrifying for passengers, but not at all likely to occur. The outbreak of acute infectious diseases (typhus and cholera the most lethal) was instead much more frequent. Besides the length of the voyage, major causes were overcrowding (at the "age of sail" European emigrants to the United States were crowded at rates of about 0.4 per gross tonnage and each passenger disposed of an area roughly corresponding to the size of a berth)[8] and inadequate ventilation. Sanitary conditions aboard were extremely poor, and medications, if available, were administered by the captain. There were other crucial variables in addition, such as age and gender and, even more importantly, the disease environments of the countries of origin or crossed during the journey and the health situation in the ports of departure. A well-established scholarship has extensively dealt with the interaction of all these aspects in determining the passengers' sanitary standards (Cohn, 1989, 2003, 2009). Later on we will deal with the importance of pre-boarding medical screenings, which at the age of sail were absolutely exceptional events.

Starting from 1819, the United States, followed by some other European countries throughout the first half of the nineteenth century, passed laws to prescribe inspections at ports of departure and improve conditions aboard vessels carrying emigrants, but with very little effect (Moltmann, 1989; Jones, 1976, 1989).

Including those deaths that occurred shortly after arrival for a disease contracted by healthy individuals during the crossing, shipboard loss was estimated at slightly over 1 percent (between 1820 and 1860 on the route England–United States). The mortality rate on sailing ships was about four times higher than that experienced at the time by non-migrants (Cohn, 2003, p. 18). Given that, compared to the average population, young adults were overrepresented on board, this rate is somehow underestimated.[9]

In sum: overseas migration had great "potential" and "future" benefits in terms of improving one's economic well-being. In exchange, migrants "under sail" were confronted with "certain" and "immediate" costs. Dying due to an epidemic on the high seas, or having just disembarked, was in every respect included.

The hazard of the transatlantic passage aboard the "floating hells", one of the many deadly nicknames (others were "coffin-ships", "floating lazar-houses" and the like) of sail ships, was real but it did not prevent many hundreds of thousands of European emigrants from arriving safely (Moltmann, 1989, p. 311). However, it is as much true that "to the extent that migration was related to benefits and costs, changes in shipboard mortality may then help to explain changes that occurred in the volume of migration overtime" (Cohn, 1989, p. 160).

Apart from the number of Europeans willing to emigrate despite the multiple risks involved, the room for passengers on sail ships was reduced according to their reduced tonnage.

Steam navigation: a maritime and migration revolution

The change from sailing to steamships for passenger travels from Europe to North America started in the 1850s: in 1850 the first steamer carrying emigrants left Liverpool for the United States. Equally important technological (namely, the introduction of iron hulls and stern screw) and economic (namely, the imbalance between the demand for passenger travels and the supply of steamers, more costly and longer to assemble than sailing ships) reasons, made the transition take a long period of time. It was fully accomplished in the 1870s: "in the 1873 the last sailing ship with emigrants aboard made its voyage from Hamburg to North America" (Moltmann, 1989, p. 311). Contemporary (the 1870s), the same happened on the routes to south America from Portugal and the Atlantic coasts of Spain (Gonzáles, 1994, 2002; Costa Leite, 1991, 1996; Valdaliso, 1992).

Ocean-going steamships made possible the development of the Great Migration.[10] Marine-engine-powered, so not subservient to winds and tides, and operated on regularly-scheduled services, they were much larger (from 1850 to 1914 the size of ships increased tenfold), much more comfortable and safer, not least because they were progressively staffed by expressly trained crews. Nevertheless, misfortune, as destruction in collisions or serious damages in gales, "was not unknown to them" (Moltmann, 1989, p. 312).

Transatlantic liners significantly shortened travel times, which passed initially from a minimum of 45 days to two weeks and then, from the dawn of the twentieth century until the outbreak of the First World War, to 9–12 days, depending on the port of embarkation, both for north and south American destinations (Costa Leite, 1991, 1996; Gonzáles, 1994, 2002). Ticket prices, after an initial decrease, did not fall since the last quarter of the nineteenth century and remained stable (amounting to about 50 per cent of the estimated total costs of one move from Europe to the United States) throughout the remainder of the pre-First World War era (Keeling, 2007, pp. 168–169). Thus, the substantial contraction of "idle time" on overall emigration costs, along with lowered sanitary risks (i.e. the restraint of infectious diseases aboard) and hardships (i.e. the supply of comfortable accommodation) of the oceanic journey, played a major role in making overseas migration an economically rational option.

Jointly considered, these new conditions eased return emigration and permitted repeated transatlantic passages. In other words, the revolution of maritime transport concealed "the terror of distance" (Gabaccia and Hoerder, 2011, p. 371) and allowed the inclusion of transatlantic migration into the pattern of seasonal, rural-to-urban/rural-to-rural, labour movements that Europeans had experienced for centuries.

As a consequence, the swarming of New emigrants induced a growing public concern in all countries involved in the process on both sides of the Atlantic. In other words, the strengthening of the "maritime ring" of chain migration trig-gered a chain reaction (Miller, 2007, p. 179).

Starting approximately from the 1880s and throughout the period prior to the First World War, sending and recipient countries revised and reinforced their migration legislation. The former, very often east and southeast European coun-tries with no direct coastal connections nor shipping interests, were concerned about the protection of their citizens before embarkation and their welfare during the passage. The latter, and first and foremost the United States, were most worried about the risk of the social integration of the increasing wave of the New Immigration, with the aim to control but not shut off it,[11] at least until the mid-1920s "country-quotas" regulations.

Owing to the rapid and massive involvement of states in the emigration process, drastic legislation measures were enacted to fix minimum standards of ventilation, hygiene and health (ship's doctors and infirmaries, toilets and washing facilities, centralized kitchens and appliances to disinfect linens and tableware), passengers' accommodations and diet. New emigrants came in most cases from backward, rural countries and such standards were incomparably more comfortable than those they were used to having at home.[12]

Thanks to these radical improvements, passage on the modern steamers was made tolerable but it did not become a pleasure trip for emigrants (McCarthy, 2006): decks were overcrowded, dormitories overheated, the sea was a com-pletely alien environment, and so bewilderment and seasickness were daily suf-ferings. This is not at all surprizing, considering the extreme hardship of labour conditions suffered by contemporary seamen (Fury, 2007).

As became apparent during the "age of sail", the spreading of epidemics during the crossing was of major concern. This concern became even more grounded, given the high-risk disease environments of the New emigrants' coun-tries of origin, where health treatments were less than deficient. Therefore, to prevent the embarkation of ill or disabled individuals, extensive and accurate preliminary medical assessments at ports of departure and arrival were enforced.

To guarantee the landing of healthy immigrants, steamship companies were charged with the responsibility of the sanitary conditions of their passengers. In case of refused entry on arrival, repatriation was at their expenses along with all other refunds. So, to defend the reputation of "their" emigrants, avoid heavy eco-nomic sanctions in the case of refused entry, and as much to attract passengers on their ships, navigation companies funnelled migration flows into a limited number of home ports. In order to ease the implementation of the state-required health screening, they promoted the building of new lodging and inspection facilities.[13] Besides, they opened offices in New York and elsewhere in the Americas; coordinated with local institution and governmental actors, like consuls; recruited and disseminated all over Europe droves of agents to sell tickets and organize all-inclusive voyages from the village of departure to over-seas destinations (Miller, 2002; Evans, 2007; Feys, 2007a, 2007b).

Ports have always been intersections of hinterland and foreland networks of multi-modal transportation infrastructures and clusters of human expertise (shipping companies and their agents; consuls, port authorities and local governments) (Miller, 2012). "Human cargos" deeply influenced their activities and port cities' authorities modernized their maritime infrastructures (piers, wharves and passenger stations) not to be cut out of the increasing demand of emigration services.[14]

Emigrants, who in the large majority of cases had never gone through a medical check, felt humiliated (women especially) since doctors were often rude and their inspections harsh, and unceasingly complained about mistreatment. Since the fear of being rejected prevailed, they made any effort to hide their possible, and frequent illnesses. Some among the most widespread, as measles or malaria, had a long incubation; others, such as trachoma or tuberculosis, had preclinical stages that were difficult if not impossible to detect. Consequently, and so confirming the very poor starting health conditions of emigrants, not imputable to their transatlantic movers and on the contrary very unfavourable to their business economics, liners were often transformed into "floating hospitals".[15] Owing also and chiefly to substantial advances in epidemiology and diagnostics,[16] deaths during the voyages were reduced by 90 per cent and progressively became a tragic but residual occurrence.[17]

Some data quantify the revolutionary impact of steam navigation on Euro-Atlantic migration flows. From 1899 to 1914, when the exodus peaked, about 14 million Europe-borne migrants crossed the Atlantic to the United States and six million did the same route eastwards (Keeling, 2012, pictures at pp. viii–ix). From 1881 to 1914 over six million embarked to Argentina and Brazil.[18]

Until shortly before the introduction of steam, the US merchant marine monopolized the migrant trade on the north Atlantic. Then, manifold causes such as, for example, the much higher profitability of investments in the West than in the shipping industry and the very negative effects of the Civil War (1861–1865), determined the end of its domination. By the 1870s, leadership passed to the European lines,[19] a sign of the opening of the long reign of Europe over the twentieth-century maritime global world. Until the 1920s, emigrants and passenger steamship companies were a substantial component of the Eurocentric maritime network that embraced and connected the whole world (Miller, 2012).

Throughout the period 1899–1914, four large and long-established British and German companies, whose principal business was not freight but passengers (i.e. emigrants), transported over half of the European emigration to the United States.

They were the Liverpool-based Cunard Line and White Star, the Hamburg–America Line and the Bremen-based Norddeutscher Lloyd (on the "Big Four" see Broeze, 1991; Keeling, 2012). The Le Havre-based Compagnie Générale Transatlatique, which also ran a railway line with carriages tailored to the needs of emigrants (Moltmann, 1989, p. 316; Rössler, 2010, p. 89), and the Rotterdam-based Holland–America Line were also top players of the set of companies of the "northern range" (extend from Hamburg to Le Havre). Since the decade prior to the turn of the century and to the eve of the First World War, the impressive wave of New emigration coming from Southern European countries, Italy followed at long distance by Greece, created a very crowded and profitable "Mediterranean migrant market".[20]

From 1900 to 1914 emigrants leaving from the Mediterranean Sea to the United States amounted to over four million, about one-third of the total (Keeling, 2012, pp. viii–xi). So, the map of the most important migration gateways (Bremen and Hamburg jointly considered, Liverpool and some others of the European north shore like Antwerp, Le Havre and Rotterdam) was integrated by the emerging of the Mediterranean emigration area. Naples and Genoa were at the top of the Mediterranean ranking, followed (in alphabetic order) by Marseille, some Ottoman harbours, Palermo, Patras and Trieste.

The "Big Four" were prompt to shift a sizeable part of their large and diversified fleets to the Mediterranean migration route and so held their overall supremacy. In 1892, when the immigration station of Ellis Island in New York harbour opened as a substitute for Castle Garden,[21] the Italians leaving from Genoa (then the most important Italian migration port) travelled on German and British ships (Tonizzi, 2000, pp. 39–58; Gibelli, 2004).

From 1901 the Navigazione Generale Italiana, supported by state intervention (D'Angelo and Tonizzi, 2004, pp. 69–76), gained its ground on the Italy–New York route and maintained its predominance to Latin American countries (Argentina and Brazil). South Atlantic destinations had not the same strategic importance of the United States, battleground of the "Big Four",[22] but were still demanded, for similarity in language and culture, by European emigrants from Italy, Spain and Portugal.[23] Therefore, the migrant trade to south America raised the attention of the Hamburg–America Line, which in 1899 funded the Italia Navigazione a Vapore, registered in Italian partners' names so to benefit from protectionism. By 1906 it was absorbed by the Navigazione Generale Italiana (Doria, 2009).

In short, the Great Migration brought about the development of a global and cartelized transportation industry, operating gigantic fleets of steel "Atlantic greyhounds" that brought overseas millions of Europeans, and was managed as other big firms of the time. The outbreak of the "Great War" of 1914–1918 and restrictive 1920s US laws brought the "Great Migration" and its related transport business to an end.

Not at all surprisingly, "the haves" and their lifestyle have always attracted much more attention than the "have-nots". In the common imagination, the stereotypes of the early-twentieth century liners are first class cabins, luxuriously furnished dining rooms and ball halls. *Titanic*, by James Cameron (1997), is the most famous example. If Leonardo Di Caprio had not been the boyfriend of a lady (or such considered) of the upper deck, he would not have been the "hero" of the movie but only one of the 513 emigrants (709 out of 1,318 passengers) who died in the iceberg scraping and consequent sinking on 19 April 1912 (Gleicher, 2006, pp. 41–43).

There is a massive literature, easily available (so we can avoid quoting it in detail) and very informative, though different in scientific quality, on individual steamship companies and entrepreneurs, their fleets, single liners and oceanic routes. In all these studies "steerage passengers" (i.e. emigrants accommodated in the "steerage"[24] below the main deck, location of the wealthy travellers) are indicated as their dominant revenue source and the main, or better only, factor in establishing satisfactory profitability. Indeed, migration from Europe to the United States is correlated closely to the steamship companies' profits, and most of the capital investment in technological upgrading occurred during the Great Migration years.

Steamship companies and transatlantic migrations: new insights

As mentioned above, our aim is to argue the importance of expanding the list of "factors" to be considered for a comprehensive understanding of the Great Migration. Two signal and brand-new books have turned the spotlight on the interaction between transatlantic migration and the migrant transport business. Their authors, who have previously published many articles on the topic,[25] belong to different sub-fields of historical investigations. Therefore, they follow different analytical paths and suggest divergent conclusions. Nevertheless, both adopt a transnational approach and bring to the fore the importance of steamship companies in the European mass migration story.

Drew Keeling's book, *The Business of Transatlantic Migration between Europe and the United States, 1900–1914* published in 2012, examines the seaborne transport business that made the Great Migration possible. His study concerns the 20 million or so European steerage passengers travelling back and forth to the United States. The choice is more than grounded, given that from 1900 to 1914 the United States absorbed as many immigrants as all other countries combined (Keeling, 2012, p. xvi). Keeling gathered an impressive mass of quantitative data, produced by all European donor countries and provides a substantial set of numerical information. The author, on his own admission, considers only in passing the "voice" (letters and personal reports) of emigrants because other kinds of sources are more useful to his purpose (Keeling, 2012, ch. 7 and p. xvii).[26]

The book focuses on the business structures of passenger steamship lines, their plans, policies, functioning and organizational innovations. Major attention is given to the risks of the travel business, highly sensitive to the downturns of the economic cycle, and to the process of cartelization, by means of the so-called Shipping Conferences, which companies adopted to regulate the north Atlantic passenger trade.[27] Pool agreements stabilized prices, and as a consequence fares did not decrease throughout the period under consideration, but fostered a "service competition" to improve the quality of the voyage and so to the advantage of migrants.

With regards to our major point of interest, the role of steamship companies and their related maritime networks in the decision-making process of emigration, Keeling's conclusion is that they were central but as mere "facilitators". Even though the fluctuating state of the US economy was far beyond their reach, migration chains, family and friend connections able to provide individuals with a good job just after the arrival and so mitigate the risk of relocation, were the key factor.

Torsten Feys' book, *The Battle for the Migrants: The Introduction of Steamshipping on the North Atlantic and its Impact on the European Exodus*, was published in 2013. Unlike Keeling, Feys has been brought up as a maritime historian and programmatically aims at integrating maritime and migration history so to provide a comprehensive investigation on the social, political and economic interests and institutional decisions that lay behind the impact of shipping companies operating on the north Atlantic migration market. To attain this object, the author chiefly uses non-quantifiable sources, for instance letters, periodicals, pamphlets, diplomatic correspondence, governmental memoranda, etc. Nevertheless, the book is complete with detailed appendices of quantitative data (Feys, 2013, pp. 323–378).

Feys considers transatlantic mass migration as a multi-dimensional trade issue and broaches it both at a micro-and macro-level of analysis. His conclusions are opposite to Keeling's. Steamship companies, and their dependent maritime network tightly entangled in migration chains, played a pivotal role not only as enablers and facilitators but also as stimulators of the process. Through prepaid tickets, shipping agents and agencies, located on both sides of the Atlantic, connected "moving" and "movers", arranged land travel to the ports and assisted emigrants during the passage and at their destinations, providing a job and accommodation. More importantly, besides supplying the seaborne information and all the services necessary to achieve already-decided migration strategies, they constantly advertised in the local papers and so brought the New World a lot closer in the mental map of Europeans, and also those travelling outside migration chains. In short, the definition of "travel agents" does not mirror their actual role.

To defend their business, i.e. prevent or at least put off the adoption of restrictive migration laws in the United States, shipping companies, throughout the Progressive Era, hired lobbyists and journalists; promoted press campaigns to influence policymakers and public opinion; put their men in the US Congress investigation committees; and generously funded the anti-restrictions Immigration Protective League (Feys, 2013, 2010). The United States closed the doors only in the 1920s and the shipping companies' "visible hand" was of crucial importance to determine such a long delay.

Conclusion

Maritime historians, as much as colleagues of other sub-fields of historical investigation working on quantitative and qualitative maritime-related primary sources, have done much, and with signal results, to intertwine maritime and migration history. We are now aware that migration chains and maritime networks operated at the same time, which in itself would not be such a great scientific acquirement. But, and most importantly, we definitively know that the latter was not less effective than the former as an emigration "factor" or "stimu-lator", as one prefers to define it.

Steamship companies were not mere suppliers of technologically-updated "vehicles" of the transatlantic crossing. For a start, as so disclaiming the philanthropic-humanitarian depiction still rooted in historiography (Italian in particular, owing to the persisting influence of the poverty-motivated Socialist and Catholic interpretation of the phenomenon),[28] they were not ruthless exploit-ers of masses of poor emigrants travelling with their bundles of rags and dreams. Their intense process of cartelization, begun in the1880s and culminating after 1900, avoided a cutthroat fares competition and improved steerage passengers' accommodation and safety. In other words, it was a rare and endorsed case of a cartel with no deleterious effects on consumers.

Besides, shipping lines had a strong clout on American migration policies and their intense lobbying activities prevented the early approval of US restrictive migration laws. Since they were charged with the enforcement of national regu-lations, they improved clinical screenings on land and so prevented debarments and assured the landing of nearly all their passengers, as it was their major busi-ness interest.

If the largest-scale historical experiment of ethnic and social transformation was achieved and emigrants became a vital part of the most intense phase of transformation of the US "way of life" (the 1900–1914 period), it must be also traced to the lucrative business they represented for the steamship companies.[29] Neither shipping companies nor involved governments were philanthropists but both operated according to their convenience: their combined action improved "moving" conditions in favour of "movers".

Now it is up to the historians of migration to value "the maritime ring" of migration chains and include it in their research work so to enhance the under-standing of the fundamental processes of the Great Migration. They have a vast body of literature to draw on.

Notes

1 These figures and the distribution per country of origin and destination are well-known. Among the many possible references Ferenczi and Willcox, 1929–1931; Woodruff, 1966; Baines, 1991.
2 Sailors and traders of the Savoy Kingdom (Liguria and Piedmont), with many desert-ers of the army on the occasion of the Crimean War (1852–1855), formed an extended social network that favoured the establishment of a permanent and populated com-munity (Vangelista, 1992). For a study on the "hidden migration" of deserters from the British merchant navy throughout the late nineteenth century to 1913, see Fischer, 1989.
3 Much earlier on the Pacific shore. The Chinese Exclusion Act was passed in 1882.
4 Focused on the shipping industry as a key component of the history of globalization, Starkey and Harlaftis, 1998; Harlaftis *et al.*, 2012; Miller, 2012.
5 Steidl, 2007. Drawing on the sociologist Mark Granovetter's theory (published in 1973) on "the strength of weak ties", the author's investigation of ship records from the ports of Hamburg and Bremen in 1910 stresses the importance of a wider

migration chain within the framework of emigration to the United States from the Austrian-Hungarian monarchy after 1870.

6 For instance McKeown, 2004: for an overview see also Manning, 2005. Gabaccia and Hoerder, 2011 for an integration between migration and world history accomplished by centring the analysis around the four oceans/seas.

7 Single total costs of that route since 1815 to 1914 are split, also chronologically from 1815 onwards, and estimated in Keeling, 2007, pp. 168–169.

8 At that time a berth was much smaller than today's single bed.

9 However high the emigrants' mortality was, it was incomparably below that of slave and convict voyages of the same period (mid-nineteenth century), Cohn, 1989, pp. 160, 182. Nevertheless some literature has alluded to a similarity, for example Greenhill, 1968.

10 "An event of enormous significance for the history of immigration", Jones, 1960, p. 157.

11 Not recent but still useful overviews of European legislations on migration transport are in Moltmann, 1989; Jones 1989.

12 As noted in many letters of emigrants coming from southeastern Europe, who had never seen a toilet or a washbasin nor had ever slept in a "real" individual bed complete with mattress and sheet. See, for instance, *BallinStadt Port of Dreams: The Emigration Museum Hamburg*. Meat, included in ships' menus twice a day with other proteins and varied carbohydrates, deeply altered the almost exclusively vegetarian diet of New emigrants, as in the case of Calabrian peasants studied by Bevilacqua, 1981.

13 The Hamburg's BallinStadt, built in 1898 by Albert Ballin, the general director of the Hamburg–America Line, and able to house 5,000 persons at one time, is the most famous.

14 Even though late with respect to North European ports, also Genoa, with Naples the most important migration hub of the Mediterranean Sea, underwent extensive structural works to handle migrant trade, see Tonizzi, 2000, 2002.

15 On sanitary conditions on Italian vessels (whose qualitative standards were lower than their North European competitors) during the Atlantic crossing at the age of the Great Migration, see Molinari, 1988, 1990, 2005.

16 Unanimously the most important factor. See, for example, Jones, 1989, p. 331.

17 As for Italy, Commissariato Generale Emigrazione 1926, *ad indicem*.

18 See Note 1.

19 On American companies before the introduction of steam, Moltmann, 1989, p. 313. Afterwards, the only US company was the American Line and it always struggled to be profitable, Feys, 2013, p. 6.

20 Evoked but not quantified by Kardassis, 1997; Manitakis, 2007.

21 Located on the southern tip of Manhattan, it was the first port of immigration to New York. Between 1855 and 1890, Castle Garden received an estimated eight million immigrants and its passenger records are invaluable research documents. See *The German Emigration Center Book*, 2009, pp. 108–110; not updated but informative Svejda, 1968. As a starting point for research on Ellis Island, Yans-Mclaughlin and Lightman, 1997.

22 For the high barriers of entry for newcomers into the oligopolistic transatlantic passenger market see Sebak, 2011.

23 Naranjo, 1995; Bernasconi, 1995, who bases her study on the passenger ship records of the port of Buenos Aires. She uses the same source, with others, to detect the immigrants to Argentina from the Republic of San Marino so to separate them from the Italian emigrants coming from other surrounding regions, Bernasconi, 2009. A recent contribution on Italian emigration to Brazil, that contemplates the role of steamship companies, is Gonçalves, 2012.

24 Steam navigation borrowed many words, and trade routes, from sail navigation. The "steerage" was the location of mechanisms for steering sailing ships.
25 Their previous contributions are listed in the references of their books and so, for brevity, we will not quote all of them.
26 Emigrants' letters very frequently, if not always, tell of the voyage and are a staple of contemporary social history of migration and of all Euro-Atlantic museums of emigration. See for instance Yans-Mclaughlin and Lightman, 1997; *(La) Merica! 1892–1914*, 2008; *The German Emigration Center Book*, 2009; *BallinStadt Port of Dreams* undated. For an updated review of the international historical literature on letters from emigrants see Sanfilippo, 2008.
27 For a previous investigation of the topic see also Greenhill, 1998.
28 As an example, for a long time the Italian historiography considered emigration agents as traffickers. For a different approach see Martellini, 2001.
29 Despite their divergent conclusions, both Keeling, 2012, p. xv, and Feys, 2013, p. 322, agree on this point.

References

Baines, D. (1991). *Emigration from Europe, 1815–1930*. Houndmills-Hampshire: Macmillan.

BallinStadt Port of Dreams. The Emigration Museum Hamburg (undated). Hamburg: Emigration Museum BallinStadt.

Bernasconi, A. (1995). Aproximación al estudio de las redes migratorias a través de las listas de desembarco. Possibilidades y problemas. In Bjerg, M. and Otero, H. (eds). *Inmigración y redes sociales en la Argentina moderna*. Buenos Aires: Cemla.

Berbasconi A. (2009). *"... luego de 35 días de mar lega a una nueva tierra". L'emigrazione sammarinese in Argentina, 1882–1956*. Repubblica di San Marino: Aiep editore.

Bevilacqua, P. (1981). Emigrazione transoceanica e mutamenti nell'alimentazione contadina calabrese fra Otto e Novecento. *Quaderni storici*, 47: 520–550.

Boyce, G. and Gorsky, R. (eds) (2002). *Resources and Infrastructures in the Maritime Economy, 1500–2002*. St. John's, Newfoundland: Research in Maritime History, no. 22.

Broeze, F. (1991). Albert Ballin, the Hamburg–Bremen Rivalry and the Dynamics of the Conference System. *International Journal of Maritime History*, iii (1): 1–32.

Broeze, F. (ed.) (1995). *Maritime History at the Crossroads: A Critical Review of Recent Historiography*. St. John's, Newfoundland: Research in Maritime History, no. 9.

Canny, N. (1994). In search of a better home? European overseas migration, 1500–1880. In Canny, N. (ed.). *Europeans on the Move. Studies on European Migration 1500–1800*. Oxford: Clarendon Press.

Cohn, R. L. (1989). Maritime mortality in the eighteenth and nineteenth century: a survey. *International Journal of Maritime History*, i (1): 159–191.

Cohn, R. L. (2003). Passenger mortality on antebellum immigrant ships. *International Journal of Maritime History*, xv (2): 1–19.

Cohn, R. L. (2005). The transition from sail to steam in immigration to the United States. *Journal of Economic History*, 65 (2): 469–495.

Cohn, R. L. (2009). *Mass Migration under Sail: European Migration in the Antebellum United States*. New York: Cambridge University Press.

Commissariato Generale Emigrazione (1926). *Annuario statistico dell'emigrazione italiana dal 1876 al 1925*. Rome.

Costa Leite, J. (1991). O transporte de emigrantes: da vela ao vapor na rota do Brasil 1851–1914. *Análise Social*, 112–113: 741–752.

Costa Leite, J. (1996). Os negócios da emigração (1870–1914). *Análise Social*, 136–137: 381–396.

D'angelo, M. and Tonizzi M. E. (2004). Recent maritime historiography on Italy. In Harlaftis, G. and Vassallo, C. (eds). *New Directions in Mediterranean Maritime History*. St. John's, Newfoundland: Research in Maritime History, no. 28.

Doria, M. (2009). Dal trasporto degli emigranti alla crociera. La travagliata storia della Società di navigazione "Italia". In Massa P. (ed.). *Andar per mare*. Genova: De Ferrari.

Evans, N. J. (2007). The role of foreign-born agents in the development of mass migrant travel through Britain, 1815–1924. In Feys, Fischer, Hoste and Vanfraechem (eds). *Maritime Transport and Migration*. St. John's, Newfoundland: Research in Maritime History, no. 33.

Ferenczi, I. and Willcox, W. (1929–1931). *International Migrations*, vol. 1, *Statistics*, vol. 2 *Interpretations*. New York: National Bureau of Economic Research.

Feys, T. (2007a). The battle for the migrants: the evolution from port to company competition, 1840–1914. In Feys, Fischer, Hoste and Vanfraechem (eds). *Maritime Transport and Migration*. St. John's, Newfoundland: Research in Maritime History, no. 33.

Feys, T. (2007b). Where all passenger liners meet: New York as a nodal point for the transatlantic migrant trade, 1885–1896. *International Journal of Maritime History*, xix (2): 245–272.

Feys, T. (2010). The visible hand of shipping interests in American migration policies 1815–1914. *Tijdschrift voor Sociale en Economische Geschiedenis*, 1: 38–62.

Feys, T. (2013). *The Battle for the Migrants: The Introduction of Steamshipping on the North Atlantic and its Impact on the European Exodus*, St. John's, Newfoundland: Research in Maritime History, no. 50.

Feys, T., Fischer, L. R., Hoste, S. and Vanfraechem, S. (eds) (2007). *Maritime Transport and Migration: The Connections between Maritime and Migration Networks*. St. John's, Newfoundland: Research in Maritime History, no. 33.

Fischer, L. R. (1989). The sea as highway: maritime service as a means of international migration, 1863–1913. In Friedland, K. (ed.). *Maritime Aspects of Migration*. Köln-Wien: Böhlau Verlag.

Friedland, K. (ed.) (1989). *Maritime Aspects of Migration*. Köln-Wien: Böhlau Verlag.

Fury, C. A. (2007). Labour conditions for seafarers. In Hattendorf, J. B. (editor in chief). *The Oxford Encyclopedia of Maritime History*. New York: Oxford University Press, vol. 2.

Gabaccia, D. R. and Hoerder, D. (eds) (2011). *Connecting Seas and Connected Ocean Rims: Indian, Atlantic, and Pacific Oceans and China seas Migrations from the 1830s to the 1930s*. Leiden and Boston: Brill.

(The) German Emigration Center Book (2009). Bremerhaven: Edition Dah.

Gibelli, A. (2004). Emigranti, bastimenti, transatlantici. Genova e la grande ondata migratoria. In Campodonico, P., Fochessati, M. and Piccione, P. (eds). *Transatlantici. Scenari e Sogni di mare*. Milan: Skira.

Gleicher, D. (2006). *The Rescue of the Third Class on the Titanic: A Revisionist History*. St. John's, Newfoundland: Research in Maritime History, no. 31.

Gonçalves, P. C. (2012). *Mercadores de braços. Riqueza e acumulação na organização da emigração europeia para o Novo Mundo*. São Paulo: Alameda Casa Editorial.

Gonzáles, A. V. (1994). De la vela al vapor. La modernización de los buques en la emigración gallega a América. *Estudios Migratoriós Latinoamericanos*, 28: 569–596.

Gonzáles, A. V. (2002). Os novos señores da rede commercial da emigración a América por portos galegos: os consignatarios das grandes navieiras transatlántica. *Estudios Migratoriós*, 13–14: 9–49.

Greenhill, B. (1968). *The Great Migration: Crossing the Atlantic under Sail*. London: National Maritime Museum.

Greenhill, R. B. (1998). Competition and co-operation in the global shipping industry: the origins and impact of the conference system for British ship-owners before 1914. In Starkey and Harlaftis (eds). *Global Markets: the Internationalization of the Sea*. St. John's, Newfoundland: Research in Maritime History, no. 14.

Harlaftis, G. and Vassallo, C. (2004). Maritime History since Braudel. In Harlaftis, G. and Vassallo, C. (eds). *New Directions in Mediterranean Maritime History*. St. John's, Newfoundland: Research in Maritime History, no. 28.

Harlaftis, G., Tenold, S. and Valdaliso, J. M. (eds) (2012). *World's Key Industry. History and Economics of International Shipping*. London, New York: Palgrave Macmillan.

Hatton, T. and Williamson, J. G. (1998). *The Age of Mass Migration. Causes and Economic Impact*. New York: Oxford University Press.

Hoste, S. and Fischer, L. R. (2007). Migration and maritime networks in the Atlantic economy: an introduction. In Feys, T., Fischer, L. R., Hoste, S. and Vanfraechem, S. (eds) *Maritime Transport and Migration: The Connections between Maritime and Migration Networks*. St. John's, Newfoundland: Research in Maritime History, no. 33

Jones, M. A. (1960). *American Immigration*. Chicago: University of Chicago Press.

Jones, M. A. (1976). Immigrants, steamships and governments: the steerage problem in transatlantic diplomacy, 1868–1874. In Allen, H. and Thompson, R. (eds). *Contrast and Connection: Bicentennial Essays in Anglo-American History*. London: Bell.

Jones, M. A. (1989). Aspects of north Atlantic migration: steerage conditions and American Law, 1819–1909. In Friedland, K. (ed.). *Maritime Aspects of Migration*. Köln-Wien: Böhlau Verlag.

Kardassis, V. (1997). Greek steam liners companies, 1858–1914. *International Journal of Maritime History*, ix (2): 107–127.

Keeling, D. (1999). Transatlantic shipping cartels and migration between Europe and America, 1880–1914. *Essays in Economic and Business History*, 17: 195–213.

Keeling, D. (2007). Costs, risks and migration networks between Europe and the United States, 19004–1914. In Feys, T., Fischer, L. R., Hoste, S. and Vanfraechem, S. (eds). *Maritime Transport and Migration: The Connections between Maritime and Migration Networks*. St. John's, Newfoundland: Research in Maritime History, no. 33

Keeling, D. (2012). *The Business of Transatlantic Migration between Europe and the United States, 1900–1914*. Zurich: Chronos.

Lucassen, J. (1987). *Migrant Labor in Europe: The Drift to the North Sea*. London: Croom Helm.

Lucassen, L. (1997). Eternal vagrants? State formation, migration and travelling groups in Western Europe, 1350–1914. In Lucassen, J. and Lucassen, L. (eds). *Migration, Migration History, History. Old paradigms and New Perspectives*. Bern: Peter Lang.

McCarthy, A. (2006). Migrant voyages to new worlds in the twentieth century. *International Journal of Maritime History*, xviii (1): 79–101.

McKeown, A. (2004). Global migration, 1846–1940. *Journal of World History*, 15 (2): 155–189.

Manitakis, N. (2007). Transatlantic emigration and maritime transport from Greece to US, 1890–1912: a major area of European steamship company competition for migrant traffic. In Feys, T., Fischer, L. R., Hoste, S. and Vanfraechem, S. (eds). *Maritime Transport and Migration: the Connections between Maritime and Migration Networks*. St. John's, Newfoundland: Research in Maritime History, no. 33.

Manning, P. (2005). *Migration in World History*. New York and London: Routledge.

Martellini, A. (2001). Il commercio dell'emigrazione: intermediari e agenti. In Bevilacqua, P., De Clementi, A. and Franzina E. (eds) *Storia dell'emigrazione italiana. Partenze*. Rome: Donzelli.

(La) Merica! 1892–1914. Da Genova a Ellis Island il viaggio per mare negli anni dell'emigrazione italiana (2008). Genova: Sagep.

Miller, M. B. (2002). Ship Agents in the Twentieth Century. In Boyce, G. and Gorsky, R. (eds). *Resources and Infrastructures in the Maritime Economy, 1500–2002*. St. John's, Newfoundland: Research in Maritime History, no. 22.

Miller, M. B. (2007). Conclusion. In Feys, T., Fischer, L. R., Hoste, S. and Vanfraechem, S. (eds). *Maritime Transport and Migration: The Connections between Maritime and Migration Networks*. St. John's, Newfoundland: Research in Maritime History, no. 33.

Miller, M. B. (2012). *Europe and the Maritime World. A Twentieth-Century History*. Cambridge and New York: Cambridge University Press.

Moch, L. P. (1992). *Moving Europeans: Migration in Western Europe since 1650*. Bloomington: Indiana University Press.

Molinari, A. (1988). *Le navi di Lazzaro. Aspetti sanitari dell'emigrazione transoceanica italiana: il viaggio per mare*. Milan: Franco Angeli.

Molinari, A. (1990). Fuentes para la historia de la emigración transoceánica italiana: la documentación sanitaria de a bordo. *Estudios Migratoriós Latinoamericanos*, 15–16: 533–545.

Molinari, A. (2005). *Traversate. Vite e viaggi dell'emigrazione transoceanica italiana*. Milan: Selene.

Moltmann, G. (1989). Steamship transport of emigrants from Europe to the United States, 1850–1914: social, commercial and legislative aspects. In Friedland, K. (ed.). *Maritime Aspects of Migration*. Köln-Wien: Böhlau Verlag.

Naranjo, C. (1993). Relaciones entre España y América Latina: movimientos migratorios y compañías navieras. In Bahamonde Magro, A., Martínez Lorente, G. and Otero Carvajal, L. E. (eds). *Las comunicaciones entre Europa y América 1500–1993*. Madrid: Miniterio de Obras Públicas.

Rössler, H. (2010). "The time has come, we are going to America". the main travel routes and emigrant ports. In Knauf, D. and Moreno, B. (eds). *Leaving Home. Migration Yesterday and Today*. Bremen: Edition Temmen.

Sanfilippo, M. (2008). Un'occasione mancata? A proposito di un libro di David A. Gerber sulle lettere degli emigranti. *Studi emigrazione/Migration Studies*, 170: 475–488.

Scholl, L. U. (1998). The global communications industry and its impact on international shipping before 1914. In Starkey and Harlaftis (eds). *Global Markets: the Internationalization of the Sea*. St. John's, Newfoundland: Research in Maritime History, no. 14.

Sebak, P. K. (2011). The Norwegian–American Line: state incentives and mediations with dominant market players. In Fischer, L. R. and Lange, E. (eds). *New Directions in Norwegian Maritime History*. St. John's, Newfoundland: Research in Maritime History, no. 46.

Starkey, D. J. and Harlaftis, G. (eds). (1998) *Global Markets: the Internationalization of the Sea Transport Industries since 1850*. St. John's, Newfoundland: Research in Maritime History, no. 14.

Steidl, A. (2007). "The relative and friends effect": Migrations networks of transatlantic migrants from the late Habsburg monarchy. In Feys, T., Fischer, L. R., Hoste, S. and Vanfraechem, S. (eds). *Maritime Transport and Migration: The Connections between Maritime and Migration Networks*. St. John's, Newfoundland: Research in Maritime History, no. 33.

Svejda G. J. (1968). *Castle Garden as an Immigration Depot, 1855–1890*, online, available at: www.nps.gov/history/online_books/elis/castle_garden.pdf.

Tonizzi M. E. (2000). *Merci, strutture e lavoro nel porto di Genova tra '800 e '900*. Milan: Franco Angeli.

Tonizzi M. E. (2002). Economy, traffic and infrastructure in the port of Genoa, 1861–1970. In Boyce, G. and Gorsky, R. (eds). *Resources and Infrastructures in the Maritime Economy, 1500–2002*. St. John's, Newfoundland: Research in Maritime History, no. 22.

Valdaliso, J. M. (1992). La transicíon de la vela al vapor en la flota mercante española: cambio tecnico y estrategia empresarials. *Revista de Historia Económica*, 1: 63–98.

Vangelista, C. (1992). Traders and workers: Sardinian subjects in Argentina and Brazil. In Pozzetta, G. E. and Ramirez, B. (eds). *The Italian Diaspora. Migration across the Globe*. Toronto: Multicultural History Society of Ontario.

Veraghtert, K. (1989). The infrastructure and equipment of the harbours in Western Europe around 1880. In Friedland, K. (ed.). *Maritime Aspects of Migration*. Köln-Wien: Böhlau Verlag.

Woodruff, W. (1966). *Impact of Western Man: A Study of Europe's Role in the World Economy, 1750–1960*. New York: St. Martin's Press.

Yans-Mclaughlin, V. and Lightman, M. (1997). *Ellis Island and the Peopling of America: The Official Guide*. New York: The New Press.

4 "We are all transnationals now"

The relevance of transnationality for understanding social inequalities

Thomas Faist

From global vs. national to transnational

A spate of recent scholarship in globalization studies has made far-reaching claims regarding the importance of cross-border interactions for social positioning and thus for social inequalities. In the words of Ulrich Beck, "the most important factor determining position in the hierarchies of inequality of the global age ... is opportunity for cross-border interaction and mobility" (Beck, 2008, p. 21). In many cases, the global is even juxtaposed with the national and the local; and the latter two are often used interchangeably. The local/national then denotes an unfavourable position in a system of inequalities in that "local in a globalized world is a sign of social deprivation and degradation" (Bauman, 1998, pp. 2–3). The global–local binary is thus used to attribute life chances and social positions on different scales, connected to the claim that this is a relatively new development brought about in the course of globalization over the past few decades. Here, social inequalities refer to the disparities of opportunity to wield resources, status and power, all of which emerge from regular and differentiated distribution and access to scarce yet desirable resources via power differentials (Tilly, 1998).

However, empirical research findings on this and related phenomena show that patterns of inequality in general and career patterns in labour markets in particular still tend to be organized mainly nationally or locally and not globally (Goldthorpe, 2002). For example, studies of top managers of multinational companies in France, the United Kingdom, Germany and the United States, conducted over many years, suggest that even the positions at the highest decision-making echelons are still organized mainly nationally, that is, following nationally-bound career paths. Education and training would have typically been carried out in the country of the company's headquarters (Hartmann, 2007). In light of this finding, the claim of the existence and importance of coherent cross-border social positions seems to be premature. Empirical research on educational and occupational careers has not supported the identification of any relatively cohesive social positionings that extend beyond borders. By implication, moreover, the very geographical mobility of certain categories of the "global elite", such as highly mobile professionals and managers, may even limit their opportunities for developing the consciousness of a transnational class.[1]

While this latter stream of research is highly critical of claims advanced about the importance of cross-border interaction and mobility, this does not suggest that transnational spillovers are to be dismissed. Rather, those cross-border transactions need to be captured more clearly, going beyond the global–local binary in the debate. Moreover, we need to cast the net more widely and go beyond a small albeit influential managerial elite. It should also be noted that the very fact that a transnational class may be in the making does not mean that national or local affiliations and ways of living and production are becoming obsolete (Carroll, 2010, p. 1).

In any case, there are three arguments indicating that the global–local binary does not suffice to capture the importance of cross-border transactions, processes and structures for generating and reproducing social inequalities. First, the fact that social mobility patterns are (still) organized mainly along national lines does not imply that cross-border interactions do not play a role. It may mean that social groups, such as networks of businesspersons or natural scientists working in laboratories and linked across borders may indeed cooperate transnationally but that these transactions have not concatenated and evolved into a common group or even class consciousness. Second, by implication, there may be clusters of social positions that do not correspond to the idea of class. Strikingly, the literature on social stratification and inequalities often has no connection with the literature on cross-border social formations, such as diasporas, transnational communities, epistemic communities, or migrant and migration networks. Differences or heterogeneities between individual or collective actors that are relevant for social inequalities may run along lines other than class, for instance, ethnicity, gender, religion, or legal status. Third, and most important, the literature making claims about the importance of the global and the local frequently lacks an analysis of actual cross-border transactions of persons, groups and organizations. For example, it is rare that factors such as years of education, training spent abroad, or social contacts across borders are included in standard analyses of social structure and social inequalities.

While the literature on cross-border social structures, the transnational (capitalist) class and the various criticisms thereof lack a sophisticated understanding of cross-border ties, the transnational perspective – sometimes erroneously called "transnationalism", as if it were an ideology – suffers from an overly simplistic understanding of social inequalities. The transnational literature is quite limited in this respect because it often conflates transnationality as a marker of difference or heterogeneity with the outcome. For instance, transnational ties are portrayed as "globalization from below", that is, migrants and their significant others eking out a living in a globalized economy through mobility strategies (Rees, 2009). Thus researchers devoted to a transnational optic sometimes treat cross-border ties themselves as a resource. This constitutes an unwarranted short circuit because transnationality can have quite diverse outcomes: in certain circumstances, transnational transactions could be a conduit for the transfer of much needed positive resources for people in immigration and emigration countries – for example, financial remittances. For migrants in immigration countries, these may be used to obtain legal documents, or for those left behind in emigration countries, to pay tuition for children's schooling. In situations of international migration, however, financial remittances may also serve to establish new dependencies and exacerbate existing social inequalities between and within countries (Guarnizio, 2003). Remittance-dependent economies might avoid much needed structural reforms as money transfers from abroad create space for the inaction of governments which should otherwise be responsible for balancing current account deficits.

The key difference or heterogeneity here is transnationality, namely, whether or not, and if so to what extent, individual and/or collective agents are characterized by cross-border transactions. This concept can provide an entry point into how such cross-border ties work and into the different kinds of transactions across borders, such as education abroad, professional experience abroad, or interlocking directorates in business companies. In short, the term "transnational" has to be disaggregated into various types of activities (financial, political, social and cultural) and clearly defined in order to be of use for inquiry into its relevance for social inequalities. Transnationality is thus context-dependent and is not to be freighted with positive or negative meanings a priori. The concept of transnationality suggests that – in addition to the better known and analysed heterogeneities such as age, gender, social class, ethnicity, legal status, sexual orientation – the very fact of being involved in cross-border transactions of some kind may be of relevance as one of the analytical starting or vantage points for the production of social inequalities. Transnationality as a term is used here from the observing social scientist's perspective in capturing cross-border transactions of agents, be they persons, groups, or organizations.

The intention of this analysis is mainly conceptual and typological, with the empirical material serving the purpose of illustrating the conceptual suggestions made here. The first section of this sketch explores key terms such as mobility and, above all, transnationality. The second section discusses in more detail how to conceptualize the relationship between heterogeneities and inequalities. Combining transnationality with varieties of social, economic and cultural capital as proxies for unequal status helps to clarify the social position of persons with respect to life-chances and thus inequalities. This effort results in a preliminary typology of social positions in cross-border spaces. The third section discusses a crucial research frontier arising from the issue of simultaneity. The evaluation of inequality in a transnational social space poses the particular problem of the frame of reference chosen by the researcher and the persons researched – (inter)national, global, or another one altogether.

Mobility and transnationality

The term "transnational" refers to cross-border processes, which sometimes involve spatial mobility of persons and which in some respects transcend national states and their regulations, but in others must deal with them. More specifically, here "transnational" means (1) trans-local, that is, connecting localities across borders of states and, by implication, also (2) trans-state, that is, across the borders of nominally sovereign states. Thus transnational does not mean *trans-national*, that is, across nations as ethnic collectives, since trans-national in this sense would theoretically also apply to relations between nations within one state. In contrast, the term *global* refers to truly world-spanning social processes and horizons within the framework of a single world, or specific sub-systems thereof, such as the global economy.

Transnationality constitutes a marker of difference, referred to here as hetero-geneity. Taking transnationality into account is important because mobility research in general and migration research in particular often focuses primarily on ethnicity as a boundary line. Heterogeneities (Blau, 1977, p. 77), such as tran-snationality, are at the very origin of the process of the creation of inequalities themselves. Inequalities here refer to categorizations of heterogeneities that lead to regularly unequal access to resources, status (recognition of roles associated with heterogeneities), and power (decision-making, agenda setting and the shaping of belief systems). Although heterogeneities are not devoid of inequality, it is helpful to distinguish analytically between the two concepts. As such, tran-snationality signals difference. And difference or heterogeneity is not the same as inequality. Think of peasant communities between which there are not neces-sarily great differences of wealth (Chase, 1980), but inequalities may arise if repeated transactions across the boundaries of categories of persons regularly result in advantages for one side. By implication, difference or heterogeneity only results in inequalities if such transactions reproduce a rather stable and enduring boundary between categories. Hence, the term "categorical inequality" (Massey, 2007) is appropriate, meaning that processes of binary categorizations, such as migrant[2]–non-migrant, black–white, men–women, young–old, etc., are involved that yield benefits systematically to those on one side of the boundary.[3] Ultimately, the transnationality–inequalities nexus needs to be captured as mul-tiple and recurrent feedback loops.

In approaching the issue of transnationality and social inequalities – namely, categorizations of heterogeneities involving transnationality that are stable and regular over a certain period of time – it is useful to start with categorizations found in public debates and in the academic literature. A common one in mass media and even academic analyses is the dichotomous distinction between highly skilled mobile persons and professionals from a particular country moving abroad on the one hand, and labour migrants and irregular migrants on the other. While the latter are frequently considered migrants in OECD countries and are responded to in terms of social problems, the former are not labelled as such and are frequently cast in terms of economic competitiveness (Faist and Ulbricht, 2015). The highly skilled are considered to be in a "win–win–win" situation, which benefits migrants, emigration and immigration states alike by increasing wealth and efficiency (GCIM, 2005). Labour migrants who practise transnationality, however, are often thought to be involved in social, residential, and occupational segregation, a form of ethnic self-isolation. In their case, transnationality is thought to be synonymous with deficits in language, education, and employment. In other words, with respect to those perceived as migrants transnationality is seen as a mobility trap (Wiley, 1967). What is striking in such accounts is that they focus in a dichotomous way on the "elite" and the "marginalized". At the very least, they exclude the "middle" social positions in between (Smith, 2000).

The central conceptual proposition here is that transnationality is a particularly important heterogeneity with respect to cross-border transactions and their consequences for inequalities. To situate transnationality, it is useful to begin by distinguishing between general processes of cross-border transactions (transnationalization), cross-border structures spanning the borders of several national states (transnational social spaces), and the extent of cross-border transactions of agents (transnationality).[4] Transnational social spaces comprise combinations of ties and their substance, positions in networks and organizations, and networks of organizations located in two or more states. The ties and positions in transnational spaces must thereby be understood not as static, but as dynamic processes. Depending on the degree of formalization of transnational ties, three ideal-type forms of transnational spaces can be distinguished. These are: reciprocity in transnational kinship groups, exchange in transnational circuits, and solidarity in transnational communities (Faist, 2000, pp. 199–210).

With respect to transnationality, three characteristics must be noted: (1) though it often refers to geographical mobility, this is not a sufficient condition for transnationality; (2) it lies on a continuum from low to dense; (3) it includes various dimensions, such as personal relations, financial transactions, identification and socio-cultural practices.

Spatial mobility

Any sustained analysis of transnationality has to deal with mobility, which is a strategically important subject of research with regard to social inequalities.[5] We need to be aware that cross-border ties are not restricted to physically mobile agents, that is, only to migrants/mobile persons and their often relatively immobile significant others, mostly families. We may also encounter, more generally, geographically immobile persons who engage in cross-border transactions (Mau, 2010). And for (relatively) immobile persons it may make a crucial difference whether or not they have ties with geographically mobile persons who have migrated either inside the state or across borders – for example, for remittances but also for knowledge of migration opportunities.

In addition, social and geographical mobility are intrinsically connected in that the latter is often a means to advance the former. It is evident that geographical mobility, frequently but not exclusively across borders, is a form of addressing social inequalities. In a way, migration is "the oldest action against poverty" (Galbraith, 1979, p. 64). It is thus possible to distinguish between those who seize opportunities such as geographical mobility across the borders of states to improve their social position, and those who stay put and relatively immobile – thus sedentary persons are also implicated. We often find mobile and immobile persons in one and the same group. Take families as an example. Sometimes a single family member engages in short- or long-distance migration, internally or cross-border, while the others remain in the place of origin. The migrant may or may not be joined later by other members of the family, relatives, friends, or acquaintances. Whether a person within such a group is engaging in migration or is relatively immobile usually has significant implications for his or her social position within the family. Migration may entail changes in the household division of labour, control over material resources, and availability of social and emotional support. Moreover, while mobility usually brings additional resources, it also incurs costs for the kinship group in that the migrant ceases to fulfil certain roles, for example, in situ child rearing or caring for elderly relatives. In a nutshell, mobility is implicated in the creation of both benefits and costs, which are unequally distributed in the respective collectives.

It is then important to know whether geographical mobility is generally a step in the direction of upward social mobility. While many migration studies answer this question affirmatively (Goldin *et al.*, 2011), this is by no means a foregone conclusion when we take into account that quite a few international migrants return "home" over the course of time or engage in onward migration. While mobility such as return migration may be an expression of goals achieved, it could also be a consequence of failing to fulfil the dream of better life chances. A similar consideration would apply to mobile persons who remain in the country of immigration. Settlement does not necessarily mean successful realization of better life chances but could also be an expression of lack of alternatives and thus a step toward socio-economic, cultural and political marginalization.

Another question is how exactly geographical mobility across borders relates to paths of mobility that do not involve crossing borders. An obvious case in point is mobility internal to states, in which the numbers of people involved are far greater than the absolute number of international migrants. For example, it is often noted that the number of internal migrants in China alone is higher than the global figure for international migrants. Other, non-geographical forms of mobility could include social mobility through social and political struggles, for example, groups pushing for a political redistribution of resources. Here, we enter the terrain of social movements. Historically, the labour movement has been instrumental in changing the very institutions of the state. Reciprocal or solidary relations could lead migrants to engage in cross-border practices, for example, by remitting money or changing political practices.

Yet geographical or spatial mobility is not a necessary prerequisite for engaging in transnational transactions although the two are often associated. For example, exchanging professional information across borders does not necessitate spatial mobility. Therefore, the net needs to be cast wider, a task for which the concept of transnationality is suited.

Transnationality as a continuum

Transnationality can usefully be conceived of not as a dichotomous characteristic but as a variable that ranges from low to dense. To use an interval scale avoids the dichotomizing use of transnational vs. national and allows for a systematic mapping of transnationality for diverse groups.

Transnationality as domain-specific

Depending on the questions asked, various dimensions need to be considered to capture transnationality; these may include items such as cross-border financial exchanges, personal relationships, transnational identification and cultural practice in domains such as politics, labour market, health, or education. In most of the studies conducted so far, transnationality has not been sufficiently disaggregated to take account of the fact that the realms of labour, education, politics, religion, etc. work according to their own logic and may involve very different kinds of transnationality. What is more, persons may be transnational to varying degrees in each of these domains.

In sum, we need to specify what needs to be operationalized and measured in order to chart inequalities across borders. The heuristic value of the concept of transnationality lies in the insight that we need to operationalize cross-border transactions systematically instead of adding potential implications for inequalities to some distant *deus ex machina* called globalization.

A transnational perspective on heterogeneities and inequalities

A transnational perspective on cross-border inequalities does not necessarily take a fixed unit of reference as a starting point but looks at a number of different ones, that is, it takes into account various scales, depending on the question to be answered (Faist, 2012). This perspective is distinct from national, international, and global approaches.

First, the national perspective is primarily concerned with inequalities between citizens or between citizens and non-citizens (the latter often migrants) within a single state and, by implication, with comparisons between national states, as in comparative cultural, economic and political analysis. Given that inequality is most often discussed in public spheres that are predominantly nationally bounded, and given that inequality is relative in that the standard of comparison is by individual in a particular socio-political community (and not those in faraway countries), it is – at first sight – not surprising that most work is done on this scale.

Second, there is an international perspective that examines inequalities between states, for example, comparing median per capita income between different states or using other, more sophisticated sets of indicators, such as the Human Development Index (HDI) which looks at income, child mortality and education. There are various forms of international comparisons, including some that take into account population size and some that do not. International comparisons figure prominently in all debates taking place in international organizations in the United Nations (UN) system and are used by organizations such as

the World Bank or the United Nations Development Program to measure disparities between countries and world regions (UNDP, 2005).

Third, there is a global perspective that takes individuals across the world as
the unit of comparison and is not bound by national borders. At this level of analysis household data are required (Milanovic, 2005). While this perspective constitutes an advance over the first two, it needs to be supplemented by a view that
looks at the interstices of various geographical units.

Fourth, there is the perspective privileged here, namely, a transnational approach
to inequalities. It deals with inequalities in the context of cross-border transactions
of groups, persons and organizations. The units of analysis and of reference are
empirical matters. These units could be family or kinship networks, village or
professional communities – in short, any kind of social formation transcending the
borders of national states. This approach is appropriate because cross-border transactions may take place on different levels, such as the family, friendship cliques,
business networks, local communities, or organizations, and it is by the very practices themselves that agents constitute these scales in the first place.

As Figure 4.1 indicates, inequalities and the perceptions of inequalities
regarding resources and status could relate to regions of emigration or to regions
of immigration or to both. Here inequality is thought to be unbounded: while
borders between states and above all boundaries of membership are of crucial
importance for the life chances of a person, social, economic, political, and cultural borders and boundaries are not coterminous. For example, the social life
worlds of transnationally active persons span several states and extend to various
locales in these states. It is to be expected that the standards of comparison differ
between regions, such as national states, and locales of emigration and immigration. In addition, standards of comparison could also be internal to social formations spanning the borders of national states. For instance, the points of reference
could be internal to transnational village communities, and villagers may
compare themselves primarily with fellow villagers. It is an empirical question
whether and to what extent this would be the case. What is certain, however, is
that comparisons regarding inequalities among the persons themselves are
always relative, i.e. relational, and that comparisons are not normally made
between persons in categories considered remote (e.g. a labour migrant and an
executive in a transnational corporation) but within those considered similar (e.g.
migrants in one region and migrants from a similar region; cf. Panning, 1983).

In a nutshell, Figure 4.1 suggests that there are not only relations between
states that are relevant but also relations that do not involve state agents primarily, although states may actively seek to regulate and shape such relations. One
crucial issue arising in such a context is how agents relate the frames of reference, for example, notions of inequality in one state to those in another, or even
genuine transnational standards to be found across several or even many states.
In other words, the task of conceptual and empirical analysis is to determine the
horizon that agents, the researched and researchers alike, use to evaluate social
position in inequality hierarchies. Such a horizon may or may not encompass
more than one state.

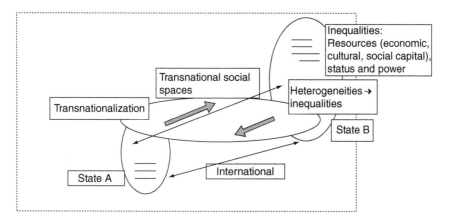

Figure 4.1 Transnational social spaces.

Note
For reasons of presentation, transnational transactions are restricted to two states in the above figure. Of course, the networks could also extend across several state borders.

Through their regulation of border controls and access to membership, national states exert a particularly important influence in reproducing social inequalities which determine cross-border social and geographical mobility patterns. Transnational social spaces are often marked by stark social inequalities, since international migration frequently occurs between regions of unequal economic development, as is evident, for example, in South–North migration flows. Two sets of institutions are of importance in this regard. First, there are migration (admission) policies and citizenship policies. Migration policies in particular, together with trade policies, have for decades acted as powerful instruments to uphold socio-economic differences between the world's regions. According to standard economic theory, free mobility of labour would result in an equalization of the factors of production, in this case increasing wages in emigration countries and decreasing wages in immigration countries (Hamilton and Whaley, 1984). In addition, barriers to citizenship and denizenship (permanent status) largely determine the set of rights available to persons crossing borders. The extent to which individuals may move across borders and thus entertain transnational ties, or the degree to which they are able to engage simultaneously in the economic and political activities of two regions, is shaped not only by immigration states but also by emigration countries through policies of citizenship, including dual citizenship, repatriation, external voting, special political representation for emigrants, special economic incentives, e.g. investment, taxation, return and re-integration programs, visa regulations, and welfare benefits. Second, national state institutions and frameworks – but also more local institutions on other scales, especially in federal political systems – such as labour policies, wage-setting institutions, as well as institutions in fields shaping life chances, such as education, childcare, and health, affect mobile and non-mobile persons alike.

(diPrete, 2007)

Mobility in transnational social spaces is thus an integral part of macro-structures of inequalities. With respect to income, for instance, there is evidence that low inequality in rich countries is achieved by using state resources and policies to exclude, limit, or control competition via migration and/or trade from low-wage workers, and through this process, low inequality in one region may be directly associated with high inequality in another. Nonetheless, there is also evidence that even in this context persons and groups moving in transnational social spaces can achieve some sort of social mobility.

Transnationality and social inequalities: a preliminary typology

When it comes to transnationality, we have to distinguish between two forms of inequality dimensions. The necessary focus of inquiry is the nexus between resources and transnationality in order to understand how power is (re)produced.[6] Transnationality can be conceptualized as consisting of various social practices, and resources can be distinguished along the lines of economic, cultural and social capital (on capital: Bourdieu, 1983). By looking at the combination of transnationality and various forms of capital we can situate persons in the webs of inequalities in a very preliminary way. It is important to point out that Figure 4.2 uses both transnationality and forms of capital as abstracted indices. The purpose is to span a conceptual space associating transnationality and capital endowments. It is not to argue that the quadrants I to IV constitute clear-cut categories of persons, such as highly skilled (I), socially integrated with little or no transnationality (II), marginalized without (III) or with (IV) high degrees of transnationality. Instead, in the end, the intersections of both axes have to be conceived of as a continuum of possible social positions.

As to capital, the basic idea is that agents usually dispose over different types of resources. If such resources are convertible, for example, from economic into cultural resources, we speak of capital (Bourdieu and Wacquant, 1992, p. 99). In other words, the convertibility into other forms of capital – economic, social, cultural respectively – distinguishes capital from mere resources and thus interlinks different forms of capital.

Capital, and this is crucial from a transnational perspective, is usually not simply transferred as a whole in an unchanged way from one country to another. Consider, for example, the observation that persons who are mobile across borders may have outstanding amounts of institutionalized cultural capital, even credentials that need to be validated cross-nationally (e.g. equivalency confirmation) in order to allow the owner to use it. However, migrants often are disappointed by their slow career progression. One way to approach this problem is to

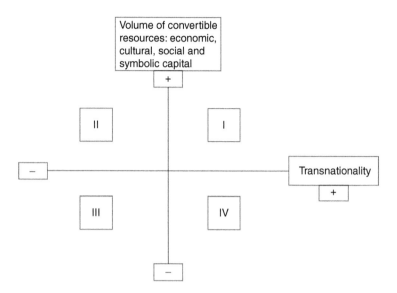

Figure 4.2 Transnationality and capital.

abandon a simplistic goodness of fit approach to capital transfer. A goodness of fit approach would assume that migrants bring with them a package of cultural, social and economic resources that may or may not fit with the culture, economy, society and status system of the country of residence as distinct from the state of origin. Such a view is very prominent in what are called human capital approaches, which posit that, for example, "different ethnic groups possess identifiable characteristics, encompassing cultural values, practices, and social networks that were formed in the homeland and transplanted with minor modifications by immigrants in the new land and there transmitted and perpetuated from generation to generation" (Zhou, 2005, p. 134). Such a goodness of fit view would be problematic for at least two reasons. First, it assumes that group boundaries can be assigned in a straightforward manner. Instead, intra-group differentiations need to be taken into account, so as not to reify national identity as the key organizing category for creating cultural, social, economic and symbolic capital(s). Ethnicity or nationality should not be the sole or necessarily the main criterion of categorizing mobile persons. Second, such an approach would assign social positions without exploring the process through which resources are made convertible, i.e. how they constitute capital. Instead, it is more fruitful to view the various sorts of capital as treasure chests that can be employed to various degrees.

As to the resources available to agents, the total volume of capital needs to be disaggregated and related to transnationality. Three forms of capital are expected to be of particular relevance for overall resources and thus for social positioning:

economic capital, above all, income and wealth; cultural capital in its incorpor-ated form, for example, degrees earned from educational institutions and occu-pational status; and social capital, in particular access to resources of other agents in one's network and – from the point of view of groups – networks of reciprocity and trust. Ideally, one could then look both at inequalities in the life-world and at every field of practice separately – for instance, education, labour market, politics, and health – since the hierarchy of the importance of the types of capital may be field-specific. The volume of various forms of capital, either individually or jointly, can be considered as useful proxies for the social position(ing) of persons and groups, and thus a helpful way to conceptualize social inequalities.

Though cognizant of all the different aspects of transnationality and of various forms of capital, it may nonetheless, as an initial step, make sense to think about potential combinations of capital and transnationality along the four quadrants indicated in Figure 4.2. This will give us a preliminary, albeit static and very provisional, idea of how transnationality and types of capital may cluster to denote certain constellations of opportunities for participation. A four-fold distinction emerges.

In field I, characterized by high degrees of transnationality and large volume of capital, we expect to see the winners of globalization, such as the mobile, highly skilled professionals, managers and entrepreneurs. The "middle class" mobility of skilled workers in the EU – a growing phenomenon – could also be included (Verwiebe, 2008). In field II, the combination of relatively large resources and low degrees of transnationality, we expect to find those who are geographically relatively immobile but (still) hold high volumes of various forms of capital. It is an empirical question whether transnational ties matter for their positioning, and if so, to what extent persons and groups in this category experience relative downward social mobility as a result of an absence of trans-national ties. In field III, it could well be that we find those truly excluded from one or various fields, such as inhabitants of slum dwellings who do not have access to the welfare state or political rights. They are normally multiply excluded. These marginalized persons would also lack the means to be geo-graphically mobile over long distances, not to speak of cross-border or even intercontinental transactions. These persons are the truly destitute, and we would expect them to constitute a higher share of the population in "developing" or transition countries than in OECD countries. In field IV, we could imagine persons who have cross-border ties but not a high capital volume of the social, cultural, and economic sorts. Labour migrants with regular status could be among those. Here, the differentiations of kinds of capital mentioned above could be extremely important. Labour migrants could be low on institutional cul-tural capital – especially considering the frequent devaluation of their educa-tional and occupational credentials in immigration countries – and have somewhat higher economic capital but could compensate for some of these defi-ciencies with high degrees of social capital, as evidenced by family networks across borders in which relatives in various countries are involved in child rearing. It is thus questionable whether persons in field IV constitute only those who live segregated lives, that is, lives separate from, for instance, immigrant societies. If that were true, then transnationality would simply be coterminous with social segregation (Esser, 2003). By looking at the relationship of transnationality to various forms of capital – social, economic and political – we may, however, gain a different insight. At the opposite pole of marginalization, we need to consider that various types of capital – most obviously economic capital – have different valences in different states. For example, it could be that Turkish migrants would be unable to muster the financial means to set up a hotel in Germany but could do so in Turkey. Opportunities to partake are consequently determined not only by the volume of different forms of capital but the context in which they can be used.

Thus, to conceptualize the relationship between transnationality as heterogeneity and resources as indicated by various forms of capital is to go beyond comparisons of migrants vs. non-migrants and allow for comparisons of mobility vs. non-mobility. The distinctive criterion is therefore not migrant vs. non-migrant, but having or lacking transnational ties, that is, fields I and IV vs. fields II and III. This is so because persons engaged in short-term mobility and relatively immobile persons could also partake in transnational transactions. Note that this fourfold distinction expands the universe of possibilities usually discussed in migrant integration research. In the latter, fields II and III are the main focus; with fields I and IV marginal phenomena.

Transnational inequalities: horizons for comparison

In all considerations of cross-border inequalities from a transnational perspective, the overarching issue of simultaneity arises. Transnationality is characterized by the potential for simultaneous membership in different countries and in groups and organizations located in these states. Simultaneity also applies to the evaluation of one's social position and windows of opportunity. The social position is then placed in a comparative cross-border frame. On the one hand, we would expect that many migrants interpret the prospects for upward mobility comparatively, with prospects perceived to be, on balance, most often better in the immigration country or countries of onward migration. There is therefore a straightforward comparison of life chances and future prospects between the immigration and emigration countries. On the other hand, a person's social position in the immigration country may not be the primary factor in her understanding of the positional effects of migration and transnational practices. Such effects on the prospects for those left behind in the emigration countries may also be significant. For example, cross-border engagement has been represented in the language of religious pilgrimage and passion in the Philippines – a necessary sacrifice for the benefit of others (Aguilar, 1999).

Yet in both of these cases, how (and where) one's social position is objectively assessed (for example, by researchers using predefined criteria) may not be the way in which assessments of social position are constructed by other social actors, namely those researched. This difference may arise for two reasons. First, when migrants compare social positions in a transnational frame, they do not simply compare the position in one hierarchy with the position in another. Rather, mobile persons may also consider the prospect for mobility within that hierarchy, either across a career or across generations, to be a major factor. Second, the social positioning can subjectively refer to the person, to the wider familial network, or to an even higher aggregate such as the village or professional community or a nation: while cross-border migrants themselves may be degraded in social positional terms, the outcome for those left behind might be upward mobility in terms of income and consumption patterns.

Overall, the frame of reference for social positioning is shifted through transnational linkages and comparisons. Transnationality shifts the frame of reference for other heterogeneities and, ultimately, for inequalities. For instance, transnationality raises the question of which standards of comparison are used. Inequality in Germany might be evaluated by migrants in relation to Turkey as a whole, or in a comparative frame that takes into account certain elements of inequalities in both countries. Furthermore, inequalities might also be evaluated in relation to the Turkish immigrant population, a comparison that is not to be dismissed. Turkish immigrants in Germany, for example, could easily find similar experiences of social positioning. For many Turkish immigrants such a perspective may make it much less daunting to have to "start over". Peer groups can change their assessment of experienced inequality owing to the emergence of new standards in terms of, say, cross-border lifestyle and social relations (Shibutani and Kwan, 1965, p. 510). A transnational approach is therefore of value also because it raises the question as to the frame of reference for making comparisons. This problem not only arises when analysing the frames held by mobiles and non-mobiles but it also refers to the categories used by researchers. In South–North migration, for instance, there is frequently an incompatibility of categories: the "middle class" may mean very different lifestyle, consumption, status and resource patterns in countries as diverse as, for example, Ghana and the Netherlands.

The perceptions of inequalities within and across the countries of emigration, immigration, and possibly countries of onward movement play an important role in the politics of inequality at the level of mobile agents. Agents tend to evaluate inequalities according to standards for equality. In other words, inequalities as such are without meaning. Their social importance derives from the meta-norm of equality (Hondrich, 1984). Ironically, one of the most important means of exclusion and root causes of the reproduction of cross-border inequalities is national citizenship. In its inward-looking guise, it is a standard for equality for all members of a nationally-bounded society, in various realms – political, social (welfare) and economic, civil, and even cultural, as in claims for multicultural citizenship.

Transnationality as a heterogeneity thus meets national citizenship as a status-defined heterogeneity in manifold ways. For mobile persons who are engaged politically, it is important to unearth which standards of comparisons they use in political practices. There is initial evidence, for example, that politically active Filipino groups in Canada have tended to adopt a discourse that sees their positions in Canada as explicitly linked to the underdeveloped plight of the Philippines. Thus, the treatment of Filipinos in Canadian society is directly linked to the perception that the Philippines play a subordinate role in the global political-economic system. While mobilization around development issues in the Philippines is not widespread in the Filipino community, it is noteworthy that activists who advocate on issues concerning immigrant settlement in Canada are at pains to link these issues to an identity based on Third World status (Pratt and Yeoh, 2003). The analysis of transnationality is therefore an important aspect in linking national citizenship to cross-border social inequalities.

After all, citizenship is a prime mechanism of social closure, which implies that the value of resources depends on group membership. In short, the naturalization of national citizenship as an ascriptive heterogeneity – ascribed by legal means – is one of the clearest roots of categorizations resulting in inequalities. The chances of living a life free from destitution are much higher in OECD countries. Importantly, viewed from a transnational perspective, national citizenship is a morally arbitrary heterogeneity, which is not rooted in merit, such as hard work, the right work ethic, and efficiency – although these are touted as factors for successful economic development and wealth. It is essential to remember this basic insight on the inequality-relevance of national citizenship because much of income inequality, for example, is on an inter-country scale. For instance, Milanovic (2005) calculated that income inequality between countries accounted for roughly two-thirds of overall world inequality in 1993. Although there is much debate about countervailing trends, this pattern has been remarkably stable over the past 200 years (Korzeniewicz and Moran, 2009, ch. 2).

In order to advance our understanding of transnationality and inequality beyond pure associations and correlations, we would need to look at the processes by which transnationality, in conjunction with other heterogeneities, is implicated in the (re)production of inequalities. Such a move is beyond the scope of this analysis, but would start from the groundwork laid here. Beyond the macro-political settings such as national citizenship it is essential to consider the specific transnational social spaces in which migrants (and other forms of mobile persons) are involved. It may indeed make a difference as to the kind of transnational social space in which cross-border transactions occur – within families, within circuits or networks, or within communities or organizations. These social entities are integrated through different social principles, such as reciprocity, exchange, or solidarity. What needs to be further specified is the different conditions under which processes of inequality production proceed, and the social mechanisms that are at work, starting from meta-mechanisms such as exploitation, opportunity hoarding, or social closure, etc.

Outlook: unbounding transnationality

Transnationality and inequality – to take up the leads by, among others, Ulrich Beck, Zygmunt Bauman and John Goldthorpe but to push them one step forward – constitute not only an issue to be debated in migration and geographical mobility studies but within a much broader scope and are thus relevant for all societal categories. It is therefore essential to bring in those (considered) immobile and consider transnationality as a potentially more widespread societal heterogeneity. After all, transnationality is not restricted to transactions arising from geographical mobility, whether short- or long-term. Therefore, it is not a concept that is restricted to migrants or other mobile categories only. It has arrived as a main heterogeneity at the core of societal affairs.

Ultimately, the issue of transnationality is an aspect of the transnational social question, that is, the perception of worldwide inequalities and injustices. In addition to the mobility of persons it also refers to commodity chains and social movements. By thus expanding the initial conceptualization, transnationally oriented mobility research can link up with and contribute to other fields in sociology, for example educational, employment and policy research, and to do so as a cross-disciplinary field. Last but not least, migration and mobility research (Yeates, 2008) can be integrated conceptually into other areas dealing with cross-border exchanges, like social movements (Tarrow and della Porta, 2005), advocacy networks (Keck and Sikkink, 1998), or religious communities (Levitt, 2007). Transnationality is not only a potential attribute of heterogeneity among migrants and their families, but also affects other categories of individuals and groups in the context of transnational processes.

The study of inequalities in this wider transnational perspective has significant implications since it ultimately promises to deliver insights into the legitimation and de-legitimation of social inequalities. Cross-border transactions of individuals suggest that inequalities between countries become comparable, at least for mobile and immobile persons who are involved in cross-border ties. This is important because the national-state principle implies that inequalities are not, especially through the institution of national citizenship where the social component is primarily tied to state-citizen ties, as in the idea of social citizenship (Marshall, 1964). From this perspective it seems that each country or welfare regime has its distinct set of rights and regulations. While this claim is the basis for a flourishing research industry of comparative welfare state analysis, the concept of transnationality opens our horizon and will allow researchers to focus on how agents compare their situation across different states and regimes. Persons who espouse transnationality are thus perhaps among the practitioners of the norm of equality that is now the benchmark by which social inequalities are perceived in both public debates and academic analyses. The question of the legitimacy of social inequalities is inextricably linked, albeit often indirectly and outside public spheres, to standards of equality that can be found in proclamations of social norms with a global reach.

Notes

1 In terms of collective agents and the potential for collective action, there have even been claims for the existence of a "transnational class" (Sklair, 2001). This concept implies that a dominant group of capital owners, professionals and managers has

emerged that transcends the borders of national states, has begun to develop a consciousness of its own, and is controlling political and economic processes across the
borders of states on a world scale.

2 There is no universally agreed-upon definition of the term "migrant". Often, the term
connotes persons who stay abroad for more than one year, an understanding that is in
line with the UN definition (UN, 1998, p. 18). Yet there are other forms of mobility,
for example, international students, seasonal workers, posted or seconded workers, or
expatriates – some of which involve periods abroad of less than a year. Here, both the
concepts of "migrant" and "mobile person" are used.

3 The processes by which categorical inequalities are produced are beyond the scope of
this analysis and involve a social mechanism based account.

4 For a detailed discussion of the concepts transnationalization and transnational social
spaces, see Faist *et al.* (2013, ch. 1).

5 Ideally, geographical mobility implies two extensions beyond the conventional migration literature. We need to enlarge the scope from migrants to geographically mobile
persons, including immobility–mobility as a continuum. Thus, this continuum includes
settled migrants on the one end, and short-term visitors and tourists on the other. Here,
geographical mobility will be restricted to migration.

6 The focus on resources leaves out for the moment two important additional dimensions of inequality: First, it occludes status, that is, the recognition of roles distributed along heterogeneities such as occupation, gender, religion and also citizenship
as status. Second, power is not dealt with systematically. Ralf Dahrendorf (1967)
famously addressed the perennial problem of the origins of inequality (Rousseau
1754) by focusing on power and authority. Power can be considered as crucial for
making categorizations – for instance, along the lines of transnationality – and
drawing boundaries between categories of persons, and also as the precondition for
categorical inequalities.

References

Aguilar, Filomeno (1999). Ritual passage and the reconstruction of selfhood in international labour migration, *Sojourn*, 14, 1: 98–139.

Bauman, Zygmunt (1998). *Globalization: the Human Consequences.* New York: Columbia University Press.

Beck, Ulrich (2008). *Die Neuvermessung der Ungleichheit unter den Menschen.* Frankfurt aM: Suhrkamp.

Blau, Peter M. (1977). *Inequality and Heterogeneity: a Primitive Theory of Social Structure.* New York: The Free Press.

Bourdieu, Pierre (1983). Ökonomisches Kapital, kulturelles Kapital, soziales Kapital, in
Kreckel Reinhard, ed., *Soziale Ungleichheiten (Soziale Welt, Sonderheft 2)*. Göttingen:
Otto Schwartz & Co., pp. 183–198.

Bourdieu, Pierre and Loicq Wacquant (1992). *An Invitation to Reflexive Sociology.*
Chicago: University of Chicago Press.

Carroll, William K. (2010). *The Making of a Transnational Capitalist Class: Corporate
Power in the 21st Century.* London: Zed Books.

Dahrendorf, Ralf (1967). Über den Ursprung der Ungleichheit zwischen den Menschen,
in Pfade aus Utopia: Arbeiten zur Theorie und Methode der Soziologie. München: R.
Piper & Co., pp. 352–379.

DiPrete, Thomas (2007). What has sociology to contribute to the study of inequality
trends? A historical and comparative perspective, *American Behavioral Scientist*,
50: 603–618.

Esser, Hartmut (2003). Ist das Konzept der Assimilation überholt? *Geographische Revue*, 2: 5–22.

Faist, Thomas (2000). *The Volume and Dynamics of International Migration and Transnational Social Spaces*. Oxford: Oxford University Press.

Faist, Thomas (2012). Toward a transnational methodology: methods to address methodological nationalism, essentialism, and positionality, *Revue Européenne des Migrations Internationales*, 28, 1: 51–70.

Faist, Thomas and Christian Ulbricht (2015). Doing national identity through transnationality: categorizations and mechanisms of inequality in integration debates. In Foner, Nancy and Patrick Simon (eds), *Fear and Anxiety over National Identity*. New York: Russell Sage Foundation.

Faist, Thomas, Margit Fauser and Eveline Reisenauer (2013). *Transnational Migration*. Cambridge: Polity Press.

Galbraith, John Kenneth (1979). *The Nature of Mass Poverty*. Cambridge, MA: Harvard University Press.

GCIM (2005). *Migration in an Interconnected World: New Directions for Action*. Geneva: Global Commission on International Migration.

Goldin, Ian, Geoffrey Cameron and Meera Balarajan (2011). *Exceptional People: How Migration Shaped Our World and Will Define Our Future*. Princeton, NJ: Princeton University Press.

Goldthorpe, John (2002). Globalization and social class, *West European Politics*, 25, 3: 1–28.

Guarnizio, Luis (2003). The economics of transnational living, *International Migration Review* 37, 3, pp. 666–699.

Hamilton, Bob and John Whaley (1984). Efficiency and distributional implications of global restrictions on labor mobility, *Journal of Development Economics*, 14, 1: 61–75.

Hartmann, Michael (2007). *Eliten und Macht in Europa. Ein internationaler Vergleich*. Frankfurt aM: Campus.

Hondrich, Karl Otto (1984). Der Wert der Gleichheit und der Bedeutungswandel der Ungleichheit, *Soziale Welt*, 35, 3: 267–293.

Keck, Margaret E. and Kathryn Sikkink (1998). *Activists beyond Borders*. Ithaca, NY: Cornell University Press.

Korzeniewicz, Roberto P. and Timothy P. Moran (2009). *Unveiling Inequality: A World-Historical Perspective*. New York: Russell Sage Foundation.

Levitt, Peggy (2007). *God Needs No Passport: Immigrants and the Changing American Religious Landscape*. New York: The New Press.

Marshall, T. H. (1964 [1950]). *Citizenship and Social Class*. Cambridge: Cambridge University Press.

Massey, Douglas S. (2007). *Categorically Unequal: the American Stratification System*. New York: Russell Sage Foundation.

Mau, Steffen (2010). *Social Transnationalism: Lifeworlds beyond the Nation State*. London: Routledge.

Milanovic, Branko (2005). *Worlds Apart: Measuring International and Global Inequality*. Princeton, NJ: Princeton University Press.

Panning, William H. (1983). Inequality, social comparison, and relative deprivation, *American Political Science Review*, 77, 2: 323–329.

Pratt, Geraldine and Brenda Yeoh (2003). Transnational (counter) topographies, *Gender, Place and Culture*, 10, 2: 159–166.

Rees, Martha, ed. (2009). Special issue: the costs of transnational migration, *Migration Letters*, 6, 1.

Rousseau, Jean Jacques (2012 [1754]). *A Discourse on a Subject proposed by the Academy of Dijon: What is the Origin of Inequality among Men, and is it Authorised by Natural Law?* Online, available at: www.constitution.org/jjr/ineq.htm, last accessed 15 March 2012.

Shibutani, Tamotsu and Kian M. Kwan (1965). *Ethnic Stratification: A Comparative Perspective.* New York: Macmillan.

Sklair, Leslie (2001). *The Transnational Capitalist Class.* Oxford: Blackwell.

Smith, Michael P. (2000). *Transnational Urbanism: Locating Globalization.* New York: Wiley-Blackwell.

Tarrow, Sidney and Donatella della Porta (eds) (2005). *Transnational Protest and Global Activism.* Lanham, MD: Rowman and Littlefield.

Tilly, Charles (1998). *Durable Inequalities.* Berkeley, CA: University of California Press.

United Nations (1998). Department of Economic and Social Affairs, Statistics Division: *Recommendations on Statistics of International Migration.* Statistical Papers Series M, No. 58, Rev. 1, New York: United Nations.

UNDP (2005). Human development report 2005. *International Cooperation at a Crossroads: Aid, Trade and Security in an Unequal World.* New York: United Nations Development Programme.

Verwiebe, Roland (2008). Migration to Germany: Is a middle class emerging among intra-European migrants?, *Migration Letters,* 5, 1: 1–19.

Wiley, Norbert F. (1967). The ethnic mobility trap and stratification theory, *Social Problems,* 15, 2: 147–159.

Yeates, Nicola (2008). *Globalizing Care Economies and Migrant Workers: Explorations in Global Care Chains.* Houndmills, UK: Palgrave Macmillan.

Zhou, Min (2005). Ethnicity as social capital: community-based institutions and embedded networks of social relations. In Loury Glen, Tariq Modood and Steven M. Teles (eds), *Ethnicity, Social Mobility, and Public Policy: Comparing the US and Europe.* Cambridge: Cambridge University Press, pp. 131–159.

5 Immigration, diversity and the labour market outcomes of native workers

Some recent developments

Gianmarco I. P. Ottaviano

Introduction

"It is not best that we should all think alike; it is a difference of opinion that makes horse races."

(Mark Twain)

The debate on immigration is often heated as it triggers instinctual reactions by natives to the perceived "invasion" of their physical, social and cultural territories by alien newcomers. This brief essay is about the "invasion" of the economic territory. In particular, it focuses on the labour market, providing a selective discussion of how in recent years economists in the neoclassical tradition have addressed the questions whether and how immigration affects natives' wages and employment levels.[1]

The answers to these questions much depend on the role "diversity" is understood to play in a market economy. On this point neoclassical economics has straightforward implications based on the main tenet of general equilibrium analysis: in a perfectly competitive environment without distortions there are gains from trade (in goods/endowments/factors) if and only if agents are "different" (in terms of preferences/endowments/technology). Indeed, if they were all identical, sharing and valuing everything in the same way, there would be no incentive for them to exchange anything and each of them would be an autarkic island. This is wittily captured by Mark Twain's famous quote cited above.

While defining what the "diversity" of immigrants actually means continues to be a matter of endless discussions, applied studies in economics have taken a pragmatic approach building on what can be actually measured in the available datasets. In this respect, "diversity" has been captured through aggregate indices based on objectively observable markers (such as ethnicity, language spoken at home or country of birth), which may affect individual economic outcomes beyond standard labour market attributes (such as educational attainment or working experience). A variety of alternative indices has been proposed with the aim of capturing both the "richness" and the "evenness" of the immigrant population. The former concept broadly refers to the number of identifiable immigrant groups while the latter concerns the relative number of their members.[2] The basic idea is to relate the chosen diversity index to the economic performance of natives in places exposed to immigration.

A general issue is that unfortunately, even from the narrow economics viewpoint of the labour market, immigration remains a complex multi-faceted phenomenon. In particular, immigration is the outcome of an endogenous location choice by mobile workers, driven by economic and noneconomic reasons, that causes economic and non-economic responses by firms and other workers both in the place of origin and in the place of destination. This chapter focuses on a specific methodological approach that cuts through such complexity by studying the labour market responses in the places of destination when immigration can be considered an "exogenous shock" driven by noneconomic reasons, to which firms and native workers react by entering and exiting the local labour market.

The basic analytical framework is laid out in the first section after this introduction. It is extended in the second section to highlight some potential "identification" problems that are relevant for empirical investigation and their possible solutions. The corresponding empirical findings are surveyed in the third section where the importance of different dimensions of "diversity" between natives and immigrants is also discussed. The fourth section debates the issue of how to distinguish a causal impact of immigration on native labour market outcomes from a correlation between them. The last section concludes.

Immigrants and wages

At the core of the specific methodological approach discussed here is the textbook version of the neoclassical equilibrium of a local labour market with full employment. This is depicted in Figure 5.1, with the solid labour demand curve (*D*-curve) and the solid labour supply curve (*S*-curve) respectively representing the wage local firms are willing to pay and the wage local workers are willing to accept for an additional hour of work at each level of employment. The *D*-curve is downward sloping because, when the wage increases, firms are willing to hire fewer workers. The *S*-curve is, instead, upward sloping because, as the wage increases, workers are willing to offer more hours. The market is in equilibrium when it "clears": at the going wage, firms demand exactly the number of hours offered by workers and, vice versa, workers offer exactly the number of hours demanded by firms. This happens at the crossing between the *D*-curve and the *S*-curve, corresponding to wage w^0 and employment L^0. Since for the equilibrium wage there are no workers that would like to work more hours than they do, there is no (involuntary) unemployment. Moreover, since for the equilibrium wage there are no firms that would like to hire more hours than they do, there are no vacancies.

The *D*-curve shifts rightwards (leftwards) when labour productivity increases (decreases), as firms are willing to hire more (fewer) workers at any given wage. The *S*-curve moves rightwards (leftwards) when the number of workers increases (decreases), as there are more (fewer) workers willing to work at any given

Wage

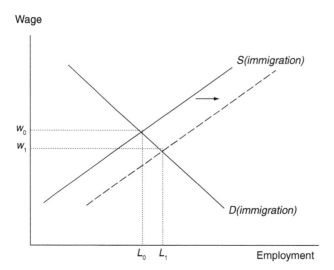

Figure 5.1 The effects of immigration when natives and immigrants are identical.

wage. Hence, if immigration does not affect firm productivity, and natives and immigrants are identical in all attributes relevant for the labour market, by increasing the number of local workers immigration causes a rightward shift of the *S*-curve while leaving the *D*-curve unaltered. In Figure 5.1 the result of this shift is depicted by the dashed upward sloping curve corresponding to the new *S*-curve. The new equilibrium at the crossing between the D-curve and the new S-curve exhibits higher employment $L_1 > L_0$ and lower wage $w_1 < w_0$. Accordingly, if the labour market characteristics of immigrants and natives are the same, immigration increases overall employment but depresses the wage, as a lower wage is needed to convince firms to absorb the additional supply of labour. This is the direct "displacement effect" of immigration on native workers.[3]

But the labour market characteristics of immigrants and natives need not be the same due to education, experience or culture heterogeneity. In this case, as firms do not perceive the two types of workers as perfectly substitutable, two parallel diagrams like Figure 5.1 become relevant, one for immigrants and one for natives, as the two types of workers effectively operate in two distinct, though interconnected, labour markets. These parallel diagrams are represented in Figure 5.2. The upper panel (a) shows the impact of newcomers on pre-existent immigrants under the assumption that they share the same characteristics and thus are perfectly substitutable in production. Just like Figure 5.1, this panel describes a displacement effect that increases immigrants' employment but reduces their wage: $M_1 > M_0$ and $w_1 < w_0$. The lower panel (b) refers, instead, to natives. There are two scenarios. In the first, under the assumption that immigrants foster native productivity, immigration makes firms willing to pay a higher native wage than before for all levels of native employment. This is captured by

(a)

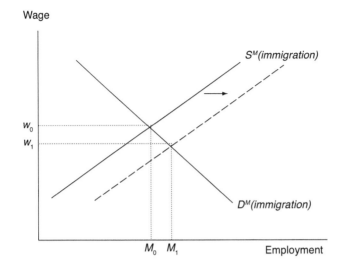

(b)

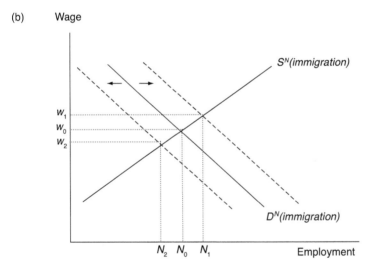

Figure 5.2 The effects of immigration when natives and immigrants are different.

the rightwards shift of the D-curve to its new dashed position, leading to both higher native employment and higher native wage: $N_1 > N_0$ and $w_1 > w_0$. In the second scenario, under the assumption that immigrants rather hamper native productivity, immigration makes firms willing to pay a lower native wage for all levels of employment. This is captured by the leftwards shift of the D-curve to its new dashed position, which leads to both lower native employment and a lower native wage: $N_2 < N_0$ and $w_2 < w_0$. Whether the immigrant inflow shifts the native D-curve (productivity effect) and, if so, in which direction are key research questions of the empirical studies on the impact of immigration on natives' labour market outcomes. Answering these questions, however, faces two types of problems, concerning the "identification" of the specific channels through which immigration and native performance interact, and the assessment of the causal impact of the former on the latter.

Identification issues when native workers relocate

When the native S-curve does not move as in Figure 5.2, looking at the change in native wage is enough to understand whether immigrants foster, hamper or do not affect native productivity. This is the case whenever native workers do not react to immigration by relocating. When instead they do react, the change in their wage on its own can be uninformative.

Figure 5.3 presents two scenarios. In panel (a) immigrants and natives are identical, as in Figure 5.1. The initial equilibrium wage w_0 in the location of interest is equal to that offered in alternative locations, so natives have no incentive to relocate. For exposition, it is useful to distinguish between the short and the long run effects of immigration. In the "short run" native workers are considered immobile. Then, as in Figure 5.1, immigration shifts the S-curve rightwards leading to lower wage $w_1 < w_0$. In the "long run" natives can relocate. Hence, faced with a wage that, due to immigration, has become lower than in alternative locations, native workers start to leave, causing the S-curve to backtrack. Their outflow goes on until the S-curve goes back to its initial position, where remaining natives have no incentive to relocate as the wage is again equal to w_0. In the end, the native wage has not changed but this does not mean that immigration has had no effect on natives' outcomes. Indeed, as also employment has not changed from its initial level L_0, it must be that each hour of work now supplied by an immigrant had been previously supplied by a native.[4] Displacement is still at work but is not revealed by the change in the wage. Observing no departure of the native wage from its pre-immigration level w_0 is, in fact, consistent with two very different stories: immigrants do not affect natives' labour market outcomes, or they actually replace them one to one. In other words, these two stories are "observationally equivalent".

A second scenario in which wage changes are uninformative when natives relocate is shown in panel (b) of Figure 5.3. The panel depicts the equilibrium in the native labour market when immigrants and natives have different characteristics (so it corresponds to panel (b) in Figure 2). Moreover, it considers a situation in which immigrants affect not only native productivity but also their quality of life. This implies that immigration shifts not only the D-curve but also the S-curve. Specifically, panel (b) of Figure 5.3 describes an example in which immigration increases native productivity (positive "productivity effect") but also reduces native quality of life (negative "amenity effect"). Improved native productivity shifts the D-curve rightwards to its new dashed position. Holding the S-curve constant, this leads to higher equilibrium wage w_1. Worsened native quality of life shifts, instead, the S-curve leftwards to its own new dashed position as, for any level of employment, natives now require a higher wage to be convinced not to leave. Holding the D-curve constant, this shift also leads to the

(a)   Wage

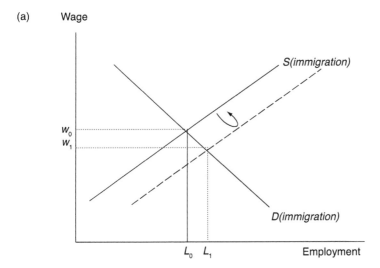

(b)   Wage

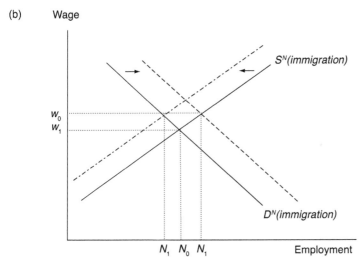

Figure 5.3 Identification problems when natives relocate.

same higher equilibrium wage w_1. Hence, an observed native wage increase to w_1 from its pre-immigration level w_0 is again consistent with two very different stories: immigration improves natives' productivity, or it actually worsens their quality of life. Also these two stories are "observationally equivalent".

To summarize, in both scenarios depicted in Figure 5.3 observational equivalence generates an "identification" issue: it is impossible to identify the exact impact of immigration on natives' labour market outcomes by looking only at natives' wage.

A way to circumvent these "identification" issues is to focus on situations on which natives' relocation is quite unlikely. This is typically the case at the national level as natives can be generally expected not to react to immigration by leaving their own country. For example, in panel (a) of Figure 5.3, taking the entire country as the spatial unit of analysis would prevent the corresponding *S*-curve from backtracking; in panel (b) it would prevent the corresponding *S*-curve from moving around. As a result, any increase (decrease) in native wage could be read as an increase (decrease) in native productivity. This "aggregate" approach, estimating the effects of immigration using national level data, has been heralded by Borjas (2003) and Borjas and Katz (2007). More recently, among others it has been adopted also by Borjas *et al.* (2012), Manacorda *et al.* (2012) as well as Ottaviano and Peri (2012).

When, instead, the analysis is performed at a finer spatial level than the whole country, natives' relocation cannot be ruled out. In this case "identification" can be achieved by complementing the observation of the change of the local native wage with parallel information on the change of the local native employment. To see this, consider Figure 5.4, which builds on panel (b) of Figure 5.3. As already discussed, in this scenario the native wage increase from w_0 to w_1 may be equivalently driven by higher native productivity (positive "productivity effect") or by lower native quality of life (negative "amenity effect"). In these two cases, however, Figure 5.4 shows that the reactions of native employment are opposite: the positive "productivity effect" comes together with the increase of native employment from L_0 to L_1 whereas the negative "amenity effect" comes together with its decrease from L_0 to L_1'. The reason is that higher local productivity attracts natives from other locations whereas lower quality of life pushes

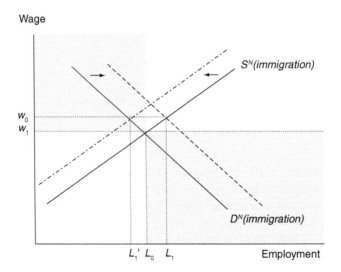

Figure 5.4 Identification strategy when natives relocate.

them away. This suggests that keeping track of not only wage but also employment reactions can help solve the identification problem.

More generally, Figure 5.4 shows how to identify the dominant effect of immigration when both the *D*-curve and the *S*-curve may move due to native relocation. If the new equilibrium at the crossing of the new *D*-curve and the new *S*-curve happens inside the white quadrants, the shift of the *D*-curve (and hence the "productivity effect") must dominate. For the new equilibrium to be in the top-right white quadrant, the *D*-curve must have shifted rightwards, thus implying a positive "productivity effect". The opposite holds if the new equilibrium falls in the bottom-left white quadrant (negative "productivity effect"). Differently, when the new *D*-curve and the new *S*-curve cross, instead, inside the grey quadrants, the shift of the *S*-curve, and hence the "amenity effect", must dominate. For the new equilibrium to be in the top-left grey quadrant, the *S*-curve must have shifted leftwards, thus implying a negative "amenity effect". The opposite holds if the new equilibrium falls in the bottom-right grey quadrant (positive "amenity effect").

Hence, when immigration is associated with higher (lower) native employment and higher (lower) native wage, this is consistent with a positive (negative) productivity effect. When immigration is associated with higher (lower) native employment but lower (higher) native wage, this is consistent with a positive (negative) amenity effect. This identification strategy builds on Roback (1982) and has been adopted by Ottaviano and Peri (2005, 2006) in order to estimate the effects of immigration using urban level data.[5]

Dimensions of diversity

An important implication of the previous discussions is that whether or not natives and immigrants are identical in terms of labour market characteristics is crucial. A first distinction concerns differences in education and experience (see e.g. Borjas, 2003; Borjas and Katz, 2007; Borjas *et al.*, 2012). The idea is that natives can be directly displaced only by immigrants with equivalent education and experience as only workers with identical characteristics compete head-to-head for the same jobs. Accordingly, the displacement argument behind Figure 5.1 should apply only to the case of immigrant and native workers within the same "education–experience cell".

A second distinction concerns any further relevant difference in "culture" between immigrants and natives with equivalent education and experience (see e.g. Manacorda *et al.*, 2012; Ottaviano and Peri, 2012). The idea here is that immigrants and natives may differ in some culture related characteristics that make then imperfectly substitutable in production even though they share equivalent education and experience. From this perspective, the displacement argument behind Figure 5.1 should apply only within the same "education–experience–culture cell". In this respect, the most commonly used markers of "culture" at the individual level are language spoken at home, ethnicity and country of birth.

The common result of studies on national data is that heterogeneity in education and experience matters as native workers are only found to suffer from a direct "displacement effect" associated with immigrants with equivalent education and experience (i.e. the *D*-curve is downward sloping). On the other hand, they are also found to benefit indirectly from a positive "productivity effect" associated with the inflow of immigrants with different education and experience (i.e. the *D*-curve shifts rightwards). Moreover, Manacorda *et al.* (2012) and Ottaviano and Peri (2012) find that also heterogeneity in country of birth is important as immigrants and natives with equivalent education and experience are still imperfectly substitutable in production, and this dampens the displacement effect.[6] Overall, considering the actual characteristics of natives and immigrants in the countries analysed, national studies conclude that there is little evidence of diffuse damages for native workers from immigration. For example, Ottaviano and Peri (2012) find that immigration into the United States from 1990 to 2006 is associated with a small increase in native wages not only on average but also individually, at least for the vast majority of native workers.

This evidence of a relevant "productivity effect" of immigration is confirmed by studies based on urban data. In these studies individual cultural markers are typically aggregated at the city level through some "diversity index" to provide a unidimensional aggregate measure of local "cultural" diversity.[7] The index is then correlated with local native wage and employment so as to check whether across cities different degrees of cultural diversity are associated with any of the quadrants in Figure 5.4. Ottaviano and Peri (2005, 2006) find evidence of a dominant positive "productivity effect" of immigration for natives living in US metropolitan areas where diversity increased between 1970 and 1990, respectively measuring diversity in terms of country of birth and language spoken at home.

Causation and reverse causation

Showing that native labour market outcomes are positively correlated with immigration, and that this is associated with an underlying positive correlation between native productivity and immigrants, does not necessarily imply that immigration *causes* higher native productivity. Causation may actually run in the opposite direction whenever some other feature makes a location more productive and thus more attractive to both native and immigrant workers ("boomtown effect").

A way to attenuate the possible relevance of such "reverse causation" is to look at "natural experiments" that closely fit the concept of an exogenous increase in the supply of immigrants to a given labour market. A famous example of "natural experiment" is the study by Card (1990) of the labour market of Miami after the Mariel Boatlift, that is, after the arrival in 1980 of 125,000 Cuban immigrants following Fidel Castro's declaration on 20 April 1980 that Cubans wishing to do so were free to emigrate to the United States from the Cuban port of Mariel. This resulted in a 7 percent increase in Miami's labour force as between 50 and 60 percent of the boatlifted decided to stay in Miami. There are two features of this exodus that are appealing in terms of "exogeneity". On the one hand, reportedly, refugees largely consisted of undesirables who were pushed out of Cuba ("exogenous push"). On the other hand, they disproportionately settled in Miami rather than elsewhere in the United States due to the presence of a relatively large local community of previous Cuban immigrants ("exogenous pull"). The analysis of Card (1990) focuses on the direct "displacement effect" for pre-existent less-skilled workers. Even though most of the boatlifted were relatively unskilled, he finds virtually no effect of the Mariel influx on the wage and employment of non-Cuban less-skilled workers in Miami from 1979 to 1985.[8]

The interpretation of these results, however, has been questioned based on the "identification" issue presented in panel (a) of Figure 5.3 (see, e.g. Autor, 2003). For example, it has been noted that after the boatlift the population growth rate slowed down much more in Miami than in the rest of Florida, possibly suggesting that natives and older immigrants were deterred from migrating to Miami. According to the logic of panel (a) of Figure 5.3, such response could have muted the "displacement effect". More fundamentally, the study of the Mariel Boatlift, as all natural experiments, faces the challenge of generalization. Autor (2003) points out that Miami was extremely well set up to absorb Cuban immigrants due to its established Cuban employment and social networks, its occupational structure and its long experience in accommodating Cuban immigration.

An alternative standard strategy to solve the problem of reverse causation is to use econometric techniques to separate the exogenous component of immigration from the endogenous one driven by the "boomtown effect". The idea is to substitute actual local immigration with some "instrumental variable" correlated with it but not with local productivity. In their studies of the impact of cultural diversity in US cities from 1970 to 1990, Ottaviano and Peri (2005, 2006) "instrument" the exogenous component of immigration in two ways. First, they use the distances of each city from the international border, from the coast, and from the closest main "gateway" into the United States (i.e. New York, Los Angeles or Miami). The underlying idea is that, in the period of observation, immigrants came to the United States for reasons exogenous to the local events of any particular city and, due to pre-existent immigrant communities, tended to settle disproportionately close to their points of entry into the United States. Hence, simply by geographic accident and not because of local productivity shocks, cities closer to the coast, the border or the main gateways received larger immigrant inflows.

The second way to proxy the exogenous component of immigration borrows the so-called "shift-share" methodology from Card (1999). This alternative "instrumental variable" is constructed by grouping foreign-born workers according to language spoken at home (Ottaviano and Peri, 2005) or country of birth (Ottaviano and Peri, 2006) and calculating the initial share of each group in each city in 1970. A group in a city is then imputed the growth experienced at the national level (due to immigration) from 1970 to 1990 according to its initial share in the city in 1970. This gives an "imputed" change in the size of each group in any given city that does not depend on the actual immigration of that group in that city after 1970. For example, a city with a large initial Mexican-born population in 1970 would be "imputed" a large share of Mexican immigrants in 1990 independently of whether and how the city actually attracted them. The idea is that using the initial local shares of immigrant groups in 1970 together with the national immigration trends for those groups from 1970 to 1990 should insulate the "imputed" changes in a city from any city-specific productivity shocks, as long as the initial presence of a given group of immigrants makes the city attractive to newcomers of the same group independently of any productivity advantage.

Both "instrumental variables" lead to the same conclusion: from 1970 to 1990 immigration caused a positive "productivity effect" on natives in US cities, associated with higher native wage and higher native employment.[9]

Conclusion

Observing how the local wage of native workers changes after an inflow of immigrants can be uninformative of the actual impact of immigration on the local labour market. The reason is that the actual composition of the natives' workforce and the actual composition of the immigrants' inflow, as well as their tastes, matter a great deal. Natives are harmed by the competition of immigrants with equivalent skills as their services become relatively more abundant, hence less valuable (negative "displacement effect"). But they may benefit from the inflow of immigrants with different skills as their services become relatively scarcer, hence more valuable (positive "productivity effect").

At the same time, cultural differences between immigrants and natives may raise barriers to effective interactions in the workplace, turning the "productivity effect" from positive to negative. But cultural differences may also generate a positive or negative "amenity effect" as natives may simply like or dislike having immigrants around. On the one hand, cultural diversity may give rise to conflicts of preferences, barriers to communication, outright racism, prejudice or fear of other groups, leading to a sub-optimal provision of private and public goods.[10] On the other hand, it can generate benefits in terms of the variety of goods, services and skills available for consumption and production.[11] By pooling different skills, abilities and solutions, cultural diversity can also help creativity and innovation.[12]

Whether the "displacement effect" and the "productivity effect" of immigration on natives have any practical relevance, whether they are positive or negative, and which eventually dominates are then empirical issues. The studies discussed in this chapter provide evidence of a negative "displacement effect" and a positive "productivity effect", with the latter dominating for the average native worker as well as for the majority of native skill groups in the countries analysed.

Notes

1 See Alesina and La Ferrara (2005), Okkerse (2008) and Pekkala Kerr and Kerr (2011) for recent surveys; Borjas (1994) and Friedberg and Hunt (1995) for overviews of the earlier literature.
2 See, e.g. Maignan *et al.* (2003) for a survey of alternative diversity indices.
3 When, differently from the textbook neoclassical model, the wage cannot adjust (for example, because of labour market institutions), the displacement effect materializes in higher unemployment rather than lower wage (D'Amuri *et al.*, 2010).
4 This is sometimes called the "skating rink mobility model", whereby each immigrant who skates into an area knocks one native off the ice. See Autor (2003) who attributes the labelling to David Card.
5 Ottaviano and Peri (2005) follow the exact identification procedure described in Figure 5.4. Closer to Roback (1982), Ottaviano and Peri (2006) use land rent instead of employment to complement wage information. The two procedures follow the same logic and are mutually consistent.
6 Other recent studies finding imperfect substitutability between immigrants and natives with equivalent education and experience include Card (2007) and Raphael and Smolensky (2008) for the United States as well as D'Amuri *et al.* (2010) for Germany.
7 See, e.g. Maignan *et al.* (2003) for a discussion of alternative indices.
8 Other examples of "natural experiments" include Carrington and de Lima (1996) on repatriations from Africa to Portugal in the 1970s and Friedberg (2001) on immigration from the Soviet Union to Israel in the early 1990s.
9 Bellini *et al.* (2013) reach comparable conclusions in the case of European regions.
10 See, e.g. Alesina *et al.* (1999) and Alesina *et al.* (2004).
11 See, e.g. Lazear (1999a, 1999b), O'Reilly *et al.* (1998) and Kahane *et al.* (2013).
12 See, e.g. Berliant and Fujita (2008) and Florida (2002a, 2002b).

References

Alesina, A. and E. La Ferrara (2005). Ethnic diversity and economic performance, *Journal of Economic Literature*, 43: 762–800.
Alesina, A., R. Baqir and W. Easterly (1999). Public goods and ethnic divisions, *Quarterly Journal of Economics*, 114: 1243–1284.
Alesina, A., R. Baqir and C. Hoxby (2004). Political jurisdictions in heterogeneous communities, *Journal of Political Economy*, 112: 349–396.
Autor, D. (2003). Lecture note: the economics of immigration, MIT 14.661, Fall 2003.
Bellini, E., G. Ottaviano, D. Pinelli and G. Prarolo (2013). Cultural diversity and economic performance: evidence from European regions. In R. Crescenzi and M. Percoco, eds, *Geography, Institutions and Regional Economic Performance*, Berlin: Springer.
Berliant, M. and Fujita, M. (2008). Knowledge creation as a square dance on the Hilbert Cube, *International Economic Review*, 49: 1251–1295.
Borjas, G. (1994). The economics of immigration, *Journal of Economic Literature*, 32: 1667–1717.
Borjas, G. (2003). The labor demand curve is downward sloping: re-examining the impact of immigration on the labor market, *Quarterly Journal of Economics*, 118: 1335–1374.
Borjas, G. and L. Katz (2007). The evolution of the Mexican-born workforce in the United States. In G. Borjas (ed.), *Mexican Immigration to the United States*, Cambridge, MA: NBER Conference Report.
Borjas, G., J. Grogger and G. Hanson (2012). Comment: on estimating elasticities of substitution, *Journal of the European Economic Association*, 10: 198–210.

Card, D. (1990). The impact of the Mariel Boatlift on the Miami labor market, *Industrial and Labor Relation Review* 43: 245–257.

Card, D. (1999). The causal effect of education on earnings. In O. Ashenfelter and D. Card, eds, *Handbook of Labor Economics*, Vol. 3A, Amsterdam: North-Holland.

Card, D. (2007). How immigration affects US cities, CReAM Discussion Paper no. 11/07, London: University College.

Carrington, W. and P. de Lima (1996). The impact of 1970s repatriates from Africa on the Portuguese labor market, *Industrial and Labor Relations Review*, 49: 330–347.

D'Amuri, F., G. Ottaviano and G. Peri (2010). The labor market impact of immigration in Western Germany in the 1990s, *European Economic Review*, 54: 550–570.

Florida, R. (2002a). Bohemia and economic geography, *Journal of Economic Geography*, 2: 55–71.

Florida, R. (2002b). The economic geography of talent, *Annals of the Association of Economic Geographers*, 92: 743–755.

Friedberg, R. (2001). The impact of mass migration on the Israeli labor market, *Quarterly Journal of Economics*, 116: 1373–1408.

Friedberg, R. and J. Hunt (1995). The impact of immigrants on host country wages, employment and growth, *Journal of Economic Perspectives*, 9: 23–44.

Kahane, L., N. Longley and R. Simmons (2013). The effects of co-worker heterogeneity on firm-level output: assessing the impacts of cultural and language diversity in the National Hockey League, *Review of Economics and Statistics*, 95: 302–314.

Lazear, E. (1999a). Globalization and the market for team-mates, *Economic Journal*, 109: C15–C40.

Lazear, E. (1999b). Culture and language, *Journal of Political Economy*, Supplement: 95–125.

Maignan, C., G. Ottaviano, D. Pinelli and F. Rullani (2003). Bio-ecological diversity vs. Socio-economic diversity: a comparison of existing measures, FEEM Working Paper n.13.2003.

Manacorda, M., A. Manning and J. Wadsworth (2012). The impact of immigration on the structure of wages: theory and evidence from Britain, *Journal of the European Economic Association*, 10: 120–151.

O'Reilly, C., K. Williams and S. Barsade (1998). Group demography and innovation: does diversity help? In D. Gruenfeld, ed., *Composition. Research on Managing Groups and Teams*, Vol. 1, Greenwich, CT: Elsevier Science/JAI Press.

Okkerse, L. (2008). How to measure labour market effects of immigration: a review, *Journal of Economic Surveys*, 22: 1–30.

Ottaviano, G. and G. Peri (2005). Cities and cultures, *Journal of Urban Economics*, 58: 304–337.

Ottaviano, G. and G. Peri (2006). The economic value of cultural diversity: evidence from US cities, *Journal of Economic Geography* 6: 9–44.

Ottaviano, G. and G. Peri (2012). Rethinking the gains of immigration on wages, *Journal of the European Economic Association*, 10: 152–197.

Pekkala, Kerr S. and W. Kerr (2011). Economic impacts of immigration: a survey, *Finnish Economic Papers*, 24: 1–32.

Raphael, S. and E. Smolensky (2008) Immigration and poverty in the Unites States, Institute for Research on Poverty Discussion Paper no. 1347–08, UC Berkeley.

Roback, J. (1982) Wages, Rents and the Quality of Life, *Journal of Political Economy*, 90: 1257–1278.

Part II
Migrations and politics

6 European migrants after the Second World War

Francesca Fauri

Introduction

From the nineteenth century to the 1920s millions of ordinary working people from Northern and later Southern Europe travelled thousands of miles to improve their lot by either permanent or temporary settlement in a new country or continent. In the words of Foreman-Peck: "The surprise is less that they were willing to migrate than that they were allowed to do so" (Foreman-Peck, 1995, p. 140). South and North American policy towards migration remained extremely liberal until the 1920s, and for many decades in the nineteenth century no passports were required, documents were provided on arrival and only migrants with contagious diseases were excluded. Land-abundant Latin American countries with landowner-dominated oligarchies encouraged immigration: Brazil and Argentina paid for transport across the Atlantic in order to expand the labour supply in agriculture. Europe, too, maintained a relatively liberal stance for a long time with regard to migrant flows; the main immigration countries such as France, Great Britain and Germany merely passed a number of weak restrictions limiting, for instance, the proportion of immigrants that could be employed in public works. Finally, in the case of the United States, the reason for the persistence of such a liberal immigration policy lay in the great variety of immigrant groups that were drawn to the country and the ease with which they could become enfranchised. The first general restriction was passed only in 1921 with the Quota Act, limiting access to historically determined and extremely narrow quotas based on national origin.

The free movement of labour became a memory of the past during the interwar years, and after the Second World War Europeans eager to migrate had to undergo lengthy bureaucratic procedures and comply with rules set by ad hoc bilateral agreements. In addition, the movement of labour within Europe was hampered by specific agreements; workers were not free to move abroad and seek employment on their own. If they did, they would be considered clandestine. National labour agreements were signed between countries and witnessed the re-opening of European borders for set numbers of migrant workers. The purpose of this research is to study which institutions helped European emigrants at the international level after the Second World War, and will devote particular attention to their effort to support, protect, and liberalize labour movements.

Two broad categories of migrants travelled across Europe after the war: displaced people and refugees, and those who voluntarily left their homes to seek better work and life prospects abroad. At the international level, the first category enjoyed immediate protection through a non-permanent UN agency: the International Refugee Organisation (IRO).[1] When the IRO was dissolved in early 1952 the legal protection of refugees was entrusted to the UNHCR. In the same year Western countries opted for the creation of an international body – the Provisional Intergovernmental Committee for the Movement of Migrants (PICMME) from Europe – whose mandate was not limited to displaced persons, but extended also and foremost to individuals wishing to emigrate from Europe (Ladame, 1958, pp. 268–269). In October 1953 the Provisional Committee changed its name to the Intergovernmental Committee for European Migration (ICEM) with the objective of arranging the transport of migrants from Europe to overseas countries and promoting a greater volume of migration from Europe via the provision of services that no other international organization was in a position to supply. ICEM member states contributed to its overall budget and decided on practical tools and operating policy. In its peak years the ICEM helped defray the transport costs of 120,000 emigrants: the largest numbers came from Italy and we will see why Italy was a special case. It will also be shown how large-scale migration opportunities sprang up within Europe itself, thus leading to a dramatic reduction in the number of movements to overseas countries in the 1960s.

In 1957 the European Economic Community (EEC) was established with the aim of liberalizing not only the movement of goods, but also of labour (and capital) between its six founding members. Yet free circulation of manpower, although accepted in principle, had to be phased in gradually. Fears of excessive mobility were still too strong among EEC partners. In spite of pressure exerted by Italy, no right for the unemployed to seek jobs abroad was contemplated, thus making migration a largely demand-induced phenomenon (Romero, 1991, p. 52). Such limited liberalization of manpower movements also meant that, under the treaty, the Italian government had no legal instruments to force other member states to hire Italian rather than non-EEC workers (Fauri, 2006). Only at the end of the 1960s did the EEC comply with its status of a customs union and introduce the free movement of labour.

Organizations responsible for European population movements (refugees, displaced persons and migrants)

After the Second World War the problem of refugees, displaced persons and migrants was tackled by several organizations. The IRO was concerned with the problem of repatriating and re-settling refugees and displaced persons, while the International Labour Organization (ILO) continued its pre-war effort to internationalize social legislation for workers, demanding equal treatment for migrant and national workers (Fumi, 2008, p. 136) and also issued memorandums on "How to break migration bottlenecks"; the Organisation for European Economic

Co-operation (OEEC) established a manpower committee to work on improving workers' circulation among its members. Last but not least, also the Council of Europe in its first consultative assembly (1949) urged all nations to grant foreign workers the same social standards enjoyed by national workers (Delpérée, 1956, pp. 111–112).

The only European country that, in international conferences, "perpetually" raised the question of surplus population and the international solutions to her problem was Italy.[2] This is easily explained: according to official estimates Italy's excess manpower totalled around two million unemployed, in addition to hidden unemployment estimated at between one million and four million people. The Italian government was convinced that the problem of unemployment was to be solved (also) through emigration and had to be "tackled at the international level [in the conviction that] ... it affected not only Italy, but the entire Western Community" (CIR, 1952, p. 337). The OEEC set up a manpower committee in 1948, which enjoyed the active participation of the Italian delegation. As a result of Italian pressure in 1950 it issued a recommendation addressed to all member countries that stressed the necessity for bilateral or multilateral agreement for the liberalization of manpower movements. Three years later the OEEC approved a "liberalization code" for the standardization of the rules concerning the employment of foreign workers between its member countries. Yet, in the words of the OEEC itself: "It was still impossible to talk of a European labour market" since the solutions proposed were mere statements of intent (OEEC, 1955, p. 19; Romero, 1991, pp. 51–57)

In 1950 the OEEC also decided to offer the ILO[3] a grant of $988,000 to undertake an extended programme of international action to facilitate European migration ($788,000 was appropriated from the Marshall Plan and $200,000 were subscribed in OEEC currencies by member countries in proportion to their subscription to the organization).[4] The work of the ILO consisted largely in setting up ILO missions in countries of immigration and emigration to advise governments on the best methods of recruiting and settling migrants.[5] The ILO migration office in Italy, for instance, was set up in September 1950 and held monthly meetings with immigration countries for the purpose of simplifying and coordinating emigration procedures; as regards employment much work was devoted to compiling an occupational classification handbook and to arranging facilities for improving the technical side of vocational training.[6] In May 1951 the manpower committee was asked by the ILO to continue and expand this programme. However, many delegations believed that this kind of technical assistance made no substantial contribution to solving Europe's overpopulation problem, while the US delegation was reluctant.[7]

The fact was that a few ILO members were no longer on the US list. When the IRO was going out of business at the end of 1951, it seemed natural that, of the existing international organizations, the ILO, which had always retained an interest in population and migration matters, should become the competent organization to deal with European problems of surplus population. Accordingly the ILO convened a large and imposing conference in Naples in September 1951 to lay plans for future action. Very shortly before the Naples conference met, the US congress decided that American money (which was the key to any serious attack on Europe over population) should not be made available to any body in which the Soviet Union or its Satellites were represented. Czechoslovakia, Poland and Albania were members of the ILO. This decision was announced by the US delegate at the opening of the Naples conference, which was thus "deprived of its raison d'être".[8] The ILO lost its influence and the money needed to go on with its programme, and was denied approval for the organized transfer over a period of five years of 1,700,000 people from overpopulated countries in Europe to other countries, mostly overseas (International Labour Review, 1952, 163–183).

Thus before the liquidation of the IRO in early 1952 the legal protection of refugees was entrusted to the UNHCR and the movement of people to a new international body (Ladame, 1958, pp. 268–269).

The birth of the PICMME

Shortly after the ILO was ruled out, the Brussels conference of December 1951 was convened at the instigation of the US government and the PICMME was set up for the purpose of making arrangements for the transport of migrants for whom existing facilities were inadequate and who could not otherwise be moved from certain European countries with surplus population to countries overseas offering opportunities of permanent resettlement.

Operations began on 1 February 1952 and by the middle of the same year 49,317 Europeans had emigrated under the sponsorship of PICMME. These migrants included many different categories of people: (1) eight million refugees of German origin from Eastern European countries and Russian-occupied eastern Germany plus hundreds of thousands of returning prisoners of war mainly from Russia were received by Western Germany and had to be re-settled; (2) the Jews who survived were offered a new home by the State of Israel, while some 430,000 European Jews emigrated to countries outside Europe: 350,000 relocated to Palestine, 40,000 to Canada and the United States and another 40,000 to Latin America and Australia; (3) the disruption of migratory movements during seven years of war had created a backlog consisting largely of families of pre-war emigrants who had left their families behind and of intending emigrants who had been prevented by the war from carrying out their plans. Finally, Italy's population pressure was helped by the new committee to find an outlet abroad, the only post-war phenomenon "which wasn't new" (Isaac, 1952, pp. 192–193).

As can be seen from Table 6.1, the largest group of migrants to be assisted was the ethnic German group – 27,400 – who were relocated to the United States on PICMME-chartered US vessels, while Italian emigration to Brazil and movements of refugees were entirely financed by the committee.[9]

The generous intake of German migrants on the part of the United States was based on the Displaced Persons act of 1948 authorizing the admission of 416,000

Table 6.1 ICEM assisted movements in 1952

Movements requiring the committee's financial assistance	
Italian migrants to Brazil	700
Refugee migrants to Australia	300
Refugees	4,600
German migrants to Venezuela	40
Total	5,640
Movements requiring shipping space the committee was able to provide	
Dutch migrants to Australia and New Zealand	3,700
Dutch migrants to Canada	400
German migrants to United States	27,700
German migrants to Australia	2,000
Displaced persons to United States and other destinations	8,200
Dependents of refugee migrants	1,300
Migrants to Canada by government-assisted passage	800
Total	44,100
Movements requiring the technical services of the committee	
Displaced persons to the United Kingdom	250
Refugees from Shanghai to various destinations	500
Total	650

Source: PRO (Pubic Record Office), FO report minutes on PICMME June 1952.

immigrants belonging to various categories of displaced persons and refugees, whose trip was financed by the committee.

In the case of Australia, the restrictive policy adopted during the interwar period was reversed and, with the help of PICMME, considerable efforts made to attract emigrants from Great Britain and other countries. Australia's intake was higher than ever before: 200,000 immigrants in 1950, 150,000 in 1951 and 80,000 in 1952 (Isaac, 1952). More than half were sponsored by PICMME which helped the transfer of 250,000 immigrants to Australia (for a total cost £32 million) and upon request the Australian minister for immigration, Holt, co-financed pilot schemes for land settlement since 1952.[10] In 1953 the ICEM portrayed itself as a "catalytic agent in the development of land settlement projects which could help the maintenance of peace".[11]

The other significant immigration country in terms of numbers admitted was Brazil: the committee subsidized the movement of dependents,[12] supported land settlement projects in Brazil in order to develop the production of agricultural commodities (such as dairy products and bread-grains)[13] and co-financed with the sending country the training of workers at home (it applied in particular to Italy, which organized pilot projects for training in the building construction trade). These latter projects were considered particularly interesting since they provided "the skills required by the immigration government which participated in the selection of the trainees and the direction of the training and agreed to accept migration persons who completed the course satisfactorily".[14]

Member countries and financial contributions

PICMME had 19 founding members (Australia, Austria, Belgium, Brazil, Canada, Chile, Denmark, France, the Federal Republic of Germany, Greece, Israel, Italy, Luxembourg, the Netherlands, Paraguay, Sweden, Switzerland, the United States and Venezuela), joined by Denmark, and Paraguay in May 1952 and by an increasing number of countries afterwards. The main European power conspicuous by its absence was Great Britain, which merely enjoyed an "observer status" within the committee. The main objection to joining was financial:

> membership would cost us 200,000 pounds which we can ill afford. Furthermore, if the money could be found the Secretary of State would rather see it spent on British emigration than use it to finance the movement of foreigners to Commonwealth countries under PICMME's auspices ... we have just cut our contribution to the Australian assisted passage scheme (under the Empire Settlement Act) from 500,000 to 150,000.[15]

However, with the undeniable fall in the number of British citizens wishing to leave and the continuing improvement in the UK's balance of payments in successive years it was becoming "more and more difficult to justify our failure to join on our inability to pay £70,000 a year.... Our refusal to join is becoming ... increasingly difficult to defend".[16] Great Britain finally joined in 1961, after a "wait and see" attitude, which it often adopted at the European level as well (it did not join the ECSC (European Coal and Steel Community) in 1951 or the EEC in 1957, eventually joining only in 1973).

The ICEM's budget consisted of an administrative budget and an operational budget. The former was covered by pre-determined, mutually agreed financial contributions paid annually by each member country, as shown in Table 6.2. The operational budget, on the other hand, was covered by a number of different allocations: member states' voluntary contributions which could be either a fixed amount for every emigrant leaving (from $40 to $60)[17] or occasional contributions unrelated to migratory movements, migrants and their sponsors' payments, international assistance and above all, US intervention, whose contributions came from many sources including the US Escapee Program (CIME, 1958).

The United States was the only country that did not contribute to the operational budget of the ICEM in proportion to the number of migrants leaving. Indeed, it was the financial force behind it: approximately one-third of its operational budget and one-third of its administrative budget were covered through US contributions; its political and financial support was a vital factor in the sponsorship and maintenance of the committee. "Since PICMME commenced operations in February 1952 [to the end of the decade] the US has appropriated $12.5 million annually for the operational budget and 1,000,000 Europeans have been re-settled overseas of whom 250,000 in Australia."[18]

Table 6.2 The ICEM budget (in $) in 1952 and 1964

		1952	*1964*
1	United States	785,567	706,900
2	Canada	198,161	0
3	France	198,161	192,100
4	Germany	198,161	192,100
5	Italy	198,161	192,100
6	United Kingdom	*65,000	178,090
7)	Australia	146,262	178,090
8	Brazil	103,798	47,016
9	Belgium	61,336	59,600
10	Netherlands	61,336	94,982
11	Switzerland	61,336	45,116
12	Austria	33,027	20,421
13	Greece	33,027	10,448
14	Chile	23,590	11,873
15	Bolivia	18,872	2,850
16	Luxembourg	2,359	2,850
17	Argentina		46,066
18	South Africa		45,116
19	Spain		39,180
20	New Zealand		23,033
21	Venezuela		23,033
22	Denmark		20,658
23	Norway		16,147
24)	Colombia		11,873
25	Israel		11,398
26	Costa Rica		2,850
27	Ecuador		2,850
28	Malta		2,850
29	Panama		2,850
30	Paraguay		2,850
Administrative budget	Total allocations	2,359,060	2,185,290
	Total expenditure	2,656,784	2,199,300
Operational budget (1953)	Total expenditure	34,608,475	

Source: PRO, FO 371/10027623, May 1953 Third session PICMME and European Historical Archives Fiesole, MC/44.

Note
* Prior to membership as ad hoc contribution for refugees.

In the 1952 budget, governmental administrative contributions reached a total of $2.4 million, while the operational budget (the cost of moving migrants) for 1953 was $34.6 million (see Table 6.2). This proportion stayed the same for the following years: in 1956 the operational budget was $41.4 million and administrative expenses $2.7 million. In its first ten years of operation, the committee financed the movement of 1.6 million European migrants, mainly to Australia (512,934) and Latin America (Argentina and Brazil were the main beneficiaries, with 117,291 and 109,587 assisted passages respectively).[19]

ICEM since 1953

In April 1953 PICMME became the ICEM and underwent a slight shift in terms of perspective and aims. The Latin American, Italian and Greek representatives brought all possible pressure to bear on the other delegations that the activities of the committee should not be confined to the mere transport of migrants but also to their assimilation in the countries of reception and their preparation for migration in the emigration countries. Their efforts were rewarded.[20] The founding charter of the ICEM established as its main goals both the transport of poor migrants unable to leave for land-abundant overseas countries and the provision of essential activities aimed at their preparation, reception and settlement, services no other international organization was providing. In Italy the ICEM financed the setting up of six National Migration Centres, with the task of selecting and directing the emigrants overseas but also to other European locations (Belgian mines, German or French factories etc.). The ICEM centre in Trieste hosted and organized the trip for those emigrants leaving for Australia: in two years (1955–1957) 10,000 migrants left the region (Friuli) for Australia (Lorenzon, 1962, p. 61).

In August 1953, President Eisenhower signed the Refugee Relief Act: more than 200,000 European refugees were allowed to enter the United States and ICEM provided for transport. At the same time, many Latin American governments offered ICEM to collaborate on land settlement schemes. ICEM experts were sent to Argentina, Brazil, Bolivia, Venezuela and also Rhodesia to help finalize each scheme. Yet the problem was not so much lack of land or manpower, but lack of capital. An enormous financial effort was in fact necessary to invest in the creation of roads, railroads, hydroelectric networks, schools and hospitals. Inadequate social overhead capital was the problem and ICEM did not possess sufficient means to carry on vast and expensive programmes such as land settlement schemes. Nonetheless, Brazil requested support for a programme aimed at receiving 3,370 peasant families for a total cost of $45 million, while Argentina offered 250,000 ha for European agricultural workers, soon followed by similar proposals on the part of Chile and Venezuela. When the ICEM met in Venice at the end of 1953, the picture was clear; even the ordinary programme covering movement of migrants was in dire straits. The provisional budget for 1954 was to be cut by $5 billion, transport costs could be covered only for only 117,000 emigrants (as opposed to 130,000). The ICEM proposed that all emigrants going overseas should contribute to the cost of the passage. It wasn't just a question of increasing the number of potential emigrants, but it was a "moral issue: each migrant was to reflect on his deeper motivation to leave and look for a better life for himself and his family overseas" (CIME, 1958, pp. 273–289). Based on the experience of the different countries involved, it began to emerge that emigrants who contributed to the total cost of the passage took their decision to migrate more seriously and were more likely to stick to it. Data showed that Dutch emigrants, who paid the highest contribution among European migrants ($85, co-sponsored by $150 from the Dutch government and $100 from the ICEM), rarely returned because of failure (2 per cent).

However it should be underlined that their chances of success were increased by proper training at home: "[The Dutch emigrant] was well prepared at home for his final destination and was given language courses and professional skills over one year before leaving."

In general, ICEM-assisted emigration increased from to 22 per cent to 40 per cent of total emigration over the 1950s. At the end of the decade, almost half of migrants leaving Europe were assisted by the ICEM. The data on Italy confirm ICEM's progressive engagement, as Figure 6.1 shows.

Nonetheless, this situation changed completely in the space of a few years. In the second half of the 1960s Europe was generally experiencing conditions of full employment, and the principal beneficiaries of the ICEM's work were the receiving countries.[21] Europe's economic miracle made it possible to find work at home for large numbers of workers for whom, previously, only emigration to another continent – the Americas or Australia – seemed to offer prospects of an acceptable future. On the one hand, large-scale migration opportunities sprang up within Europe itself and on the other even greater migratory movements were taking place within some of the states that had previously made a very significant contribution to overseas emigration. Thus the number of movements to overseas countries fell dramatically.[22]

The ICEM changed again. In 1980 it became the International Organization for Migration (IOM), whose objective since has been to ensure the orderly

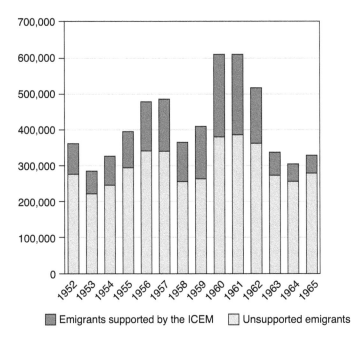

Figure 6.1 Italian migration and ICEM assistance (source: own calculations from ISTAT Annuario, various issues).

migration of persons in need of international migration services, the geograph-ical restriction to European migrants therefore being eliminated (Perruchoud, 1989).

European emigration: why Italy was a special case

Italy was a special case since most European migrants wishing to leave were Italians (Colucci, 2008; Sala, 2009; Romero, 2004). The second half of the 1940s saw increasing diplomatic efforts on the part of Italy to ease the way for her migrants abroad. After the fascist years, people were now free to emigrate, but not anywhere and only through international agreements with recipient states or a recruitment contract with a foreign ministry or private enterprise. Rinauro (2009, p. 148) calculates that up to 50 per cent of Italians working in Europe – the highest average in the case of France – were clandestine in the 1950s.

The United States, which had represented the main outlet for Italian migrants before the First World War, held on to its 1921 Quota Act (which allowed a very limited number of people to reach its borders) and, despite acknowledging its interest in "plans for the migration of surplus population from Western Europe ... since this idle people are extraordinarily susceptible to propaganda designed to undermine our indulgence upon and help to these countries", only allowed a set amount of refugees to enter (but set up and generously financed PICMME and ICEM as we have seen) (Foreign Relations of the United States FRUS, 1951b, p. 179).

After the Second World War, Italy feebly hoped for a revision of this policy and was highly critical of the failure of the US administration to open its doors slightly: "They had even rejected the proposal to accumulate the annual Italian quota of 5,000 odd over the war years which would have let in over 20,000 Ital-ians straight away ... an immense outlet for Italian farmers".[23] Prime Minister De Gasperi's efforts to internationalize Italy's surplus labour problem are well known: he rarely made a public speech without dwelling upon it (at a conference with the US Deputy Representative of the North Atlantic Council De Gasperi held that "The Americans should not lose sight of the fact that Italy's biggest surplus are babies") (FRUS, 1951a, p. 608). The British Embassy in Rome was convinced that

> These millions of unemployed and underemployed miserably poor and the ideal breeding ground for Communism must inevitably form a gigantic spectre which never ceases to haunt the Italian government and all thought-ful Italians, and which should always be present in the minds of those who are anxious to keep Italy on the Western Side of the Iron Curtain.[24]

Despite the diplomatic efforts of all government officials and Prime Minister De Gasperi, the United States kept its borders closed (formal requests on the need to re-open US borders to Italian emigrants were constantly made by De Gasperi during his official visits to the United States) (FRUS, 1951a, pp. 699–719; Adsands, 1953).

On the other hand, many European countries were experiencing a labour short-age after the war and showed a genuine interest in Italy's surplus manpower; talks started as early as the summer of 1945 (Colucci, 2012, p. 163) and the first agree-ments were signed at the end of that year and in 1946.[25] Particular interest was aroused by the approaches of the Belgian government to the Italian ambassador in Brussels in August 1945 when it was intimated that employment could be found in Belgium for 30,000 Italian coal miners. As a British Foreign Office Report tes-tifies, despite the fact that coal mining was a very small industry in Italy, the Italian government viewed the proposal to transfer its workers to the Belgian mines very favourably, not only in the general interest of emigration but because it was hoped to obtain special allocations of Belgian coal for Italy. The first 500 men recruited (350 in Lombardy and 150 in Veneto) were to be allocated to the five mining districts (100 men each) and included a small number of skilled underground and surface workers with sufficient unskilled workers to be trained for work in the Belgian mines. If the first experiment were successful, considera-tion was to be given to an increased rate of recruitment. In order to save time and avoid lengthy negotiations, Italy and Belgium decided to ratify the pending treaty of 29 September 1938, which guaranteed that Italian workers received the same pay and conditions of employment as the Belgian workers.[26] By mid-June 1946, 20,000 Italians had travelled to Belgium for work in the mines, and between June and October 1946 an endeavour was made to despatch 1,000 Italians a week to Belgium for work in the mines.[27] In July 1946, a Belgian delegation visited Rome and after consultation with the government and General Confederation of Labour agreed to increase the number of workers to be transferred to work in Belgian mines from 30,000 to 50,000. Living and working conditions in the mines were terrible, yet good, regular wages kept attracting an increasing amount of workers (Bertucelli, 2012; Cumoli, 2013). Salaries were extremely high by Italian stand-ards, for hewers and drillers a salary of 1,500 lire a day was promised – the daily agricultural salary in Italy varied greatly according to province, yet from an average of 500 lire in the south it rose to 900 lire in the north and ranged from 800 to 1,000 lire in the manufacturing industry in 1949 (ISTAT, 1951) – while remittances of any individual were not to exceed 25,000 lire a month. As reported by the British representative: "Of particular satisfaction to Italian industry is the promise that the Belgian government will send to Italy between 3,500 and 5,000 tons of coal per month for every 1,000 Italians employed."[28]

Belgium was soon followed by France, which sent a delegation to Rome on 31 January 1946 to arrange the recruitment of Italian labour. The director general of the National Office for Migration, Mr Auffay, (received by Italy's minister of labour on 1 February) said that the French government was not prepared to honour the Franco-Italian agreement operating before the war and the intention was to negotiate a new agreement and start emigration to France. The initial migration would be of 20,000 miners, this figure to be brought to 60,000 within a period of 18 months. France was also ready to employ strong unskilled workers and a percentage of skilled ones. Being aware of the negotiations proceeding between the Italian and Belgian governments, the negotiators said that they would be glad to share the Italian skilled workers who might be available with the Belgians. Skilled Italian workers were a rare item, as everyone in Europe knew. Italian workers in France would also receive all the usual social insurance and welfare benefits from the French authorities.[29] Finally the recruitment of 20,000 Italians to work in the French coal mines was agreed; difficulties arose in agreeing the amount of remittances, family allowances and a minimum period of service.[30] In the end, according to the agreement of 29 April the employer was to pay recruitment bonus of 2,000 lire plus travelling expenses to France and family allowances as soon as the worker's family arrived in France.[31]

Also the steady seasonal migration that normally took place in peace time from Italy to Switzerland was revived in 1946 and new agreements signed to transfer approximately 7,000 men and women for various types of seasonal employment in industry and agriculture. Many more just left on their own making Switzerland the most important emigration country for Italy, see Table 6.3 (Fauri, 2015).

In March 1946, the Labour Division of the Allied Military Government approached allied authorities in Italy with a view of arranging the transfer of workers in Udine and Northern Italy for employment in Western Austria: the immediate need was for brick and tile workers, building trade workers and labourers for agriculture. After lengthy negotiations it was finally agreed that Italian workers would be able to remit to their families in Italy at least 200 lire per day or 5,000 lire per month. The Italian government would arrange for this payment to be made currently to the families provided that the Austrian government would guarantee the despatch of timber or other commodities to Italy to the value at least of 5,000 lire per worker per month. On these general agreements the Italian government sent workers to Austria during the week ending on 15 June 1946.[32]

In the case of Germany, the 1955 bilateral agreement started an influx that soon saw the German labour market become one of Italy's favourite destinations. The German government considered Italian workers temporary guests, a purely transitory phenomenon based on a simple money for labour exchange. Yet, in the end, half a million Italians chose to stay on (Bevilacqua *et al.*, 1993; Bade, 1993).

The United Kingdom started to advertise the availability of employment for Italian foundry workers in November 1946. Initially the British government used official recruitment schemes to attract Italian workers. Through these schemes foreign labour abroad was recruited by the Ministry of Labour on a large scale but without a definite job in view of each person recruited. This type of recruitment was highly successful in meeting the urgent demand of the undermanned industries in 1947–1948. The workers were brought to the United Kingdom at the government's expense and in the interval between landing and being placed with suitable employers in essential industry they were accommodated at government expense.[33] In 1946 instructions on "how to apply for Italians" were sent to the British iron foundry industry, anticipating that:

> Owing to the shortage of foundry labour in this country, the Ministries concerned, employers, the ironfounders' federation and the trade unions agreed

to employ imported Italian foundry workers, up to 800 skilled and 2,000 others, on terms and conditions similar to those of British workers.

The recruitment of Italians was carried out by technical, experienced foundry-men, who visited Italy for the purpose at the end of 1949.[34] Medical examina-tions were to be performed by Italian authorities, proper winter clothes were to be sent by the United Kingdom by January 1947. Workers were to be transported on troop trains, which "make little concession to comfort" for a 50-hour journey, despite some concern that it would represent the "worst possible introduction of Italians to British conditions ... they will arrive in England disgruntled and exhausted after a trying experience".[35] Finally, the British government offered the same wage level as British foundry workers (not less than £6 per week for skilled men and no less than £4.10 per week for unskilled) and the possibility to remit to Italy up to a maximum of £10 monthly (9,000 lire).[36] Other schemes for the employment of Italy's surplus population (as they were called) were put in effect by 1949: for recruiting domestic servants, male and female textile workers and quarrymen.[37]

In 1951 two more arrangements followed: the first was meant to recruit from 1,000 up to 7,000 Italian workers for employment on track maintenance and repair and as labourers in the signal and tele-communication departments of the British railways.[38] The second started in April 1951, and by the middle of January 1952, 1,619 Italians had been recruited for coalmining at the expense of the British government (at a recruitment cost £9 per man).[39] Ad hoc recruiting missions – for coalmining, brick-making and tinplate industries and for the rail-ways – were arranged and sent to Italy.[40] However, a temporary suspension of recruitment of Italians for coalmining was put into effect at the beginning of 1952. Italians recruited for underground coalmining had not been placed in the mines because of opposition from the local miners' lodges. The resident com-mittee demanded a withdrawal of all Italians from the miners' hostel, since Ital-ians "made life intolerable for the others (they were violent, brought women to the hostel, enjoyed preferential treatment)".[41] Of the 2,418 men brought to the United Kingdom, 1,027 failed to get jobs in British mines (and were transferred to other employments). It was a problem of "human relationships" as had been correctly envisaged, but 1,100 Italians had to be turned away from work in the British pits. However, official recruitment schemes were to end soon: by 1949 demands from undermanned industries had been met and employers who wished to recruit foreign workers were urged "do so at their own expense under a Min-istry of Labour permit".[42]

As to Latin America, Argentina was the non-European country that absorbed the largest influx of Italian emigrants: between 1946 and 1948, 97,000 Italians had already moved there. On 2 May 1949 Pietro Campilli left for Buenos Aires on a special mission, the main goal of which was to arrange for an increase of trade and a higher flow of Italian emigrants. His tour lasted two months and covered many South American countries.[43] On 8 October 1949 Brazil and Italy signed an agreement for increased Italian immigration.[44] In June 1951 a new commercial agreement (superseding the agreement of 13 October 1947) was signed with Argentina to allow the settlement of 500,000 persons over five years:[45] Italian migrants would enjoy equal status with Argentine workers and special financial help.[46] Yet the peak was reached between 1949 and 1951 when 232,000 Italians left for Argentina, thereafter, due to Italy's economic miracle and Argentina's recurrent economic crisis the flow steadily decreased to a few hundred people per year by the beginning of the 1960s (see Table 6.3) (Roncelli, 1987).

Australia, too, had been ready to take 20,000 Italians (half women, half men) since the summer of 1948. On 29 March 1951 a new five-year immigration agreement was signed in Melbourne providing for assistance to suitable peasants in Italy wishing to emigrate to Australia for permanent settlement. The two governments contributed to the cost of transportation (they each paid a quarter of the fare with the emigrant paying the other half – approximately £57 – which could be loaned by the Italian government), migrants had to remain in employment for a minimum of two years while Italy was to facilitate the transfer of reasonable funds from Italy by the migrants in order to assist them in their settlement in Australia. To this end, the Italian government allotted 1.5 billion lire in the 1951–1952 budget for emigration to Australia. Between July and August 950 emigrants left, to be followed later by their families. According to the British Embassy in Rome, the Australian selection team who came to Italy in 1951 demanded "extravagantly high qualifications"[47] and in the end the largest contingent came from Friuli and Veneto (due in part to the lack of seasonal work in France and Austria).[48] In the case of Australia (and other overseas destinations), the selection process started in the migration centres (set up with the assistance of ICEM, as we have seen) where emigrants underwent a medical and professional examination in order to be sent to the foreign national selection teams. It was a new Australian commissioner named Mr Hill who adopted very stringent criteria for Italians wishing to go abroad and dismissed half of the candidates.[49] However, between 1946 and 1970, 336,386 Italians moved to Australia under stringent bilateral arrangements.

Finally, brief mention should be made of the existence of the ICLE (*Istituto per il credito del lavoro italiano all'estero*) which was established under Fascism but kept alive after the Second World War to foster land settlement projects for Italian migrants. As shown in Table 6.4, until the middle of the 1950s the ICLE sent study missions in Latin America in order to evaluate the possibility to initiate industrial or agricultural projects (this part of the budget was financed with Marshall Plan money). The ICLE also helped 14,000 workers leave the country, spending $4.4 million to buy them a ticket for an overseas destination (most of them went to Australia). Finally it invested almost two-thirds of its budget in the organization of agricultural settlement projects in various Latin American countries (which included the purchase of the land, infrastructure works, agricultural machinery, cattle and seeds and starting capital).

The land settlement projects were not only very expensive but also very unsuccessful, the farm areas purchased with ICLE funds were located in remote

Table 6.3 Italian emigration and main destination countries

Years	France	Belgium	Germany	Switzerland	Canada	United States	Argentina	Brazil	Australia	Total	Returnees (%)	Rate (×1,000)	% to Europe
1946	28,135	24,653	—	48,808	—	5,442	749	603	4	110,286	4	-2.3	93
1947	53,245	29,881	—	105,112	58	23,471	27,379	4,137	50	254,144	26	-4.2	76
1948	40,231	46,365	—	102,241	2,406	16,677	69,602	4,697	2,047	308,515	39	-4.2	63
1949	52,345	5,311	—	29,726	5,991	11,460	98,262	6,949	10,939	254,469	47	-3.0	37
1950	18,083	4,226	74	27,144	7,135	8,998	78,531	8,980	13,516	200,306	36	-2.8	27
1951	35,099	33,308	431	66,040	21,467	10,225	55,630	9,183	17,453	293,057	31	-4.3	51
1952	53,810	22,441	270	61,593	18,742	7,525	33,366	17,026	26,802	277,535	35	-3.9	52
1953	36,687	18,368	242	57,236	22,610	9,996	21,350	14,328	12,865	224,671	46	-2.6	50
1954	28,305	14,377	361	65,671	23,440	26,231	33,866	12,949	16,960	250,925	43	-3.0	43
1955	40,713	17,073	1,200	71,735	19,282	34,975	18,276	8,523	27,689	296,826	40	-3.7	50
1956	87,552	10,395	10,907	75,632	28,008	36,386	10,652	6,022	25,631	344,802	45	-4.0	60
1957	114,974	10,552	7,653	78,882	24,536	16,805	14,928	6,157	17,003	341,733	48	-3.7	69
1958	72,469	4,304	10,511	57,453	28,502	25,302	9,523	4,528	12,375	255,459	54	-2.4	62
1959	64,259	2,290	28,394	82,532	23,734	10,806	7,549	3,874	14,149	268,490	58	-2.3	72
1960	58,624	4,915	100,544	128,257	19,011	15,208	4,405	2,976	19,606	383,908	50	-3.9	81
1961	49,188	3,718	114,012	142,114	13,461	16,293	2,483	2,223	16,351	387,123	54	-3.6	85
1962	34,911	3,152	117,427	143,054	12,528	15,348	1,817	1,205	14,406	365,611	63	-2.7	86
1963	20,264	3,141	81,261	122,018	12,912	13,580	945	528	11,535	277,611	80	-1.1	85
1964	15,782	1,036	75,210	111,863	17,600	8,866	621	233	10,888	258,482	74	-1.4	84
1965	20,050	1,182	90,853	103,159	24,213	11,087	436	295	10,320	282,643	69	-1.7	82
1966	18,370	3,885	78,343	104,899	28,541	31,238	592	384	12,523	296,494	70	-1.8	74
1967	15,517	3,939	47,178	89,407	26,102	17,896	794	554	13,667	229,264	74	-1.2	73
1968	13,100	3,749	51,152	81,206	16,745	21,693	723	419	14,505	215,713	70	-1.3	73
1969	10,741	3,517	47,563	69,655	9,441	15,470	1,389	749	8,740	182,199	84	-0.6	76
1970	8,764	3,338	42,849	53,658	7,249	15,490	1,179	573	6,362	151,854	94	-0.2	76
Total	991,218	279,116	906,435	2,079,095	413,714	426,468	495,047	118,095	336,386	6,712,120			

Note
Own calculations from ISTAT, Annuario, ISTAT, Annuario statistico dell'emigrazione italiana and ISTAT, Un secolo di statistiche italiane.

Table 6.4 The ICLE budget 1951–1954

Projects	Destination	$
Study missions	Brazil, Chile, Peru, Ecuador, Paraguay, Bolivia, Mexico	1,300,000
Tickets	Australia, Chile, Venezuela, Canada, South Africa	4,401,000
Land settlement projects	Latin American countries, France, Canada	9,186,000
Stock holdings		250,000
Total		15,137,000

Source: Archivio INSMLI, Fondo Parri, busta 15 fascicolo 42.

places, infrastructure works proved extremely costly and in most cases with no contribution from the local government. Many of the Italian settlers after a few terrible years decided to go back (Fauri, 2009, pp. 257–280). In this respect, the land settlement projects envisaged by the ICEM and ICLE suffered the same problematic constraints and rarely thrived.

From labour recruitment contracts to the free movement of labour

A permanent solution to Europe's surplus population was to shift from bilateral manpower agreements to the free circulation of workers. A proposal for a multilateral quota system was submitted to the OEEC by Italy: workers admitted under the quota were to be free of all employment restrictions and would have the right to settle permanently. The quotas were to be increased every two years with the object of obtaining a smooth transition to complete freedom of movement among OEEC countries after ten years. The same proposal was discussed by the Working Group on Labour Mobility in NATO in 1953, to which Italy added another two forms of intervention: the revision of immigration regulations with a view to increasing facilities for the employment of foreign workers and fostering the work of the ICEM. However, the free circulation of workers was "quite unacceptable" to the United Kingdom, France and Belgium, who offered to improve the existing system of individual work permits.[50]

During the same years, when negotiations concerning supranational European organizations (ECSC, European Defence Community (EDC), EEC) began, the Italian delegation persistently proposed the free movement of workers as part of the deal. From an economic point of view, it represented a good and radical solution to the problem of migration, which would thus become "an internal movement of workforce" aimed at balancing the European labour market and absorbing external shocks (Gini, 1955, p. 994). During the EEC negotiations, in the subcommittee on social problems, the Italian delegation made clear from the beginning the movement of labour had to be as free and ample as possible (Doumulin, 1989). Still, while the idea could be accepted in principle, the reports from Brussels spoke of the difficulties that arose in trying to reach an agreement on the "the time and means to allow the free movement of labour" (Fauri, 2006). Fears of excessive mobility were still too strong among the other participants and "in spite of Italy's pressure, no right for the unemployed to seek for jobs abroad was contemplated. The guiding principle remained the primacy of demand-induced migration" (Romero, 1993, p. 52). The directives putting into effect the EEC articles of the free movement of labour (Art. 3, 48, 49) only came through in 1968–1969 (yet, in the meanwhile, new instruments to help migrant workers were introduced as the Sío-López–Tedeschi chapter shows).

The right granted by Article 48 was the right to accept any job that was available (although not in the public sector) plus a conditional right to remain in the territory of a member state after having been employed in that territory. Such freedom of movement and residence was to be reached not later than the end of the transitional period, i.e. 31 December 1969 (although the regulation, directive and decision completing it were formally adopted a year in advance, in October 1968).[51] To summarize, the effect of the October 1968 instruments was that nationals of any EEC country were able to enter any other EEC country and, once they had entered, to be considered for jobs that were available there (except in the public service) on the same basis as nationals of that country. If they found employment there they had the right to reside in the country and to be joined by their families if suitable accommodation was available. The instruments were not specific as to whether they had the right to reside in a country if they did not find work. In the report of the British delegation: "The Community is clearly anxious that EEC nationals move around without regard to the availability of employment".[52] Work permits were abolished and the EEC system of labour mobility allowed workers to move freely between member states merely on production of a valid passport or national identity card. On arrival in another member state an EEC worker and his dependents had a right of residence if he took up employment and was issued with a residence permit (valid for five years and automatically renewable). One of the main provisions concerned the total and final abolition of national priority in access to employment: i.e. the privileged positions enjoyed by nationals compared to workers from other member states. Under the new system, nationals from other member states had access to employment under the same conditions as nationals, while employers were to give EEC applications the same consideration as those of nationals who were seeking work before offering jobs to workers from non-member countries (priority of EEC workers over non-EEC workers).[53] Unfortunately, as the data show, the slope of Italian emigration was already pointing downward at the end of the 1960s. Italy's economic miracle and internal migration movement had greatly contributed to the solving of its unemployment problem. For the first time since the end the war, between 1970 and 1975 the number of immigrants (returnees) exceeded the number of emigrants, by 19,000 (UN, 2012).

Conclusion

One of the most delicate issues after the war was where and how to resettle displaced persons, war prisoners and refugees. The war had drawn a new Europe, whose geography had changed yet again, physical borders had shifted and political borders had been created, dividing the continent and its successive history and economic development. Many people felt betrayed and left their country of origin, millions of refugees poured into Germany from Russia, the Jews who survived emigrated all over the globe. First the IRO and subsequently the UNHCR took care of and assisted them and provided for their protection, transport and reestablishment in countries able and willing to receive them.

Yet, seven years of war had also disrupted migratory movements, which were to start again under the rigid umbrella of bilateral treaties and international labour agreements. Many people unemployed or with low paid jobs wished to escape poverty and find better work opportunities abroad either in labour-scarce European countries or start again in a new overseas territory. While the United States had closed its borders as a receiving country and was not willing to open them again, Latin America and Australia were interested in surplus European manpower. The ILO (1919) had traditionally retained an interest in population and migration matters and after the war was identified as the competent organization to deal with European problems of surplus population. The OEEC provided the ILO with generous financing, its work consisting largely of setting up missions in countries of immigration and emigration and to advise the governments on the best methods of recruiting and settling migrants. Yet results had not been impressive and, most of all, the United States did not like the idea of financing a few members of the ILO that were not on the right side of the Iron Curtain. Therefore, the ILO was put on standby and the American government set up and financially supported the PICMME. The purpose of the PICMME–ICEM was to arrange for the transport of (poor) migrants from certain European countries with surplus population to other countries in Europe or overseas offering opportunities of permanent resettlement. ICEM progressively assisted from 22 per cent to 40 per cent of all emigrants leaving from Europe in the 1950s. Nonetheless, in the space of a few years things changed completely. In the second half of the 1960s Europe was generally experiencing conditions of full employment, and the principal beneficiaries of the ICEM's work were receiving countries or political refugees. In 1980 the ICEM became the IOM, supporting migrants all over the world (and not just those leaving Europe, as was the case previously).

As to why Italy was a special case, being the provider of most European migrants to other countries within Europe and around the world, we must consider its difficult post-war situation, when two million of its people were jobless and poor. If work was not available there, it had to be found abroad. The Italian government signed bilateral labour agreements with an increasing number of European and overseas countries. Besides solving the unemployment problem, there were two good additional reasons for signing these contracts: by improving the economic situation of many young and jobless Italians, the "gigantic spectre" of communism haunting the Italian government (and its allies) was appeased. In the second place, the first bilateral treaties regulating emigration and signed in 1946 also helped to alleviate the problematic lack of raw materials, without which the economy was stranded (Fauri, 2010, pp. 112–131). In the case of Belgium, as we have seen, manpower was exchanged for coal – between 3,500 and 5,000 tons of coal per month for every 1,000 Italians employed. In the case of Austria, timber or other commodities were to be despatched to Italy to the value at least of 5,000 lire per worker per month.

When finally free movement of workers within the EEC entered into operation at the end of the 1960s, Italy no longer needed it. Things had changed swiftly, Italy's economic miracle had pushed it to feature among the most industrialized countries and internal migration had fed the northern firms while providing employment for surplus labour leaving the south. In less than 15 years, the widespread European fear of an invasion of unspecialized Italian labour seemed a distant memory.

When the free movement of EEC labour became effective at the end of the 1960s the chance to create a European labour market was no longer there. Today only nine million Europeans work in another EU country, despite the economic crisis labour mobility has fallen abruptly to the point that it is very unlikely that the two million jobs available in the EU will be covered by an EU migrant worker (Barroso, 2013).

Notes

1 Its main functions were repatriation, identification, registration and classification, care and assistance, legal and political protection, transport, resettlement and reestablishment in countries able and willing to receive them, of refugees and displaced persons in Europe.
2 Public Record Office (from now on PRO), FO 371/105918 Letter from British Embassy in Rome to Wright FO, 4 May 1953.
3 Among the founding aims of the ILO (created in 1919, as part of the Treaty of Versailles) were the protection of workers and cooperation to obtain similarity of working conditions in countries competing for markets. At the end of the 1940s its role extended to the protection/regulation/opening of migration though its contribution focused primarily on supplying potential migrants with information on life and work conditions (Delpérée, 1956, p. 105).
4 PRO, FO 371/94358 ILO letter to OEEC 6 October 1950.
5 PRO, FO 371/94361 Mutual Aid Department Minutes 27 April 1951.
6 PRO, FO 371/94358 Progress report on technical assistance project no. 3 carried out under ILO – Note by the Italian delegation.
7 PRO, FO 371/94361 Mutual Aid Department Minutes 27 April 1951.
8 PRO, FO 371/100278 Letter from TW Garvey 7 August 1952 and also FRUS, 1951a, pp. 191–194.
9 PRO, FO 371/100278 The Provisional Intergovernmental Committee for the Movement of Migrants from Europe (PICCME) meeting, Third session 30 May 1952.
10 PRO, DO 35/6364 Extract from *Australia and New Zealand Weekly* 6 September 1952; and Extract from *Canberra Times* 20 August 1952.
11 PRO, FO 371/111221 Sixth Session of ICEM Venice 12–21 October 1953.
12 PRO, FO 371/100276 Third Session of PCIMME 30 June 1952. "The administration has been active in assisting the development of a scheme for Italian families settling in Brazil; the Brazilian government will pay transport costs to heads of families, while PICMME will subsidize the movement of dependents".

13 PRO, DO 35/6364 ICEM Fifth Session 6 May 1953 "Latin American countries want to increase agricultural production".

14 PRO, DO 35/6364 Purpose and function of ICEM.

15 PRO, FO 371/10027829 Parliamentary Question, Lady Tweedsmuir to ask why UK is not member of PICMME, July 1952.

16 Ibid.

17 PRO, FO 371/100278 Agreement between the Italian government and the PICMME. "As a contribution to the operational budget Italy shall pay $60 per migrant towards the cost of the ocean transport of all emigrants from Italy who are assisted by the Committee".

18 PRO, DO 35/10191 Letter from the Minister of Immigration (Canberra) to Lord Ferrier (House of Lords), 13 April 1960.

19 PRO FCO 61/596, ICEM migrants 1 February 1952–31 December1962.

20 PRO, FO 371/105912 Letter from UK permanent delegation in Geneva PC Pell to Christofas (Mutual Aid Dep.) 21 April 1953.

21 PRO, FCO 61/596 ICEM Letter by Hayment on GB withdrawing from ICEM 1 January 1968.

22 PRO FO 61/596 Council of Europe Sixteenth Report of the Activities of ICEM 24 Apr. 1969.

>   Last but not least, in late 1968 also the events in Czechoslovakia influenced ICEM assistance. There had not been so many refugees calling on ICEM assistance since the Hungarian crisis, out of 80,302 persons moved in 1969, 50,000 were refugees.

23 PRO, DO 35/3363 2 Oct. 1948 Letter from the FO to Commonwealth Relations Office.

24 PRO, FO 371/102087 Telegram from Rome to FO 23 November 1959.

25 PRO, FO 371/60830 Letter from the Italian Minister of Labour to FO 12 December 1945 announcing the Italo-Belgian agreement.

26 PRO, FO 371/60830 Emigration of Italian workers to Belgium (Report) 30 January 1946. On the Belgian agreement see: Oblath, 1946.

27 PRO, FO 371/60830 Emigration of Italians (Report) August 1946.

28 Ibid.

>   Family allowances have been agreed at a minimum of 900 lire for one child for a maximum of 17,300 lire a month for 10 children (if the family resides in Italy the allowances to be paid directly by the Italian authorities). After 30 years' work in the mines a worker will be entitled to a pension of 70,000 lire a year (130,000 lire for 41 years).

29 PRO, FO 371/60830 Emigration of Italian workers to France (Report).

30 PRO, FO 371/60830 Emigration of Italians (Report).

31 PRO, FO 371/60630 From Rome to FO, 8 May 1946 Italians in French mines.

32 PRO, FO 371/60830 Emigration of Italians (Report).

33 PRO, LAB 8/1741Ministry of Labour and National Service Letter from Mr Griffin 22 August 1951.

34 PRO, LAB 26/199 Ministry of Supply – Iron and Steel Control – Letter to Certain Iron Foundries 6 November 1946.

35 PRO, LAB 26/199 Letter from Mr Lewis to Mr Wilson 19 November 1946.

36 PRO, LAB 26/199 Conditions at which employment is offered to Italian foundry workers.

37 PRO, FO 371/79534 Minutes "Existing schemes of employment and emigration of Italian surplus population", 5 February 1949.

38 PRO, FO 371/102140 Letter from Ministry of Labour and Public Service "Recruitment of Italian workers", 30 November 1951.

39 PRO, LAB 3/248 Letter E. Robbie to Mr Singleton 24 January 1952.
40 PRO, FO 371/102140 Minutes, Italian Labour for the United Kingdom FC Mason 31 January 1952.
41 Manchester Guardian 19 April 1952 "Fresh moves to get Italians out of miners' hostel".
42 PRO, LAB 3/248 Letter to DJ Mitchell (Treasury Chambers) 29 October 1952.
43 PRO, FO 371/79406 Letter from Rome to FO, 3 May 1949.
44 PRO, FO 371/102087 Letter from the British Embassy Rio de Janeiro to FO, 3 October 1952.
45 PRO, FO 271/105918 Commercial agreement between Italy and Argentina envisaging the movement of 500,000 Italians to Argentina over a period of five years.
46 PRO, FO 371/102130 British Embassy Rome to FO, 9 May 1952.

   The law was passed on 30 April 1952 authorizing the Foreign Exchange office to allocate 200 million Argentine pesos for financing Italian emigration to Argentina (the funds will be released from Italian credits now frozen in Argentina). The Argentine government in its turn is to make a contribution of at least equal value.

47 PRO, DO 35/3363 Letter from the British Embassy in Rome to Ernest Bevin 6 January 1951.
48 PRO, FO DO 35/3363 Italian immigration into Australia 24 April 1949.
49 Archivio centrale dello stato, Ministero del lavoro e previdenza, Centri di emigrazione, busta 31 1951. The centres swiftly set up ad hoc courses for those Italian emigrants laid off by the Australian commission for lack of "a minimum standard of cultural preparation".
50 PRO, FO 271/105918 "Italian manpower" Italian appeal presented in NATO 1 April 1953.
51 Regulation 16/12/1968 on the freedom of movement for workers applicable from 19 October 1968. Directive 68/360/EEC on the abolition of restrictions on movement and temporary residents of workers of member states and their families applicable from 19 October 1968 Yet, it had to wait until 19 July 1969 to bring into force the necessary national legislation.
52 PRO, LAB 10/3603 The European Economic Community: the free movement of labour and immigration (report). Member states can derogate from the provisions of the directive on grounds of public policy, public security or public health and public safety.
53 PRO, LAB 10/3603 Press Release Brussels 13 April 1967 "Towards complete freedom of movement for workers".

References

Adsands, Paolo Canali (1953). *Acide De Gasperi nella politica estera italiana 1944–1953*, Verona: Mondadori.
Bade, K. J. (1993). Emigrazione-migrazione per lavoro-migrazione. Esperienze tedesche nel XIX e XX secolo. In J. Petersen (ed.), L'emigrazione tra Italia e Germania, Manduria: P. Lacaita.
Barroso, J. M. (2013). Jean Monnet ECSA-world Conference 14 November.
Bertucelli, L. (2012). *L'Emilia nel cuore dell'Europa*, Milan: Unicopli.
Bevilacqua, P., Andreina A. De Clementi, E. Franzina (1993). *Storia dell'emigrazione italiana*, 2 vols., Rome: Donzelli.
CIME, Il Comitato intergovernativo per le migrazioni europee (1958). *La sua struttura e le sue attività*, Geneva.

CIR, Comitato interministeriale per la ricostruzione (1952). *The Development of Italy's Economic System within the Framework of European Recovery and Cooperation*, Rome: Tip. Apollon.

Colucci, M. (2008). *Lavoro in movimento*, Donzelli: Rome.

Colucci, M. (2012). Il governo delle migrazioni nell'Europa del dopoguerra. In L. Bertucelli (ed.), *L'Emilia nel cuore dell'Europa*, Milan: Unicopli.

Cumoli, F. (2013). *Un tetto a chi lavora. Mondi operai e migrazioni italiane nell'Europa degli anni Cinquanta*, Milan: Guerini e Associati.

Del Gaudio, G. (1973). Libera circolazione e priorità comunitaria dei lavoratori nei paesi della CEE. In F. Assante (ed.) *Il movimento migratorio italiano dall'unità nazionale ai nostri giorni*, Geneva: Librairie Droz.

Delpérée, A. (1956). *Politique sociale et intégration européenne*, Paris: Librairie générale de droit et de jurisprudence.

Doumulin, M. (1989). (ed.), *Mouvements et politiques migratoires en Europe depuis 1945: le cas Italiane*, Brussels: Ciaco.

Fauri, F. (2006). *L'integrazione economica europea 1947–2006*, Bologna: Il Mulino.

Fauri, F. (2009). Il decollo mancato: nascita e vita travagliata dell'Istituto di credito per il lavoro italiano all'estero, in *Studi Storici*, 1.

Fauri, F. (2010). Big business and Italian industrial policies after World War II. In A. Colli and M. Vasta (eds), *Forms of Enterprise in 20th Century Italy. Boundaries, Structures and Strategies*, Edward Elgar: Cheltenham.

Fauri, F. (2015). *Storia economica dell'emigrazione italiana*, Bologna: Il Mulino.

Foreman-Peck, J. (1995). *A History of the World Economy: International Economic Relations since 1850*, New York: Harvester Wheatsheaf.

FRUS, Foreign Relations of the US (1951a). Vol. iv.

FRUS (1951b). Interest of the United States in plans for the migration of surplus population from Western Europe, vol. vi.

Fumi, G. (2008). Gli accordi internazionali di "sicurezza sociale" e la questione delle politiche sociali alle origini della costruzione europea (1947–1956). In A. Cova (ed.) *Il dilemma dell'integrazione. L'inserimento dell'economia italiana nel sistema occidentale (1945–1957)*, Milan: Franco Angeli.

Gini, C. (1955). Delle migrazioni internazionali in *Rivista di politica economica*, March.

International Labour Review (1952). *The ILO and the migration problem*, lxv, 2.

Isaac, J. (1952). International migration and European population trends, *International Labour Review*, lxvi, July/December.

Ladame, P. (1958). *Le rôle des migrations dans le monde libre*, Genève: Dorz.

Lorenzon, O. (1962). *L'emigrazione in Friuli*, Camera di Commercio di Udine, Udine.

Oblath, A. (1946). *Problemi dell'emigrazione italiana*, Rome.

OEEC (1955). *From Recovery to Economic Strength*, Sixth Report, Paris.

Perruchoud, R. (1989). Intergovernmental committee for European migration, *International Journal of Refugee Law*, 1, 1, January.

Rinauro, S. (2009). *Il cammino della speranza*, Turin: Einaudi.

Romero, F. (1991). *Emigrazione e integrazione europea 1945–1973*, Milan: Franco Angeli.

Romero, F. (1993). Migration as an issue in European interdependence and integration: the case of Italy. In A. S. Milward (ed.), *The Frontier of National Sovereignty: History and Theory 1945–1992*, London: Routledge.

Romero, F. (2004). Il problema della libera circolazione della manodopera: dalla CECA alla CEE. In R. Ranieri and L. Tosi (eds), *La Comunità Europea del Carbone e dell'Acciaio (1952–2002): Gli esiti del Trattato in Europa e in Italia*, Padova: Cedam.

Roncelli, I. N. (1987). L'emigrazione italiana verso l'America Latina nel secondo dopoguerra (1945–1960), *Studi e Ricerche di Geografia*, x, 1.

Sala, R. (2009). L'emigrazione italiana in Europa dal boom economico alla fine dei grandi flussi. In Paola Corti and Matteo Sanfilippo (eds), *Migrazioni*, Storia d'Italia, Annali, 24, Turin: Einaudi.

UN (2012). World population prospects: the 2012 revision. Online, available at: http:// esa.un.org/wpp.

7 Migrants and European institutions

A study on the attempts to address the economic and social challenges of immigration in EU member states

Cristina Blanco Sío-López and Paolo Tedeschi

Introduction

The aim of this contribution is to shed light on the motivations, the strategies and the discourses of the European institutions about migrants and, moreover, it seeks to address the evolving challenge of integrating successive waves of immigrants arriving from candidate countries, from new member states, as well as from African and Asian countries.[1] More particularly, this chapter shows the reaction of the European institutions regarding the influx of migrants from the Italian Mezzogiorno, the Iberian peninsula and Eastern Europe during the 1950s, 1960s and 1970s. It also examines the influence of the institutional and reconversion challenges posed by the Southern enlargement of the EEC in the 1980s. Furthermore, it analyses the socioeconomic implications of the political decision to go ahead with an East–West "reunification" of the continent via the Eastward enlargement of the EU that started in the early 1990s.

The main sources adopted for this study are the Historical Archives of the European Commission relating to the High Authority of the ECSC, the Historical Archives of the EU (HAEU), the governmental archives concerning some of the European countries studied here (such as Spain and Germany), the Archives of the DG Enlargement of the European Commission, amongst others.[2] These sources help to throw light on the causal relation between the evolving position of the European institution with regard to this issue, and allow us to understand the reactions and proposals of the major players and the ensuing decision to channel migration vectors. The sources also include a set of interviews with those who occupy positions of power within the European institutions and within their respective governments, the European institutions and on the topic of the risks, the opportunities and the conclusions reached in relation to the synchronized enlargements and the correlated EEC/EU migration processes from the 1980s onwards.

This chapter also takes into consideration published works relating to the phenomena of emigration towards the richest countries of the EEC. This enables us to show how the European institutions have attempted to address the social and economic challenges linked to the successive arrival of intra-European migrants and third country nationals. It shows that the approaches and rules of the European institutions varied in relation to the migrants' country (and whether or not they belonged to the EEC) on the one hand, and their professional skills on the other (level of instruction and job specialization). This chapter also analyses the experience of socialization of migrants during the 1980s and 1990s at the European level and explores the extent to which different contingents helped to disseminate a socio-political spillover effect in the communities of the migrants; an effect that contributed to the opening up of new democratic political cultures in the countries to which they returned and that had experienced dictatorships and authoritarian regimes. So, it underlines the effects of migrants on the political and diplomatic agenda of the host countries and on the relation between the EEC/EU and successive candidate countries. Furthermore, this chapter looks into the actual economic impact that migrants have had on the internal development of their native countries; it draws attention to the significance of migrant remittances and the specific professional qualifications that former immigrants have acquired. Finally, the chapter reflects upon the integration schemes affecting former and current European migrants' integration, highlighting ways in which good practices can be applied to the new present challenges that involve the migration waves still taking place in our continent, and emphasizes the salience of one of the fundamental principles of the European integration process: solidarity and its related cohesion expectations and compromises.

The ECSC and EEC encounter the "migrant problem" during the first phase of the European integration process

Before analysing how during the 1950s and 1960s, the European institutions tried to solve the main problems linked to emigration within the boundaries of the new Europe, it is important to underline the fact that different migrants arrived in the richest ECSC/EEC countries. This means that European institutions were faced with a variety of problems and, therefore had to offer different solutions (CECA, 1957a; CEE, 1966). Furthermore, it is important to note that migrants who were communitarian citizens benefited from the treaties creating the ECSC and EEC: the privileges covered by the treatise did not extend to the problems involved in finding a job or accommodation. The legal situation of communitarian migrants was certainly better than that of other migrants. Moreover, it is important to state that in the early 1950s, all ECSC countries registered a surplus of unskilled manpower, and so migrants were able to take up jobs that were physically demanding (e.g. mining) and that were often underpaid and short term (e.g. building) (Molinari, 1958; Faidutti-Rudolph, 1962; Böhning, 1972a; Salt and Clout, 1976, Martens, 1976; UN, 1979; Grassi, 1994; Schor, 1966; Goedings, 2000; Spire, 2005; Illegal, 2014).

In 1951 the PICCME was founded, indicating that Western Europe had great difficulty in assimilating immigration within its boundaries, and that it had to foster) European emigration towards North America, Latin America and Oceania.[3]

For the period under investigation, it is possible to identify several categories of migrants in Europe; to observe their positive labour skills and the benefits that migrants brought to the countries they settled in: it is also possible to detect the kind help that came from European institutions.

These migrants came from the least economically advanced regions of the EEC (in particular from Southern Italy): they often had a low level of specialization (or were unskilled) and sought a job in order to support their families (who often remained in Italy). Once they had found a job, they were able to use the extremely useful networks that had been created by Italian migrants in the period stretching from the end of the nineteenth century to the 1930s, but clearly, they needed training courses that would enable them to improve their language and labour skills. Besides, when migrants did not belong to a category mentioned in the particular agreement among the ECSC/EEC governments, e.g. they did not appear in the agreements concerning Italian migrants who arrived in Belgium to work in the mines, one of the main job opportunities for Italians until 1956 (Morelli, 1988), there existed the problem of the reunification of the migrant's family. The migrant had a job and was able to pay for the accommodation of his wife and children, but countries could not accept all members of families (Faidutti-Rudolph, 1964; Dumoulin, 1989; Romero, 1991, 1993; Besana, 2002; Blanc-Chaléard, 2003; Colucci, 2008; Rinauro, 2009).

One category of migrants included refugees from European countries governed by dictators or other forms of authoritarian government; amongst these we may count the Iberian countries (Pereira, 2012; Dreyfus-Armand, 1999; Sanchez, 2004) the East European countries under USSR authority (Dufoix, 2002), and those who had fled the military dictatorship in Greece in the period from 1967 to 1974 (Alexiou, 2004). These migrants wanted to live in democratic countries; they usually had good work skills. East European people speaking Magyar and Slavic languages typically had the necessary work skills and were able to quickly learn the language of the country to which they had immigrated. Their professional skills favoured their integration. The question of whether the influx of these particular immigrants would increase the opportunity for spying arose, and, at the same time, governments were concerned about the ideological bias of immigrants arriving from Iberia and Greece, who may have belonged to the Communist party.

Furthermore, there was the particular case of the German people who in the post war period remained in their East European countries and then decided, in the 1950s and in the early 1960s, to escape to West Germany: they arrived from German regions that became part of new socialist republic of Poland, Czechoslovakia, Hungary and East Germany. In this case they knew the language and it was easier to find a job even if they did not have any family members in West Germany. Before the "German economic miracle", it was possible to have relevant discussions between "local Germans" and "foreign Germans" in particular in the rural areas. The public authorities obviously had the problem of controlling if they were spies. In general the immigrants possessed considerable work skills. And indeed, it was in order to stop this "haemorrhaging of the best brains" that the Berlin Wall was built in August 1961 (Dreyer, 1961; Korte, 1985; Herbert and Hunn, 2001).

Other migrants from Belgium, Holland and the French former colonies had few problems with the target language (McDonald, 1965; Simon, 2002; Le, 1997; Cornet, 2004). There was no problem for people of European nationalities, who typically had good professional skills, but emigrants from Africa and Asia were faced with greater difficulties. These people often had had little education and were generally unskilled. Europeans were, on the whole, less willing to accommodate people having a different religion and/or colour of the skin. The integration of Muslim or black people was evidently more complicated and the risk of creating some ghettos in the outskirts of the main towns was high.

Finally there was a privileged category of migrants: the executives of the new European institutions. In this case governments wanted to guarantee their employment in host countries by guaranteeing high salaries, accommodation, good services, fiscal privileges and the creation of special structures for families (such as international schools where children could learn a variety of European languages including their native one).

It is interesting to explore the questions of how the European institutions attempted to address the social and economic challenges linked to the arrival of intra-European migrants and third country nationals. The European institutions had to manage the arrival and integration of migrants: this meant that they had to control the emigration flows and allow the host countries to organize their labour markets so as to avoid exploiting this new labour through excessively low wages and also overly priced accommodation, moreover they sought to avoid the segregation of immigrants in the *ghettos.* Migrants had to be fully integrated in the new countries if social problems were to be avoided: if they had regular work it was obviously easier to create conditions conducive to social peace. The aim was to develop public spaces where migrants could meet their compatriots, but also establish the necessary structures so that they could learn the language and customs of the country where they worked. These policies implied limiting the number of migrants. European institutions could not handle unlimited numbers of migrants: the arrival of too many people would not allow the ECSC and EEC to establish the rules so that migrants could become integrated in the host country. If they established that communities and factories that received migrants had to create workers' villages including accommodation, schools and leisure areas (for dancing or playing sports), it was still evident that these measures could only be achieved if the number of migrants was limited (Stoetzel, 1954; Gibellini, 2010). The European institutions affirmed the need to address the issue of health assistance (in case of workers' injuries or sickness), also for people arriving from third countries. Yet, these were mere statements of intent since many measures could not concern clandestine migrants who did not exist in official statistical prospects.[4] So, while several agreements concerning the social protection of migrant workers were signed from 1948 to the end of the 1950s and the European Institutions also envisaged the creation of new forms of assistance and pensions that might guarantee the welfare of all European workers

(Mazzetti, 1975; Bikkal, 1975; Gui, 1975; Masini, 1975), new *ghettos* of foreign workers were developed (in particular in the outskirts of the main towns) and did not allow a real European social integration. The European institutions endeavoured to create and organize a new "Europe of work" (which was linked to the activity of the ILO), but they were not able to face to the increasing number of migrants related to the economic growth of Western Europe (CECA, 1957b; Leboutte, 2006; Taccolini, 2006; Mechi, 2013).

The problem of migrants did not concern the ECSC/EEC members only: all Western European countries belonging to the Council of Europe (or European Council, EC) were involved, and the EEC countries shared their migration policies with the other EC members. All these institutions dedicated a lot of time to the solution of the most serious migrants' problems and the EC promulgated many "resolutions" concerning accommodation. Governments were supposed to check that accommodation was hygienic. They were also supposed to provide information that would give migrants the knowledge they needed. Other directives concerned the participation of migrants in the organization of the businesses and the areas where they lived and worked.[5]

In the early 1950s, ECSC members knew that finding solutions to the problems of migrants would directly impinge on the development of the processes of European integration, and would also have consequences for the future of the wider social and economic systems of Europe. So the ECSC Consultative Committee promoted the improvement and harmonization of labour conditions and the control of the real wages. Following the US advice during the European Recovery Program, the ECSC (and the EEC afterwards) tried to improve work conditions and, at the same time, increase productivity so as to reduce the unit costs and final prices. This result could allow European institutions to create an economic and social system which could be an alternative to the USSR Marxist model and also to US capitalism (even if the US army protected Western Europe).

The existence of good political and economic relations between the six EEC members depended on the kind of living conditions available to migrants. Italy exported workers, and the country demanded that their rights be respected. The problem of integration depended on solving the problems of migrants and so those countries who took in migrants were expected to improve conditions for Italian workers. This expectation was not related to any "contractual power" possessed by the Italian government, rather, it related to the general political conditions that existed in the 1950s and 1960s. European institutions were concerned to demonstrate to EEC citizens that the "Western choice" offered a better way than the "Marxist solution" to be found in the Eastern European countries. In Italy existed the greatest communist party in Western Europe and it could gain power if the Italian government (led by the Christian Democracy party and its allies) failed to protect those Italian emigrants who went to other EEC countries. If the Italian Communist Party (linked to the USSR) emerged victorious in Italy, a country that belonged to NATO, the process of European integration would have been endangered, and the strategic equilibrium between the United States and the USSR imperilled. The Italian government was therefore able to ask their European partners to improve the conditions of Italian workers: if Italian emigration had been interrupted, the ensuing social problems would have favoured the rise of the Italian Communist Party. So the European institutions had to allow Italian workers to move freely within the ECSC/EEC countries, which also paid for the economic development of the Mezzogiorno, the poorest ECSC/EEC region.

While OEEC members could reject Italian demands and hence prohibit the free circulation of Italian workers, the ECSC members could not act in the same manner, because Article 69 of the treaty obliged members to accept workers who were qualified to work in mines and iron and steel industries. Italy wanted to delegate to the High Authority of the ECSC all powers to manage the labour market, but the opposition of other countries led to a compromise: Article 69 only concerned those workers who had two years of experience and particular professional skills. Moreover, the High Authority established new rules for the social security of those migrants who worked in the mines and in the iron and steel factories. Furthermore new rules also concerned the organization of vocational training for workers (to facilitate their "réadaptation" and to give more opportunities to find a job, in particular if they emigrated) and the building of houses for workers (to guarantee lodgings, in particular for migrants). Finally new ECSC subsidies were established for the unemployment related to new technological innovations and the growth of the competition on the ECSC market: from 1953 to 1960, 115,000 workers benefited from European subsidies and in 1965 this number reached 500,000. All these new rules clearly implied that ECSC members had to invest in the improvement of the quality of life of migrants and of their professional skills (Mechi, 2000; Leboutte, 2005; Locatelli, forthcoming).

The Treaties of Rome and the creation of new instruments to develop the economies of Western Europe and to reduce unemployment and migrants

New ECSC rules about the free circulation of workers affected few people. They took effect as from 1957, when the Treaties of Rome were signed. The problem of Italian migrants clearly inspired the new articles relating to the issue of the economic and social cohesion of Europe. This process required greater economic development in the more backward regions of Europe. The Italian government obtained from the EEC greater liberty for its unskilled migrants in the European labour market, but also more European funds for the improvement of the professional skills of jobless people and for investment in the Mezzogiorno.

Article 48 of the EEC treaty permitted the free circulation of workers when and where demand for such workers existed. New articles belonging to title XVII of the Treaties of Rome also provided a new way to promote the economic development of the Mezzogiorno. Integrating migrants was recognized to be one of the most important issues in European economic and social cohesion. In order to achieve this aim, the Treaties of Rome also envisaged the creation of the European Social Fund (ESF) and the European Investment Bank (EIB). It became clear that in order to promote a better way of life for migrants, new financial resources would be needed, and new programmes would have to be created to guarantee that the money invested would be spent appropriately. The EEC assigned to the ESF and EIB several aims concerning the solution of the "migrants problem". The EIB had to reduce the number of migrants facilitating the creation of new enterprises in the European backward regions. The ESF had to help those communities that received migrants to build houses and the necessary infrastructures for the utilities. It also invested to organize training courses to raise professional standards, and sought to enable migrants to learn new language.

The ESF sought to boost the professional skills of workers so that they could adapt to the requirements of the new EEC market. It contributed up to 50 per cent of the finance required by projects that would improve employment opportunities. It attempted to find solutions to facilitate the transition from school to the work of young people. This involved financing vocational training for less-skilled people seeking a job. This policy gave EEC migrants more opportunity to find better jobs.

Besides, as from the early 1970s, a new awareness within European societies led to projects that would help hitherto disadvantaged groups, the ESF also aimed to facilitate the prospects for unskilled women and for unemployed people who had no experience in the labour market. It also sought to help those who had worked in agriculture or those industrial sectors that were now in decline. So the ESF organized training courses for more people and this implied increasing the financial resources invested in ESF projects by EEC members. This policy improved the labour skills of a large number of EEC citizens who, sometimes, found a new job in their countries and so did not emigrate. Finally, from the 1970s, the ESF also financed training courses for people with a physical handicap and laws were passed that facilitated their employment in both the public and private spheres (Collins, 1975, pp. 40–70; Laffan, 1983; Mechi, 2006; Leboutte, 2008, pp. 653–663; Tomé, 2013)

The building of new infrastructure and the creation of new industrial areas were in part financed by the EIB in less economically developed areas of the EEC and in particular in the Italian Mezzogiorno (Kipping, 2002; Dumoulin *et al.*, 2008; Coppolaro, 2009; Leboutte, 2009): this led to a reduction of unemployment and thus of the number of migrants. In addition, the EIB financed other infrastructures connecting the Mezzogiorno to the EEC countries and this helped the economic development of Italian regions, where new motorways and railways passed through. Thanks to this new infrastructural network, these regions (in the centre and north of Italy) could absorb a great share of migrants arriving from the Mezzogiorno (Tedeschi, 2008).

A new advisory body was founded, entitled the Economic and Social Committee (ESC). It grouped the representatives of European industrial and rural workers, entrepreneurs, consumers. It advised on issues relating to the EEC economy and also EEC policies for the labour market. Although it had no financial resources, in the 1960s it assumed a relevant role in the development of the EEC social policies and the new rules for migrant workers (Varsori, 2000, 2006a).

The EC also decided to create, in 1956, a special *fund de reétablissement*, whose aims included the financing of projects for the integration of refugees, the development of infrastructure and the modernization of the unfavoured European rural regions, the creation of schools for vocational training and foreign language learning solely reserved for migrants, as well as the construction of social housing and shelters for migrants.[6]

So, by the end of the 1950s, the EEC and the EC had more instruments to analyse and solve the juridical, economic and social problems arising from the presence of migrants in their new countries. They were also concerned to solve those problems relating to the return of migrants and their families to their native countries, which involved their re-integration. During the 1960s the rise of incomes allowed some migrants to return to their native countries. This meant that the EEC and the EC felt obliged to organize and facilitate the social reintegration and the re-placement of such citizens into their native countries.[7] Many migrants preferred to accumulate foreign currency rather than being promoted. They preferred to earn more rather than take training courses and even gave up holidays, working in a second job. They sought to buy property in their native countries or to restructure their old family home (they also purchased agricultural instruments to cultivate the old family arable land or vines or orchards). On the contrary, the children of migrants, who only knew their parents' dialect, preferred to seek social amelioration in the country where they were growing up. Young women in particular had no desire to return to the South of Italy, to a way of life which no longer satisfied their aspirations. They considered that their grand-parents' sunny land was perfect only for holidays.[8]

The EEC and the EC also had to solve the problem of seasonal migrant workers who enabled the "receiving" countries to maintain a more flexible labour market. These workers obviously helped the "exporting" countries to partially reduce the negative effects of unemployment: so they assumed an important role for a lot of Western European countries. Adequate plans had to be set in place to cope with fluctuations in the workforce. New laws were passed regulating sickness subsidies and benefits for involuntary and temporary unemployment.[9]

Such issues led to the realization that some kind of social statute should be created in order to define the rights of migrant workers in countries belonging to the EC. Issues also arose relating to the "naturalization" of refugees and the organization of aid for those people who did not want to gain refugee status as they hoped to return home sooner or later. So the EC suggested the creation of the "Centres Europe" for giving migrants lodgings and also a place to facilitate the meeting between foreigners and natives.[10] However, the European institution's attitudes on refugees and their integration were not always coherent with this aim: Europe could be heaven or hell for refugees and this depended on the country and the shelter where they arrived (Joly, 1996; Lindstrøm, 2005; *Rifugio Europa*, 2006; Cherubini, 2012).

The ESF was the means by which problems in the EEC labour market were addressed and, until the early 1970s, this body was especially useful in solving problems arising from intra-communitarian emigration. From 1958 to 1971 the ESF financed projects dealing with the problem of unemployment in southern Italy; it also sought to improve the professional skills of migrants (in particular Italian workers) in West Germany, France and Belgium. The ESF financed vocational training; it provided 50 per cent of the costs, the rest being paid by the country that organized such processes, whether the "exporting country" (Italy) or the "importing countries". From 1961 to 1973, 1,713,650 workers benefited from the ESF projects: Italy received 65 per cent of the funds and West Germany 25.5 per cent of the funds. Such data shows that Italy exported the majority of workers in the EEC and required substantial investment in order to finance these projects. From the early 1950s to the early 1970s there were more than 5,580,000 Italian emigrants, 75 per cent of these came from the Mezzogiorno. From 1946 to 1957 the difference between those immigrating and those emigrating came to a total of 1,941,000. This number was reduced to 780,000 at the time of the Italian economic miracle (1958–1963), and further reduced to 387,000 between 1964 and 1969.[11] The ESF data also show that West Germany got more than a quarter of the ESF funds: it received the majority of workers arriving from other EEC members and it had to invest to facilitate their integration.

The EEC effort to support ESF action was significant: from 1961 to 1972, the ESF budget received 420 million "unités de compte" (1 u.c. = 0.88867088 grammes of gold), and this very considerable investment demonstrated how important it was considered to solve the immigrants issue and to help migrants to participate in the European social and economic development. Underlying the ESF budget was the idea that solidarity between EEC members was of fundamental importance. So Italy contributed only 20 per cent of the budget, while West Germany paid 32 per cent as did France, meaning that these countries were subsidizing Italy (Leboutte, 2008, p. 654). Helping the poorest country was not only a philanthropic choice, but such solidarity aimed also at showing that the West European model actually worked. Such pragmatic approach reduced the risk that the delay in the social and economic development of the Mezzogiorno favoured the increase of the electoral consensus for the Communist Party.

However, such policies were no longer viable after the fall of the international monetary system and in particular after the oil shock of autumn 1973. West Germany and France temporarily closed their frontiers to all immigrants, accepting only those coming from EEC countries or those covered by special cooperation agreements. The need for new policies to come with the increasing number of immigrants coincided with the economic downturn. Comparing the situation of the early 1950s with that of the early 1970s (before Denmark, Eire and the United Kingdom joined the EEC), we note that foreigners living in EEC countries totalled about 2,881,000 persons, while 20 years later the number had risen to 6,945,000. While this number had more than doubled, the total EEC population had risen by only 19 per cent. Clearly, there were consequences in those EEC regions to which migrants had transferred. In November 1972, the two main issues considered were "young people in the labour world" and "the condition of migrant workers in Europe". Concerns related to vocational training for young people, security in the workplace and the rate of unemployment for young people and women. Although 20 years had passed since the founding of the ECSC, it was still essential to create policies to integrate migrants and their families in the host countries, to enable them to learn languages, to unite their families and find accommodation. Attempts had to be made to reduce clandestine work and social protection had to be extended during economic decline. Despite all the work that had been accomplished by European institutions, many targets had not been reached and future prospects did not appear promising.[12] Data concerning migration flows partially justified this result and in particular showed how the demographic panorama of some EEC countries had changed dramatically. Luxembourg represented the country with the higher rate of immigration: from the early 1950s to the early 1970s migrants increased from 29,000 to 63,000 (that is from less than 10 per cent to 18.5 per cent of total population). Belgium also registered a great growth in the number of migrants: they rose from 368,000 to 886,000 (that is from 4 per cent to 9 per cent of total population). As only a small share of the migrants worked in the European institution, it was evident that the main aim consisted in the improvement of life conditions of migrants and their families. Most migrants obviously moved to the main EEC members, that is France and West Germany: in the early 1950s foreigners living in France totalled 1,765,000 (more than 4 per cent of total population), while in West Germany they numbered 568,000 (1 per cent, including people living in Saarland and West Berlin); in the early 1970s foreigners numbered 2,621,000 in France (5 per cent) and 2,976,000 in West Germany (almost 3.5 per cent). Numbers of migrants also increased in the Netherlands where, in the same period, they rose from 104,000 to 255,000 (from 1 per cent to almost 2 per cent). A positive trend was registered in Italy too: there were 47,000 immigrants in the early 1950s, 62.800 in the early 1960s and 144,000 in the early 1970s: however they represented an inappreciable percentage (between 0.1 per cent and 0.25 per cent), because Italy continued to be a country that exported workforce and had a low appeal for foreign migrants.[13]

The international migration debates in the 1970s and their influence on EEC institutional positions

Since the beginning of the 1970s, new political and scholarly considerations on the social and economic effects of immigration entered the public discourse, causing a lasting influence on the evolution of EEC policies and measures in this realm. One important example is constituted by the Conclusions of the Committee for International Coordination of National Research on Demography (Tapinos, 1974), in which it is stated that "all economic growth, indeed, involves some form of mobility (internal or international). There is, accordingly, a clear relation between international migration and economic development". From this mindset, Western European countries promoted freer mobility in this period, resulting in migration becoming fully liberalized within the boundaries of the Scandinavian labour market and the European Community member states. In addition, migrants coming from outside these areas were granted different privileges codified in agreements between the receiving and sending states. Nonetheless, such measures did not result in making migration advantageous to all parties involved, since they were mainly designed to serve the instant needs of the receiving labour markets. Indeed, they greatly overlooked the promotion of development within a larger region, a view that particularly stood in contradiction with the self-stated cohesion aspirations of the European integration process.

The preference for short-term considerations in EEC migration policy at that time was also evident in the restrictions that some countries (for example West Germany) imposed in response to the effects of the oil crisis in that period. As a matter of fact, many nationals of industrialized countries who formerly considered leaving the continent under more stringent economic conditions decided to stay, and many Southern Europeans preferred then to move and work just temporarily in nearby relevant industrial nodes. Despite these trends, an upsurge of overseas migration, comparable in scale and structure to the then rapidly evolving intra-European migration, would have been rather unlikely. Against this backdrop, the receiving countries in Western Europe competed mainly for skilled rather than for unskilled labour, which made up the bulk of intra-European migrants.

Coming down to the illustration of migration figures in this period, it should be noted that there were, approximately, "11.5 million foreigners living in OECD countries in 1972, among them 7.7 million workers. Most of them were employed in the West Germany (2.3 million), in France (1.65 million), and in Great Britain (1.55 million)" (Tapinos, 1974). This distribution reflected both longstanding affiliations between specific sending and receiving states, as well as newly-established connections. Following such new tendencies in the 1970s, we can observe that most immigrants to Sweden come from Finland. In Switzerland, Italians dominated over other nationalities. France was the preferred destination of migrants from North Africa and Portugal, and Great Britain continued to employ large contingents of Irish workers. Furthermore, in West Germany (which started to attract foreign migrants much later than the other states) Yugoslavs and Turks outnumbered Italians, who formerly were the largest group. However, the network of flows within Western Europe was much tighter. There were, indeed, large population flows coming from Greece to West Germany and Sweden and from Spain to West Germany, France and Switzerland, as well as intensive return migrations from all parts of Western Europe to all regions of Southern Europe. Besides, migration among industrialized countries gained in significance, although less than it could be expected as a result of the fact that citizens coming from EEC members and the Scandinavian labour market could move freely within these areas. In addition, there were many connections with other continents (especially those coming from North Africa, but also from the Middle East and the Caribbean) and even with Eastern Europe.

Apart from France, the Netherlands and the United Kingdom, which were then the main destinations for migrants from their former colonies, West Germany also admitted increasing numbers of non-European migrants under various recruitment and assistance schemes.

Nevertheless, foreign workers in most West European countries did not face very advantageous conditions in this period: they were often forced to accept unskilled, low-paid jobs; they usually could not bring their families with them and their sojourn was strictly limited by contract; they were not supposed to stay in the receiving country to fully integrate; they were regularly discriminated against by the nationals of each given host country and sometimes even by national trade unions (Böhning, 1972b). In order for them go through all these impending difficulties, it meant that the economic advantage of emigration had to be really high. And that seemed to be the case: the possibility of securing employment at wages three and four times higher than, for instance, in Spain, was a strong inducement for migration for workers whose consumption standards did not adjust to such high wages on a permanent basis and who saw emigration as a way to fund their families' well-being in their home country. If such was the motivation in Spain and other sending countries, their development rate was at least below the level required to adequately use their labour potential (Tapinos, 1974). In other words, if the space of development was going to be accelerated, emigration was expected to decrease. As ILO analysts then stated: "With continued economic growth it may be anticipated that emigration from Italy will continue to decline" (ILO, 1972). It should have been the same also for other Southern European countries, but in some, like Spain and Greece, the repression of any organized labour movement kept wages artificially low in contrast to most West European industrialized countries. In such conditions, emigration went on longer, despite gradual, internal development. Especially suggestive of the rapidly increasing labour surplus in the least developed sending areas such as Turkey, Tunisia or Morocco was the incidence of clandestine migration, not only towards key industrial nodes, but also toward Southern Italy and parts of Greece and Spain, which became short of certain kinds of low-paid agricultural labourers as a result of excessive outward migration.

In this context, EEC industrialized countries were, hence, faced with a choice of three possible options to enhance GNP growth:

(a) to substitute capital for labour, as annual production generated a constant share of savings to be invested (assuming a constant propensity to save); (b) to invest abroad; or (c) to invest in the domestic economy but to import foreign labour to man the factories.

(Castles and Kosak, 1972; Becker *et al.*, 1971; Schiller, 1971)

Since the end of the Second World War, Western European industrialized countries were more in favour of the last option. Indeed, it was for this reason that the challenges of migrant workers was posed once full employment was attained and industry became incapable of guaranteeing further reserves from the agricultural sector.

From a more global perspective, it is important to bear in mind that both inward and outward migration flows were institutionalized during this period within the framework of multilateral treaties, including those consolidated by various international organizations such as the ILO, the UN and the Council of Europe, which were engaged in the coordination and unification of treaties in this field. The aim of these agreements was to avoid conflict between different systems and to ensure some basic common standards. On the one hand, the "ILO Agreement 97" in this period aimed at promoting an appropriate free service designed to assist migrant workers and, in particular, to provide them with accurate information. Moreover, the Council of Europe adopted a European Social Security code and incorporated in the *European Social Charter* a section on the rights of migrant workers and their families to protection and assistance: this code comprised facilities for departure, travel and reception of migrants, regulations on equal treatment and special provisions for the maintenance of established rights (European Social Charter, 1966). These bodies also made recommendations to their member states aimed at unifying and coordinating action undertaken by the various national authorities. Some examples include ILO recommendations on the housing of workers and the EEC recommendation on social services for migrants (Kamp, 1971; CICM, 1974, p. 252).

Furthermore, also the influence of the judiciary at the EEC level left a lasting trace in the implementation of EC-wide measures regarding intra-European migration. One significant example could be that of the 1975 *Rutili Judgment*, in which the European Court of Justice provides a strict interpretation of the public policy reservation that may possibly restrict the free movement of workers in the EEC member states. As an exception to a fundamental principle of community law, its application must comply with all community rules. Accordingly, any measures that may be taken by a member state must be based exclusively on the personal conduct of the individual posing a genuine and sufficiently serious threat, and must apply indiscriminately to nationals of the member states and to other community nationals (Rutili Judgment, 1975). However, it is important to note that a new and more open line was defined in contrast to this judgment when Eduardo García de Enterría was elected: he was the first Spanish judge at the European Court of Human Rights in April 1978, a position he held until 1986. Indeed, he upheld that Spain also became party to the various conventions and treaties adopted by the Council of Europe, such as the *European Convention on the Legal Status of Migrant Workers*, thus introducing leverage, as well as a tempering measure with respect to previous and more restrictive rules in community migration issues.

Political transitions and socioeconomic dimensions of European migration from the 1970s to the new millennium: challenges and trends in EU migration policy

The context of change of the mid-1970s in Southern European non-EEC member states, such as Portugal and Spain, was also defined by an important trend, namely, return migration (Address by Ernâni Lopes, 1985), which coincided with a major parallel process of transition to democracy and of political negotiations for EEC accession. This trend was explained by the economic impact of the oil crisis, especially in West Germany and in France, which temporarily closed their frontiers to immigration, leaving them accessible only for migrants coming from EEC member states and for other national collectives under the aegis of special cooperation agreements (Latorre Catalán, 2006). Within this context, the number of Spaniards regarded as emigrants in 1970 has been estimated at about 3.5 million. The majority, especially as far as emigration to EEC member states is concerned, represented a rural mindset, both in relation to the level of occupation, attitude, and as to geographical origin, employment and career plans, etc. Similar features could be evidenced from the emigration records of other states in the Mediterranean area, like Italy, Greece, Turkey and the former Yugoslavia. In relation to the very notion of return migration, Mediterranean migrants seemed to prioritize the accumulation of foreign currency over occupational promotion and career concerns. At the same time, the paradigmatic Mediterranean migrant of this period seemed to prefer

> the multiplication of hours of overtime to the sacrifice of some time and money to various training courses. He does not appear to be as much interested in social mobility in the host society, in relation to which he feels himself in a fringe situation, as in economic and social improvement in his society of origin.

Against this backdrop,

> his frequent aims are generally related to the purchase of an apartment and of agricultural machinery, to generating bank savings and self-employment, etc. This explains why only 6% of foreign workers employed in the Federal Republic of Germany in the mid-seventies were in the specialist grade.
>
> (Del Campo and Garmendia, 1974)

However, the Mediterranean migrant was usually considered, in this context, merely as a labourer both as a result of lack of technical know-how and due to the fact that he was more useful and profitable in practical and low-skilled tasks.

As the flow of Spanish emigration to other EC countries developed, it underwent a period of crisis as the potentiality of accumulating savings gradually decreased. That was the case of Spanish migration to France, where migration policies encouraged longer stays. Spanish citizens moulded to this new context by means of associative activities, which gathered good numbers of Spaniards living and working in France (Díaz-Plaja, 1974). Such associations, also promoted integration tools within a variety of EC initiatives, provided a space for socialization and a means of recreating the culture of origin. Some of them, furthermore, even acquired a critical awareness of the emigrant condition (Garson and Loizillon, 2003; Babiano, 2002). In addition, these activities played a fundamental role in offering radically different transnational civic values, as well as a socialization and politicization experience to migrant workers coming from countries under dictatorships, since it allowed them to contact and participate in labour organizations, in democratic political parties and in political organizations centred on the particular conditions of economic and political exile. This also had a remarkable influence on activism patterns during transition periods in return migrant communities.

The Spanish first migration wave to the EEC, from 1973 to 1986, also coincided with the first oil crisis and with a general lack of contracts for Southern European migrants in the most developed EEC member states. In the next phase, from 1986 to 1992, Spanish and Portuguese migrants ceased to be considered as such to become EEC workers, holding equal rights to those of EEC member states, even if free circulation was dependent on transition periods. From this moment on, Southern European workers started moving to other EEC member states as highly qualified professionals (Pioneur, 2006), and also benefited from an high educational capital to develop transnational careers and to seek particular working environments, innovative lifestyles and diverse consumption patterns (Alaminos Chica and Santacreu Fernández, 2010, pp. 201–211; Straubhaar, 1984). This trend was remarkably consolidated via EEC/EU diploma recognition schemes, which gradually implemented a harmonized method of professional qualifications recognition in old and new EU member states, constituting a key socioeconomic factor of European integration deepening (Alaminos Chica, 2006). In this respect, it is also fundamental to address the political and socioeconomic impact of the Schengen Agreement and of the Amsterdam Treaty (1997),[14] as well as the special attention paid to the *EU Social Policy Agreement*, and to the subsequent EU-wide provisions on the free movement of persons with regard to visas, asylum and immigration.

As already mentioned, the Spanish economy had experienced a very significant development in the mid-1970s. In this context, migrants' remittances became an actual trigger of economic growth (Powell, 2011). By contrast, the overall economic growth that followed EEC accession fed a wave of extra-European migration during the late 1980s, specially focused on agricultural labour from the Mediterranean basin, which became socially acknowledged only at the end of the 1990s. In this respect, Spain started following the pattern of Greece and Italy, notably characterized by low fertility rates, population aging as well as increasing education levels. This resulted in a refusal of younger generations to concentrate on the primary sector, thus prioritizing a search for more qualified jobs. Hence, the internal demand coming from sectors such as agriculture, household jobs, construction work and catering increased accordingly. This new extra-European migration provided manpower mainly to SMEs but fell, in many occasions, into the realm of the informal economy. From this viewpoint, it is important to bear in mind that "in highly segmented labour markets, immigrants occupied and still occupy the worst positions, not only regarding salaries and work conditions, but also in terms of instability and lack of Social Security protection" (Álvarez, 2006).

In the period that goes from the 1990s to the beginning of the twenty-first century, Southern Europe, but very particularly, Spain, became the main destination of a new wave of extra-European migration in the EU. Indeed, according to Eurostat, "Italy and Spain received 56% of total EU immigration that arrived during the period 1997–2008, while Spain alone received 50% of the total during the past decade, 2000–2009".[15] The fact that Spain was at the forefront of a new wave of extra-European migration deeply transformed its role and attitude in relation to the measures taken by the EU in this field. For instance, Spain gradually acquired a more proactive role in the design of an evolving EU migration policy and promoted the establishment of Frontex in 2004. At the same time, Spain gradually demanded an increasing involvement of Northern EU member states in addressing the challenges of migration in the EU. Indeed,

> the establishment in 2007 of a European financial fund for the return of irregular migrants or the launching of European repatriation joint flights were also results of this Spanish demand for a bigger involvement of Northern countries in the financial cost of immigration management.
>
> (González Enríquez, 2011)

It was also remarkable that integration initiatives and associate activities regarding extra-European migration in Spain were mainly encouraged and maintained within the sphere of Spanish civil society.

In 2008, Spain was also actively involved in the elaboration of the *European Pact on Immigration and Asylum*, resulting from a French proposal, which included a restrictive notion of creating an "immigration contract". However, such initiative was later refused by the Spanish government of the time, despite the acceptance to incorporate an institutional blocking of mass regularizations within the pact. In this respect

> the European Union has played a double role in the Spanish immigration process: Spain has obtained EU support in the financial and political effort to reduce irregular migration, especially coming from Africa, and has used EU decisions as external legitimization for the introduction of domestic policies that could arouse opposition.
>
> (González Enríquez, 2011; Drozdz, 2011; EEC, 2007; Luedtke, 2005; Herz, 2003; Cornelius *et al.*, 2002; Lu, 1999; Callovi, 1992)

From a different perspective, it is essential to take into account that the 2004 and 2007 EU enlargements implied radical political and socioeconomic transformations in Europe that also affected intra-European migration flows. Above all, they directly influenced common European prospects and definitions of welfare systems, especially within the framework of the *European Employment Strategy and the Social Agenda*.

Scholarly analysis in this field shows that

(a) EU enlargement had a significant impact on migration flows from new to old Member States, (b) restrictions applied in some of the countries did not stop migrants from coming, but changed the composition of the immigrants, (c) any negative effects in the labour market on wages or employment are hard to detect, (d) post-enlargement migration contributes to EU growth prospects, (e) these immigrants are strongly attached to the labour market, and (f) they are quite unlikely to be among welfare recipients. These findings point out the difficulties that restrictions on the free movement of workers bring about.

(Kahanec and Zimmermann, 2010; Carrera and Merlino, 2010;
Shafagatov and Aygun, 2005; Messina, 2002)

Following the 2004 EU enlargement, Ireland, the United Kingdom and Sweden opened access to their labour markets immediately. As for social benefits, access to the welfare systems in Ireland and the United Kingdom depends on the duration of residence and employment. Sweden was deeply in contrast with these trends by applying European Union rules. In the second phase of these arrangements, eight more member states opened their labour markets by November 2008: Spain, Finland, France, Greece, Portugal, Italy, the Netherlands and Luxembourg (Kahanec and Zimmermann, 2010). Restrictions in national access regimes continued in some economic sectors in Belgium, Germany and Denmark, which felt a fear of mass migration similar to that of past EEC/EU enlargements. Also, similarly to these past cases, mass migration never became a reality and the potentialities of economic development coming from migration (specially from high skilled labour) never seemed to be fully explored, encouraged and discussed in an EU-wide dialogue analysing also positive interdependencies. Last but not least, in a context characterized by the socioeconomic challenges of debt crisis and the shrinking of a European social dimension, it would be advisable to openly address the issue of how regional imbalances could be more easily superseded through a coordinated action towards free circulation of workers within the EU. In sum, a more European wide perspective, beyond national interests, would be auspicable to find articulated migration strategies in line with the evolution and potentialities of the European integration process.

Conclusion: preserving the "fortress Europe"?

The EEC/EU institutional initiatives to address the social and economic challenges related to the intra-European and extra-European migrations were developed to a remarkable degree. From the first steps of European integration to the new millennium, the main targets of the policies of the European institutions with regard to migrants and their families included: a full integration in the host countries, the teaching of European languages, the finding of healthy accommodation and workplaces, the reunification of families with respect to European laws, the fight against clandestine work (which also concerned illegal immigrants) and the establishment of a possible social welfare during periods of economic decline and difficulty (Ireland, 1998; Trépant, 2002; Kaelble, 2007; Fassmann *et al.*, 2009; Hamida, 2010).

In the 1990s all Western European countries had a positive balance for migration (only Eire sometimes had a negative balance, but for 5,000–6,000 persons only) and received migrants arriving from Eastern Europe as a result of the end of the Cold War: for the first time all Western European countries had the same problems concerning migrants and the new migration flows needed new European policies (King and Black, 2002; EU enlargement, 2002; The New Face, 2008; Cuschieri, 2007; Black *et al.*, 2010). Furthermore, a new phenomenon arose in the EU: an increasing number of retired people decided to retire to Mediterranean countries (and in recent years in the new Balkan EU members too) where the weather conditions were better, and the real value of their pensions allowed for a higher quality of life. These factors increased the transfer of money towards the Southern EU countries and also modified the redistribution in the EU economies of welfare costs: retired people did not spend their pensions in their native countries, but the costs of their welfare (in particular hospital services) were charged to their native countries (*Older Migrants*, 2004).

In any case, such new migrant flows did not produce sufficient economic advantage to the Mediterranean countries to counteract the disadvantages deriving from the influx of migrants from Balkan countries, as well as those from the Third World. These migrants considered all EU countries the perfect destination: the quality of their lives would be improved and, as had happened to European migrants from the West previously, they risked their lives in order to attain their objectives. A growing consensus for movements against immigration emerged amongst European countries (and in particular those countries with land or sea frontiers with Africa and Asia): however, the hard discussions about the real impact of migrants on the EU labour market showed that positive effects were prevalent on negative ones and that the European institutions continued to help all migrants (Angrist and Kugler, 2003; Livi Bacci, 2005; Dupâquier and Laulan, 2006; Venturini and Villosio, 2006, 2008; Papademetriou *et al.*, 2009; D'Amuri *et al.*, 2010; Keereman and Szekely, 2010; Eichhorst *et al.*, 2011; Brücker and Eger, 2012). Migrants and their families helped not only the European social and economic development with their work, but they also influenced the attempts of European institution to create a new European common identity, which had to coexist with the "old" national cultures. This was, and remains, a very strong challenge for its implications concerning the EU society (different religions and "ways of life") and moreover the EU economy (common currency, common welfare, and common agrarian and industrial policies in the new world markets) (Beers and Raflik, 2010; Spohn and Triandafyllidou, 2001; Milza, 1994). A new European culture could come into being only if European institutions promoted teaching projects dedicated to the migrants and their families: the improvement of migrants' professional skills depends on a better education too (Bekemans and Ortiz De Urbina, 1997; Varsori, 2006b; Dustmann and Glitz, 2011).

All the initiatives of the European institutions were the result of the programmes and policies demanded both at the international level (OIT, OCDE, etc.) and at the domestic level. These initiatives depended on the evolving political spectrum and on the growing and diversifying civil society of the new EEC/

EU members: they were also linked to European political transitions and global socio-economic transformations. The EU welfare systems and domestic social policies had to change and to include new prospects for migrants' integration.

The evolution of migrant flows toward the Western European countries also influenced and modified the existing correlation between migration waves and EEC/EU accession negotiations both at the level of the European institutions regulations on migrants' integration measures and at the level of the relationship between migration and economic development. European institutions first focused their attention on the feedback of employment-related migration: this was evident during the post war reconstruction and it was progressively reduced during the "golden age" until the early 1970s. New rules were linked to the attainment of European solidarity: ECSC and EEC members had to show that the "Western choice" was winning and they did not allow that parties linked to the USSR won in the backwards regions. So European institutions tried to help the poorest regions to reduce their unemployment rate and, at the same time, to guarantee a good quality of life for migrants. Second, from the mid-1970s onward, the European institutions had to face the social and economic impact of the oil crisis, which provoked new migration arrangements in parallel with new requests for EEC accession arriving from countries that "exported" workers. So, during the 1980s, the European institutions reassessed the impact and foreseeable long term effects of return migration, not only in economic terms, but also with regard to transfers of political culture and of democratization of socioeconomic relations at the domestic level. At the same time, the European institutions focused on the role of migrants in the EEC labour market, which helped shape new legal frameworks towards the constitution of a strongest political union: it was clear that only this latter, established with the Single Act in 1986, could guarantee more opportunities for the best workers in a wider and regulated new European market.

The reform of the ESF in 1988, and moreover the doubling of its budget, increased the effort of the EEC to help all European workers, including migrants. Conversely, during the decade of the 1990s, the issue of extra-EU migration, increasingly linked to irregular migration flows forced a shift of EU policies from an economic dimension to the realm of justice, security and home affairs which was evidently very difficult to realize. This period was also characterized by the migration challenges of an enlarged Europe after the end of the Cold War, which implied a renewed attention in the establishment of transition periods concerning the Eastern European countries (which became EU members in the new millennium). Moreover, European institutions also stressed the existence of important asymmetries in the development of EU countries regarding migration flows: the lack of solidarity among EU countries and the holding on to different national policies concerning migrants (as the EU immigration policy continues to seem a "phantom" or a "fantasy") provoked the transfers of migrants towards the countries having "lighter" laws or showing more difficulties in their real application. So only a small number of migrants went to the countries with an economy that could better support migrants' needs: in contrast some migrants could receive some subsidies to survive, but not a job for improving their future

(Philip, 1994; Brochmann, 1996; Guild, 1998; Guiraudon, 2000a, 2000b; Givens and Luedtke, 2004, 2005; Geddes, 2005, Bendel, 2007; Schain, 2009).

Furthermore, even if some relevant changes were established in the Amsterdam and Lisbon treaties, the new world crises that set in after the birth of the euro currency implied a strong return of employment-related migration, as well as a preference for skilled workers and for temporary migration. At the same time, the number of non-skilled migrants increased (in particular the clandestine ones). The EU tried to consolidate new integration measures in a difficult dialogue with national policy preferences: in any case, unemployment rates affected more foreign workers than native workers, despite manipulative discourses in a different direction and the public opinion asking for new laws consolidating the "fortress Europe" and strongly reducing migration flows toward the EU countries (Geddes, 2000; Caviedes, 2004; Bendel, 2005; Korf, 2008; Triandafyllidou, 2010). Finally the new nature of intra-European migration posed new challenges, but it also offered the opportunity to increase European integration and to adopt the best measures for improving the economic trend and the European citizens' living conditions, migrants included: the alternative was obviously a policy preserving and reinforcing the walls of the "fortress Europe".

Notes

1 Even if this chapter is the result of common researches, analysis and reflections by the authors, the third and fourth sections have to be attributed to Cristina Blanco Sío-López (*Centre Virtuel de la Connaissance sur l'Europe*) and the remaining text to Paolo Tedeschi (University of Milan-Bicocca).

2 See in particular the records concerning the High Authority of the ECSC and the ESF in the European Commission Historical Archives: CEAB 1, 1649–1673, CEAB 7, 1316, 1484, 1863 (free circulation of workforce, 1953–1963), CEAB 1, 1680 (Italian workers in Belgian mines, 1955–1956), CEAB 4, 634, 720, 948–949, 1166, 1168, CEAB 7, 1402, 1485, 1607–1608 (social security for migrant workers, 1953–1968), CEAB 1, 669, 1790, 1816–1832, 1834–1852 (ECSC financial helps for building houses for workers, 1952–1968), CEAB 1, 134–136, 656, 1718–1722, CEAB 4, 385–388, 1127–1128, CEAB 7 1651, 1634–1648 (ECSC policy for vocational trainings and "réadaptation", 1953–1968). See also EEC, BAC 1/1962, BAC 1/1968, BAC 26/1969, BAC 30/1969 (ESF and European social policies). Besides see HAEU: BAC-042/1991 (27, 29), CENYC (83); CES (7208–7209); CPPE (1448); GJLA (246, 280); PE0 (2445, 2711, 12921, 18080); OEEC (27.037, 261); WEU (106.016). Finally see DG Enlargement, EC, (doc 7688/94, 7955/97, 11329/94), and Archives of the Ministry of Foreign Affairs (Spain), MAE, Leg. 12557, Exp. 60(E)77–1, CEE 1977.

3 About the birth of PICMME and its members see the contribution of Francesca Fauri in this volume.

4 For an example concerning the integration between EEC rules and EEC members' national laws about the welfare for migrants and their families see Mongé, R., *Le travailleur espagnol et la famille espagnole en France*, and *Le travailleur portugais et la famille portugaise en France*, and *Le travailleur italien et la famille italienne en France*, published in 1966 by the Service Social d'Aide aux Émigrants.

5 See the EC resolution 69/8 and 69/9 in *Ici l'Europe* (the bulletin edited by the EC), 1969, 2: 24. During the 1950s and 1960s all west European countries gave their adhesion at the EC, which was founded in 1949: Denmark, Eire, United Kingdom, Sweden, Norway were among the founders. Switzerland acceded in 1963 and was the

European country with the highest share of migrants after Luxembourg (285,000 and more than 6 per cent of the total population in the early 1950s and 1,080,000 and more than 17 per cent of the total population in the early 1970s). See the special issue for the twentieth anniversary of the EC birth in ibid., pp. i–xv.

6 From its birth to the spring of 1969 the fund invested more than 57 million US dollars for financing almost 50 projects. See ibid., p. vi.

7 The number of returns progressively increased during the 1960s and in the spring of 1969 the Committee of Ministers of the EC recommended new measures for facilitating these returns as the creation of a special office for their placement and also the organization of courses for the children to allow them to know the history, the geography and the language of their parents' countries. See resolution 69/7 in ibid., p. 23.

8 Please note that until the 1970s there were also some problems concerning the rules for giving the nationality to migrants' sons and daughters (laws privileged the *jus sanguinis*) and for wives (most of countries attributed to them the nationality of their husbands and moreover wives did not receive the reversion pension if their husband died). See ibid., 1973, 1, pp. 13–14.

9 See resolution 69/9 in ibid., 1969, 2, p. 24. The Committee of EC Ministers also suggested to establish some different holiday periods for people working in different industrial sectors and in the public offices: this allowed to reduce the jobless time in tourism. However the suggestion had no relevant applications.

10 See ibid., 1969, 4, pp. 60–62. Please note that the debate about the statute continued for a lengthy period and in 1971 the Commission of Population and Refugees proposed that the rights concerned all migrants arriving in Western Europe even if their native country did not subscribe the statute. See ibid., 1971, 1, p. 8. Finally, note that in 1972 the EC refused to finance Greek refugees: see ibid., 1972, 1, p. 19.

11 In Italy from 1951 to 1971 more than ten million inhabitants were involved in regional migrations and more than 4.2 million left the Mezzogiorno (that is more than 23 per cent of the total population). Other data about Italian emigration in this period are in the contributions of Francesca Fauri and Sandro Rinauro in this volume.

12 See *Ici l'Europe*, 1972, 4, pp. 74–75; ibid., 1973, 3, pp. 51–52.

13 Please note that data about real migrant flows in EEC countries change depending on the sources used, so the figures are indicative only. For example the data in the text concerning the number of foreigner workers in West Germany (Kaelble, 2007, p. 185) are not compatible with other data which put in evidence an increase from 280,000 in 1960 to 2.6 million in 1973 (Romero 1991, p. 91).

14 See "European Parliament resolution on the Schengen Agreement and political asylum", 6 April 1995; "Treaty of Amsterdam", 2 October 1997.

15 In comparative terms, the effect of this migration wave is bigger in Spain than in Italy, as the size of the native population is much smaller. All in all, Spain received more than five million new migrants (i.e. net migration) during the 2000s, over a population of 40 million at the beginning of the period in a process of unknown intensity in Europe. From 0.5 per cent of the population in 1985, the number of immigrants amounted to 14 per cent in 2010.

References

Address given by Ernâni Lopes to the Assembly of the Republic (Lisbon, 9 July 1985). Online, available at: www.cvce.eu.

Alaminos Chica, A. (2006). *Living abroad. Intraeuropean migrations*, Alicante: Pioneers of Europe, WP 14.

Alaminos Chica, A. and Santacreu Fernández, O. (2010). *La emigración cualificada española en Francia y Alemania*, Universidad de Alicante, Instituto Universitario de Desarrollo Social y Paz. Papers, 95/1.

Alexiou, A. (2004). L'immigration grecque en Belgique. In Morelli, A. (ed.), *Histoire des étrangers et de l'immigration en Belgique de la préhistoire à nos jours*, Brussels: Couleur livres, pp. 297–318.

Álvarez, A. (2006). La transposición de directivas de la UE sobre inmigración. *Documentos CIDOB Migraciones*. 8.

Angrist, J. D. and Kugler, A. (2003). Protective or counter-productive? Labor market institutions and the effect of immigration on EU natives, *Economic Journal*: 302–331.

Babiano, J. (2002). Emigración, identidad y vida asociativa: Los españoles en la Francia de los Años Sesenta. *Hispania*, 211.

Becker, R., Dörr, G. and Tjaden, K. H. (1971). Fremdarbeiterbeschäftigung in Deutschen Kapitalismus. *Argument 68*, 13: 741–756.

Beers, M. and Raflik, J. (eds) (2010). *National Cultures and Common Identity. A Challenge for Europe?*, Brussels: Peter Lang.

Bekemans, L. and Ortiz De Urbina, Y. (1997). *The Teaching of Immigrants in the European Union*, Brussels: EDUC, European Parliament.

Bendel, P. (2005). Immigration policy in the European Union: still bringing up the walls for fortress Europe? *Migration Letters*, 1: 20–31.

Bendel, P. (2007). Everything under control? The European Union's policies and politics of immigration. In Faist, T. and Ette, A. (eds), *The Europeanization of National Policies and Politics of Immigration*, Hampshire: Palgrave Macmillan, pp. 32–48.

Besana, C. (2002). Accordi internazionali ed emigrazione della mano d'opera italiana tra ricostruzione e sviluppo. In Zaninelli, S. and Taccolini, M. (eds), *Il lavoro come fattore produttivo e come risorsa nella storia economica italiana*, Milan: Vita e Pensiero, pp. 3–17.

Bikkal, D. (1975 [1956]). Per un Istituto Pensioni Europeo. In *50 anni di studi nella rivista "Previdenza Sociale" dell'Istituto Nazionale della Previdenza Sociale*, Rome, INPS, pp. 267–278.

Black, R., Engbersen, G., Okólski, M. and Pantîru, C. (eds) (2010). *A Continent Moving West? EU Enlargement and Labour Migration from Central and Eastern Europe*, Amsterdam: Amsterdam University Press.

Blanc-Chaleard, M. C. (2003). Les italiens en France depuis 1945, Rennes: PUR.

Böhning, W. R. (1972a). *The Migration of Workers in the United Kingdom and the European Community*, Oxford: OUP.

Böhning, W. R. (1972b). The social and occupational apprenticeship of Mediterranean workers in West Germany. In Livi Bacci, M. (ed.), *The Demographic and Social Pattern of Emigration from Southern European Countries*, Florence: Dipartimento Statistico-Matematico dell'Universita.

Brochmann, G. (1996). *European Integration and Immigration from Third Countries*, Oslo: Scandinavian University Press.

Brücker, H. and Eger, T. (2012). The law and economics of the free movement of persons in the European Union. In Eger, T. and Schäfer, H. B. (eds), *Research Handbook on the Economics of European Union Law*, Cheltenham: Elgar, pp. 146–179.

Callovi, G. (1992). Part II: Western Europe: new, old and recast of immigration questions in the post-Cold War period: regulation of immigration in 1993: pieces of the European Community jig-saw puzzle. *International Migration Review*, 2: 353–372.

Carrera, S. and Merlino, M. (eds) (2010). *Assessing EU Policy on Irregular Immigration under the Stockholm Programme*, Brussels: CEPS.

Castles, S. and Kosak, G. (1972). The function of labour immigration in Western European capitalism. *New Left Review*, 73.

Caviedes, A. (2004). The open method of co-ordination immigration policy: a tool for prying open fortress Europe? *Journal of European Public Policy*, 11: 289–310.

CECA (1957a). *Rapport sur la migration et la libre circulation des travailleurs dans la Communauté*, Luxembourg: CECA.

CECA (1957b). *Obstacles à la mobilité des travailleurs et problèmes sociaux de réadaptation*, Luxembourg: CECA.

CEE (1966). *La libre circulation de la main d'œuvre et le marché du travail dans la CEE*, Brussels: CEE.

Cherubini, F. (2012). *L'asilo dalla Convenzione di Ginevra al diritto dell'Unione Europea*, Bari: Cacucci.

CICM (1974). Social policy of the European Community considered in the context of migration: study on the free circulation of workers from the European Economic Community – Werquin: recommendations from the Commission of the EEC to the member states concerning the work of the social service departments with workers migrating within the community: summary 1960 – follow-up to the recommendation August 1962 to December 1964–1969 to 1970. In Tapinos, G. (ed.), *International Migration: Proceedings of a Seminar on Demographic Research in Relation to International Migration. Held in Buenos Aires, Argentine, 5–11 March*, Paris: CICRED (World Population Year).

Collins, D. (1975). The European Communities: the social policy of the first phase, vol. 2, *The European Economic Community 1958–72*, London: M. Robertson.

Colucci, M. (2008). *Lavoro in movimiento: L'emigrazione italiana in Europa, 1945–57*, Rome: Donzelli.

Coppolaro, L. (2009). Setting up the financing institution of the European Economic Community: the creation of the European Investment Bank (1955–1957). *Journal of European Integration History*, 2: 87–104.

Cornelius, W., Martin, P. L. and Hollified, J. F. (eds) (2002). *Controlling Immigration: A Global Perspective*, Stanford: Stanford University Press.

Cornet, A. (2004). Les Congolais en Belgique aux XIXe et XXe siècles. In Morelli, A. (ed.), *Histoire des étrangers et de l'immigration en Belgique de la préhistoire à nos jours*, Brussels: Couleur Livres, pp. 375–400.

Cuschieri, M. A. (2007). *Europe's Migration Policy towards the Mediterranean: The Need of Reconstruction of Policy-Making*, Bonn: Center for European Integration Studies, Discussion Paper.

D'Amuri, F., Ottaviano, G. and Peri, G. (2010). The labor market impact of immigration in Western Germany in 1990s. *European Economic Review*, 4: 550–570.

Del Campo, S. and Garmendia, J. A. (1974). The return of emigrants. In Tapinos, G. (ed.), *International Migration: Proceedings of a Seminar on Demographic Research in Relation to International Migration. Held in Buenos Aires, Argentina, 5–11 March*, Paris: CICRED (World Population Year).

Díaz-Plaja, G. (1974). *La condición emigrante. Los trabajadores españoles en Europa*, Madrid: Cuadernos para el Diálogo.

Dreyer, H. M. (1961). Immigration of foreign workers into the Federal Republic of Germany. *International Labour Review*: 1–25.

Dreyfus-Armand, G. (1999). *L'exil des républicains espagnols en France: de la Guerre civile à la mort de Franco*, Paris: A. Michel.

Drozdz, J. (2011). Spanish leadership in developing a "common" European immigration policy: intergovernmentalist supranationalization approach, College of Liberal Arts and Social Sciences Theses and Dissertations, Paper 92.

Dufoix, S. (2002). *Politiques d'exil: Hongrois, Polonais et Tchécoslovaques en France après 1945*, Paris: PUF.

Dumoulin, M. (1989). *Mouvements et politiques migratoires en Europe depuis 1945: le cas italien*, Louvain la Neuve: Ciaco.

Dumoulin, M., Bussière, E. and Willaert, E. (eds) (2008). *The Bank of the European Union: The EIB 1958–2008*, Luxembourg: Imprimerie Centrale.

Dupâquier, J. and Laulan Y. M. (eds) (2006). *Immigration/Intégration: un essai d'évaluation des coûts économiques et financiers*, Paris: L'Harmattan.

Dustmann, C. and Glitz, A. (2011). Migration and education. In Hanushek, E. A., Machin, S. and Woessmann, L. (eds), *Handbook of the Economics of Education*, Amsterdam: Elsevier, vol. iv, pp. 327–439.

EEC (2007). *Regularisation Programmes for Irregular Migrants*, Parliamentary Assembly, July 6, 2007.

Eichhorst, W., Giulietti, C., Guzi, M., Kendzia, M. J, Monti P., Frattini, T., Nowotny, K., Huber, P. and Vandeweghe, B. (2011). *The Integration of Migrants and its Effects on the Labour Market*, Brussels: EMPL, European Parliament.

Ernâni Lopes to the Assembly of the Republic (Lisbon, 9 July 1985). Online, available at: www.cvce.eu.

EU Enlargement and East–West Migration (2002) special issue of *Journal of Ethnic and Migration Studies*, 4: 581–742.

European Social Charter, Council of Europe "Research 1966" (1966). *Recommendations of the Committee of Ministers – Reports from the Social Committee of the special representative for refugees and surplus population*, Strasbourg: ESC.

Faidutti-Rudolph, A. M. (1962). L'évolution de l'immigration en France de 1946 à 1960. *L'information géographique*, 4: 152–160.

Faidutti-Rudolph, A. M. (1964). L'immigration italienne dans le Sud-Est de la France. *L'information géographique*: 179–182.

Fassmann, H., Haller, M. and Lane, D. (eds) (2009). *Migrations and Mobility in Europe: Trends, Patterns and Control*, Cheltenham: Elgar.

Garson, J. P., and Loizillon, A. (2003). Changes and challenges: Europe and migration from 1950 to present. In *Proceedings of the Conference: The Economic and Social Aspects of Migration*, Brussels: OECD.

Geddes, A. (2000). *Immigration and European Integration: Towards Fortress Europe?*, Manchester: Manchester University Press.

Geddes, A. (2005). Getting the best of both worlds? Britain, the EU and migration policy. *International Affairs*, 4: 723–740.

Gibellini, E. (2010). *Gli strumenti di politica sociale nel trattato della CECA*, online, available at: www.cvce.eu.

Givens, T. and Luedtke, A. (2004). The politics of European Union immigration policy: institutions, salience, and harmonization. *Policy Studies Journal*, 1: 145–165.

Givens, T. and Luedtke, A. (2005). European immigration policies in comparative perspective: issue salience, partisanship and immigrant rights. *Comparative European Politics*, 1: 1–22.

Goedings, S. (2000). Labour market developments, national migration policies and the integration of Western Europe, 1948–1968. In Leboutte, R. (ed.), *Migrations and Migrants in Historical Perspective: Permanencies and Innovations*, Brussels: Peter Lang, pp. 311–329.

González Enríquez, C. (2011). Spain: the making of immigration policies in the Southern frontier of the EU, 1985–2010. In Roy, J. and Lorca-Susino, M. (eds), *Spain in the European Union: the First Twenty-Five Years (1986–2011)*, Miami: Miami-Florida European Union Center/Jean Monnet Chair.

Grassi, V. (1994). Le politiche migratorie nei principali paesi dell'Europa occidentale dal secondo dopoguerra agli anni '80. *Affari sociali internazionali*, 2: 57–80.

Gui, L. (1975 [1957]). La convenzione europea per la sicurezza sociale dei lavoratori emigranti. In *50 anni di studi nella rivista "Previdenza Sociale" dell'Istituto Nazionale della Previdenza Sociale*, Rome: INPS, pp. 315–317.

Guild, E. (1998). Competence, discretion and third country nationals: the European Union's legal struggle with migration. *Journal of Ethnic and Migration Studies*, 4: 613–625.

Guiraudon, V. (2000a). European Integration and Migration Policy: Vertical Policy-making as Venue Shopping. *Journal of Common Market Studies*, 2: 251–271.

Guiraudon, V. (2000b). *La politique d'immigration en Europe (Allemagne, France, Pays-Bas)*, Paris: L'Harmattan.

Hamida, C. (2010). Quels défis pour la libre circulation des travailleurs? Limites et enjeux des politiques de migration économique dans l'UE. In Di Sarcina, F., Grazi, L. and Scichilone, L. (eds), *Res Europae. Attori, politiche e sfide dell'integrazione europea*, Florence: CET, pp. 155–166.

Herbert, U. and Hunn, K. (2001). Guest workers and policy on guest workers in the Federal Republic: from the beginning of recruitment in 1955 until its halt in 1973. In Schissler, A. (ed.), *The Miracle Years: a Cultural History of West Germany, 1949–1968*, Princeton: PUP, pp. 187–218.

Herz, D. (2003). *European Immigration and Asylum Policy: Scope and Limits of Inter-governmental Europeanization*, Nashville: Archives of European Integration (AEI).

Kipping, M. (2002). La Banque Européenne d'Investissements, de l'idée à la réalité (1949–1968). In *Le rôle des ministères des finances et de l'économie dans la construction européenne (1957–1978)*, Paris: CHEFF, pp. 525–542.

Illegal Mediterranean Migrations to Western Europe after World War II (2014). Special issue of *Journal of Modern European History*, 1.

ILO (1972). *Future ILO Action on Migrant Workers, Report to the Governing Body*, Geneva: ILO.

Ireland, P. R. (1998). Migrations, liberté de circulation et integration des immigrés dans l'Union: une réponse politique ambivalente. In Leibfried, S. and Pierson, P. (eds), *Politiques Sociale Européenne. Entre intégration et fragmentation*, Paris: L'Harmattan, pp. 261–301.

Joly, D. (1996). *Haven or Hell? Asylum Policies and Refugees in Europe*, Houndmills: Macmillan.

Judgment of the Court of Justice, Rutili, Case 36/75 (28 October 1975). Reports of Cases before the Court, 1975, [s.l.].

Kaelble, H. (2007). L'héritage de l'immigration en Europe. In Geremek, B. and Picht, R. (eds), *Visions d'Europe*, Paris: Odile Jacob, pp. 181–194.

Kahanec, M. and Zimmermann, K. F. (2010). Migration in an enlarged EU: a challenging solution? In Keereman, F. and Szekely, I. (eds), *Five Years of an Enlarged EU: A Positive Sum Game*, Heidelberg: Springer, pp. 63–94.

Kamp, K. (1971). Population registers, individual-data banks, and official population statistics. In Brass, W. and Cillov, H. (eds), *Report on Population Data Needs and the Use of such Data in Demographic and Social Analysis*, Strasbourg: EEC, pp. 30–36.

Keereman, F. and Szekely, I. (eds) (2010). *Five Years of an Enlarged EU: A positive sum game*, Heidelberg: Springer.

King, R. and Black, R. (eds) (1997). *Southern Europe and the New Immigrations*, Brighton: Falmer Press.

Korf, H. (2008). *Fortress Europe or a Europe of Fortresses? The Integration of non-European Union Immigrants in Western Europe.* Brussels: Peter Lang.

Korte, H. (1985). Labor migration and the employment of foreigners in the Federal Republic of Germany since 1950. In Rogers, R. (ed.), *Guests Come to Stay: the effects of European labor migration on sending and receiving countries*, Boulder: Westview Press, pp. 29–49.

Laffan, B. (1983). Policy implementation in the European Community: the European Social Fund as a case study, *Journal of Common Market Studies*: 389–408.

Latorre Catalán, M. (2006). Ciudadanos en democracia ajena: aprendizajes políticos de la emigración de retorno española en Alemania durante el Franquismo. *Migraciones y Exilios*, 7: 81–96.

Le, H. K. (1997). *L'immigration du sud-est asiatique en France*, Paris: ADRI.

Leboutte, R. (2005). Coal mining, foreign workers and mine safety: steps towards European integration. In Berger, S., Croll, A. and La Porte, N. (eds), *Towards a Comparative History of Coalfield Societies*, Aldershot: Ashgate, pp. 219–237.

Leboutte, R. (2006). L'action des Communautés européennes dans la politique de réadaptation des travailleurs et la reconversion industrielle, 1950–2002. Aux origines de l'Europe sociale. In Eck, J. F., Friedemann, P. and Lauschke, K. (eds), *La reconversion des bassins charbonniers. Une comparaison interrégionale entre la Ruhr et le Nord/Pas-de-Calais*, special issue of *Revue du Nord*, 21: 335–356.

Leboutte, R. (2008). *Histoire économique et sociale de la construction européenne*, Brussels: Peter Lang.

Leboutte, R. (2009). La Banque européenne d'investissement: cinquante ans de cohésion économique et sociale. In Devaux, S., Leboutte, R. and Poirier, P. (eds), *Le Traité de Rome: histoires pluridisciplinaires. L'apport du Traité de Rome instituant la Communauté économique européenne*, Brussels: Peter Lang, pp. 81–104.

Lindstrøm, C. (2005). European Union policy on asylum and immigration: addressing the root causes of forced migration: a justice and home affairs policy of freedom, security and justice? *Social Policy and Administration*, 6: 587–605.

Livi Bacci, M. (ed.) (2005). *L'incidenza economica dell'immigrazione*, Turin: Giappichelli.

Locatelli, A. M. (forthcoming). The cost of social security in European integration. In Bussière, E. *et al.* (eds), *National Economies and European Integration: Ways and Phases*, Stuttgart: Franz Steiner Verlag.

Lu, C. Y. (1999). *Harmonization of Migration in the European Union: A State-Centric or Institutionalist Explanation?*, Pittsburgh: Archives of European Integration (AEI).

Luedtke, A. (2005). *One Market, 25 Stats, 20 Million Outsiders? European Union Immigration Policy*, Washington: Archives of European Integration (AEI).

McDonald, J. R. (1965). The repatriation of French Algerians, 1962–63. *International Migration*, 3: 146–157.

Martens, A. (1976). *Les immigrés: flux et reflux d'une main-d'œuvre d'appoint. La politique belge de l'immigration de 1945 à 1970*, Louvain: PUL.

Masini, C. A. (1975 [1973]). I regimi generali obbligatori di vecchiaia per i lavoratori dipendenti nei Paesi membri della CEE. In *50 anni di studi nella rivista "Previdenza Sociale" dell'Istituto Nazionale della Previdenza Sociale*, Rome: INPS, pp. 657–689.

Mazzetti, G. (1975 [1951]). Verso una sicurezza sociale europea. In *50 anni di studi nella rivista "Previdenza Sociale" dell'Istituto Nazionale della Previdenza Sociale*, Rome: INPS, pp. 173–177.

Mechi, L. (2000). L'action del Haute Autorité de la CECA dans la construction des maisons ouvrières. *Journal of European Integration History*, 1: 63–85.

Mechi, L. (2006). Les États membres, les institutions et les débuts du Fonds Social Européen. In Varsori, A. (ed.) *Inside the European Community. Actors and policies in the European Integration 1957–1972*, Baden-Baden: Nomos, pp. 95–116.

Mechi, L. (2013). Du BIT à la politique sociale européenne: les origines d'un modèle. *Le Mouvement Social*, 3: 17–30.

Messina, A. (ed.) (2002). *West European Immigration and Immigrant Policy in the New Century*, Westport: Praeger.

Milza, P. (1994). Les migrants dans la formation de l'identité européenne. In Girault, R. (ed.), *Identité et conscience européennes au XXe siècle*, Paris: Hachette, pp. 47–64.

Molinari, A. (1958). Manpower and the Common Market. *BNL Quarterly Review*: 484–510.

Morelli, A. (1988). L'appel à la main d'oeuvre italienne pour les charbonnages et sa prise en charge à son arrivée en Belgique dans l'immédiat après-guerre. *Revue Belge d'Histoire Contemporaine*, 1–2: 83–130.

Older Migrants in Europe (2004). Special issue of *Ageing and Society* 3: 307–475.

Papademetriou, D. G., Sumption, M. and Somerville, W. (2009). *Migration and the Economic Downturn: What to Expect in the European Union*, Washington: Migration Policy Institute.

Pereira, V. (2012). *La dictature de Salazar face à l'émigration. L'État portugais et ses migrants en France (1957–1974)*, Paris: SciencesPo Les Presses.

Philip, A. B. (1994). European Union Immigration Policy: Phantom, Fantasy or Fact? *West European Politics*, 2: 168–191.

Pioneur (2006). *Project: Pioneers of Europe's Integration "from Below": Mobility and the Emergence of European Identity among National and Foreign Citizens in the EU*, European Commission, Fifth Framework Programme, Key Action "Improving the Socio-economic Knowledge Base", Brussels 2006.

Powell, C. (2011). The long road to Europe: Spain and the European Community, 1957–1986. In Roy, J. and Lorca-Susino, M. (eds), *Spain in the European Union: The First Twenty-Five Years (1986–2011)*, Miami: Miami-Florida European Union Center/ Jean Monnet Chair.

Rifugio Europa? (2006). Special issue of *Studi Emigrazione*, 160: 267–358, 379–436.

Rinauro, S. (2009). *Il cammino della speranza. L'emigrazione clandestina degli italiani nel secondo dopoguerra*, Turin: Einaudi.

Romero, F. (1991). *Emigrazione e integrazione europea 1945–1973*, Rome: Edizioni Lavoro.

Romero, F. (1993). Migration is an issue in European interdependence and integration: the case of Italy. In Milward, A. S., Ranieri, R., Lynch F. M. B., Romero, F. and Dorensen, V. (eds), *The Frontier of National Sovereignty: History and Theory 1945–1992*, London: Routledge, pp. 33–57.

Salt, J. and Clout, H. (eds) (1976). *Migration in Post-War Europe: Geographical Essays*, Oxford: OUP.

Sanchez, M. J. (2004). Les Espagnols en Belgique au XXe siècle. In Morelli, A. (ed.), *Histoire des étrangers et de l'immigration en Belgique de la préhistoire à nos jours*, Brussels: Couleur livres, pp. 279–296.

Schain, M. A. (2009). The state strikes back: immigration policy in the European Union. *European Journal of International Law*, 1: 93–109.

Schiller, G. (1971). Die Auswanderung von Arbeitskräften als Probleme der Wirtschaftlichen Entwicklung. *Argument 68*, 13: 800–809.

Schor, R. (1996). *Histoire de l'immigration en France. De la fin du XIXe siècle à nos jours*, Paris: A. Colin.

Shafagatov, R. and Aygun, M. (2005). *Immigration Policy as a Challenging Issue in the EU Policy-making Process: A Study of Immigrant Integration Policy*, MA thesis, Linkopings University.

Simon, J. (2002). *L'immigration algérienne en France: de 1962 à nos jours*, Paris: L'Harmattan.

Spire, A. (2005). Étrangers à la carte. L'administration de l'immigration en France (1945–1975), Paris: Grasset.

Spohn, W. and Triandafyllidou, A. (eds) (2001). *Europeanisation, National Identities and Migrations. Changes in boundary constructions between Eastern and Western Europe*, London: Routledge.

Stoetzel, J. (1954). *Français et immigrés: nouveaux documents sur l'adaptation. Algériens, Italiens, Polonais: le service social d'aide aux immigrants*, Paris: PUF.

Straubhaar, T. (1984). The Accession of Spain and Portugal to the EC from the Aspect of the Free Movement of Labour in an Enlarged Common Labour Market. *International Migration*, 3: 228–238.

Taccolini, M. (2006). *La costruzione di un'Europa del lavoro. La Commissione per gli affari sociali dalle origini all'applicazione del Trattato di Roma (1953–1960)*, Milan: Angeli.

Tapinos, G. (ed.) (1974). *International Migration: Proceedings of a Seminar on Demographic Research in Relation to International Migration. Held in Buenos Aires, Argentine, 5–11 March*, Paris: CICRED (World Population Year).

Tedeschi, P. (2008). The EIB and the economic and social development of Italy from 1958 to the beginning of the 1970s. In Dumoulin, M., Bussière, E. and Willaert, E. (eds), *The Bank of the European Union. The EIB 1958–2008*, Luxembourg: Imprimerie Centrale, pp. 73–90.

The New Face of East–West Migration in Europe (2008). Special issue of *Journal of Ethnic and Migration Studies*, 5: 701–841.

Tomé, E. (2013). The European Social Fund: a very specific case instrument of HRD policy. *European Journal of Training and Development*, 4: 336–356.

Trépant, I. (2002).*Pour une Europe citoyenne et solidaire. L'Europe des traités dans la vie quotidienne*, Brussels, De Boeck.

Triandafyllidou, A. (2001). *Immigrants and National Identity in Europe*, London: Routledge.

Triandafyllidou, A. (ed.) (2010). *Irregular Migration in Europe: Myths and Realities*, Farnham: Ashgate.

UN (1979). *Labour Supply and Migration in Europe: Demographic Dimensions 1950–1975*, New York: UN.

Varsori, A. (ed.) (2000). *Il Comitato Economico e Sociale nella costruzione europea*, Venezia: Marsilio.

Varsori, A. (2006a). Le Comité Economique et Social Européen et ses tentatives pour influencer de la CEE, puis de l'UE. In Bussiere, E., Dumoulin, M. and Schirmann, S. (eds), *Europe organisée, Europe du libre-échange? Fin XIXè siècle – Annèes 1960*, Brussels: Peter Lang, pp. 229–242.

Varsori, A. (ed.) (2006b). *Sfide del mercato e identità europea: Le politiche di educazione e formazione professionale nell'Europa comunitaria*, Milan: Angeli.

Venturini, A. and Villosio, C. (2006). Labour market effects of immigration into Italy: an empirical analysis. *International Labour Review*, 1–2: 91–118.

Venturini, A. and Villosio, C. (2008). Labour-market assimilation of foreign workers in Italy. *Oxford Review of Economic Policy* 3: 517–541.

8 Irish immigration then and now

Cormac Ó Gráda[1]

Until the beginning of the new millennium, Ireland was a land of emigration, not immigration. Since the Great Famine, both the broad contours of, and short-term fluctuations in, Irish population change were determined by net migration, not by natural increase; and it was emigration that made Ireland, uniquely among European countries, lose population for over a century. Much has been written on the ramifications of that emigration, both for Ireland and for host countries.

Over the past decade or so, however, it is immigration that has loomed largest in Ireland. In 1991 the number of Irish residents born outside the country numbered 228,725, or 6 per cent of the total population, and only 40,341 of those had been born outside the United Kingdom or the United States. Two decades later (in 2011) the foreign-born numbered 766,770, or 17 per cent of the total, and three-fifths (or 10.6 per cent) of those were from outside the United Kingdom. The big rise in the numbers of residents of east European origin – and especially the influx from Poland – are often highlighted, but between 2002 and 2011 the number of African-born residents doubled (from 26,515 to 54,419) and that of Asian-born residents almost trebled (from 28,132 to 79,021). Not only was the influx unprecedented on Paddy's green shamrock shore; it was also massive – in relative, not in absolute terms – by present-day European standards (Figure 8.1).

Now, with the passing of the Celtic Tiger, emigration looms large again. In the year ending April 2012, over 87,000 left, more than half of them Irish, the others non-nationals seeking better opportunities elsewhere.

A century ago, a much smaller immigration was the spark for a famous passage in the "Nestor" episode in James Joyce's *Ulysses*:

> Mr Deasy halted, breathing hard and swallowing his breath.
> *– I just wanted to say,* he said. *Ireland, they say, has the honour of being the only country which never persecuted the Jews. Do you know that? No. And do you know why?* He frowned sternly on the bright air.
> *– Why, sir?* Stephen asked, beginning to smile.
> *– Because she never let them in,* Mr Deasy said solemnly.

The passage is interesting for several reasons. One for the *literati* is that Stephen's bigoted companion Garrett Deasy with "his angry, white moustache" was not a Catholic Dubliner, but a northern Protestant – a Protestant "Citizen", in effect. A second, much more important, is that she (Ireland) *did* let them in. In 1904 there were still virtually no restrictions on immigration into Ireland or any-where else in the United Kingdom – although hostility in Britain to the immigra-tion of people seen as "paupers" and "criminals" led to the Aliens Act of 1905. That legislation was directed chiefly against East European Jews.[2] A third reason why Deasy's claim, to which I will return, is interesting is that it is an exaggera-tion to say that Ireland "persecuted the Jews" when "she let them in".

A more interesting question is why did the Jews want to settle in Ireland at a time when tens of thousands were leaving it? Why didn't they go elsewhere? One answer is that, for the most part, they did. Ireland's Jewish population was always miniscule. Data on flows are lacking, but between the late 1860s and the Great War Ireland's stock of non-UK and non-American born residents fell from a miniscule 6,811 in 1861 to 6,142 (or 0.14 per cent of the population) in 1911.[3] In 1911 Russian-born Jews accounted for almost one-third of the total, and there were 5,148 professing the Jewish religion.

Thanks to one Leopold Bloom, the Jewish immigration is well documented.[4] Less is known about a much smaller but more or less contemporaneous immi-gration from Italy. On the eve of the Great War Ireland's Italian community numbered about 400; excluding transient sailors, there were 171 Italians in 1851, 255 in 1871, 340 in 1891, and 276 in 1901. Thanks to the relatively new tech-nique of web scraping, it is not difficult to construct a profile of the small Italian community in 1911.

The two migrations had some things in common. Both Jews and Italians were subject to some resentment and abuse. The treatment meted out to the Jews has been the focus of a good deal of research, but there was hostility to the Italians also, albeit of a different kind, from various quarters. Neighbourhood residents sometimes resented their fish-and-chip shops and ice cream parlours for the noisy, unruly custom they attracted. For example, the vicar of St. Anne's and others objected to Edmund Caveri's fish-and-chip shop on nearby South Anne Street for the "improper characters" it attracted, and Celeste Macari in Derry was fined for allowing gaming on his premises.[5] In Belfast, Italians were vulnerable to sectarian attacks, as when in December 1910 a crowd of youths on their way down the Shankill Road stoned the window of an Italian shop-front near Carrick Hill. One of occupants fired a shot into the crowd, and this resulted in a "regular vendetta" against all Italians in Belfast that night, with the smashing of the windows of virtually every shop in the south and west of the city. A year and a half later, Italian-run ice cream shops were again the target of gangs of anti-Catholic "youths and mill girls".[6] In the wake of more disturbances in January 1913 an *Irish Independent* report opined that the Italians were targeted because they came from "the country of the Pope".[7] But the hostility that greeted Jews and Italians was not enough to prevent them from staying and making a decent living in Ireland.

In both communities later there was a shared belief or memory that the migra-tion had been, in part anyway, "accidental". The story goes that Giuseppe (or

Joseph) Cervi, who is credited with having introduced Dubliners to fish-and-chips,[8] "disembarked from an American ship in Cobh" in the late 1880s, convinced he was in New York. From there he "made his way to Dublin on foot, and, having worked for some time for an Italian stonemason called Bassi, he bought a cart, from which he would sell chips".[9] Another account reports that Cervi "began by selling chips from a stall in the street, on the spot where Pearse Street fire station now is". It states that he got the idea from a Russian "who used to run a hot potato stall on Tara Street", but adds that he had also seen chips in England "and decided to launch them on the Irish". The shop that an illiterate Giuseppi (Joseph) Cervi opened almost across the street from the old Queen's Theatre was still operated by his grandson in 1960.[10]

Similar themes crop up in Jewish oral accounts. Gerald Goldberg, son of an immigrant Litvak, described the arrival of Jews in Cork as an accident. Reaching the port of Queenstown, they were duped by the colloquial claim that "America is the next parish". Another more colourful version of this tale recounts that calls of "Cork, Cork" were mistaken for "New York", prompting "befuddled, bedraggled, wandering Jews" to disembark in Cobh.[11] But specialists on migration dismiss such tales about "accidental" destinations.[12] And so there is no need to wonder why Giuseppe Cervi believed Queenstown was New York. Indeed, the implication that he had spent some time in England before coming to Ireland begs the question why he would have landed in Queenstown.

Similarly, if Cervi learned from a Russian (possibly Jewish?) immigrant, it is said that some of the early Jewish immigrants in Dublin took to selling holy pictures after seeing Italians producing them; and one story, which I owe to the late Asher Benson, mentions a Jewish family discovering a shed full of pictures and statues in the back yard of a newly occupied house on the South Circular Road, and starting off trade in that way.[13] And other cameos reveal curious parallels. Thus, in May 1908, a Roscommon man got a month's hard labour for assaulting an Italian decorator named Brinteni with a thatcher's knife. His excuse was that Brinteni refused to drink with him. This recalls an incident in Cork two decades earlier, when a trades council delegate complained in the course of anti-Semitic tirade that local Jews "would not eat or shake hands with a Christian".[14] Otherness was a two-way street.

In both communities, the migrations had been associated in communal memory with a small place in the home country; the tiny village of Akmeyan/Akmene (with a population of 2,800 today) in northwestern Lithuania in the case of the Jews, and Lazio's Val di Comino, about 100 km from Rome, and in particular the small community of Casalattico (population 700 today) in the case of the Italians. One strong hint of an early Casalese presence is that two of the four organ grinders convicted of assaulting two Irishmen on Dublin's Chancery Lane in November 1887 had surnames closely linked to the village.[15] The links underline an important characteristic of both flows – the key role of chain migration.

The link with Casalattico would seem to find further corroboration in the remarkably high proportion of Italians – nearly four in every five – in Ireland in the mid-1980s who had been born in the region of Lazio. Next in importance of

Italy's 18 regions came Lombardy, which accounted for only 72 of the total of 2,312 Italian-born residents.[16] Yet this exaggerates the Casalattican component in Italian immigration in the interim.

In 1911 Ireland contained fewer than 400 immigrants of Italian stock. Their surnames imply that were a varied bunch, by no means exclusively from Casalattico. Interestingly, too, 93 of the 104 of those identified as Casalatticans by their surnames lived in County Antrim or in the neighbouring counties of Down and Armagh. The 1911 census suggests that all of Ireland's 28 Fuscos then lived in Belfast, as did all but two of the 44 Fortes. In 1911 only a dozen with common Val di Comino surnames – including the Cervis – lived in Dublin. Salazar (1912) reckoned that there were about 300 Italians in Dublin, a few less in Belfast, about 50 in Cork, and another 100 or so scattered around the island. This is an exaggeration the total, but he may have included the children of those born in Italy. According to Salazar the community included two groups. One came from Lucca and was made up of artisans, plaster workers, and woodworkers, with surnames like Bassi, Corrieri, Deghini, Giuliani and Nanetti. The second came from the Val di Comino and in this group Salazar counted 40 Fortes, 19 Fuscos, and other typical Casalattican names, all either street-sellers of ice cream or café owners.[17]

That the north of Ireland had been the original focus of Casalese immigration is corroborated by Reynold's research in Casalattico in the early 1990s (Reynolds, 1993, p. 99). Dublin's Italians were more likely to have had Tuscan connections a century ago; they included Joseph Patrick Nanetti MP, one-time lord mayor of Dublin, son of Giuseppe, a sculptor from Lucca. Those who settled in Belfast formed their own little ghetto, much like the Jews did.[18] But this was not a ghetto in the literal sense, any more than Dublin's Little Jerusalem, since from the outset the Italians lived cheek by jowl with the locals.

A century ago Belfast was Linenopolis – and more – and a far more dynamic place than Dublin. It also contained more people, even allowing for Dublin's middle-class suburbs of Rathmines and Pembroke. On that basis it should have been more likely to attract immigrants than Dublin. On the eve of the Great War, indeed, Belfast contained more Italians than Dublin, but the Jews settled mostly in Dublin. The paradox is explained by the Jews' specialization in activities that targeted mainly the less well off. Both Italian and Jewish immigrants catered to non-overlapping niches as classic "middleman minorities". So the Jews concentrated at the outset on peddling, on selling goods on credit through their so-called "weekly" system, and on moneylending, whereas the Italians specialized successively in organ grinding, ice cream and confectionery, and fish-and-chips.

The communities also, for a few years at least, had a street in common. Members of the Dublin Metropolitan Police found accommodation for some of the first Litvak settlers in a tenement next to the police station in Chancery Lane. There they lived "in a little square wherein stood the police station, Chancery Lane, joining the other foreigners – Italian organ-grinders, bear-leaders, one-man-band operators, and makers of small, cheap plaster casts of the saints of the Catholic church". By the 1870s Chancery Lane, originally a small but elegant street of three- and four-storey buildings, was already in a state of dilapidation, and home to "a miscellaneous population whose avocations it would be difficult to describe".[19] The Jews left quickly for what would become Little Jerusalem, but the Italians stayed on: there were almost as many of them and their Irish-born families there in 1911 (49) as there had been in 1901 (52).

In 1911 Ireland had 12 Italian-born organ grinders or street "musicians", five (again judging by surnames) from Casalattico and seven from elsewhere. This emblematic employment had long been associated with Italian immigrants. The number of Italian-born "musicians" recorded in the census rose from ten in 1851 to peak of 42 in 1891. The organ-grinders emerge in press cameos such as that of the murder in February 1841 of an organ-grinder Domenico Garlibardo in Rathfarnham[20]; or the court case taken in May 1888 by a woman named Marcella, wife of an organ-grinder, against another organ-grinder named Violante and his wife, which was attended by "about a dozen from what might be called the Italian colony"; Signora Marcella's claim that she was assaulted by Violante and his wife was countered by Signora Violante's insistence, backed by several witnesses, that it was Signora Marcella who started the fighting.[21] An amusing gloss on organ-grinders is given by the story of two Casalatticans who were charged in 1904 with annoying the well-known writer George Moore by playing outside his house in up-market Ely Place, "and refusing to desist when asked to do so". Moore complained that the noise was intolerable but one of the musicians protested that he left when he had finished the tune, and promised not to play outside Moore's house any more. The Italians posted a £5 bond to desist from "a deliberate persecution".[22]

A long-standing custom of the organ grinders was their annual New Year's concert in Chancery Lane, epicentre of the Dublin Italian community. In 1884 this involved "over a dozen organs [being] wheeled into the thoroughfare and as twelve o'clock struck the men began to grind as many different airs". Other musicians joined in, generating a "hideous" cacophony of sound, a big crowd and "much laughter and amusement, [but] no disorder". A decade later this bois-terous annual event was on the wane, although the Italians "dressed in their pic-turesque native costumes appeared at the windows and doors of the houses with smiling faces and cheery words of salutations to the passers-by"[23] On New Year's Day 1901 the *Irish Times* rather lamented "the serenading crowds, and the sounds of squealing instruments from almost every window of the tumble-down houses, and the great fete of intolerable noise which drowned the neigh-bouring bells of the two cathedrals".

Moreover, in 1911 the occupational profile of the Casalatticans differed mark-edly from that of the majority non-Casalatticans. Of the quarter with occupations ($n=62$) who had Casalattican surnames, 26 were ice cream vendors and another 21 were confectioners or shopkeepers. Only one or two of the Casalatticans were fish-and-chip merchants, however (compare Reynolds, 1993, p. 48). They were less likely to be labourers than non-Casalatticans and also less likely to be white collar.

To return very briefly to Chancery Lane, seven of the eight Italian male household heads living there in 1901 had married Irishwomen. Moreover, they had married women who were younger than them by an average of ten years or so, and in all cases but one it was a case of Italian men who could neither read nor write marrying literate Irishwomen. If these older, illiterate Italians were considered good catches, what does this say about Irishmen? The habit of marrying out seems to have been prevalent among Dublin's Italian immigrants, whereas in Belfast marrying within a more tightly knit, mainly Casalese community was the norm. Reynolds (1993, p. 109) highlights how Casalese households in Ireland maintained their traditions, as "the second generation – that is, those who were born in Ireland – usually speak dialect to their children".

The Jewish community at the outset was also extremely close-knit and inward looking, and rich in social capital. The Italians were also clannish, but they integrated more readily. Many of the Italian men recorded in 1911 had married out, including six of the seven based in Cork. And a few even changed religion while doing so: the 1911 census records three cases of Belfast-based Italian men who had changed religion in order to marry local women, and that of mosaic worker Rego Trosone who married a Presbyterian but remained Catholic.

Finally, both immigrations, like the much bigger reverse flow out of Ireland, were overwhelmingly economic in origin. Here is an account based on the experiences of Myer Joel Wigoder, who would set up a highly successful paint-and-wallpaper retailing business in Dublin:

> When my grandfather, Myer Joel Wigoder, left Lithuania in 1891, his destination was Holland. His motivations for leaving home and family to start a new life elsewhere were entirely economic. As I read through his works of memoirs ... I find no reference to any anti-Semitic experience of to the atmosphere of pogrom and persecution.... Various business ventures had not succeeded ... so at the age of thirty-six he left his pregnant wife and four children and headed west.

It was likewise with another Dublin immigrant, Lieb Berman. A brother-in-law had set him up as a brewer in Lithuania, but "he made it so good that he lost heavily on every brew". When he switched to peddling, "his horse ate up every groschen he had". The final straw was the spoilage of a cartload of fish on a sweltering day en route to Wexna market. His exasperated wife, hearing about a kinsman's success in Ireland, sent her husband packing. And Louis Wine's spur was a letter home from a stepbrother who, "having found his way to Ireland wrote glowingly of the country, saying he felt it was a land of great opportunity".[24] As often happens, such plausible, matter-of-fact accounts do not square with collective or folk memory.

Back to Mr Deasy

Mr Deasy's "she never let them in" is far from the truth a century later. As noted at the outset, Ireland's immigrant inflow in the 2000s, sudden and big, was unmatched in relative terms anywhere else in Western Europe (Figure 8.1).

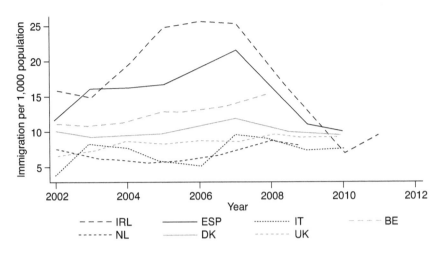

Figure 8.1 Immigration per 1,000 population, 2002–2011.

Some of it, it is true, consisted of returning Irish immigrants, but most did not. The acid test of Irish tolerance, then, is not what happened in Mr Deasy's day, but what is happening a century later. At first sight the impact of immigration on Irish attitudes is curious and ambivalent. On the one hand, it has not – so far at least – given rise to the xenophobic brand of politics currently in the ascendant across much of Europe. Ireland lacks a Front National, a Northern League, or a Geert Wilders, and the established political parties, including Sinn Féin, have given a wide berth – again, so far – to representatives seeking to capitalize on anti-immigrant sentiment.

On the other hand, incidents of ill treatment meted out to Jewish or Italian immigrants a century or so ago pale into relative insignificance compared to those inflicted on Irish immigrants in the recent past.[25] In mid-June 2009 20 Roma families consisting of about 100 people were forced out of their homes in the Village area of south Belfast. Most of them returned home to Romania, although by mid-July they were waiting to hear if it was safe to return.[26] To my knowledge nothing as violent was inflicted on the Italian or Jewish communities a century ago, nor was any Italian or Jewish immigrant was murdered for racist reasons.

No physical harm was inflicted on the Belfast Roma. But on a wet evening in January 2002, English-language student and Chinese national Zhao Liutao (29) was murdered in Beaumont in north Dublin on his way home from a night out. The BBC described this as Ireland's "first racially motivated murder". In February 2008 two Polish migrant workers in their late twenties were murdered in Drimnagh; over two years later a youth from the area was found guilty of their murder. A 15-year-old of Nigerian origin from Tyrelstown in west Dublin was murdered 2 April 2010, as he tried to stop an altercation. In March 2012 three men were jailed for having killed a Polish national in Coolock in the north of the city on his way to work on 2 October 2010. One of the culprits said they did it for a "buzz". In November 2011 a Nigerian taxi driver was brutally attacked by a white passenger on Dublin's Pearse Street and died of his injuries a few days later. Some at least of these murders were racially motivated. Mr Deasy would have said "I told you so".

Nor has Northern Ireland been immune. In Carrickfergus on June 24 1996 the owner of a Chinese takeaway was robbed and murdered in an attack deemed racist by the police. And in Newry in July 2009 a 40-year-old Pole was the victim of a racially motivated murder.

Successive opinion polls also point to significant anti-immigrant feeling. A September 2008 poll[27] found that two-thirds of respondents wanted more restrictive immigration laws, whereas only 7 per cent favoured less restrictive laws. This provoked the *Irish Examiner* to editorialize, "Our attitude towards immigrants maybe about to face a sterner test than before. Let us hope we pass it".[28] Another poll just over a year later[29] reported a big majority (72 per cent) wanting to see a reduction in the number of immigrants. Over two-fifths declared that they would like to see some, but not all, immigrants leave, while 29 per cent would like to see most leave, and just over one in four was happy to leave the number as it was.

Further insight into attitudes to immigration may be gained from the Irish National Election Study (INES), a panel survey carried out by the ESRI between 2002 and 2007. The main focus of INES was voting behaviour in two general elections, but it included some questions that bear on immigration. Three of the relevant variables (V0245–V0247) required responses on a scale of 1 (strongly disagree) to 7 (strongly agree) to specific statements about travellers and immigrants. The first (V0245) stipulated that people should not have to put up with halting sites in their area; the second (V0247) that there should be strict limits on immigration; and the third that immigrants should adapt to Irish customs (V0246). The other two refer to age (V0906) and educational level attained (V0921). Table 8.1 describes the raw correlations between these five variables. The high correlations between V0245, VO246, and V0247 show that hostility to immigrants was strongly correlated with hostility to travellers, implying that apart from any economic threat they presented, immigrants were perceived by some as undesirables as "others" or "different".

Age was not a good predictor of attitudes, but the level of education was. More educated people tended to be more tolerant of difference but perhaps this was because they did not live cheek by jowl with either travellers or immigrants.

Since 2003 Eurobarometer pollsters have asked citizens the question: What do you think are the two most important issues facing (country X) at the moment? Respondents were asked to choose two of 14 possible answers (unemployment, the economy, terrorism, crime, housing, healthcare, immigration, inflation, pensions, taxation, education, the environment, public transport, other).[30] Before the collapse of the Celtic Tiger in Ireland, neither immigration, nor unemployment, nor the state of the economy mattered very much, but in recent years people have begun to worry a lot about unemployment and the

Table 8.1 Irish attitudes to immigration in the 2000s

	V0245	V0906	V0921	V0246	V0247
V0245	1.000				
V0906	−0.064	1.000			
V0921	−0.179	0.406	1.000		
V0246	−0.140	−0.037	0.129	1.000	
V0247	0.270	−0.064	−0.235	−0.343	1.000

Source: INES N = 3,844.

Key to variables used in the table above
V0245 Anti-traveller halting sites.
V0906 Year of birth.
V0921 Educational level.
V0246 Pro rights for asylum seekers.
V0247 Strict limits on number of immigrants.

economy. However, the proportion of people listing immigration as one their top two concerns has remained small. This is in sharp contrast with some other European economies such as the United Kingdom. In Ireland immigration featured among the top two concerns only in a small minority of cases, less than almost anywhere else.

According to *Eurobarometer 66* (2006), 56 per cent of Irish people still believed in 2006 that "immigrants contribute a lot" to the country. This represented a much more positive view of immigration than the European average (40 per cent). In that poll Swedes were most pro-immigration (79 per cent), followed by the Portuguese (66 per cent), and then the Irish. Most hostile were Estonians, Latvians and Slovaks. A very recent (June 2012) Eurobarometer survey asked for an opinion on the statement "Immigration enriches (our country) economically and culturally". A majority of Irish respondents still expressed a positive opinion (Table 8.2) but they were further down the pro-European pecking order than in 2006.

Table 8.2 Replies to statement: "immigration enriches (our country) economically and culturally"

Country	Rank	Agree	Disagree
Sweden	1	81	18
Luxembourg	2	72	25
Netherlands	3	67	30
Ireland	10	55	37
Czech Republic	26	23	73
Cyprus	27	23	75
Latvia	28	19	78

Source: Special Eurobarometer 380: QB9.1 (June 2012; fieldwork December 2011), online, available at: http://ec.europa.eu/public_opinion/archives/ebs_380_en.pdf.

Figures 8.2a and 8.2b summarize Irish responses to questions about immigration in the European Social Survey (ESS). The ESS is a population representative cross-national survey that has been conducted every two years across the continent since 2002. Over 30 countries currently participate. Typically, data collection takes place over a period of about eight months, spanning two calendar years. The ESS contains six questions about immigrants: three about how many immigrants should be allowed in (depending on race, country of origin, etc.), and three more general questions about whether the respondents thought immigration was good for the country in different domains. Using factor analysis, we used these six questions to generate a synthetic measure of whether people were for, or against immigrants, and immigration in general. Normalized to a mean of zero and a variance of 1 over the three waves, our measure, ATTIM, can be used to analyse the trend in Irish attitudes to immigrants, and what sort of people are more, or less sympathetic to immigrants. These responses are analysed in more detail in Denny and Ó Gráda (2013). Figures 8.2a and 8.2b describe the shifts in our measure of public acceptability of migration (ATTIM) and xenophobia (Z) between 2002 (Round 1) and 2012 (Round 6). Between 2002 and 2006, as immigration rose rapidly, ATTIM rose in tandem. The sharp fall in the wake of economic collapse – Irish GDP fell by 13 per cent between 2007 and 2010, and the unemployment rate rose from 4.8 to 13.9 – is perhaps not so surprising, but the reversal to 2012 is.

Denny and I also generated a second variable, Z, to measure xenophobia, and it attempts to capture that particular hostility reserved for immigrants who differ ethnically/racially from the host population. The ESS first asks respondents about their attitude to immigrants from the same race/ethnicity as the majority of residents. It then asks the same question about immigration from different race/ethnic groups than the majority. The possible responses to both questions were "Allow many to come and live here", "Allow some", "Allow a few", and "Allow none". We set

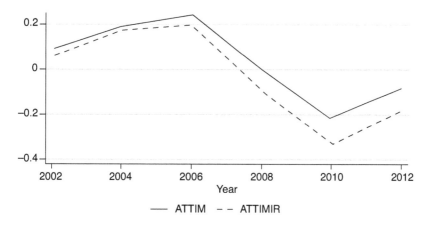

Figure 8.2a ATTIM 2002–2012.

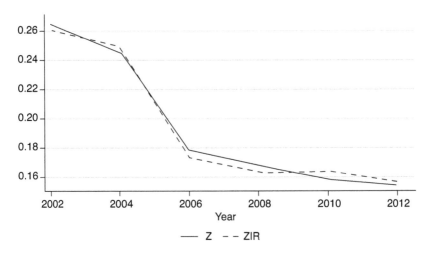

Figure 8.2b Z, 2002–2012.

xenophobia to one ($Z=1$) if respondents wanted to allow fewer from the non-majority race/ethnic group than from the majority, and equal to zero otherwise.

In the Irish context, which is our sole focus here, Z may be interpreted as a measure of a respondent's preference for returning Irish immigrants, and for immigrants from the United Kingdom and the United States, over immigrants from elsewhere. In the case of other economies, where return migration is unimportant, it might indicate instead a preference for Caucasian over black or Muslim immigrants – or, in the case of Israel, for Jewish over all other immigrants. Figure 8.2b describes the trend in Z, our measure of xenophobia, between 2002 and 2012. Note in particular the sharp fall between 2004 and 2006, when immigration was at its highest. The decline since – slow, but persistent – offers an interesting and rather surprizing perspective on the Irish response to globalization in an era of recession.

Public opinion as reflected in opinion polls is not articulated much in the media, in intellectual discourse, or in politics. Perhaps hostility is held in check by evidence that the vast majority of Irish immigrants are relatively young, healthy, at work, and net contributors to the exchequer; perhaps too that most of the immigrants are European and not black may also be a factor. One might want to add "not Muslim either", although Islam today is Ireland's third largest faith, and the country has about 40,000 foreign-born Muslims (compared to less than one-tenth of that in 1991).

Friedman's dilemma

Economist Milton Friedman's assertion that "you cannot simultaneously have free immigration and a welfare state" has been interpreted as an argument against immigration by some commentators and an argument for curbing or harmonizing welfare systems by others. A century ago this dilemma did not arise, but the growth of the welfare state has led to fears in host countries that some immigration is welfare- rather than employment-driven. A "blue card" system that excludes non-citizen immigrants from some or all welfare entitlements, as in the cases of Kuwait and Singapore, has sometimes been invoked as a solution. The exclusion of Italian immigrants from social security benefits unless they have being paying for them, and from healthcare apart from emergency hospital treatment, is in this tradition – although you might not think so from anti-immigrant propaganda –, as are the recent proposals by UK Labour spokesperson on immigration Yvette Cooper.[31] Friedman, an implacable enemy of the welfare state, declared his opposition to such measures, but supporters of immigration such as Lant Pritchett and Tito Boeri,[32] view them as the only way of reconciling two desirables.

Most studies of present-day immigration find that immigrants are net contributors to the public purse. Nevertheless, the sense that immigration entails welfare tourism is real,[33] and opinion polls that reveal that those who believe that there are "too many" immigrants are much more likely to declare that they constitute a fiscal burden. The image of immigrants as welfare tourists has been the most important cause of hostility to immigration in Europe, outstripping fears of job market competition and crime. Tim Hatton and Jeff Williamson[34] have found that the richer and more unequal the host country and the more extensive its welfare system, the greater is the hostility towards immigrants.

The unease tempered by equanimity about half-a-million non-nationals contrasts sharply with the panic and consternation in Ireland caused by one relatively small category of asylum seekers in the early 2000s. In Ireland the perception that some immigrants were abusing the welfare and citizenship systems was inextricably linked to the controversy surrounding the twenty-seventh referendum on citizenship, voted on in June 2004. The story goes back to 1987, when a High Court ruling involving Nigerian-born Bankole Lawrence Fajujonu and his Moroccan-born wife Zohra Fajujonu, both illegal residents, and their Irish-born daughter Miriam, recognized Miriam's right to citizenship under Articles 40–42 of the constitution, thereby opening the way – on the premise that children would not be separated from their parents – for what Attorney General Michael McDowell would later call "citizenship tourism".[35] The Supreme Court confirmed the decision of the High Court in 1989. First to take advantage of the door opened by the Fajujonu judgment were Nigerians resident in other EU countries, who realized that residency status in Ireland would mean freer movement within the EU; they were followed by mothers-to-be from Nigeria itself, often from wealthy families, who sought to capitalize on the benefits of having a family member with Irish citizenship; these women did "not depend on the Irish government for support throughout their stay in Ireland [but] often reside[d] in a hotel till they deliver[ed] their baby"; once they obtained the baby's birth certificate, they returned home.[36] Finally, pregnant women from other countries also began to avail of the loophole in increasing numbers.

In January 2000 Peter McKenna, master of the Dublin's Rotunda maternity hospital, expressed wonder at how women, "mainly Nigerians but also Eastern Europeans,... can manage to travel half way across the world pregnant and walk in the door to us at 39 weeks". He was "past the stage of being surprized at the number of refugees giving birth in Ireland but [he had] no doubt whatsoever that the system [was] being exploited".[37] The Annual Clinical Report of the Coombe, another maternity hospital, for the year 2000 (p. 90) noted that "media reports continue to draw attention to the number of pregnant asylum seekers attending maternity hospitals throughout the country for delivery". The head of Garda Immigration in Dun Laoghaire explained:

> They're coming in very close to birth and seem to be waiting until the very last minute to make the trip over. Most of them would be seven or eight months pregnant and can be very distressed. It would look like they are coming here to have their baby and get Irish citizenship.[38]

In 2002 a report compiled by the Eastern Regional Health Authority highlighted the stress on staff in maternity hospitals, and noted that staff members were sometimes verbally abused by patients and accused of being racist. The hospitals claimed that "the vast majority of pregnant asylum seekers are from Nigeria".

In April 2002 the High Court overturned its own 1987 ruling and in January 2003 the Supreme Court upheld its verdict. This meant that Irish-born children could be deported with their non-citizen parents, unless the latter agreed to be deported alone. In June 2004 this ruling was superseded by the Citizenship Referendum, which sundered the link between birth in Ireland and citizenship. Henceforth the constitutional right to citizenship would be restricted to those with at least at least one parent who is an Irish citizen or entitled to be an Irish citizen.

The 1937 constitution unknowingly embodied Leopold Bloom's response to the Citizen's barbed question in *Ulysses*, "What is your nation if I may ask?", to which Bloom replied, "Ireland. I was born here. Ireland". In the eyes of those who enacted and supported the citizenship referendum welfare tourism made the definition parlous. The rhetoric of the referendum campaign pitted "good" immigrants who came to Ireland to work against "bad" immigrants who sought to take advantage of its welfare regime.

The referendum passed overwhelmingly, by a margin of 4 to 1. There was very little variation across the country in the proportions for and against, unlike in, say, the case of the referenda on the Nice Treaty in 2001, Crisis Pregnancy in 2002, or Fiscal Stability in 2011.

Data described in detail elsewhere[39] confirm both the motive for the rise in births up to the 2004 referendum and the effectiveness of the closing the loophole. The impact of the Fajujonu judgment is evident in the very different booking pattern of women in the early 2000s, and there is evidence too of the effectiveness of the referendum in putting a stop to the practice. The data also suggest that Nigerian women were not alone in seeking entry by this route. Comparing the distribution of booking dates before and after the referendum indicates that Russians, Romanians and "Other Africans" were also wise to the constitutional loophole. But Nigerian women were more adept at exploiting the constitutional loophole provided by the 1987 case than any other national group.

Nigerian immigrants differed in other ways too. In a comparative study of recent immigrants from India, China, Nigeria and Lithuania, Feldman *et al.*[40] found that Nigerians' recourse to medical care exceeded that of the other three nationalities by a wide margin. The Nigerians also felt most discriminated against of the four groups yet, paradoxically or not, were also most resolved to remain.

Irish Independent journalist Kevin Myers, moreover, was quick to point out that the 2006 census revealed that the labour force participation rate of Nigerian immigrants was far lower than that of other immigrant groups (compare Table 8.3). But Myers overlooked the likelihood that many of the Nigerians, unlike the Poles and the Lithuanians, were not allowed to work.[41] Moreover, five years on, while Nigerians are still outliers as regards labour force participation and unemployment, they are far less so now than they were in 2006 (see Table 8.4). And the number of Nigerians in Ireland remains

Table 8.3 Employment status of immigrants by nationality in 2006, ages 15+ only (%)

	At work	Unemployed	At school	Home	Retired/other
Latvian	83	8	3	5	1
Polish	84	9	2	4	1
Lithuanian	83	8	3	5	1
Filipino	85	6	3	5	1
French	78	5	10	5	1
German	69	4	9	9	9
British	56	7	7	13	17
American	51	5	17	14	13
Nigerian	38	31	16	11	4
Chinese	44	7	43	5	1

Source: Census 2006, *non-nationals living in Ireland.*

Table 8.4 Employment status of immigrants by nationality in 2011

Nationality	Population 15+ (%)			LFPR (%)	UER (%)
	At work	Unemployed	Other		
Latvian	63.7	20.8	15.6	84.4	24.6
Polish	69.2	18.8	12.0	88.0	21.3
Lithuanian	65.3	20.6	14.1	85.9	24.0
Filipino	73.3	9.5	17.1	82.9	11.5
French	72.6	7.9	19.5	80.5	9.8
German	63.4	7.8	28.9	71.1	10.9
British	46.4	14.9	38.7	61.3	24.3
American	46.1	9.5	44.3	55.7	17.2
Nigerian	41.6	26.0	32.3	67.7	38.5
Chinese	47.4	9.9	42.7	57.3	17.3

Source: 2011 Census: table CD354.

small – about 8,000 in 2000, 16,300 in 2006, and 17,642 in 2011 – and certainly much smaller than, say, the number of Irish illegals currently in the United States.

Concluding thoughts

In their attitudes to immigrants, are the Irish any different? Mr Deasy's jibe more a century ago was that they *thought* they were different, but that this was only because the challenges they faced were different. And, ultimately, claims that one group or community is inherently more or less prejudiced or racist than another are dubious, if not dangerous. In Ireland, there is no room for complacency, and the threats and hostility endured by Nigerian and Roma immigrants today dwarf those faced by Italian and Jewish immigrants a century or so ago. At the same time, there is a role for initiatives that minimize and pre-empt friction between native and newcomer, and there is a case for seeing the 2004 Citizenship Referendum in that light. There is a case too for transparency about the facts. Research elsewhere[42] comparing perceptions and reality suggests that public opinion has an exaggerated and distorted impression of immigration's impact on unemployment, living standards, and crime.

Finally, Ireland has built up a reputation, not undeserved, for its relatively generous foreign aid programme. Perhaps there is a case for regarding some immigration from less developed countries as a complement to foreign aid? Irish history suggests that, by and large, emigration benefited both those who left and those who remained at home. Emigrants not only relieve pressures on the domestic labour market; they also send back remittances and some return with their human capital enhanced. Insofar as the same applies to less developed economies today, foreign aid and immigration could be seen as substitutes. UN data underline the important role of remittances in boosting incomes; in many less developed economies today, remittances exceed both foreign aid and foreign investment (UNDP, 2010). Of course, aid and immigration are imperfect substitutes, particularly when it is the relatively better off in the sending countries who benefit from both the migration and the remittances. Still, as a recent World Bank study (Mohapatra *et al.* 2010) argues:

> Harnessing the development potential of migration and remittances by increasing the awareness of the decision makers and improving data on remittances and migration; facilitating labor mobility and recruitment across borders, while allowing for safe and affordable mechanisms for sending money back; and combating the increase of fear-based xenophobia and overregulation are some ingredients along the way towards a migration policy that benefits both migrant-sending and receiving countries.

Given that Ireland cannot absorb all those who might want to come and the latent hostility described earlier, which would-be immigrants should get preference? What kind of migration maximizes remittances; what kind promotes human capital formation in the sending country; what kind reduces inequality and poverty in the sending country most? These are hard questions, but they are surely not insoluble.

In October 2007, in one of his most extreme rants about immigration columnist Kevin Myers – Ireland's answer to Enoch Powell – warned in the *Irish Independent*:

> The bridge stands unmanned as Lars Porsena's legions approach, and this time there is no Horatio. Ireland, as Ireland, is about to vanish, just as Leicester, Bradford, Luton, Rotterdam, *et cetera*, have already Six years later there were no signs that Ireland had vanished, although the country had changed for the worse for other well-known reasons. And as a result, net immigration, which was a sign of the good times and which Myers implied would continue at pace indefinitely, has turned into net emigration on a considerable scale. The turnaround at its most dramatic is reflected in the number of immigrants from the EU12: from 85,300 in 2007 and 54,700 in 2008 to 10,100 in 2011 and 10,400 in 2012. As the economy continues to stagnate and welfare regimes tighten, there is little reason to believe that this pattern will not continue.

Notes

1 Thanks to Kevin Denny, Bryan Fanning, David Madden, Bairbre Ní Chiosáin, and Brian Reynolds for comments and help on various points.
2 Gainer, 1972.
3 Excluding the 1,620 Indian-born residents in 1861 as presumably in the main the children or relatives of Irish natives – in 1911 there were only 198 who had been born in all of Asia – would not alter the balance much.
4 Hyman, 1972; Keogh 1988; Ó Gráda, 2006.
5 *Freeman's Journal*, 4 January 1908; *Irish Times*, Alleged gaming in ice cream shop, 2 May 1913.
6 Revolver firing in Belfast: ice cream shops and public houses wrecked, *Irish Times*, 10 December 1910; Intimidation in Belfast: more workers attacked, *Irish Times*, 6 July 1912.
7 Belfast scenes: more revolver firing, *Irish Independent*, 20 January 1913.
8 On the early history of fish-and-chips, see Walton, *Fish and Chips*.
9 Reynolds, 1993, p. 46; Power, 1988, p. 23.
10 Italy in Dublin (1960) *Irish Times*, 21 May. Cervi was recorded as "Chervie" by the enumerator in 1911. He was still renting a boarding-house on Little Ship Street in 1911, as he had been a decade earlier.
11 Ó Gráda, 2006, pp. 25–26.
12 Cesarani, 1996; Klier, 1996. Compare Patrick O'Farrell's scathing dismissal of oral history (O'Farrell, 1979) as "image, selective memory, later overlays and utter subjectivity".
13 Ó Gráda, 2006, p. 56.
14 *Irish Times*, 7 May 1908; Ó Gráda, 2006, p. 187.
15 *Irish Times*, 8 November 1887. Their names were Forti and Macari. The others were Scantori (*sic, recte* Scantore) and D'obriolo. For lists of Casalattico/Val di Comino

surnames see All Things Italian website, online, available at: www.allthingsitaliane. com/surname_database.htm and Archiver website, online, available at: http://archiver. rootsweb.ancestry.com/th/read/anglo-italian/2002–12/1040297141.

16 As reported in Reynolds, 1993, p. 56.

17 As reported in Casalattico.com, online, available at: www.casalattico.com/index. php?option=com_content&view=article&id=11&Itemid=121].

18 In its heyday Belfast's Little Italy "consisted of the city end of Nelson Street, Great Patrick Street, Little Patrick Street, Carolina Street, Academy Street, and the lower end of Frederick Street" (Doherty, n.d.).

19 *Irish Times*, 26 December 1889. See too Ó Gráda, 2005.

20 Garlibardo, a young man, lived in Maiden Lane off Wood Street with two compatriot organ-grinders, Vernice and Giovanni Fraco. On the day he was murdered he was in the company of two other Italians, Giovanni Bianco and Giovanni Rivere. Several Italians were taken into custody: their names were given as Michele Cecile, Giovanni Stello, Giovanni Caslarino, Tomaso Riva, Giovanni Rivere, Giovanni Beauchitte, Giuseppe Muchette, Giuseppe Fraco (*Freeman's Journal*, 5 March 1841, 3 November 1842).

21 Power, 1988, p. 29; Chapters of Dublin website, online available at: www.chaptersofdublin.com/books/Neighbourhood/chapter10.html; *Irish Times*, May 11 1888. For details of another inter-family fracas see *Irish Times*, August 21 1882.

22 *Irish Times*, 2 January 1904.

23 *Freeman's Journal*, 1 January 1894.

24 Ó Gráda, 2006, pp. 16–7.

25 Compare Edmund Sanders, "African refugees in Israel get a cold shoulder and worse" (2012) *Los Angeles Times*, May 27.

26 Henry McDonald (2009a) "Romanian gypsies beware beware, loyalist C18 are coming to beat you like a baiting bear", *Observer*, June 1; Henry McDonald (2009b) "Pipe bomb threat to Roma discovered", *Observer*, June 28; "Hard times for Roma who fled Belfast" BBC News, online, available at: http://news.bbc.co.uk/2/hi/uk_news/northern_ireland/8143368.stm.

27 Conducted by Amárach Research.

28 *Examiner*, 10 September 2008.

29 *Irish Times*, 11 November 2009.

30 For the most recent data see Europa website, online, available at: http://ec.europa.eu/public_opinion/archives/eb/eb78/eb78_anx_en.pdf.

31 "Labour outlines measures to restrict benefits for new EU arrivals in UK" (2013) *Guardian*, 7 March.

32 Pritchett, online, available at: http://reason.com/archives/2008/01/24/ending-global-apartheid/4; Boeri, 2009.

33 In August 2012 a district court judge had to apologize for having suggested in court that "social welfare [w]as a Polish charity" (*Irish Times*, 2 August 2012).

34 Hatton and Williamson, 2008.

35 Breen *et al.*, 2006; Ní Chiosáin, 2007.

36 Kómoláfé, 2002.

37 *Irish Independent*, 24 January 2000.

38 *Irish Independent*, 24 January 2000.

39 Ó Gráda, 2012.

40 Feldman *et al.*, 2010; more generally see Fanning, 2011.

41 "Risible lies about immigrants no substitute for honest debate" (2008) *Irish Independent*, 15 August.

42 Gomellini and I discuss some of the Italian evidence on this in Gomellini and Ó Gráda (2012).

References

Boeri, Tito (2009). *Migration to the Land of Redistribution, IZA Discussion Paper No. 4273.*

Breen, Michael, Amanda Haynes and Eoin Devereux (2006). Citizens, loopholes and maternity tourists: media frames in the citizenship referendum. In Mary P Corcoran and Michel Peillon, eds. *Uncertain Ireland*, Dublin: IPA, pp. 59–70.

Cesarani, David (1996). The myth of origins: ethnic memory and the experience of emigration. In Newman and Massil, *Patterns of Migration*, London: Jewish Historical Society, pp. 247–254.

Denny, Kevin and Cormac Ó Gráda (2013). Irish attitudes to immigration during and after the boom. University College Dublin Centre for Economic Research Working Paper No. 13/14.

Dietz, Angelika (2011). *Dimensions of Belonging and Migration by Choice: Contemporary Movements between Italy and Northern Ireland*, Muenster: Waxmann.

Fanning, Bryan (2011). *Immigration and Social Cohesion in the Republic of Ireland*, Manchester: Manchester University Press.

Feldman, Alice, Mary Gilmartin, Stephen Loyal and Bettina Migge (2010). *Getting on, from Migration to Integration: Chinese, Indian, Lithuanian and Nigerian Migrants' Experiences in Ireland*, Dublin: Immigrant Council of Ireland.

Gainer, Bernard (1972). *Alien Invasion, the Origins of the Aliens Act of 1905*, London: Heinemann.

Gomellini, Matteo and C. Ó Gráda (2012). Migrations. In Gianni Toniolo, ed. *Handbook of the Formation of the Italian Economy*, Oxford: Oxford University Press, pp. 271–302.

Hatton, Tim (2009). The rise and fall of asylum: what happened and why? *Economic Journal*, 119: F183-F213.

Hatton, Tim and J. G. Williamson (2008). The impact of immigration: comparing two global eras. *World Development*, 36 (3): 345–361.

Hyman, Louis (1972). *The Jews of Ireland: From Earliest Times to the Year 1910*, Shannon: Irish University Press.

Keogh, Dermot (1998). *Jews in Twentieth-Century Ireland: Refugees, Anti-Semitism and the Holocaust*, Cork: Cork University Press.

King, Russell and Brian Reynolds (1990). Italiani in Irlanda: note storiche-geografiche, *BollettinodellaSocietàGeograficaItaliana* (ser. XI) 7: 509–529.

King, Russell and Bryan Reynolds (1994). Casalattico, Dublin and the fish and chip connection: a classic example of chain migration, *StudiEmigrazione*, xxxi (115): 398–426.

King, Russell and Brian Reynolds (1996). Casalattico: storiamigratoria e trasformazionigeografiche di uncomunedella Val di Comino, *Geografia 29*: 15–27.

Klier, John D. (1996). Emigration mania in late-imperial Russia: legend and reality, in Newman and Massil, *Patterns of Migration*, London: Jewish Historical Society, pp. 21–30.

Kómoláfé, Julius (2002). Searching for fortune: the geographical process of Nigerian migration to Dublin, Ireland. *Ìrìnkèrindò: a Journal of African Migration*, 1. Online, available at: www.africamigration.com.

Marantonio, Katia (1998). L'emigrazione italiana in Irlanda. *Studi Emigrazione*. 35 (129): 127–135.

Mohapatra, Sanket, Dilip Ratha and Elina Scheja (2010). Impact of migration on economic and social development: a review of evidence and emerging issues, online, available at:

http://siteresources.worldbank.org/TOPICS/Resources/214970-1288877981391/Migration&Development-Ratha-GFMD_2010a.pdf.

Newman, A. and S. W. Massil, eds. (1996). *Patterns of Migration, 1850–1914*, London: Jewish Historical Society.

Ní Chiosáin, Bairbre (2007). Passports for the New Irish? The 2004 citizenship referendum, *Etudes Irlandaises* 32 (2).

O'Farrell, Patrick (1979). Oral history: facts and fiction. *Quadrant* 23 (148): 4–8.

Ó Gráda, C. (2005). Settling in: Dublin's Jewish immigrants of a century ago. *Field Day Review*, 1: 87–98.

Ó Gráda, C. (2006). *Jewish Ireland in the Age of Joyce: A Socioeconomic History*, Princeton: Princeton University Press.

Ó Gráda, C. (2012). Because she didn't let them in: Irish immigration a century ago and today. Unpublished.

Power, Con (1991). A little bit of Italy in heart of Dublin. *Sunday Press*, 4 August.

Power, Una (1988). *Terra straniera: the Story of Italians in Ireland*, Dublin: Club Italiano.

Reynolds, Brian (1993). *Casalattico and the Italian Community in Ireland*, Dublin: UCD Foundation for Italian Studies.

Salazar, Lorenzo (1912). Gli Italiani in Irlanda, *Rivista Coloniale* 2 (1):15–17.

UNDP (United Nations Development Programme) (2010). Overcoming barriers: human mobility and development, *Human Development Report 2009*. Online, available at: http://hdr.undp.org/en/reports/global/hdr2009/.

Walton, John K. (2000). *Fish and Chips and the British Working Class 1870–1940*, London and New York: Leicester University Press.

9 Italian illegal emigration after the Second World War and illegal immigrants in Italy today

Similarities and differences

Sandro Rinauro

Illegality in cross-border movements is a long-lasting phenomenon. It has existed at least since European migration reached a mass dimension in the second half of the nineteenth century. Until the end of intra-European mass movements of individuals, during the 1970s, it impacted mainly Southern European workers in the Northern European developed countries. The decline of intra-European mass migrations, the advent in the 1960s of the Community Code on the Free Movement of Communitarian Workers and the birth of the EU put an end to the phenomenon only for communitarian persons within the EU. At the same time, the increase of extra-communitarian immigration strongly renewed illegal movements and involved also the Southern European nations as receiving countries. What has changed in regards to the causes and the dimension of the phenomenon? What has changed as to the concern and the attitude towards it by public opinion and rulers? Is there a continuity both for the immigrant and receiving countries' practices involved in this issue?

Before I try to answer these questions, I will describe the main aspects of Italy's illegal emigration in the past and nowadays. Italy is, in fact, one of the most representative European countries as to both these dimensions.

Illegal expatriation in liberal Italy

Illegal expatriation of Italians was already widespread in the decades of the "Great Migration" around the turn of the twentieth century, but during the Italian mass migration era (1870s–1970s) its dimension changed considerably.

As a matter of fact, during the "Great Migration" illegal expatriation was relatively huge in number, but small compared with the great number of legal migrants. The first semi-official statistics on migration, carried out by Leone Carpi, give the figure of illegal migrants (people without passport) in 1870 as 8,643, compared with 101,815 legals, thus they were slightly less than 8 per cent of the total number of migrants. In 1871, 11,068 illegal migrants were apprehended out of a total of 122,479 migrants (9 per cent), and in 1873 the figure was 11,833 out of a total of 147,003 (8 per cent). However, these are uncertain and incomplete figures. The reasons for illegal expatriation mentioned by Carpi were primarily failure to report for military service, followed by the lack of funds to pay for the ocean crossing and, last, the lack of a work contract abroad, without which the Italian authorities would not issue a passport (Carpi, 1874, p. 233; Rinauro, 2010, pp. 393–418).

In those years, the legal restrictions that led to illegal emigration were thus not so much due to immigration policies in the countries of destination, which were quite liberal, so much as to hostility towards the exodus among the ruling classes in Italy and, less, to the protection aims of Italian law. The most important Italian legal obstacles to free migration were the ban on expatriation for those who could not demonstrate a job contract abroad or sufficient means of subsistence, for adults suspected of avoiding their family responsibilities, for minors without parental consent, and for women who, emigrating alone or without the legal consent of their father or husband, were suspected of entering the international prostitution market. Sporadic prohibition to reach countries where the treatment of immigrants was particularly inhumane (as was the case in 1911 towards the La Plata countries) also led to illegal expatriations (Ostuni, 2001, pp. 309–310; Manzotti, 1962). The migration law of 1888 and especially the 1901 law made a license compulsory for emigration agents and for carriers. Thus, illegal migration grew even further because, beside the undocumented migrants, also those who had been recruited by unlicensed agents and carriers, or who embarked at foreign ports or with foreign shipping companies that were not authorized by Italy for the transport of migrants were considered illegal (Martellini, 2001, pp. 303–308; Commissariato generale per l'emigrazione, 1926, pp. 347–368).

At any rate, France and Switzerland were the main destinations of Italian illegal migration because of their geographical proximity, the many informal paths crossing the Alps and because the most active agencies illegally recruiting migrants for Europe and the Americas were based there. The illegal passage crossing the ocean was encouraged also by foreign shipping companies. At the same time, criminal migrant-smuggling organizations and document forging workshops were already appearing in these decades (Frescura, 1904; Sori, 1979, pp. 320–324; Cioli, 1989, pp. 43–48; Porcella, 1998; Lupo, 1996, pp. 153–154; Borruso, 2001, pp. 141–161; Sanfilippo, 2011, pp. 227–236). Thus, illegal expatriation grew so rapidly from the end of the 1870s, involving at least 20,000–30,000 individuals each year (Sori, 1979, pp. 320–324), but that still meant only 5 per cent of the annual expatriation during the first 15 years of the twentieth century (600,000). The scale of illegality in the seasonal migration from the Italian Alps was however incalculable, for these migrants had little care for passports and frontiers in their centuries-old traditional coming and going (Molinari, 1995, p. 142).

As a consequence of the growing illegal migration, Law no. 1075 of 2 August 1913 increased the powers of control and investigation by the Commissariato Generale per l'Emigrazione (CGE) against illegal recruitment. The US "quota laws" of 1921 and 1924, which radically reduced the access to Italian migrants, led to an even greater wave of illegal migration and an enormous rise in the price demanded by recruiters. Despite the law of 1913, a great deal of illegal migration managed to elude the Italian controls. The official number of Italians who left from foreign ports illegally (without a passport) was thus incomplete but nevertheless conspicuous: 26,801 Italians, at least 8,000 of whom were illegal emigrants, reached the United States from the port of Le Havre in 1912, 6,187 in 1913, and at least 10,565 Italians entered Brazil illegally in 1910 and 1911. Around 1907 at least 20,000 Italians crossed the Italian–Swiss border on their way to the Swiss and French recruitment agencies who would then smuggle them across the ocean (Commissariato generale per l'emigrazione, 1926, pp. 349–357).

Illegal migrants also boarded ships at Italian ports, where fake forwarding companies helped them on board by disguising them as sailors or porters with the bribed connivance of the crew, and sometimes even of the captain, as well as forging passports for them. Stowaways were often discovered and reported to the CGE agent on board, but many of them managed to land on the other side of the ocean (Franzese, 1996, pp. 129–157; Masi, 2003, p. 127). In the 1910s the CGE intensified its preventive and law-enforcement activities, especially to prevent illegal migration of deserters during the First World War, monitoring alpine passes and ports and checking expatriation documents. At the same time, in collaboration with Italian consuls abroad, the CGE collected data on foreign and internal illegal agents and recruiters. These multiple activities enabled the Commissariato to present thousands of complaints to court against illegal recruiters and swindlers of migrants, but the sentences were rare and fairly light because the magistrates were unaware of the dramatic situation faced by stowaways and swindled migrants (Commissariato generale per le migrazioni, 1926, pp. 360–368).

Illegal migration between the wars

From the 1920s, the first blanket restrictions came into force with the adoption of ethnic "quotas" to limit access to the United States, Canada and Brazil. However, it was mainly the Great Depression that drastically reduced expatriation (Divine, 1957; Higham, 1965; Martellone, 1980; Hutchinson, 1981; Tichenor, 2003; De Clementi, 2002, pp. 428–434; Audenino and Tirabassi, 2008, pp. 79–83). In addition, in the late 1920s the Fascist regime in Italy also adopted a restrictive emigration policy, in line with its demographic and military policies (Cannistraro and Rosoli, 1979; Labanca, 2000; Luconi, 2000; Bertonha, 2001; Franzina and Sanfilippo, 2003). In reaction to all these limitations, illegal emigration shot up. The political exile of many anti-fascists – about 60,000 individuals – often illegal in the eyes of the Fascist law and of the receiving countries, also increased the flow of clandestine migrants. As a result of the racial laws (in 1938) thousands of Italian Jews and foreign Jews passing through Italy were obliged to migrate, sometimes illegally (Audenino and Tirabassi, 2008, pp. 107–121; Tombaccini-Villefranque, 1999, pp. 80–86; Rapone, 2008; Veziano, 2002; Istituto storico della Resistenza e della società contemporanea in provincia di Cuneo, 2007).

The restrictions on migrants in the inter-war years had a strong impact on the illegal emigration of workers, as the extremely high number of illegal Italian immigrants in France in particular clearly shows: between 1920 and 1933, next to an average annual inflow of about 10,000–15,000 legal Italian immigrants, another 20,000–25,000 illegal and irregular Italians entered the country each year. Under the pressure from local employers, the French authorities were so tolerant that no less than a third of foreign workers (all nationalities) who arrived in France in the 1920s were illegal immigrants (Henneresse, 1978, p. 62, 155; Maltone, 1988, pp. 103–118; Mauco, 1932, p. 132; Demangeon and Mauco, 1939, p. 628; Gani, 1972, pp. 13–14, 29).[1]

Illegal emigration during the years of the reconstruction

Immediately after the Second World War, the illegal flow of political emigrants – war criminals, Fascist Party officials, particularly ruthless republican Fascists and public and private managers who had collaborated in the war economy of the regime and of the Nazi occupiers – was important in political terms but involved just a few hundred people. Their destinations were mainly Latin America and Switzerland, from which many returned to benefit from amnesties and frequent acquittals (Bertagna, 2006; Devoto, 2000; Capuzzi, 2006, pp. 243–264; Sezzi and Sigman, 2003; Van Dongen, 2008; Setta, 1993). The Italian and foreign Jews who sailed from Italy to Israel before its constitution as an independent nation, were also illegal emigrants (Villa, 2005; Sereni, 1994; Toscano, 1990).

Anyway, it was in the post-war period that labour illegal emigration really took off. In fact, Western democracies valued "full employment" as the fundamental tool for maintaining international peace and democratic consent at home. Thus, in order to assure "full employment" at home, immigrant-receiving countries adopted a restrictive migration policy. The basic measure was that nobody could go abroad to look for a job, the only legal way to work abroad was to be called by a foreign employer or a relative. At the same time, the receiving countries imposed the quantity, quality, employment sector and short duration of immigration. These countries also established the sole place of work and residence and even the size of the remittances that immigrants could send back to their families in Italy. Workers going abroad spontaneously were automatically clandestine migrants and, as for the regular ones, once they were abroad, those who changed the district of residence assigned to them or their profession or even only their employer, or who stayed beyond the terms of their contract, became illegal immigrants and were thus immediately repatriated. The process of setting up such a precise system for managing foreign labour proved to be highly complex and lengthy (Rinauro, 2005b; Romero, 1991; Colucci, 2008). These limitations, the ignorance of the complex bureaucratic procedure for recruitment and its excessive length encouraged large numbers of Italians to avoid the official recruitment process and to expatriate illegally, or to change their profession and place of residence from those assigned to them, which meant they were abroad unlawfully.[2]

In addition, the host countries often hindered family reunions, both to prevent workers from becoming rooted in the country and to maintain a high percentage of economically active people in the population. Very often the result was that reunions took place illegally. Coupled with this was the interest of foreign business owners, and sometimes also of their governments, to receive illegal immigrants who were thus docile, cheap and precarious and, in any case instantly adaptable to the economic situation by getting rid of them at any time.

The flow of illegal migrants across the oceans started up again and also led to bereavements. The majority of these migrants, lacking a work contract or a legal call from their relatives abroad, went overseas with just a tourist passport and then stayed on illegally. More frequent still was illegal migration made possible by Italian and foreign swindlers who procured false work contracts, especially for land settlements, building and transport (Rinauro, 2009, pp. 100–112).[3]

In any case, illegal migrants mainly headed to European countries. The main destinations were France and Switzerland and, less important, Belgium, Luxembourg and West Germany. In the case of Belgium, many Italians entered France legally or illegally and then went to Belgium without permits in search of a job. More frequently Belgian companies recruited in Italy directly, eluding checks by the Italian authorities in order to find cheaper, more flexible manpower. In addition, often immigrants put themselves into a state of illegality by abandoning their most common job as underground workers in coal mines, in order to avoid the frequent mortalities and silicosis (Morelli, 2002, p. 167).[4]

During periods of greatest demand, the collieries sent their own recruiters to Italy and to mining areas in France to illegally hire Italian migrants. When, after the mine accident occurred in Marcinelle (1956), where 136 Italian miners died, Rome indefinitely suspended recruitment for Belgian mines, the collieries got round the prudent measure of the Italian authorities by hiring illegal workers en masse (Rinauro, 2009, pp. 115–124).

In Switzerland there were still many private recruitment agencies who provided migrants with work contracts, in exchange for money and violating contractual principles. However it was mainly Swiss companies that recruited directly in Italy without respecting the recruitment and labour conditions agreed upon with Rome. Their aims were to select workers more skilled than those recruited by Italian authorities among unemployed persons, to avoid peoples from the South of Italy and to offer contracts less favourable than the official ones. In 1954, the Italian Ministry of Labour ascertained that irregular recruitment by Swiss companies constituted "the highest contingent of Italian migrants to Switzerland".[5] The other most significant cause for migration and illegal residence was the extremely restrictive immigration policy: to avoid a high and permanent presence of strangers into the national population ("*überfremdung*"), the Confederation favoured seasonal and annual labourers, hindering permanent residence and family reunions. A significant number of illegal immigrants were therefore women and children (Meyer Sabino, 2002, p. 152; Castelnuovo Frigessi, 1977, p. xxxiv; Frigerio Martina, 2012; Frigerio Martina and Burgherr, 1992; Ricciardi, 2010).

Another important cause of illegal immigration was the demand of many Swiss employers for moonlighting. That led to the arrival of a large numbers of Italian workers with just tourist passports. Surprisingly, they were allowed in by the Swiss border guards after a medical selection. This practice demonstrated the tolerance and complicity of the authority. After 20 years of tolerance, in 1965 the Confederation decided to block the influx of illegal immigrants and "false tourists" in order to restrict the "*überfremdung*" and the high level of economic activity due to the many cheap foreign workers. On that occasion it was stated that, together with the arrival of 1,500 regular Italians per day, there were at least 700 Italian "false tourists" per day who were blocked at entry, that is to say 32 per cent of all arrivals.[6] In the previous years too, the ratio of illegal migrants was quite high: according to the Italian consulate in Brig, among the 3,336 Italian workers entered by that border post during August 1961, 701 of them had no work contract, 18 were going to well-known employers, but without contract and with the simple tourist passport, and 206 were looking for a job, they had neither passport, nor contract, that is to say they were real clandestine migrants: the illegal migrants were, thus, 28 per cent of all arrivals. Among the 7,014 Italians workers who entered that same month through the border post of Chiasso, 675 were unemployed persons looking for a job and lacking in all the due documents, that is to say complete stowaways. In 1961, among the 161,293 Italians entered by Chiasso, 20,189 were "lacking in prescribed documents and looking for a job", that is to say 12.5 per cent.[7]

The illegal arrival of Italian immigrants to the German Federal Republic consisted both of persons coming directly from Italy, and of Italians residing in neighbouring European countries. The presence of women, who were mainly sought for domestic work, was considerable. However, this illegal flux lasted only a few years from the beginning of the mass immigration in Germany (late 1950s). In fact, the introduction in the 1960s of free movement of European workers within the Community made it unnecessary to have a work contract before entering (Romero, 1991, pp. 104–108; Rinauro, 2009, pp. 112–115).

In any event, it was in France that illegal Italian immigration reached its highest number, and this was due mainly to the more than tolerant attitude of the French authorities. Between 1946 and the end the of the 1950s, about 50 per cent of workers from Italy entered illegally or as "false tourists", and about 90 per cent of the families who joined them in France did so illegally. There were many reasons for such an extensive flow of migrants: during negotiations for the first migration agreements, Paris accepted the illegal immigrants en masse in order to oblige Rome to accept inferior conditions for legal immigrants in the treaties. Until 1948 Rome prohibited the recruitment of emigrants by name to prevent France from taking its most qualified workers, who were most useful for the reconstruction. This meant that French businesses resorted to recruiting them illegally. At the same time, the legal recruiting system was too impersonal, it selected workers unknown by French employers in Italy and sent them to employers unknown by Italian workers. Thus, both often preferred to meet informally by means of illegal expatriation in order to choose one another.

Generally French authorities regularized this kind of work relationship, but for Italians apprehended crossing the Alps illegally their frequent regularization was a painful process. Apart from those who died in the attempt, those apprehended were placed in concentration camps ("camps de rassemblement"), selected and regularized on condition that they accepted to work in mines, as day labourers on farms, or to enrol in the French Foreign Legion to fight in Indochina and in Algeria. Those who refused these jobs or arrived during economic recessions were thrown out back to Italy.

There were also "ethnic engineering" objectives that induced the French authorities to encourage illegal arrivals: in 1947 the Algerians were declared French citizens, thus obtaining freedom of immigration into France as well as priority over foreign immigrants in access to work. Since it could not prevent this process legally, Paris decided to discourage the influx of Algerians, considering them "unassimilable", and allowing illegal Italian immigrants to saturate the market. As for the enormous illegal influx of the Italians' families, the law allowed family reunions only if there was suitable accommodation: due to the scarcity and appalling quality of housing for immigrants, many Italians were obliged to bring in their families in violation of the law. The authorities tolerated that practice in order to favour the demographic aim they attributed to the Italian family immigration. What is more, through its official recruiting service the state-controlled economy in France imposed the profession, employer and sole district of residence, so many Italians preferred to enter illegally in order to choose their own job freely.

Nevertheless, the causes that mostly led the French authorities to encourage illegal immigration were the bureaucratic delays in official recruiting and the terrible living and work conditions for legal immigrants: because of these conditions, regular immigration was far lower than that required by the migration treaties, so Paris decided to make up for the lack of regular immigrants by taking in illegal ones. In the end, the tolerance of illegal immigration became the means with which France competed with other immigrant-receiving countries in getting its hands on foreign workers.

Demand for manpower and the migration of Italians to France reached its height at the start of the European "economic miracle", between 1956 and 1958, and it was paradoxically at that very time that illegal immigration from Italy reached its apex: of the 80,000 Italians who arrived in 1957, almost 36,000 – in other words, 45 per cent – entered illegally or as regular "tourists".

This entry through the side door of illegality had an extremely high cost, however: apart from the insecurity and exploitation to which many illegal immigrants were subjected, crossing the Alps on foot cost many Italians their lives, and women and children in particular, and over 1,000 Italians died in the Indochina War. Most of these were illegal immigrants who had been convinced to join the Foreign Legion by the threat of repatriation for illegal immigration (Rinauro, 2009, pp. 148–410; 2005a, pp. 4–48; Gastaut and Hanus, 2011).

In conclusion, in Switzerland and in France the restrictive nature of the migration policies was designed to reduce the number of foreign workers and to get rid of them during the economic crisis, but it was an obstacle to attracting foreign workforce during growth phases. Illegal migration managed by the state aimed, therefore, to give the necessary flexibility to the rigid legal framework.

One can suppose that illegal migration was exclusively a matter of Italian workers, perhaps inscribed in their traditional custom and impatience regarding bureaucratic rules. In reality, when the Community Code on Free Movement of the communitarian workers led to the decline of Italian illegal migration in Europe, the workers of some European nations not yet included in the Community began the first supply of illegal manpower in Western Europe. Among the 900,000 Portuguese workers that entered France between 1957 and 1974, 600,000 were illegal migrants or "false tourists", that is to say 67 per cent, and during the 1960s about 50 per cent of the Spanish workers in West Germany had no resident or work permit. Therefore, illegal migration in the European receiving countries during "Les Trente Glorieuses" was deeply inscribed in the nature of their migration policies, in the familiarity of their labour market with moonlighting and in a large and sometime planned tolerance by the state (Pereira, 2012; Sanz Díaz, 2004; Babiano and Fernández Asperilla, 2002).

The initial lack of an immigration policy and the spontaneous arrival of foreign workers in Italy: the size of the dimension of illegal immigration

After more than a century of mass emigration, during the 1970s and the 1980s Italy had some difficulties to conceive herself as an immigrant country. Otherwise, in that period foreign workers were few, mainly seasonal and quite invisible in many areas of the country. Thus, with the exception of the articles of the Testo Unico di Polizia of 1931 on stay permit for foreign citizens, the first law on immigration was promulgated only in 1986. At the same time, because of the economic crisis during the 1970s and the early 1980s, the traditional receiving nations of Europe officially closed the recruitment of foreign workers. The closing of North Europe and the lack of immigration laws and, consequently, of border surveillance in South Europe was one the first causes of the arrival of migrants in Italy and of their often illegal status of residence (Pugliese, 2006, pp. 82, 114–115, 120, 125–126).

As a result of that deficiency in border controls and of the long-lasting general low interest in immigration, surveys of the number of clandestine immigrants and of irregular ones (persons that entered with a tourist passport and stayed after its expiration, *overstayers*) were very hypothetical, varying between 500,000 and one million in the late 1980s, an enormous proportion considering that the first reliable number of regular stay permits was, in 1992, 650,000. According to Istat (National Institute of Statistics), on the contrary, in 1989 irregular immigrants were 30–35 per cent of all extra-communitarian persons (Bade, 2001, pp. 357–358; Barbagli, 2008, pp. 87–88).

Since the late 1980s Italian public opinion has voiced increasing worry regarding the rapid increase of both legal and illegal immigration. At the same time the government claimed for the regularization of those who could present a legal work contract, both for taxation aims and to hinder the informal economy. Thus, the first Italian law on immigration, Law 943 of 30 December 1986, established equality of treatment (as for labour and welfare rights) for Italian and foreign workers and promulgated the first general regularization of clandestine and irregulars foreign workers ("*sanatoria*"). Thus, the many following general and partial regularizations (1986, 1990, 1995, 1998, 2002, 2009) were among the means to survey the size of illegal migrants. The ratio of undocumented migrants regularized on those occasions in the total foreign born population in Italy varied considerably, from 14 per cent in 1986 to 32.6 per cent in 2002 (Fasani, 2010, p. 170; Fasani, 2009, pp. 92–93; Istat, 2008).

In reality, these proportions deeply underestimated the real size and ratio of undocumented foreign workers, indeed not every undocumented stranger decided to apply for regularization and, above all, many employers did not give them the legal work contract required for their regularization. Moreover, till the first half of the 1990s data on the total foreign presence in Italy were quite inaccurate. As a matter of fact, the most reliable investigations on undocumented migrants registered a higher number and percentage of them. In 1986 they were estimated being 294,000–355,000, comprising 41–46 per cent of the total foreign presence; in 1990 307,000–604,000, 31–47 per cent; in 1994 465,000–564,000, 38-43 per cent; in 1998 176,000–295,000, 18–24 per cent (Fasani, 2009, pp. 92–93; Strozza, 2004, p. 313). These data relate to the stocks of undocumented and irregular immigrants. As for the inflow, the Italian Ministry of Internal Affairs estimated an average yearly inflow of 176,000 undocumented and irregular immigrants between 1998–2002 (Ministero dell'Interno, 2007, p. 337).

The frequent regularizations (typical device of the Italian migration policy aimed to correct the illegal effects of the official policy of recruitment) caused the recurrent falls in the number of illegal strangers. Even if, after a few years and also because of the many false work contracts allowed to regularize the undocumented strangers, their number quickly increased, thus requiring a new general regularization.[8] Anyway, the general effect of the mass regularization is a constant fall in ratio – but not in number – of the undocumented immigrants, especially since the greater regularization of 2002. According to the more reliable investigations, by Fondazione ISMU (Iniziative e Studi sulla Multietnicità), between 2005 and 2008 the number of undocumented migrants rose from 541,000 to 651,000, that is to say from 16.1 per cent to 15.00 per cent of the total foreign presence (Fasani, 2010, p. 170).[9]

In conclusion, during the 1980s and the 1990s the ratio of the undocumented immigrants to the total number of immigrants was very high (about 40–50 per cent) and roughly the same as that experienced by the Italians in France and in Switzerland and by the Spanish migrants in West Germany during "Les Trente Glorieuses", while less than that experienced by the Portuguese in France. Since the beginning of the 2000s the ratio of the current undocumented migrants in Italy (about 15 per cent) has been much reduced and, above all, far less than the one of the Southern European migrants in Europe after the Second World War. The yearly average inflow of 176,000 undocumented and irregular immigrants (1998–2002) in Italy is high, but it must be noticed that it is the result of many of the foreign nationalities entering Italy, while only about 30,000 Italian clandestine workers entered France between 1946 and 1947. Thus, if we consider each national group and not the total inflow, Italian illegal migration frequently was higher than currently not only in ratio, but also in number.

Nonetheless, the number of illegal persons regularized from 1986 to 2002–2004 (1,486,398) is very important. Moreover, with regard to Italian migration policy, also the official procedure for asking new immigrants by means of the annual "flow decree" is, in part, a procedure of regularization of the illegal immigrants still present in Italy. Thus, it is certain that more than half of the actual legal immigrants in Italy were once illegal and obtained legal status through the amnesties or the "flows decrees" (Barbagli *et al.*, 2004, p. 8; Pugliese, 2006, p. 135; Fasani, 2010, p. 171). Moreover, the Romanians were the first national group of undocumented migrants, but their inclusion in EU free circulation, since 2007, automatically regularized those who were undocumented. This is one of the reasons for the decrease in the ratio of illegal migrants in recent years.[10]

As for the general regularization, there are similarities with the Italian experience, in fact the French government used to establish recurrent collective regularizations of all foreign undocumented persons who could show a legal work contract or accepted jobs by the authorities or accepted to enlist in the French Foreign Legion. In contrast, in Switzerland regularizations were individual and quite unofficial: during the periods of tolerance towards the "false tourists", the Swiss border agents only advised illegal Italians to reach the nearest Italian consulate to apply for a work passport. Especially since the early 1960s Italian diplomacy began to largely support this procedure (Rinauro, 2009, pp. 148–410).[11]

The geography of undocumented immigrants: entry routes, countries of origin, geographical distribution in Italy

One may think that most undocumented immigrants come to Italy by landing on its shores. Indeed, this is the more frequent image in the media and political discourse because of its evocative power. In reality, between 2000 and 2006 only 4–16 per cent of undocumented immigrants came in this way, 15–34 per cent crossed the land borders in the North of Italy, arriving especially from Slovenia and France, or comfortably landed in ports and airports with false papers. By far the majority of the illegal migrants (65–70 per cent) arrive legally as tourists and stays beyond the expiration of their visas (*overstayers*) (European Migration Network, 2005, pp. 16–18; Fasani, 2010, pp. 172–174; Ministero dell'Interno, 2007, p. 336). This is another similarity with the Southern European illegal migrants during the first decades after the Second World War, but it is difficult to know the ratio between the completely undocumented migrants and the *overstayers*. The ratio of completely clandestine immigrants in France seems larger than in Switzerland, where the "false tourists" prevailed. Indeed, with the exception of the asylum seekers, who have no possibility to get a tourist passport from their persecutor authorities or foreign consulates and, consequently, are obliged to migrate in a clandestine way; since hidden crossing of the sea and land borders is a very dangerous and expensive way, it is thus chosen by a minority of migrants.

As we saw, many undocumented Italians died crossing the Alps, but it is difficult to count them and determine their ratio. Anyway, one can suppose that crossing the Alps, especially with the help of a smuggler, was less dangerous and fatal than crossing the 355 km of sea between Tripoli and Lampedusa, especially with a tramp ship (*carretta del mare*) or a dinghy. As for the number of illegal migrants who died crossing the Mediterranean towards Italy, the more reliable figures are those collected by means of the international press by the private organization Fortress Europe. According to this, among the 19,372 persons who died since 1988 trying to reach Europe, 7,999 died in the Mediterranean on their voyage to Italy, the majority coming from North Africa to Sicily and a minority crossing from Albania to Apulia. However, these data deeply underestimate the real number of victims and don't include the thousands of persons who died in the Sahara Desert trying to reach the North Africa coast to board for Italy, and in addition the data do not include those persons who died crossing the Alps (Fortress Europe, 2014). Moreover, it is difficult to establish the ratio of the victims to the total number of the undocumented immigrants. Thus, as for the victims, we can ascertain the similarity with the Italian illegal migrants' experience only at a qualitative and moral level.

At a regional level the proportion of the undocumented migrants in the total number of regional immigrants (legal and illegal) is higher in the South of Italy (due to the local higher level of moonlighting), but at a national level they are much more present in the North and Central Italy (75 per cent of them in 2005), because in general most of the strangers live there. In 2005 more than half were Eastern European citizens, especially Romanians and Albanians; one-sixth were from North Africa and one-tenth from Asia, Oceania, sub-Saharan Africa and Latin America (Fasani, 2010, p. 173; European Migration Network, Italian National Contact Point, 2005, p. 14). In fact, this is another similarity with the Italian illegal immigrants, most of whom went to the nearest countries (France, Switzerland, Belgium, West Germany), but only in part is this due to geographical reasons: they went there especially because those countries were the most developed and were looking for immigrants. Indeed, Portuguese and Spanish migrants went to the same receiving countries even if for them they were further than for Italians, and generally were not border nations. On the contrary, geography today is more determining, for Italy is geographically the compulsory path to Europe from sub-Saharan regions and North Africa.

The causes of illegal immigration and the Italian policy of recruitment

Apart from the geographical cause (Italy is the compulsory door of Europe for migrants coming from Africa), scholars agree with three main causes of illegal immigration. First, the large scale of the underground economy and moonlighting in Italy (Reyneri, 2003, 2004; Carchedi *et al.*, 2003; Barbagli, 2008, pp. 104–104; Maroukis *et al.*, 2011; Ambrosini, 1997, 1999; Chiuri *et al.*, 2007). If employers didn't hire persons without official papers, such persons wouldn't come. On the contrary, the underground economy looks especially for them for they are needier and, consequently, open to blackmail and willing to accept work off the books. In 2008 the size of the underground economy in Italy was 17.5 per cent of the GDP or 20.6 per cent considering only the GDP of market activities (exclusive of the public administration activities), that is to say one of the bigger in the EU (Istat, 2010). In 2010 the rate of irregular work was 12.3 per cent, which means 2,600,000 workers (Istat, 2010, pp. 6–8, 2011, pp. 256–260; CNEL, 2011, p. 135). Due to the many amnesties, the units of irregular work of clandestine foreign citizens reduced from 721,000 in 2001 to 377,000 in 2009, which means from 22.0 per cent to 12.7 per cent of the total irregular workers (Italians and strangers). But in addition are the uncertain number of regular foreign citizens working without a work contract (Istat, 2010, pp. 6–8). Anyway, according to ISMU in 2009 32 per cent of the foreign workers were not in possession of a legal work contract, but the legal contract is the condition required by the prefectures to give and to renew the residence permit. Thus, work off the books is the first cause of entering an illegal stay for those who entered legally by means of official recruitment and tourist visa (ISMU *et al.*, 2010, pp. 17, 117). The economic branches where irregular work is more widespread are farming, services for persons and building, that is to say the most important jobs for the presence of foreign citizens.[12]

In conclusion, underground economy and moonlighting as a cause of illegal immigration has a strong analogy with the causes of Italian illegal migration in Europe after the Second World War.

The second important cause of illegal immigration is the great disproportion between the demand for foreign workers by firms and families and the official restrictive recruitment system. Here we can observe the most important similarity with the causes of the Italian illegal emigration in Europe: according to Italian law, nobody can enter Italy to look for a job, foreign citizens can come only if they are requested individually. Italy, thus, adopts the same principle that in vain she opposed for her emigrants till the advent of the Community Code on the Free Movement of Communitarian Workers. Indeed, Law 40 of 6 March 1998 (*legge Turco-Napolitano*) established a quota system of recruitment: every autumn the Ministry of the Interior enacts the "flow decree" establishing the number of new immigrant workers. The annual quota was around 60,000 between 1998 and 2000, then increased to 80,000 and reached 550,000 in 2006, 170,000 in 2007 and 150,000 in 2008. Then, because of the crisis, it vastly decreased or was addressed only to the seasonal workers. But in general, except for 2006, the demand for foreign workers was far bigger than the annual quota, so many of the candidate immigrants for whom employers applied too late to include them in the quota had the mathematical certainty to find a job in Italy, even if they entered without a resident permit. At the same time – and this is another strong similarity with the legal recruitment system faced by Italian emigrants in Europe – the official system is very impersonal: the employer who does not know nominally the foreign worker he needs, has to ask for him by means of the Italian Ministry of the Interior and the diplomacy; once the diplomacy finds a candidate with the professional skill required, sends him to Italy, he/she meets the Italian employer, signs the work contract and, consequently, receives the residence permit. The problem is that the employers generally don't want to hire workers that they have never seen or tested, so they prefer to find workers from the pool of clandestine workers and false tourists still present in Italy and submit them to a probation period. Then, the honest employers try to regularize them by the general amnesty (but the amnesty occurs every four or five years), or by the annual "flow decree". In the last case, the illegal foreign worker goes back to his country and undergoes the official recruitment system, pretending to have never worked in Italy before for the employer who is asking for him. This is the reason why the great majority of illegal immigrants are "false tourists" in *overstayer* status (Borgna, 2011, pp. 17–24, 76–79; Fasani, 2010, pp. 175–177; Einaudi, 2007).

The third cause of illegal immigration is the great number of asylum seekers landing in Italy. Naturally, they cannot ask their persecutor governments, and often the Italian diplomacy in their country, for a passport. Thus, they are obliged to arrive by the most dangerous and expensive entry routes: a hidden crossing of the northern borders and landing on shores of Southern Italy. They travel by the same means of transport of the clandestine workers and mix with them. Their great size in the total number of irregular and undocumented migrants is one of the bigger differences with the Italian emigration experience where, as we saw, the number of illegal migrants for political reasons was quite small, except in the fascist period. Sometime it is impossible to prevent such dangerous and fatal journeys because the political causes of their escapes are quite unpredictable and sudden. Nevertheless, many of them plan to arrive in an illegal and dangerous way because of the very restrictive European and Italian laws on asylum. Once arrived and intercepted, especially since 2005, they are detained in camps (CPT, Centri di permanenza temporanea, now called CIE, Centri di identificazione ed espulsione) waiting for a decision on their application for asylum. In case of refusal (which occurs in the majority of cases) they must be expelled, but the expulsion is often impossible because of its cost and due to humanitarian reasons. So, many of them remain illegally or go abroad illegally (Boldrini, 2013; ICS, Consorzio italiano di solidarietà, 2005; Medici senza frontiere, 2006; Ambrosini and Marcheti, 2008; Hein, 2006; Cherubini, 2012).[13]

The Italian policy on illegal immigration and the attitude of public opinion

Law 39 of 28 February 1990 on immigration (*legge Martelli*) established the expulsion in 15 days of the irregular (*overstayer*) and illegal foreign citizens by an administrative decree of the prefect. In case of refusal by the stranger, he undergoes compulsory transfer to the airport by the security forces. The problem is that no nation accepts to welcome unidentified people, thus, generally the intercepted illegal strangers hide their identity and country of origin and, consequently, Italy succeeds to expel only a small minority of them. In order to get around this device, Law 40 of 6 March 1998 (*Legge Turco-Napolitano*) established their stay for a month in the CPT, Law 189 of 30 July 2002 (*legge Bossi-Fini*) extended the period to two months, and extended further to six months in 2009 and to 18 months in 2011. The idea was that a longer detention could help the investigators to find the real identity of the illegal stranger or induce him to confess it in order to leave the CIE. At the same time Italy established treaties of return of clandestine immigrants with many of the countries of origin in exchange of a preferential quota of legal migrants. At the same time, the law *Turco-Napolitano* established the immediate compulsory transfer to the border of the illegal migrants intercepted during or just after the crossing of the border (the law *Martelli* reserved this procedure only for the recidivists), and the law *Bossi-Fini* established the collection of the fingerprints of any migrant receiving and renewing the residence permit. Nevertheless, the ratio of the irregular and undocumented migrants expelled increased but rarely approached 50 per cent of the intercepted ones, especially since the security forces generally tolerate the irregular migrants working off the books and prosecute only those who commit crimes (Barbagli, 2008, pp. 122, 93–129; Sciortino, 2000, 2004, pp. 91–101). Finally, Law 94 of 15 July 2009 established the crime of clandestine immigration, but overlaps with the previous administrative procedure of expulsion and, in any case, because of lack of men and means, it led neither to a higher rate of expulsions, nor to a deterrent against illegal arrivals, leading to the abolition of the crime in April 2014 (Borgna, 2011, pp. 79–88).[14] As for the Italian control of the labour market against work off the books, the great ratio of the strangers involved in it (32 per cent, as we saw) testifies its deep inadequacy (Barbagli, 2008, pp. 102–104).

In conclusion, the real causes of the relatively lower rate of illegal immigrations of the 2000s and the 2010s compared to the 1990s are the general amnesties and the inclusion of some of the main countries of origin of undocumented migrants in the EU free circulation. On the contrary, the immigration laws and controls failed to limit illegal immigration not only because they lacked the men and the means to implement them, but especially because they didn't face the real causes of illegality: the restrictive official recruitment system, the restrictive policy of asylum, the great size of the underground economy and the lack of inspections of work contracts.

As for the current Italian policies of control, we can easily recognize some other similarities and differences with the Italian illegal emigration during "Les Trente Glorieuses": a similarity is the use of concentration camps (CPT and CIE), but the "camps de rassemblement" of France had the sole aim to permit the sanitarian and professional selection of the illegal Italians and the expulsion of the workers of no use, consequently those migrants were detained as little as possible. The main aim of the French camps was to include, not to exclude foreign workers. Clandestine immigration was a crime in France as it was in Italy from 2009 to 2013. Contrary to the Italian law, the French law stated imprisonment before expelling the illegal migrants, even if imprisonment was uncommon. As in today's Italy, there were expulsions of undocumented migrants crossing the border during the economic crisis, but the receiving countries of Italian migrants never turned them to third and totalitarian nations to do so, as was the case in the rejections of illegal migrants from Italy to Libya (Human Rights Watch, 2009; Messineo, 2006; Vassallo Paleologo, 2009, 2010; Paoletti, 2011).

Anyway, the main difference is cultural: the attitude of the public opinion (and politicians and media) towards the undocumented migrants. Italian migrants suffered xenophobic prejudice in their host countries regardless of legality of their status. In France public opinion rarely worried about the illegal status of the Italian migrants, and when it did happen it was for fear of disloyal competition on the labour market. This led to the demand for their expulsion, but for their regularization too. The equation: clandestine migrant = criminal was absent. Above all, till the 1970s in France illegal immigration was never a central argument for electoral campaigns as it is in Italy since the beginning of mass immigration (Tapinos, 1978, p. 215). In Switzerland the fear of *überfremdung* led in 1970 to a referendum for the limitation of the foreign presence, which meant especially of Italians. Also because of the xenophobic movement, in 1965 the Swiss government established the stop to the arrival and the expulsion of false tourists and undocumented migrants. That xenophobic movement became a political party, the *Schweizer Demokraten,* and later many of its leaders and electors flew into the *Schweizerische Volkspartei* that is today no less than the first party of Switzerland. But in 1965 the stop of the illegal Italian migrants aimed to reduce the presence of foreign citizens regardless to their illegal status. The target was not illegal immigration as it is in today Italy and Europe.

In general, no politician or opinion leader in Italy would openly say today what the director of the Réglementation et des Étrangers of the French Ministry of Interior, Pagès, wrote in 1947 to the prefect of Savoy about Italian illegal immigrants:

Personally I have always been opposed to the systematic expulsion of the clandestine workers, since I believe that the great majority of them, after a medical check and a meticulous examination by the police, could be a useful contribution to our economy.

(Rinauro, 2009, p. 214)[15]

Notes

1 Centre des Archives Contemporaines, Fontainebleau (CAC), Pos. 19900544, Art. 3: programme d'immigration.
2 L'emigrazione clandestina in Francia (1948). *Bollettino quindicinale dell'emigrazione.* 2 (16–17): 331.
3 Emigrazione clandestina (1956). *Bollettino quindicinale dell'emigrazione.* 10 (24): 363.
4 State Central Archives, Rome (ACS), Ministry of Labour and Social Security (MLPS), General Direction of Labour Placing (DGCM), Division of Migration Treaties for Communitarian Countries (DAEPC), b. 386, f. Emigrazione clandestina in Belgio 1946–'51; ACS, MLPS, DGCM, DAEPC, b. 364, f. 1 Emigrazione italiana in Belgio – Informazioni e notizie.
5 MLPS, Servizio per l'Emigrazione Div. X – reclutamento, alla Div. IX, "Svizzera – Reclutamenti abusivi", Rome, 4 June 1954, in ACS, MLPS DCM, DAEPC, b. 385, fasc. Emigrazione clandestina per la Svizzera 1946–1957.
6 ACS, Presidency of the Ministers Council (PCM) 1965–1967, fasc. 2–7 61995.2 "Emigrazione in Svizzera".
7 Emigrazione italiana in Svizzera (1961). *Bollettino quindicinale dell'emigrazione.* 15 (19) 19: 297. Lavoratori italiani in Svizzera (1961). *Bollettino quindicinale dell'emigrazione.* 15 (21): 330. Lavoratori italiani entrati in Svizzera attraverso il valico di Chiasso (1962). *Bollettino quindicinale dell'emigrazione.* 16 (3–4) 3–4: 40–41.
8 As for the illegal tricks and general effects of the Italian regularization of 2002, the largest in Europe, see (Barbagli *et al.*, 2004) and (Ambrosini and Salati, 2004).
9 See the trend (1990–2007) of the estimated undocumented migrants in Italy in Fasani, 2010, p. 171.
10 About the fall in number of illegal workers in the Italian construction industry because of the inclusions of the Romanians in the EU, see data of CRESME: "Nel 2007 + 2.9% gli occupati nel settore edile" (2007). Online, available at: www.edilportale.com/news/2008/11/mercati/nel-2007-+29-gli-occupati-nel-settore-edile_13347_13.html.
11 MLPS, DGOIM, Div. IX to Div. XI, Rome 23/6/1949, "Assistenza ai lavoratori in transito a Briga", in ACS, MLPS, DGCM, DEPE, b. 484, f. "Emigrazione italiana in Svizzera. Informazioni e notizie – Dati statistici. Licenziamenti ecc. – anni 1945–57"; "Concessione del passaporto agli emigranti italiani che giungono in Svizzera muniti della sola carta d'identità" (1961). *Bollettino quindicinale dell'emigrazione.* 15 (1): 11; Italian Embassy in Bern to the Italian Foreign Office (MAE), Bern 14/1/1965, "Nuove misure limitative dell'ingresso e impiego dei lavoratori stranieri", in ACS, PCM 1965–1967, b. 474, f. 2–7 61995.2 "Emigrazione. Assistenza emigranti italiani all'estero 1965–67", f. "Emigrazione in Svizzera".
12 As for the foreign citizens' irregular work in building see (CRESME, 2006, p. 87).
13 CPT, Amnesty: "Violati i diritti dei rifugiati" (2005). *Melting Pot*, 21 May. Online, available at: www.meltingpot.org/articolo5596.html.
14 Via il reato di immigrazione clandestina. Il Senato approva l'emendamento del M5s (2013). *Corriere della Sera*. 10 October 2013. Online, available at: www.corriere.it/cronache/13_ottobre_09/via-reato-immigrazione-clandestina-senato-approva-l-emendamento-m5s-fe96b7d2–310b-11e3-b3e3–02ebe4aec272.shtml.
15 For the Italian current prejudice against illegal migrants and its usefulness in the electoral campaigns see Fasani, 2010, pp. 177–181, 2009, pp. 69–82 and Barbagli, 2008, pp. 137–156.

References

Ambrosini, M. (1999). *Utili invasori. L'inserimento degli immigrati nel mercato del lavoro italiano.* Milan: F. Angeli.

Ambrosini, M. (ed.) (1997). *Lavorare nell'ombra. L'inserimento degli immigrati nell'economia informale.* Milan: ISMU.

Ambrosini, M. and Marchetti, C. (ads.) (2008). *Cittadini possibili. Un nuovo approccio all'accoglienza e all'integrazione dei rifugiati.* Milan: F. Angeli.

Ambrosini, M. and Salati, M. (eds) (2004). *Uscendo dall'ombra. Il processo di regolarizzazione degli immigrati e i suoi limiti.* Milan: F. Angeli.

Audenino, P. and Tirabassi, M. (2008). *Migrazioni italiane. Storia e storie dall'Ancien régime a oggi.* Milan: B. Mondadori.

Babiano, J. and Fernández Asperilla, A. (2002). *El fenómeno de la irregularidad en la emigración española de los años sesanta.* Madrid: Fundación 1° de Mayo.

Bade, K. (2001). *L'Europa in movimento. Le migrazioni dal Settecento a oggi.* Rome-Bari, Laterza.

Barbagli, M. (2008). *Immigrazione e sicurezza in Italia.* Bologna: Il Mulino, Bologna.

Barbagli, M., Colombo, A. and Sciortino, G. (eds) (2004). *I sommersi e i sanati. La regolarizzazione degli immigrati in Italia.* Bologna: Il Mulino.

Bertagna, F. (2006). *La patria di riserva. L'emigrazione fascista in Argentina.* Rome: Donzelli.

Bertonha, J. F. (2001). Emigrazione e politica estera: la "diplomazia sovversiva" di Mussolini e la questione degli italiani all'estero, 1922–1945. *Altreitalie.* 23 (2): 39–61.

Boldrini, L. (2013). *Tutti indietro. Storie di uomini e donne in fuga e di come l'Italia li accoglie tra paura e solidarietà.* Milan: Rizzoli.

Borgna, P. (2011). *Clandestinità (e altri errori di destra e di sinistra).* Rome-Bari: Laterza, Roma-Bari.

Borruso, P. (2001). Note sull'emigrazione clandestina italiana (1876–1976). *Giornale di storia contemporanea.* 4 (1): 141–161.

Cannistraro, P. V. and Rosoli, G. (1979). Fascist Emigration Policy in the 1920s. An Interpretative Framework. *International Migration Review.* 13 (4) xiii: 673–692.

Capuzzi, L. (2006). *La frontiera immaginata. Profilo politico e sociale dell'emigrazione italiana in Argentina nel secondo dopoguerra.* Milan: F. Angeli.

Carchedi, F., Mottura, G. and Pugliese, E. (eds) (2003). *Il lavoro servile e le nuove schiavitù.* Milan: F. Angeli.

Carpi, L. (1874). *Delle colonie e dell'emigrazione d'italiani all'estero.* Milan: Tip. Editrice Lombarda, vol. III.

Castelnuovo Frigessi, D. (1977). *Elvezia, il tuo governo. Gli operai italiani emigrati in Svizzera.* Turin: Einaudi.

Cherubini, F. (2012). *L'asilo dalla Convenzione di Ginevra al diritto dell'Unione Europea.* Bari: Cacucci.

Chiuri, M. C., Coniglio, N. and Ferri, G. (2007). *L'esercito degli invisibili. Aspetti economici dell'immigrazione clandestina.* Bologna: Il Mulino.

Cioli, M. G. (1989) Il passaporto falso. Vagabondi, clandestini, renitenti in alcuni documenti della prefettura di Genova. In Gibelli, A. (ed.) *La via delle Americhe. L'emigrazione ligure tra evento e racconto.* Genoa: Sagep.

CNEL (2011). *Rapporto sul mercato del lavoro 2010–2011.* Rome: CNEL.

Colucci, M. (2008). *Lavoro in movimento. L'emigrazione italiana in Europa, 1945–57.* Rome: Donzelli.

Commissariato generale per l'emigrazione (1926). *L'emigrazione italiana dal 1919 al 1923.* Rome: CGE.

Concessione del passaporto agli emigranti italiani che giungono in Svizzera muniti della sola carta d'identità (1961). *Bollettino quindicinale dell'emigrazione.* 15 (1): 11.

CPT, Amnesty: "Violati i diritti dei rifugiati" (2005). *Melting Pot*, 21 May. Online, available at: www.meltingpot.org/articolo5596.html.

CRESME (2006). *Lavoro e costruzioni: fabbisogni, mutamenti e mercati*. Rome: CRESME 2006.

De Clementi, A. (2002). La legislazione dei paesi d'arrivo. In Bevilacqua, P., De Clementi, A. and Franzina, E. (eds) *Storia dell'emigrazione italiana*, vol. ii *Arrivi*. Rome: Donzelli.

Demangeon, A. and Mauco, G. (1939). *Documents pour servir à l'étude des étrangers dans l'agriculture française*. Paris: Hermann & CIE.

Devoto, F. J. (2000). Inmigrantes, refugiados y criminales en la "vía italiana" hacia la Argentina en la segunda posguerra. *Ciclos*. 19 (1): 151–176.

Divine, R. A. (1957). *American Immigration Policy, 1924–1952*. New Haven: Yale University Press.

Einaudi, L. (2007). *Le politiche dell'immigrazione in Italia dall'Unità ad oggi*. Rome-Bari: Laterza.

Emigrazione clandestina (1956). *Bollettino quindicinale dell'emigrazione*, 10 (24): 361–363.

Emigrazione Italiana in Svizzera (1961). *Bollettino quindicinale dell'emigrazione*. 15 (19): 297.

European Migration Network, Italian National Contact Point (2005). *Immigrazione irregolare in Italia*. Rome: Idos, Roma 2005.

Fasani, F. (2009). *Undocumented Migration: Counting the Uncountable: Data and Trends across Europe: Country Report Italy*. Brussels: European Commission.

Fasani, F. (2010). The quest for La Dolce Vita? Undocumented migration in Italy. In Triandafyllidou, A. (ed.), *Irregular Migration in Europe: Myths and Realities*. Surrey: Ashgate Publishing Co.

Fortress Europe (2014). *La fortezza*. Online, available at: http://fortresseurope.blogspot.it/p/la-fortezza.html.

Franzese, P. (1996). L'emigrazione negli Stati Uniti d'America ai primi del '900 attraverso i documenti della Questura di Napoli, conservati nell'Archivio di Stato. In Spikes, D. (ed.) *Stati Uniti a Napoli: rapporti consolari 1796–1996*. Naples: Filema.

Franzina, E. and Sanfilippo, M. (eds) (2003). *Il fascismo e gli emigrati. La parabola dei Fasci italiani all'estero (1920–1943)*. Rome-Bari: Laterza.

Frescura, B. (1904). *Dell'emigrazione clandestina italiana diretta ai Porti Esteri e di alcuni mezzi pratici che potrebbero essere adottati per frenarla*. Genoa: Montorfano.

Frigerio Martina, M. (2012). *Bambini proibiti. Storie di famiglie italiane in Svizzera tra clandestinità e separazione*. Trento: Il Margine.

Frigerio Martina, M. and Burgherr, S. (1992). *Versteckte Kinder: zwischen Illegalität und Trennung: Saisonnierkinder und ihre Eltern erzählen*. Lucerne: Rex Verlag.

Gani, L. (1972). *Syndicats et travailleurs immigrés*. Paris: Editions sociales.

Gastaut, Y. and Hanus, P. (2011). Migrants italiens dans les Alpes françaises après 1945. Une mobilité sous surveillance? *La pierre et l'écrit*, 22 (1): 183–207.

Hein, C. (eds) (2006). *Rifugiati. Vent'anni di storia del diritto d'asilo in Italia*. Rome: Donzelli.

Henneresse, M. C. (1978). *Le patronat et la politique française d'immigration 1945–1975*. Paris: PhD dissertation, Institut d'Etudes Politiques.

Higham, J. (1965). *Strangers in the Land. Patterns of American Nativism*. New York: Atheneum.

Human Rights Watch (2009). *Scacciati e schiacciati. L'Italia e il respingimento di migranti e richiedenti asilo, la Libia e il maltrattamento di migranti e richiedenti asilo*.

New York: Human Rights Watch. Online, available at: www.hrw.org/sites/default/files/reports/italy0909itweb.pdf.

Hutchinson, E. P. (1981). *A Legislative History of American Immigration Policy 1798–1965*. Philadelphia: University of Pennsylvania Press.

ICS, Consorzio italiano di solidarietà (2005). *La protezione negata. Primo rapporto sul diritto d'asilo in Italia*. Milan: Feltrinelli.

ISMU, CENSIS and IPRS (eds) (2010). *Immigrazione e lavoro. Percorsi lavorativi, Centri per l'impiego, politiche attive*. Milan: ISMU.

Istat (2008). *Permessi di soggiorno per motivo della presenza e sesso al 1 gennaio. Anni 1992–2007*. Online, available at: http://demo.istat.it/altridati/permessi/serie/tab_1.pdf.

Istat (2010). *La misura dell'economia sommersa secondo le statistiche ufficiali. Anni 2000–2008*. Rome: Istat.

Istat (2011). *Rapporto annuale. La situazione del paese nel 2010*. Rome: Istat, Roma.

Istituto storico della Resistenza e della società contemporanea in provincia di Cuneo (ed.) (2007). *Ebrei in fuga attraverso le Alpi*. Turin: Regione Piemonte. Online, available at: www.memoriadellealpi.net/index.php?method=news&cat=57&action=zoom&id=188.

L'emigrazione clandestina in Francia (1948). *Bollettino quindicinale dell'emigrazione*, 2 (16–17): 327–349.

Labanca, N. (2000). Politica e propaganda: emigrazione e fasci all'estero. In Collotti, E. *et al. Fascismo e politica di potenza. Politica estera 1922–1939*. Scandicci: La Nuova Italia.

Lavoratori italiani entrati in Svizzera attraverso il valico di Chiasso (1962). *Bollettino quindicinale dell'emigrazione*. 16 (3–4): 40–41.

Lavoratori italiani in Svizzera (1961). *Bollettino quindicinale dell'emigrazione*. 15 (21) 21: 330.

Luconi, S. (2000). *La "diplomazia parallela". Il regime fascista e la mobilitazione politica degli italo-americani*. Milan: F. Angeli.

Lupo, S. (1996). *Storia della Mafia dalle origini ai giorni nostri*. Rome: Donzelli, Roma.

Maltone, C. (1988). L'introduction de la main-d'œuvre italienne en France, entre les deux guerres. In Cedei *L'immigration italienne en France dans les années 20. Acte du colloque franco – italien, Paris 15–17 octobre 1987*. Paris: Cedei.

Manzotti, F. (1962). *La polemica sull'emigrazione nell'Italia unita. Fino alla prima guerra mondiale*. Milan: Dante Alighieri.

Maroukis, T., Iglicka, K. and Gmaj, K. (2011). Irregular Migration and Informal Economy in Southern and Central-Eastern Europe: Breaking the Vicious Circle? *International Migration*. 49 (5): 129–156.

Martellini, A. (2001). Il commercio dell'emigrazione: intermediari e agenti. In Bevilacqua, P., De Clementi, A. and Franzina, E. (eds), *Storia dell'emigrazione italiana*, vol. I, *Partenze*. Rome: Donzelli.

Martellone, A. M. (ed.) (1980). *La questione dell'immigrazione negli Stati Uniti*. Bologna: Il Mulino.

Masi, G. (2003). Tra spirito d'avventura e ricerca dell' "agognato peculio": linee di tendenza dell'emigrazione calabrese tra Ottocento e Novecento. In Sanfilippo, M. (ed.) *Emigrazione e storia d'Italia*. Cosenza: L. Pellegrini.

Mauco, G. (1932). *Les étrangers en France. Leur rôle dans l'activité économique*. Parigi: Colin.

Medici senza frontiere (2006). *Oltre la frontiera. Le barriere al riconoscimento del diritto d'asilo in Italia*. Milan: F. Angeli.

Messineo, F. (2006). Refoulement verso il Nord Africa e diritti dei migranti. *L'altro diritto. Centro di documentazione su carcere, devianza e marginalità*. Online, available at: www.altrodiritto.unifi.it/frontier/storia/messineo.htm#9.

Meyer Sabino, G. (2002). In Svizzera. In Bevilacqua, P., De Clementi, A. and Franzina, E. (eds) *Storia dell'emigrazione italiana*, vol. II. *Arrivi*. Rome: Donzelli.

Ministero dell'Interno (2007). *Rapporto sulla criminalità in Italia*. Rome: Ministero dell'Interno. Online, available at: www.interno.gov.it/mininterno/export/sites/default/it/assets/files/14/0900_rapporto_criminalita.pdf.

Molinari, A. (1995). Storia e storie di emigrazione dal Ponente Ligure. Alcuni percorsi di ricerca. In Corti, P. and Schor, R. (eds) L'esodo frontaliero: gli italiani nella Francia meridionale. *Recherches régionales*. 35 (3) xxxv: 140–148.

Morelli, A. (2002). In Belgio. In Bevilacqua, P., De Clementi, A. and Franzina, E. (eds) *Storia dell'emigrazione italiana*, vol. ii. *Arrivi*. Rome: Donzelli.

Nel 2007 + 2.9% gli occupati nel settore edile (2007). Online, available at: www.edilportale.com/news/2008/11/mercati/nel-2007-+29-gli-occupati-nel-settore-edile_13347_13.html.

Ostuni, M. R. (2001). Leggi e politiche di governo nell'Italia liberale e fascista. In Bevilacqua, P., De Clementi, A. and Franzina, E. (eds), *Storia dell'emigrazione italiana*, vol. I, *Partenze*. Rome: Donzelli.

Paoletti, E. (2011). *The Migration of Power and North–South Inequalities: The case of Italy and Libya*. Basingstoke: Palgrave Macmillan.

Pereira, V. (2012). *La dictature de Salazar face à l'émigration. L'État portugais et ses migrants en France (1957–1974)*. Paris: SciencesPo Les Presses.

Porcella, M. (1998). *Con arte e con inganno. L'emigrazione girovaga nell'Appennino ligure-emiliano*. Genoa: Sagep.

Pugliese, E. (2006). *L'Italia tra migrazioni internazionali e migrazioni interne*. Bologna: Il Mulino.

Rapone, L. (2008). Emigrazione italiana e antifascismo in esilio. *Archivio storico dell'emigrazione italiana*. 4 (1): 53–67.

Reyneri, E. (2003). Immigration and the underground economy in new receiving South European countries: manifold negative effects: manifold deep-rooted causes. *International Review of Sociology*. 13 (1): 117–143.

Reyneri, E. (2004). Immigrants in a segmented and often undeclared labour market. *Journal of Modern Italian Studies*. 9 (1): 71–93.

Ricciardi, T. (2010). I figli degli stagionali: bambini clandestini. *Studi emigrazione*. 180 (4): 872–886.

Rinauro, S. (2005a). Percorsi dell'emigrazione italiana negli anni della ricostruzione: morire a Dien Bien Phu da emigrante clandestino. *Altreitalie*, 31 (2): 4–48.

Rinauro, S. (2005b). Politica e geografia dell'emigrazione italiana negli anni della ricostruzione. In Ganapini, L. (ed.), *L'Italia alla metà del XX secolo. Conflitto sociale, Resistenza, costruzione di una democrazia*. Milan: Guerini.

Rinauro, S. (2009). *Il cammino della speranza. L'emigrazione clandestina degli italiani nel secondo dopoguerra*. Turin: Einaudi.

Rinauro, S. (2010). Le statistiche ufficiali dell'emigrazione italiana tra propaganda politica e inafferrabilità dei flussi. *Quaderni storici*. 45 (2): 393–418.

Romero, F. (1991). *Emigrazione e integrazione europea 1945–1973*. Rome: Edizioni Lavoro.

Sanfilippo, M. (2011). La clandestinità è una storia vecchia: note su alcuni aspetti dell'emigrazione irregolare di italiani. *Giornale di storia contemporanea*. 14 (2): 227–236.

Sanz Díaz, C. (2004). *Clandestinos, Ilegales, Espontáneos. La emigración irregular de españoles a Alemania en el contexto de las relaciones hispano-alemanas, 1960–1973.* Madrid: Comisíon española de istoria de las relaciones internacionales.

Sciortino, G. (2000). *L'ambizione della frontiera. Le politiche di controllo migratorio in Europa.* Milan: F. Angeli.

Sciortino, G. (2004). Le politiche di controllo migratorio nel contesto dei sistemi migratori mediterranei. In ISMU, *Nono rapporto sulle migrazioni.* Milan: F. Angeli.

Sereni, A. (1994). *Clandestini del mare. L'emigrazione ebraica in terra d'Israele dal 1945 al 1948.* Milan: Mursia.

Setta, S. (1993). *Profughi di lusso. Industriali e manager di Stato dal fascismo alla epurazione mancata.* Milan: F. Angeli.

Sezzi, L. and Sigman, N. (2003). "Pionieri del progresso". L'impresa Borsari in Terra del Fuoco. *Storia e problemi contemporanei.* 34 (3): 113–132.

Sori, E. (1979). *L'emigrazione italiana dall'Unità alla seconda guerra mondiale.* Bologna: Il Mulino, Bologna.

Strozza, S. (2004). Estimates of the illegal foreigners in Italy: a review of the literature. *International Migration Review.* 38 (1): 309–331.

Tapinos, G. (1978). Enquête sur les perspectives des émigrations à long terme en R.F.A. et en France. *Studi emigrazione.* 50 (2): 213–245.

Tichenor, D. (2003). *Dividing Lines: the Politics of Immigration Control in America.* Princeton: Princeton University Press.

Tombaccini-Villefranque, S. (1999). La frontière bafouée: migrants clandestins et passeurs dans la vallée de la Roya (1920–1940). *Cahiers de la Méditerranée.* 58 (1): 79–95.

Toscano, M. (1990). *La porta di Sion. L'Italia e l'immigrazione clandestina ebraica in Palestina (1945–1948).* Bologna: Il Mulino.

Van Dongen, L. (2008). *Un purgatoire très discret. La transition "helvétique" d'ancien nazis, fascistes et collaborateurs après 1945.* Paris: Perrin.

Vassallo Paleologo, F. (2009). Accordi bilaterali e tutela dei diritti fondamentali dei migranti. *Progetto Melting Pot Europa.* Onine, available at: www.meltingpot.org/Accordi-bilaterali-e-tutela-dei-diritti-fondamentali-dei.html#.U0XQSPl_ugY.

Vassallo Paleologo, F. (2010). La protezione internazionale ed il respingimento alle frontiere marittime. In Bozzi, G., Sorgoni, B. (eds), *I confini dei diritti.* Bologna: Il Mulino.

Veziano, P. (2002). *Ombre di confine. L'emigrazione clandestina degli ebrei stranieri dalla Riviera dei Fiori verso la Costa Azzurra (1938–1940).* Pinerolo: Alzani.

Via il reato di immigrazione clandestina. Il Senato approva l'emendamento del M5s (2013). *Corriere della Sera,* 10 October 2013. Online, available at: www.corriere.it/cronache/13_ottobre_09/via-reato-immigrazione-clandestina-senato-approva-l-emendamento-m5s-fe96b7d2–310b-11e3-b3e3–02ebe4aec272.shtml.

Villa, A. (2005). *Dai lager alla terra promessa. La difficile reintegrazione nella "nuova Italia" e l'immigrazione verso il Medio Oriente (1945–1948).* Milan: Guerini.

10 A new Italian migration toward Australia?

Evidences from the last decades and associations with the recent economic crisis

Donatella Strangio and Alessandra De Rose

The theoretical perspective: from globalization to skilled migration and brain drain

With the rapid expansion of research and policy interest in migration over the last two decades there has been a significant paradigm shift. Following Hugo (2012), we can state that this shift has involved a move away from thinking about migration purely in terms of permanent settlement or what Ley and Koba-yashi, (2005, p. 112) refer to as the "narrative of departure, arrival and assimilation". The emergence of transnationalism theory involves a more holistic consideration of movements (Dunn, 2005; Piper, 2008) including, among others, the following elements: (a) It focuses not only on the destination but also on the origin and on migration's impact on the flows, linkages and relationships between them (Faist, 2000, Levitt, 2001); (b) It includes all forms of mobility and not just permanent displacement and resettlement; (c) It explicitly includes a consideration of diaspora and the linkages that it maintains with origin countries; (d) It recognizes that people can, and do, identify with more than one nation state (Basch *et al.*, 1994).

This paradigm shift has reinvigorated global migration research and considerably informed our understanding of the migration process and its effects. As Boyle (2002, p. 533) points out "It is the high intensity of exchanges and the new modes of contact that makes this an exciting new research arena".

In 1973, the oil crisis marked a milestone in the new world economic development and it was followed by a period of recession that caused all developed countries to rethink their economic strategies. Overcoming the crisis required the restructuring of production systems and the modification of processes, so as to bring about a complete transformation of the world economy. This led to a profound change in migration policy and, therefore, in migration patterns and directions of flows: in those years a new phase for internal and international migration began that saw some Southern European countries, traditionally sources of emigration, become countries of immigration. The process of urbanization has been gathering momentum since the 1970s, beginning in the poorest countries of the world, where millions of people left the poorest rural areas for the city, subsequently giving rise to a migratory chain that has increased over time and produced a significant impact on the international flows. The arrival of large population masses in cities still lacking the necessary economic, social and health factors necessary for a decent standard of living has prompted a growing number of people to seek their fortune in more developed countries. The destinations of these new flows have not only been those traditionally of immigration (usually the United States or Western European countries) but also those considered of emigration (namely the Southern European ones), in case the latter prove to be more easily accessible than the former.

Since the second half of the 1980s, and especially since the beginning of the 1990s, international migration has undergone further changes due to the process of political and economic globalization following the end of the Cold War and the dominance of the American and Soviet Polish people (Rosoli, 2001).

The major political and economic events of the years 1989–1993 dismantled the old political order, and its economic relations created a new model and a different structure of migration flows and produced changes in the meaning and the effects of migration themselves (see Gould and Findlay, 1994). Thus, while the political crisis of the Soviet Union and Eastern European countries and the creation of new independent states produced the interruption of a large part of the goods trade that took place within the Eastern Bloc, with a contemporary openness to Western markets, the ensuing economic crisis prompted people to seek work in richer countries (see Kupiszewski, 1994).

This crisis also affected selected countries, such as Yugoslavia, Somalia and Eritrea, which, although not belonging to the Soviet bloc, maintained privileged commercial relations with it. In some of these countries, the pressures to emigrate were fuelled by internal conflicts and the situation for ethno-religious and political minorities that forced many to leave and seek political asylum in Western countries. Frequently, the standard flow of migrants in search of employment was incremented by a substantial number of refugees who, being confused with the first, turned out to be barely distinguishable from them. The case of those who left Albania and the former Yugoslavia is without doubt the most emblematic.

Problems similar to those described above presently exist for migrants from many of the less developed or developing countries, where the political and social conflicts exacerbate the disastrous effects of the population explosion and the collapse of economies before they were able to take off.

The end of the millennium gave rise to a new stage in the migration process. The gap between rich and poor countries is increasing, that is the gap between the North and the South of the world. However, it is also within the different regions of the world that we observe important inequalities: the economies of Eastern Europe are struggling to approach those of the rest of Europe; a persistent economic "barrier" divides the United States from Mexico, as well as, in the Mediterranean, separating Europe from North Africa. All of these sources of local inequalities continue to create high migratory pressure towards the richest countries of all areas, with the result of transforming at times – as in the case of southern Italy – areas of traditional emigration experience into potential immigration ones. When this is the case, the effect is the deterioration of pre-existent economic and social issues, and the emergence of new ones. For example, we observe the emerging of new economic disputes that often fuel different forms of national protectionism, including unclearly defined defensive needs, sometime justified on ethical grounds.

Thus, we see that the process of globalization of migration flows is still limited, compared to their regionalization. It is also necessary to note that the internationalization of the economy does not exclude the geographical polarization of investment, and this explains why migration between neighbouring countries and among countries that have historical and cultural similarities is always very strong.

An important feature of the last few decades' mobility process is the role played by skilled migration. Becker *et al.* (2004) show that already in the 1990s there was an increasing volume of migration flows involving skilled workers. Over the past decade, however, the increase in migration flows is increasingly characterized by the so-called skilled migrations (OECD, 2011).

According to Hugo

> in knowledge-based economies, countries seek to maximize their stocks of human capital not only by training their own populations, but also by attracting skilled persons through migration. Hence the "global" quest for talent has become an important part of the strategies of more-developed economies.
>
> (Hugo 2007, p. 20)

The related "brain drain" phenomenon, that is to say the departure of highly qualified and educated (young) people – although difficult to define and measure (Brandi, 2001) – is nowadays becoming a source of worry, especially in the light of the recent economic crisis that is challenging many developed countries, including Italy.

The aim of this chapter is to examine the long-term trends of Italian migration to Australia according to this historical framework, within the international context and focusing on the last few years during which the flows have recovered slightly. Hugo said that

> Whereas the economic impacts of the settlement migration era were clear in terms of the benefits to the migrants themselves, Australia and Italy, the implications of the modern system are not. The Italian/Australian connection is strong, self-sustaining and expanding, forming a corridor along which people, goods, ideas and finance flow freely.
>
> (Hugo 2012, p. 24)

Following this introduction, the chapter is organized as follows: the second section deals with Italian migration to Australia in the long run; the third section focuses on the flows of very recent decades and the skilled migration process; the fourth section discusses the effect of the economic crisis on migration and on the relationship between Italy and Australia; some conclusions are drawn in the final section.

The Australian experience and the Italian emigration: relationship with economic development and institutions

Australian society has been shaped by a long history of immigration (Withers and Pope, 1993). It has been estimated that since the end of the Second World War, more than seven million immigrants have entered Australia.

Historically, in order to evaluate the permanent immigration to Australia only permanent visas granted to foreign nationals were counted. However, for a long time the status of permanent onshore was granted only to specific groups, especially family members and refugees.

Indeed, one must distinguish between those who required temporary visas and those who required permanent ones; recently, an increase in skilled migration has been observed, favoured by ad hoc programmes put in place by the Australian government.

Among the flows to Australia, those from Italy have been the most numerous. Since the end of the Second World War, despite a clear gap between the amount of permits for out-migration granted by the Italian authorities and the Australian requests, and although the numbers cannot be compared to those directed towards the Americas (see Figures 10.1, 10.2 and 10.3), Italy has been one of the major contributors to the population of Australia (Castles *et al.*, 1992; Messina, 1976; O'Connor 1996; Rando, 1992; Boncompagni, 2002; Sanfilippo, 2011). In the mid-1950s Italian migration to Oceania was still largely in surplus. In 1954 the Australian government opened some assisted inflows, albeit with some restrictions. Thanks to a special programme, only relatives and girlfriends of Italian immigrants could take advantage of the bilateral agreement. The year 1955 marked a historic high flow, with 27,699 Italians arriving in Australia (Sanfilippo, 2011, p. 488).

A great deal of the literature argues that efforts by states to regulate and restrict immigration have often failed (Bhagwati, 2003; Castles, 2004; Cornelius *et al.*, 2004; Düvell, 2005). In fact, international migration is mainly driven by structural factors such as labour market imbalances, inequalities in wealth, and political conflicts in countries of origin, factors upon which migration policies have little or no influence (Czaika and de Haas, 2013, p. 487). The limited effect of migration policies does not imply that states have a minor influence on migration processes. Czaika and de Hass (2013, p. 505) said that

> the very notion of international migration presumes the existence of national states and clearly defined territorial and institutional borders. The importance of factors such as economic growth, labour market structure, education, inequality and conflict points to the role of non-migration policies and institutions, and more generally, of nation-states, in shaping migration processes.

Italian migration has a long history, closely related to the economic characteristics and geography of its peninsula (Bonifazi, 2013). To put Italian emigration in the political framework after Unification (1861) – thanks to the first statistical surveys of 1876 – we must remember that the first Great Migration is the peak of a process begun many decades before, and that, over time, the emigration process retains many features, including the habit of returning. Indeed, the tendency of many migrants to leave and then come back again is an element that characterizes many of the flows from Europe. Another important aspect is that leaving the country of origin is common not only to respond to a new and difficult economic situation, but also to anticipate one. Many people have migrated not because they live in misery, but because they are afraid of finding themselves poor (Franzina, 1976; Sori, 1979, 2001; Corti, 2003). The 20 years of fascist dictatorship appears to be a "hinge" era, unjustly ignored by the literature (Franzina and Sanfilippo, 2003; Pretelli, 2010). After the Second World War, flows to Europe and northern Italy rose dramatically because of the interaction of push and pull factors, namely the difficult internal situation and the external demand for manpower. Italy was left in pieces by the Second World War and had to be rebuilt, but other nations lacked a labour force (Maffioletti and Sanfilippo, 2004; Colucci, 2008; see also the recent work "Outward and inward migrations in Italy" by Ó Grada and Gomellini – Bank of Italy, 2011, which is very important from a historical perspective). Up to 1958, the exodus from Southern Europe had been directed towards the Americas and Australia, and had made up the bulk of transoceanic migrations, while the internal movements remained those from the countryside to the city (Fofi, 1964; Colucci, 2008; Montaldi and Alasia, 2010). During the 1960s, also as a result of the contraction of number of departures abroad, the internal mobility from the south to the north of the country intensified. In the same period an increase in repatriations was observed. In 1973, Italy showed a positive balance in the statistics on emigration: the returns were slightly more numerous than departures. However, internal mobility never stopped (Pugliese, 2003; Colucci, 2011). In the 1990s, flows to Western Europe and the United States were increasing and a new mobility process started from Eastern Europe and the Third World towards Europe in order to encourage their commercial and industrial development. Italy, for the first time, became an attractive country for those flows. In the last decade of the millennium, many young people started leaving Italy, apparently claiming to move for tourism or education, but ultimately looking for a job position abroad. We also observe a great deal of "elite" departures (designers, graphic directors and advertisers), a phenomenon that is increasing what is called the "Brain Drain",[1] already observed in Central and Western Europe, Scandinavia, and North America (Sanfilippo, 2011).

Figures 10.1 (a, b); 10. 2 (a, b) and 10.3 (a, b) illustrate the long trend of Italian emigration flows from 1860 onward.

The decrease in Italian citizens' emigration has been particularly pronounced since the second half of the 1970s (Figure 10.4).

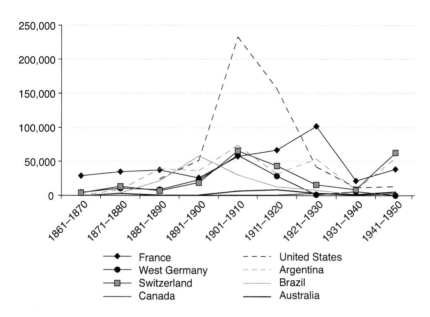

Figure 10.1a Expatriated 1861–1950: row periods.

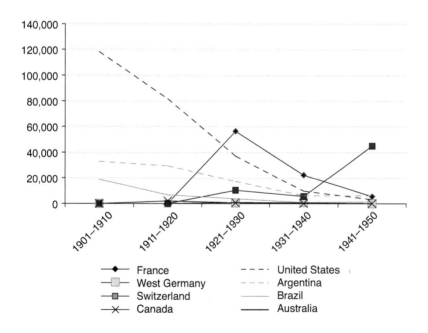

Figure 10.1b Expatriated 1926–1950: yearly details.

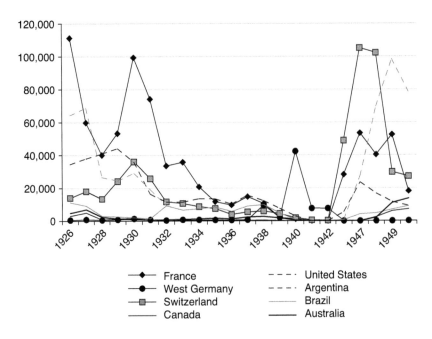

Figure 10.2a Repatriated 1901–1950: row periods.

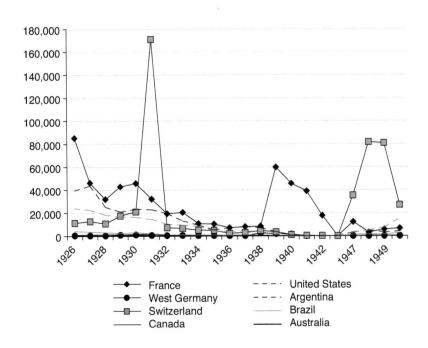

Figure 10.2b Repatriated 1926–1950: yearly details.

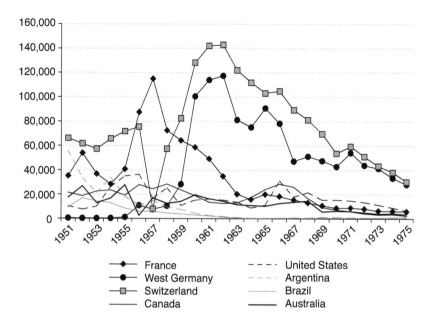

Figure 10.3a Expatriated 1951–1975.

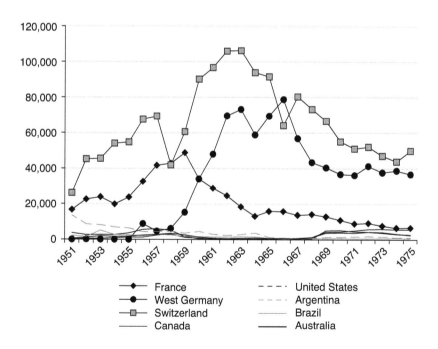

Figure 10.3b Repatriated 1951–1975 (source: ISTAT, various years).

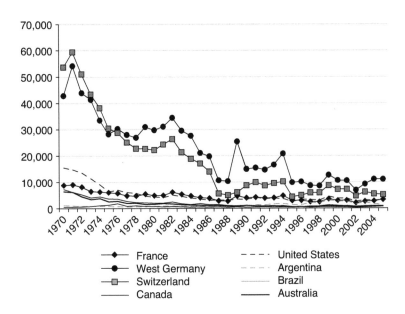

Figure 10.4 Emigration flows from Italy: main destinations, 1970–2005 (source: ISTAT/
AIRE, various years).

The slowdown has also affected the flows to Australia and this has affected the presence of Italian origin population there (Hugo, 2012).

By the 1971 Australian population census, the Italian-born community reached its peak with 289,476 persons. From then on, the amount started to decrease: already in the following year the Italian-born population numbered 280,154. Moreover, already in 1973 and 1974, the flow towards Australia had a negative balance. In any case, the Italian presence is quite solid. It is estimated that in Australia in the mid-1970s there were 220,000 second generation Italians, besides those born in Italy (first generation): the quota of total Italian-origin migration would therefore be approximately half-a-million individuals (Hugo, 2012). The federal government acknowledges the contribution of Italian immigrants to the local society, and as a result of this, in January 1975, a cultural cooperation agreement with the Italian Republic was signed (Agreement of Cultural Cooperation between Australia and Italy). Although the text refers to reciprocal actions, it is clear that its initiatives refer more to Australia, deeply interested in learning more about their new citizens. The 1980s confirmed the progressive decline of first generation Italians. By the time of the 1981 census, people born in Italy were just 275,883, and 254,780 in the 1991 census; in 2011 the Australian Italian-born community numbered only 185,402. It has to be noted, however, that in the meantime there is a persistently strong second generation (about 243,400 units) recently joined by more than 58,000 units. Thus, we can speak of a population of Italian origin, which totals about 564,000.

The drastic reduction of flows from Italy has been a function of the slowing down of permanent immigrations of Italians, a significant return migration and a progressive aging of the Italian-origin population with the gradual disappearance of the pioneers of the Second World War. It is important to note that this figure is quite different from another official source: according to the AIRE (Registry of Italians Living Abroad), in 2007, there were 117,329 Italians living in Australia: this number is much lower than the Australian population of Italian origin, cited above, since AIRE's data only include a selection of Italian citizens, those interested in maintaining strong ties with Italy (Bonifazi, 2012). A recent survey (Baldassar *et al.*, 2012) of the Italian diaspora in Australia found that other forms of connection are maintained with Italy, which act both as channels of knowledge exchange as well as cultural maintenance and identity.

The Australian migration flows of the last few decades and skilled migration

As already stated (see first section), the migration process since the last decade of the millennium has been characterized by an increasing mobility of highly skilled workers (Becker *et al.*, 2004). Guarneri (2001) noted that these new flows are "related to the new phenomena of globalization and the *new economy*, regulated by factors such as the cost of labour and the level of advancement in the technological and scientific sector". The recent literature tends to frame this phenomenon within the endogenous growth model (which starts from the 1980s) and to introduce technological innovation and the effects of human capital on economic growth (Lucas, 1988). In this type of model, growth is generated by the presence of constant or increasing returns to scale, and the migration of human capital has a significant effect on the income of the country of origin and on economic growth. This could be one of the flows of human capital factors that can explain the differences between the growth rates of different countries (see the pioneering work by Miyagiwa, 1991). Indeed, the changes in the structure of economies around the world (Caselli, 1998; Hugo, 2003–2004; Massey *et al.*, 1998) have affected the demand for skilled workers in developed countries through various trends.

In the case of Australia, it is true that the labour market is the most influenced by international migration among OECD nations. The recent government policy tends not to put many obstacles in the way of qualified immigration, while increasing the barriers to unqualified immigration (Hugo, 2004). As an effect of this policy, the number of permanent visas for categories such as Business Skills, the Employer Nomination Scheme and the Regional Sponsored Migration Scheme have increased sharply.

Under the migration programme, the number of visas granted to people who are already physically present in Australia has more than doubled in nine years, from 16,535 in 1996–1997 to 43,363 in 2005–2006. In 1996–1997, the arrivals of new immigrants (settler arrivals) were 85,752. In 2005–2006, they rose to 131,593 and reached a peak of 152,414 in 2012–2013. Permanent additions – defined as the number of settler arrivals plus the number of people granted permanent residence while in Australia on a temporary visa – started to increase again after an interruption in 2008–2009 (Figure 10.5): in 2011–2012 they totalled 245,270 and further increased in 2012–2013 to 254,734.

Of all the permanent additions to Australia in 2012–2013, 76.7 per cent were on visas under the permanent migration programme (50.6 per cent under Skill Stream, 25.7 per cent under Family Stream and 0.5 per cent under Special Eligibility). Australian citizens and New Zealand citizens from overseas who identify themselves as settlers accounted for 17.1 per cent and 6.2 per cent were those coming under the humanitarian programme (DIBP, 2013).

However, Australian research on this issue cannot focus exclusively on permanent settlement migration: recent research by Hugo demonstrates, instead, that non-permanent migration has an important impact on the Australian labour market, although such migrants are not included in standard data collections and research on migrants and the labour market. A number of data sources are utilized to estimate the labour-market impact of working holiday makers, temporary business entrants, overseas students and New Zealand temporary migrants (Hugo, 2006a, 2006b).

There were 196,450 temporary skilled visa holders in Australia on 30 September 2013. This represents an increase of 11.9 per cent when compared with 175,580 on 30 September 2012 (there were fewer than 160,000 in 2008). The temporary entry visa grants (those granted for a stay of up to four years for business purposes) rose to 126,350 in 2012–2013 with a small increase compared to 2011–2012. Italy, for the first time in this decade, is among the top 15 citizenship countries for applications granted (1,100 in 2013 and 610 in 2012). A greater increase is observed for the working holiday visas. In 2011–2012 216,644 working holiday visas were granted, the highest number on record. A strong growth in grants was recorded for citizens from Taiwan, Italy and Hong Kong. Overall, the number of working holiday visa holders passed from less than 100,000 in 2008 to more than 160,000 by September 2013 (DIBP, 2013).

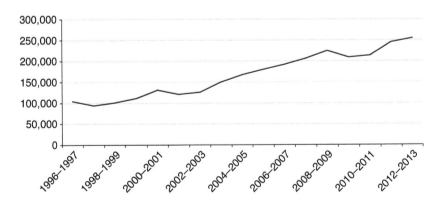

Figure 10.5 Permanent additions in Australia, 1996–2013 (source: DIBP (former DIAC), various years).

The temporary migration Australian programme increasingly involves students and highly skilled young people (Robertson, 2014),[2] and this has actually characterized Italian emigration since the beginning of the 1990s (Guarneri, 2001; IRES, 2009) as it is more and more attractive for well-educated and trained young workers. Avveduto and Brandi (2004), using ISTAT data on cancellations from the population of graduates in Italy, show that about 12,000 graduates left Italy between 1996 and 2000. Overall, the number of graduates who moved to other countries quadrupled between 1990 and 1998. They came mainly from the North even though there has been an increase in graduates emigrating from the South; indeed, even the inter-regional mobility of human capital within the country remains lively. And the phenomenon is likely to worsen in the years to come as an effect of the economic recession, as we are going to discuss in the following section.

The effect of the economic crisis on migration: in particular the relations between Italy and Australia

The 2008–2009 financial crisis and the ensuing economic recession created the sense of urgency necessary to deal with the changes that are necessary in a flexible and globalizing economy.

An important issue concerns whether and how labour migration is affected by economic downturns.

Economic recession usually creates a climate conducive to a restrictive regime of international migration. Castles and Vezzoli (2009) state that the 1929 crisis "led to a massive decline of international labour migration, sometimes compulsory, but it is difficult to separate the crisis impact from the restrictive policies adopted during and after WWI". Beets and Willekens (2009, p. 27) said that "conventional wisdom holds that times of recession and high unemployment create pressure for restrictive immigration legislation" (see also Bonjour, 2005). Beets and Willekens (2009, p. 27) also noted that

> The two major economic crises which occurred in the latter half of the twentieth century – the Asian financial crisis of the late 1990s and the 1973 oil crisis, affected migration in distinct ways. The 1997–99 Asian crisis had a relatively modest effect on migration in the region. The recession in the 1970s in Europe was a turning point in global migration which had not been predicted: guest worker migration ended, family reunions and more permanent settlements started, leading to new long-term ethnic minorities (Castles and Vezzoli 2009).... Due to the crisis, large corporations began outsourcing production to developing regions, with these new industrial sites becoming destinations for migrants over time. However, the 1973 crisis did not result in large waves of return migration from Europe among non-European migrants.

The 1997–1999 Asian financial crisis did not spread globally and was followed by a relatively quick resumption of economic growth.

On the basis of past experience, the economic downturn following the 2008–2009 financial crisis is likely to have negative effects on both migrants and nationals, although these effects will differ according to country, geographic region as well as employment sector.

In particular low-skilled migration is expected to decline, while political and environmental refugees, marriage migration and family reunions will not be much affected (Castles and Vezzoli, 2009).

Remittances are affected less than predicted. The World Bank expects money transfers to remain resilient compared to many other categories of resource flows to developing countries. This may have to do with migrants being more reluctant to transfer money through formal channels due to a lack of confidence in the stability of banking systems. Migrants probably do not want the crisis to have a harmful impact at home; therefore they continue to send remittances (IOM, 2009). If the current recession deepens and persists, the shift away from ever-increasing migration and remittances could have significant consequences for families that are dependent on that source of money (Sward, 2009). The volume of remittances to developing countries used to increase much faster than the stock of migrants. Martin (2009) expected a similar figure between 2005 and 2010 in spite of the crisis, although the stock of migrants will increase at a slower pace than before the crisis.

The 2008–2009 recession seems to have been most severe in those sectors that hire relatively large numbers of migrants, such as residential construction, light manufacturing, and financial and travel-related services (Martin, 2009). Sharply increasing unemployment has made many EU governments introduce measures to protect domestic labour markets (Frontex, 2009). The IOM expects the crisis to impact differently on male and female migrant workers, especially in affected sectors of the economy dominated by one gender. Furthermore, illegal migration has been severely hit: illegals already present in the EU are likely to try to stay (Frontex, 2009) and the highly skilled migrants, who are often young and single and usually with good language skills, may more easily stay because of their ability to quickly find another job.

In Australia, the flow of immigrants increased right after the economic crisis instead of decreasing further and this also holds for Italian emigrants, while other popular destinations such as Germany or the United States are decreasingly chosen. Permanent migration between Italy and Australia over the last two decades is presented in Figure 10.6.

Moreover, if we only count the settler arrivals of Italian citizens, they increase from 181 in 2001 to 205 in 2009 and 311 in 2013, which may reflect the impact of the global financial crisis in Italy.

Baldassar et al. (2012) state that the Italian diaspora towards Australia is not sustained so much by economic and business ties but more by personal linkages. This does not mean, however, that the diaspora does not have important economic functions. This has been seen in the global financial crisis beginning in 2008, which has been more severe in its impact in Italy than in Australia (Hugo, 2012). During the period 2005–2012, the principal Australian destinations for

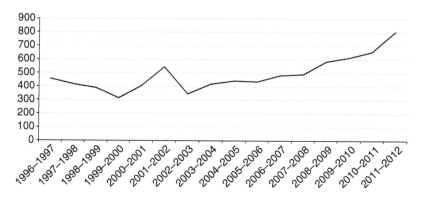

Figure 10.6 Permanent additions of Italians in Australia, 1996–2013 (source: DIBP (former DIAC), various years).

Italian migrations were (in order): the Consulate of Melbourne, the Consulate of Sydney and the Consulate of Adelaide (see Table 10.1).

To sum up, the data analysed indicates that there has been a significant upturn in temporary skilled migration from Italy to Australia since the onset of the global financial crisis. The Italy/Australia connections forged by the Australian Italian diaspora over the decades have created a situation in which Australia is seen by skilled young Italians as a potential place to work when the Italian economy is under stress. The connections, which have been primarily based on personal/family links, have been used for economic purposes. The linkages based largely on permanent migration in the 1950s and 1960s by unskilled permanent migrants have created a corridor that has been activated several generations later by temporary skilled migrants. As Baldassar *et al.* (2012, p. 72) point out: "Australia, in contrast to Europe, is once again seen as a destination that offers migrants opportunities for economic advancement, in some ways similar to their post-war predecessors".

Table 10.1 The principal destination of Italian immigrants in Australia (2005–2012)

	31/12/2005	*31/12/2012*	*% 2005 on tot. Australia*	*% 2012 on tot. Australia*
Consulate of Adelaide	13,496	14,779	11.2	11.1
Consulate of Melbourne	45,031	48,087	37.3	36.1
Consulate of Sydney	35,613	39,039	29.5	29.3
Other Consulate	26,669	31,218	22.0	23.5
Total Italian citizens in Australia	120,809	133,123	100	100

Source: AIRE (register of Italians abroad).

This is a demonstration of the potential these linkages have to take on an economic dimension. In a world where international exchanges of knowledge, skill, capital and labour are playing an increasingly significant role, the existence of such a strong, multi-faced and sustained linkage can be of economic benefit to both Italy and Australia, given appropriate policies and programmes (Agunias and Newland, 2012).

The crisis has vividly demonstrated the interdependence of the globalized economy and this applies especially to the emerging global markets for labour of all skill levels.

Conclusions

The current crisis is likely to have far-reaching effects that we cannot foresee. According to Castles and Vezzoli (2009) we are wrong to believe that migrants serve as a safety valve for developed economies, by providing labour in times of expansion and by going away during recessions. When the economic conditions deteriorate in rich countries they may be even worse in poorer origin countries. Moreover migrants are social beings who put down roots and form relationships in new countries. The post-crisis global economy is radically different from the past; we might see new patterns of migration, new sending and receiving countries and the rise of a new migration order. New systems of employment based on recruitment of cheap labour may emerge.

The lesson from the crisis is that the effects of economic downturns on migration are complex and hard to predict. The last crisis of 2008 has its own unique features and cannot easily be compared with those of 1929 or 1973 or 1997–1999; the end of the Cold War opened the way to a single global economy. The neo-liberal globalization model appears to have run its course.

The 2008 economic crisis has produced the side effect of a renewal of emigrations: in 2009 the migration balance of Italian citizens was negative (−7,418) and in 2010 the situation worsened (−11,353). In 2011 the balance reached a negative peak −18,000, a fairly clear sign that many Italian workers have been forced to expatriate (Bonifazi, 2013).

As has been shown before, Australia has returned to being a popular destination and has managed to carve out a position over time of great economic prosperity, coupled with the reputation of being a country with great respect for individuals' rights and for the environment. In the past Australia was one of the most racist societies of the Second World War, that is a country where the *White Australia Policy* even came to affect trade relations with the neighbouring countries. Yet today, despite a strict immigration flow regulation, Australia is recognized as one of the most desired destinations, even by Italy that claims to adopt quite restrictive immigration laws. Indeed, both countries have adopted stricter immigration rules and nowadays it is not easy to move to either country if you do not satisfy certain requirements. But as always happens, it is the way in which the principles are implemented that distinguishes them. Italy, under strong pressure to respect the Schengen Treaty, has adopted a number of laws gathered within the "Testo Unico sull'Immigrazione", which makes it very difficult to stay on Italian land, and includes a number of crimes such as that of illegal immigration.[3] With the economic crisis as an aggravating factor, the conditions imposed on legal immigration are prohibitive, with the result of an increase in illegal immigration. The Italian government does not have the means to effectively implement the law on immigration, an issue that could paradoxically produce an increasing number of illegal immigrants in the country.

In Australia, immigration law is even stricter than the Italian one, but more elastic in some respects and, recently, it has proved to be of great benefit to the productive system. Citizens of selected countries, such as Italy for example, can take advantage of a working holiday visa, a visa for workers under 30 years of age that lasts for one year, renewable for a further year in the case of work in farms where they produce fruit or vegetables of importance for Australian business. Other countries with less strict diplomatic relations than Italy only have access to the student visa, with which you can work up to a maximum of 20 hours per week and you are obliged to pay approximately $1,000 per month to educational institutions recognized by the government. If people are older than 30 and want to settle in Australia, they must renew their student visa, or find a sponsorship from a willing company, or respect the canons of the skill visa (a visa where the applicant meets the specific work requirements of the market at a given time), or invest the minimum sum of $500,000 with an Australian bank. The Australian approach has been successful over the years because it aims to transform the migration flows, strictly controlled, into a resource for the economy, cultural diversity and meritocracy in the country, while in Italy the same attempt is frustrated by the lack of a common policy among the successive governments, and there is no benefit from flows of equal importance.

Notes

1 The term "brain drain" was originally introduced to describe the outflows of researchers, academics, scientists, doctors and professionals from England, Germany and, more generally, Europe to the United States and Canada. The professionals quit their country of origin because their skills could not be put to proper use at home, and so they emigrated to destinations that offered them better prospects (Huges, 1977).

2 Robertson's recent work brings the various temporal dimensions of young people who are seeking an overseas work/life experience or a pathway to more permanent migration; it creates a framework for understanding the key temporal aspects of temporary graduate workers and working holiday makers.

3 Law on immigration: Italy compared with Australia, online, available at: www. geopolitica-rivista.org/20409/legge-sullimmigrazione-litalia-a-confronto-con-laustralia/Geopolica Rivista dell'istituto di alti studi in geopolitica e scienze ausiliarie Gabriele Abbondanza 19/2/2013. The current immigration policy is regulated by a law of the Italian Republic, the Bossi-Fini Law (30 July 2002, n. 189, passed by the Italian Parliament during the fourteenth legislature), to amend the consolidated law on immigration and the status of foreigners, (legislative decree 25 July 1998, n. 286), and following the previous law, known as the Turkish-Napolitano law (6 March 1998, n. 40).

References

Abella, M. (2004). The role of recruiters in labor migration. In Massey, D. and Taylor, J. (eds), *International Migration: Prospects and Policies in a Global Market*, Oxford: Oxford University Press.

Agunias, D. R. and Newland K. (2012). *Developing a Road Map for Engaging Diasporas in Development: A Handbook for Policymakers and Practitioners in Home and Host Countries*, Geneva and Washington, DC: International Organization for Migration and Migration Policy Institute.

Auriol, L. and Sexton, J. (2002). Human resources in science and technology: measurement issues and international mobility. In OECD (Organisation for Economic Cooperation and Development), *International Mobility of the Highly Skilled*, Paris: OECD Proceedings.

Avveduto, S. and Brandi, M. C. (2004). *Le migrazioni qualificate in Italia*, Studi Emigrazione, xli: 797–829.

Baggio, F. and Sanfilippo, M. (2011). L'emigrazione italiana in Australia, *Studi Emigrazione/Migration Studies*, xlviii, 183: 477–499.

Baldassar, L., Pyke, J. and Ben-Moshe, D. (2012). *Survey Report: the Italian Diaspora in Australia and Links to the Homeland*, Melbourne: Centre for Strategic Economic Studies, Victoria University, March.

Basch, L., Glick Schiller and Szanton, Blanc C. (eds) (1994). *Nations Unbound: Transnational Projects, Postcolonial Predicaments, and Deterritorialized Nation-States*, Switzerland: Gordon and Breach.

Becker, S. O., Ichino, A. and Peri, G. (2004). How large is the "brain drain" from Italy?, *Giornale degli Economisti e Annali di Economia*, 63: 1–32.

Beets, G. and Willekens, F. (2009). The global economic crisis and international migration: an uncertain outlook, in *Vienna Yearbook of Population Research*, Vienna: Vienna Institute of Demography, pp. 19–37.

Bhagwati, J. (2003). Borders beyond control, *Foreign Affairs* (January/February): 98–104.

Boncompagni, A. (2002). *In Australia*. In *Storia dell'emigrazione italiana, Arrivi*, P. Bevilacqua, A. De Clementi and E. Franzina eds., Rome: Donzelli editore, pp. 111–119.

Bonifazi, C. (2012). Un pezzo d'Italia poco conosciuto, *Neodemos*, online, available at: www.neodemos.it/index.php?file=onenews&form_id_notizia=609.

Bonifazi, C. (2013). *L'Italia delle migrazioni*, Bologna: il Mulino.

Bonjour, S. (2005). *The Politics of Migration and Development. The Migration-Development Connection in Dutch Political Discourse and Policy since 1970*, Florence: Florence School on Euro-Mediterranean Migration and Development.

Boyle, P. (2002). Population geography: transnationalism women on the move, *Progress in Human Geography*, 26, 4: 531–545.

Brandi, M. C. (2001). Evoluzione degli studi sulle skilled migration: brain drain e mobilità, *Studi emigrazione*, xxxviii, 141: 75–93.

Caselli, G. (1998). *Migrazioni internazionali*, Enciclopedia del Novecento, supplemento II, online, available at: www.treccani.it/enciclopedia/migrazioni-internazionali_%28 Enciclopedia_del_Novecento%29/.

Castles, S., (2004). Why migration policies fail, in Ethnic and Racial Studies, 27: 205–227.

Castles, S. and Vezzoli, S., (2009). The global economic crisis and migration: temporary interruption or structural change?, *Paradigmes*, 2, June: 69–75.

Castles, S., Alcorso, C., Rando, G. and Vasta, E., (1992). *Australia's Italians: Culture and Community in a Changing Society*, Sydney: Allen and Unwin.

Cobb-Clark, D. and Connolly, M. D. (1997). The worldwide market for skilled migrants: can Australia compete?, *International Migration Review*, 31: 670–693.

Colucci, M. (2008). *Lavoro in movimento. L'emigrazione italiana in Europa, 1945–57*, Rome: Donzelli.

Colucci, M. (2011). *L'emigrazione italiana negli anni '80 e '90*, in Fondazione Migrantes, *Rapporto italiani nel mondo 2011*, Rome: Idos, pp. 54–60.

Cornelius, Wayne A., Takeyuki, Tsuda, Martin, P. L. and Hollifield, J. F. (2004). *Controlling Immigration: a Global Perspective*, Standford, CA: Standford University Press.

Corti, P. (2003). *Storia delle migrazioni internazionali*, Bari-Roma Laterza, ii ed 2005, iii ed 2007, iv 2009.

Czaika, M. and de Haas, H. (2013). The effectiveness of immigration policies, *Population and Development review*, 19 (3): 487–508, September.

DIBP – Department of Immigration and Border Protection (2013). *State and Territory Migration Summary Report*, Disney: Australian Government.

Dunn, K. M. (2005). A Paradigm of Transnationalism for Migration Studies, *New Zealand Population Review*, 31, 2: 15–31.

Düvell, F. (2005). Illegal immigration in Europe: beyond control? Houndmills: Palgrave.

Faist, T. (2000). *The Volume and Dynamics of International Migration and Transnational Social Spaces*, Oxford: OUP.

Fofi, G. (1964). *L'immigrazione meridionale a Torino*, Milan: Feltrinelli.

Franzina, E. (1976). *La grande emigrazione. L'esodo dei rurali dal Veneto*, Venezia: Marsilio.

Franzina, E. and Sanfilippo, M. (2003). *Il fascismo e gli emigrati. La parabola dei fasci italiani all'estero (1920–1943)*, Roma-Bari: Laterza.

Frontex (2009). *The Impact of the Global Economic Crisis on Illegal Migration to the EU.* Frontex (European Agency for the management of Operational Cooperation at the External Borders of the EU Member States) in cooperation with EU Joint SitCen, IOM and ICMPD. Warsaw, Frontex Risk Analysis Unit, online, available at: www.frontex. europe.eu.

Gomellini, M. and Grada, C. Ó. (2011). Outward and inward migrations in Italy: a historical perspective, Quaderni di Storia economica (Economic History Working Papers) Banca d'Italia, 8, (October): 1–63.

Gould W. T. S. and Findlay A. M. (eds) (1994). *Population Migration and the Changing World Order,* Chichester: Wiley.

Guarneri A. (2001). La recente emigrazione italiana in Europa: Francia, Regno Unito e Svizzera a confronto, Working Paper 2/01, December, Istituto di Ricerche sulla Popolazione (IRP-CNR) sotto la direzione di Corrado Bonifazi.

Huges, H. S. (1977). *Da sponda a sponda. L'emigrazione degli intellettuali europei e lo studio della società contemporanea (1930–1965)*, Bologna: il Mulino.

Hugo, G. (2003–2004). A new paradigm of international migration: implications for migration policy and planning in Australia, Research Paper, 10, pp. 1–83.

Hugo, G. (2004). *Temporary Migration: a New Paradigm of International Migration*, Australian Parliamentary Paper, Parliamentary Library, Canberra.

Hugo, G. (2006a). Globalization and changes in Australian international migration, *Journal of Population Research*, 2, 23, pp. 107–134.

Hugo, G. (2006b). Temporary migration and the labour market in Australia, *Australian Geographer*, 37, 2, July: 211–231.

Hugo, G. (2007). Skilled migrants. Where will they come from? *Around the Globe* winter: 20–26.

Hugo, G. (2009). The growing significance of diasporas: an Australian example, *Around the World*: 9 20.

Hugo, G. (2012). From permanent settlement to transnationalism – contemporary population movement between Italy and Australia: trends and implications, draft paper for a special issue of *International Migration*, September.

Hugo, G. (2013). Economic and social impacts of international migration – key trends and implications, United Nations Department of Economic and Social Affairs, *Population Division – Technical Paper* 8.

Hugo, G., Rudd, D. and Harris, K. (2003). *Australia's Diaspora: Its Size, Nature and Policy Implications*, CEDA Information Paper no. 80, Victoria, December.

IOM (International Organization for Migration) (2005). *World Migration, Costs and Benefits of International Migration 2005*, vol. 3, World Migration Report Series, Geneva.

IOM (International Organization for Migration) (2009). *The Impact of the Global Financial Crisis on Migration*, Geneva, online, available at: www.osce.org/documents/eea/2009/01/35935_en.pdf.

IRES (2009). Le nuove migrazioni italiane e le attività dell'Inca all'estero: I casi Francia, Germania e Svizzera, October: 1–209.

Khoo, S.-E., McDonald, P., Voigt-Graf, C. and Hugo, G. (2007). *A Global Labor Market: Factors Motivating the Sponsorship and Temporary Migration of Skilled Workers to Australia*, IMR 41, 2, summer: 480–510.

Khoo, S.-E., McDonald, P., Voigt-Graf, C. and Hugo, G. (2008a). *Which Skilled Temporary Migrants Become Permanent Residents and Why?*, IMR 42, 1 (spring): 193–226.

Khoo, S.-E., McDonald, P., Voigt-Graf, C. and Hugo, G. (2008b). *Skilled Migration to Europe to Australia, Paper presented at the session on "European Emigration" at the European Population Conference, Barcelona, 9–12 July.*

Kupiszewski, M. (1994). *Migration from Eastern Europe to European Community: Current Trends and Future Developments*, School of Geography Working Paper n. 94/4, Leeds.

Levitt, P., (2001). *The Transnational Villagers*, Berkeley and Los Angeles: University of California Press.

Ley, D. and Kobayashi, A., (2005). Back to Hong Kong: return migration or transnational sojourn?, *Global Networks*, 5: 111–128.

Lucas, R. E. Jr. (1988). On the mechanics of economic development, *Journal of Monetary Economy*, 93: 901–18.

Maffioletti, G. and Sanfilippo, M. (eds) (2004). *Contributi sull'emigrazione italiana del secondo dopoguerra*, numero monografico di *Studi emigrazione*, 155, 2004.

Martin, P. (2005). *Migrants in the Global Labour Market*, Paper prepared for the Policy Analysis and Research Programme of the Global Commission on International Migration, Global Commission on International Migration, Geneva.

Martin, P. (2009). The recession and migration: alternative scenarios, *Working Papers 13*, Oxford International Migration Institute.

Massey, D. S., Arango, J., Hugo, G., Kouaouci, A., Pellegrino, A. and Taylor, J. E. (1998). *World in Motion. Understanding International Migration at the End of the Millennium*, Oxford: Clarendon Press.

Messina, N. (1976), L'emigrazione italiana in Australasia (1876–79). *Studi emigrazione*, 41: 102–118.

Miyagiwa, K. (1991). Scale economies in education and brain drain problem, *International Economic Review*, 32: 743–759.

Montaldi, D. and Alasia, F. (2010). *Milano, Corea. Inchiesta sugli immigrati negli anni del "miracolo" con una lettera di Danilo Dolci*, riedizione con introduzione di Guido Crainz, Donzelli, Roma.

O'Connor, D. (1996). *No need to be Afraid: Italian Settlers in South Australia between 1839 and the Second World War*, Adelaide: Flinders Press.

OECD (Organization for Economic Cooperation and development) (2004). *Country Study of Australia (part IV)*, Paris.

OECD (2005). *Trends in International Migration: Annual Report 2004*, 29th Annual Report of the OECD Continuous Reporting System on Migration, Paris.

OECD (2011). Migration in The Post-Crisis World.

Piper, N. (2008). *New Perspectives on Gender and Migration – Rights, Entitlements and Livelihoods*, London: Routledge.

Pretelli, M. (ed.) (2009). *Gli italiani in Australia. Nuovi spunti di riflessione*, numero monografico *Studi emigrazione*, 176.

Pretelli, M. (2010). *Il Fascismo e gli italiani all'estero*, Bologna: CLUEB.

Pugliese, E. (2003). *L'Italia tra migrazioni internazionali e migrazioni interne*, Bologna: il Mulino.

Rando, G. (1992). Italians in Australia: assimilation, integration, multiculturalism, *The Italian Diaspora Migration Across the Globe*, Toronto: MHSO.

Robertson, S. (2014). Time and temporary migration: the case of temporary graduate workers and working holiday makers in Australia, *Journal of Ethnic and Migration Studies*, doi:10. 1080/1369183X.2013.876896.

Rosoli, G. P. (2001). Migration movements in the world today, in Un grande viaggio. Oltre … un secolo di emigrazione italiana, saggi e testimonianze in memoria di P. Gianfausto Rosoli, edited by G. Maffioletti e M. Sanfilippo, Centro studi emigrazione Roma, Rome, pp. 161–200.

Salt, J. (2002). Global competition for skills: an evaluation of policies. In Department of Immigration and Immigration and Multicultural Affairs, *Migration: Benefiting Australia*, Conference Proceedings, Canberra.

Sanfilippo, M., (2011). Cronologia e storia dell'emigrazione italiana, Studi Emigrazione/ Migration Studies, xlviii, 183: 357–370.

Siew-Ean, Khoo, McDonald, Peter, Voigt-Graf, Carmen and Hugo, Graeme (summer 2007). *A Global Labor Market: Factors, Motivating the Sponsorship and Temporary Migration of Skilled Workers to Australia*, IMR, 41, 2: 480–510.

Sori, E. (1979). *L'emigrazione italiana dall'Unità alla seconda Guerra mondiale*, Bologna: il Mulino.

Sori, E. (2001). L'emigrazione italiana in Europa tra Ottocento e Novecento. Note e riflessioni, *Studi emigrazione*, 142: 259–295.

Sward, J. (2009). Migration and the financial crisis: how will the economic downturn affect migrants? *Briefing no. 17* of the Development Research Centre on Migration, Globalisation and Poverty. Sussex Centre for Migration Research. Online, available at: www.research4development.info/PDF/Outputs/MigrationGlobPov/BP17.pdf.

Withers, G. and Pope, D. (1993). Do migrants rob jobs? Lessons of Australian history, 1861–1991, *Journal of Economic History*, 53: 719–42.

Part III
Migrations and citizenship

11 From economic integration to active political participation of immigrants

The Belgium experience from Paris to the Maastricht Treaty (1950–1993)

Pierre Tilly

Until recently only Belgian citizens were allowed to participate in local elections. As demonstrated by an in-depth analysis and in a rather long perspective of this issue, Belgian politicians and political parties have been remarkably reluctant in allowing foreign residents more active political participation. This was, as has been extensively explained in some relevant works, mainly due to polarization and electoral struggles over the anti-immigrant vote in the 1980s and early 1990s. In addition, the Flemish-Francophone cleavage was particularly disruptive in this regard in the second half of the 1990s.[1] This cleavage lead to two divergent types of attitudes and in reaction to the inflow and settlement of immigrants. While the Flemish speaking community has pursued a multiculturalist policy, the French speaking community seems to have supported a less specific approach, more in line with "French republican assimilationism".[2] In comparison to other European immigration countries, both the Flemish and French speaking communities began to devise immigrant policies quite belatedly (Bousetta *et al.*, 2005, p. 5).

It was early 1999 before Belgium finally enfranchised EU-citizens in compliance with the Maastricht Treaty and the derived European directive. Foreign residents from EU-countries were thus able to participate in the most recent local elections, which took place in October 2000. Some of the foreign residents were for the first time able to vote and stand as a candidate in Belgian municipal elections. If non-Belgian EU-citizens were able to register as voters and participate in the local elections, that wasn't case for non-EU residents, who were not allowed to vote or stand as a candidate.

This chapter attempts to put into perspective this long course and its pathways toward the full integration and participation of foreign people in the Belgium political sphere and to determine the main cornerstones of this historical dynamic in terms of the active civic participation of immigrants in Belgium. The hypothesis assumed is that this historical process has been clearly given impetus because of the European unification process for economic reasons and the necessary labour mobility. Actually, socio-economic actors have anticipated an evolution giving more rights to the immigrants toward a greater integration. The political sphere was and remains a contentious one, despite the promotion of citizenship at the European level from the Maastricht Treaty. The political Europe makes its absence felt. In the first part of the chapter, we shall trace a general overview of the historical context of the immigration dynamic in Belgium before bringing to light the impact of the European integration process. This thematic is well embedded with a more global approach (including the European integration process) and addressed in the broadest terms considering the complexity of the issue. The main points and outcomes of the history of the integration of immigrants in Belgium is worthy of discussion. It will be our first point of analysis. Then, we more particularly address the issue of the political participation of foreign people by approaching both the theoretical framework offered by sociology and political science and by examining the way Belgium has been, not without difficulty, integrating the citizenship promotion encouraged by the Maastricht treaty and its following step by putting the citizenship at the centre of the debate.

Migration and globalization in the long run: the Belgium case

The migration of manpower within Europe is by no means a new phenomenon. But its magnitude and geographical scope have developed in a unique manner from the 1940s to early 1970s. Early in the age of mass migration, controls on it were either absent or largely ineffective. Economic interests may not be the only ones that drive immigration policy, attitudes to immigration and racial prejudice may matter independently. Wars and the interwar depression intensify the process of restriction in the short term, a process that was reversed as stability returned in the early post-Second World War period. In the early post-Second World War years, narrowing income distributions and rapid wage growth provided permissive conditions for a return to a more open immigration policy in Europe and the New World. But from the 1970s, a rising demand for migration was accompanied by slower real wage growth and widening income distributions.[3] Anti-immigration sentiment increased rapidly, and in some countries this was reflected in policy tightening aimed against labour migrants.

Since 1918, Belgium has been a country of immigration.[4] In the late 1990s, foreigners represented about 9 per cent of the total population. Diverse small groups of foreign workers, retailers, political refugees and also in some cases students, mostly "Italians", had been more active in Belgium since the end of the nineteenth century. In the past, an important part of these flows were oriented toward the labour market. After 1918, foreign manpower was recruited from Eastern Europe and Italy. These immigrants worked in the building sector, in the textile industry and in the coal mining industry. The 1930s economic depression and the resulting restrictions to foreign immigration reduced the size of immigration between 1930 and 1939. After the Second World War, immigration started again, but the flows were collectively ruled by international agreements.

The labour demand was strong in the coal industry and in the national reconstruction.[5] In 1948, annual flows reached a maximum of 4,000 people (mainly Italians). In 1949–1950 foreign recruitment was shortly brought to a halt, as the result of a cyclical recession and pressure from the trade unions. It would be taken up again in 1951. Between 1951 and 1953 in total over 44,000 (new) Italians were attracted to the Belgian – mainly to Walloon mines (Martens, 1976). In the period 1952–1955 foreign recruitment was in principle again halted – although there was some lenience for the mines in 1952 and 1953 – to be rein-stalled in May 1955. In the period 1955–1957 over 20,000 Italian miners came to Belgium. After 1955, foreign recruitment of workforce was no longer limited to the coal mines, but was gradually extended to the steel industry and the construction sector. In addition, foreign miners increasingly sought (and found) new employment in these other sectors, which in turn led to a need for other new (foreign) miners.

In February 1956 a mining accident at Quaregnon caused the death of seven Italian miners. In August 1956, another disaster at "Bois du Casier", much more serious and dramatic, led to many deaths among Italian miners (Tilly, 1996). This tragedy had a major impact on Italian immigration, as Italy asked for better security conditions for its nationals. Given the security related demands of the Italian government, Belgium decided to turn more actively to other countries to recruit foreign workers. Consequently, agreements were signed with Spain and Greece. Between 1958 and 1961, trade unions pleaded to reduce immigration flows. However, new agreements were negotiated with Morocco and Turkey in 1964.

The majority of "Italians" arrived in Belgium after 1945, and the first decade that followed had been recruited for the coal and the steel industries to make a decisive contribution to the "battle of coal" and had been brought along by their relatives and were followed by their descendants.[6] When the movement first started, it was generally understood that employment in Western Europe would be temporary and of relatively short duration. But with time, the labour-importing countries recognized that their need for foreign labour would be an ongoing phenomenon, not a temporary one. Belgium as other Western countries did not view itself in the foreseeable future as an immigration country in the strict sense of the term.

From the golden 1960s, right up until the economic crisis and migration stop in 1973, between 8,000 and 10,000 Italians emigrated in Belgium each year (Beyers, 2005). In the 1980s, the number of Italians entering Belgium remained high, increasing to 2,500 people a year, with Brussels, as the EU capital, as the most attractive destination. At this time, Italians could be considered as "integrated" after a period, during which they held marginal economic and political positions in the Belgian society. As underlined by Hassan Bousetta *et al.* (2005), Belgium, a former colonial power in Central Africa from 1909 to the 1960s (Congo but also Ruanda and Burundi in a different way), did not choose to recruit a predominantly European workforce, diverging on that specific point, from most of the great colonial powers of that time.

The turning point of the 1970s

However, the years 1973–1974 marked a major turning point in this evolution of post-war migration (Grimmeau, 1992). During the 1970s, the issue of immigration was one of the most crucial topics for social struggles and it began to re-emerge as a political problem. The growing immigrant working class became involved in massive strikes in the industry, and the specific issues of immigrant status in the economy and in society, including the issue of political rights, began to be questioned in the early 1970s. Like in other countries in Europe (e.g. local voting rights in Sweden and Ireland or consultative bodies in Germany), Belgium experienced various types of political participation for foreign workers, which led to the birth of a new form of consultative councils at a local level.

The shift was brought about by the energy crisis of 1973 and the economic recession that followed. Although the official end of workers' recruitment in Italy and elsewhere, one can observe that this didn't prevent the family regrouping. Immigration flows were strongly linked to the economic context in Belgium. Governments tend to rule on immigration much more severely during depression periods. This explains why immigration stopped in 1974. Due to the oil crisis, the foreign population structure progressively changed. Between 1974 and 1980, the number of newcomers declined. Family reunion became an important motive. Since the late 1980s, the number of asylum seekers and refugees has increased. Over the last two decades, the average flow has amounted to 50,000. Today, about 70 percent of the Belgian immigrants come from other European countries. The share of immigrants coming from less developed countries (mainly from North Africa) amounts to 22 per cent. The Moroccan community is largely represented in this context.

The impact of European integration: raising mobility

European integration was founded on the principles of the free movement of goods, capital and services – but also of people. Since the Treaty of Rome, Europeans living within what is now known as the EU have enjoyed progressively stronger rights to move freely, reside and work in other EU countries.

Table 11.1 Number of Italians within the three Belgian regions and in Belgium

	Wallonia	*Brussels*	*Flanders*	*Belgium*	*Italians % foreigners*
1961	170,232	11,357	18,497	200,086	44.1
1970	196,784	28,354	24,352	249,490	35.8
1981	213,409	35,809	30,482	279,700	31.8
1991	182,116	32,093	26,966	241,175	26.7
2001	142,574	28,771	24,241	195,586	22.7
2004	131,909	27,953	23,159	183,021	21.3

Sources: Recensement 1961, 1970, 1981; Registre national 1991, 2001, 2004: INS et Ecodata (Gouvernement Fédéral Service pour l'économie).

By 1951, Article 69 of the ECSC already contained some basic measures aimed at permitting the free movement of workers on EU territory. It explicitly refers only to qualified workers in the indicated sectors and not to the whole workforce. Belgium and Italy have played a major role in this perspective in accord with the other four founding members of the unification of Europe. Besides, most of the ancient Italian migrants were convinced they had contributed to the emergence of a European citizenship by leaving their country to go to live in another country of the EEC.

The creation of the EEC in 1957 introduced a substantial change and was the premise for relevant future developments. The legal basis of the right of free movement can be found primarily in the EU Treaty of Rome (now Art 14 TCUE). The implementation of this right has taken place in a progressive manner due to encountering several resistances. Political conflicts at the supranational and domestic levels weren't really centred on this issue of freedom of movement for EU citizens but on other issues, such as political participation for example. Since the institution of the ECC was formed in 1957, various arrangements have gradually rendered such a right a concrete reality, although not without some obstacles to intra-European mobility. The EEC and then the EU have acquired legal authority to guarantee equal treatment for migrating EU citizens and to regulate their internal movement by protecting their rights to mobility, working conditions and settlement. The EU also succeeded by overseeing transfers of social insurance claims from one country to another. A fundamental step will be the adoption of Regulation 1612/68 on the freedom of movement of workers and Directive 68/360 on the abolition of restrictions on movement and residence for workers of member states and their families. Since 1968, the European Court of Justice will promote this dynamic significantly and extend and reinforce these rights for workers in host countries.

This raises the question of political representation for these foreigners. The initial forms of participation were social, through voluntary associations and trade unions. It was only later, and often in order to tackle specific problems (segregation, academic failure, the creation of "ghetto" neighbourhoods), that issues were raised in terms of political rights, equal rights or access to full citizenship. The integration of migrants generated a strong debate at the European level from the mid-1970s in the framework of the fight against discrimination and for equal treatment of both national and foreign workers. The Council of Europe recommended a series of measures addressed to the member states in this sense. The issue was also in debate at an international level through the ILO and produced some outcomes with Convention 143: according to which, a member may take all necessary measures that fall within its competence and collaborate with other members to facilitate the reunification of the families of all migrant workers legally residing in its territory.[7]

The first consultative councils for immigrants were set up at the local level at the end of the 1960s. This initiative took place following recommendations made by the Council of Europe from 1964 onwards.[8] The European Committee on Local and Regional Democracy (CDLR) was first set up in 1967 to make it possible for the governments of member states to discuss issues of local and regional democracy and to pave the way for greater European co-operation in this area. The Council of Europe worked to achieve recognition of the social and political rights of foreigners who were legally resident in the territory of its member states. During the fifth session of the European conference of local governments in 1967, representatives from the CEE suggested new ways to promote the political participation of migrants. Several municipalities would set up Local Consultative Councils for Immigrants. The oldest national bodies (in the Benelux countries and the Nordic countries) date back to the 1970s and 1980s. Several of these early official bodies have disappeared, while some new immigration countries have renewed interest in consultative bodies (Greece, Ireland, Italy, Spain and Portugal). These bodies tend to be part of government's first attempts at a comprehensive integration strategy.

The development of local self-government everywhere in Europe has played a major role in the recognition of the need for better understanding and a new approach to foreign populations. Through this stimulus, and the commitment of local elected representatives who were directly confronted with the social realities of their populations, participative bodies for foreign residents have been introduced, often on an experimental basis and in very varied forms. And a Convention on the Participation of Foreigners in Public Life at Local Level, dated 5 November 1992, will become the reference text in this area but has so far been signed by only nine member states and ratified by only six of these: Denmark, Finland, Italy, the Netherlands, Norway and Sweden. The proposed mechanisms for participation include measures to provide foreign residents with full information about their rights and civic duties; the creation of consultative committees or other mechanisms to enable foreign residents to inform local authorities about their points of view; and give foreigners who meet specific residence criteria the right to vote and stand for election in local government.

The 1992 Maastricht Treaty provided a new impetus for the construction of a European Political Union. The integration of immigrants has only recently appeared on the European political agenda (compared with the Treaty of Amsterdam's establishment of an agenda for a common migration policy in 1997). The Council of the EU's 2004 declaration in The Hague on the principles of an integration policy is a landmark. In a broader sense, however, particularly in terms of formulating an anti-discrimination strategy, the EU and European Parliament have been active since the early 1990s.

Toward more integration and political participation: the Belgium case

In his PhD research, Marco Martiniello (1992), was among the first Belgian scholars to systematically challenge the idea that immigrants were politically quiescent.[9] Studying Italian elites and leaders, he showed that the lack of political rights had not led to a vacuum in terms of participation. Martiniello argued that the Belgian political system not only disenfranchised non-nationals, but also disempowered them.[10] Articulating a theory of power to the case in point, Martiniello showed that Italians were politically active but powerless and marginalized in the Belgian political sphere.[11]

Andrea Rea presented another account of the issue by looking at the links between integration policies and immigrant responses to them.[12] Starting from an anthropological perspective and using participant observation, Rea provides in his thesis one of the finest analyses of a specific, although exceptional, type of reaction of second generation youth to prejudice and discrimination: the "race riot".[13] As mentioned by Bousetta *et al.*, Rea uses such concepts as the notion of "racialization, which helps identify the resulting context of a process of social change marked by symbolic exclusion, domination and inferiorization".[14] Drawing on the social movement literature, Rea further argues that "the opening of the political opportunity structure at the turn of the nineties made possible this confrontational repertoire of collective action".[15] In other words, the confrontation between the youth and the police happened in the context of a reflux of institutional and political racisms in Brussels and not the converse.

In the municipal elections, held in 1994, the participation and successes of Belgians of non-EU foreign origin was marginal. Only 14 Belgians of non-EU foreign origin were elected of a total of 650 local councillors for the 19 municipalities of Brussels.[16] As argued by Jacob *et al.* "this was already progress since, until then, the representation of immigrant ethnic minorities in local political life has been non-existing even in the municipalities and neighbourhoods where immigrant origin citizens were significantly concentrated".[17] In October 2000, we can observe a strong and obvious increase of elected Belgian politicians of non-EU origin.

Putting this scheme in a historical perspective permits to underline that the reception policy of immigrants became more diverse when the first provincial immigration and reception services were set up in Liege in 1964; in Limburg in 1964 and in Namur in 1965. In addition to assistance on legal and administrative matters, these institutions offered literacy and training programmes, and also cultural activities.[18] They also informed the native population about the immigrants' way of life and organized activities to bring the communities closer together. At the national level, an advisory committee of foreigners was set up on 20 December 1965, in order to examine and issue opinions on all the social, economic and administrative problems related to immigration. Regional commissions were also launched and modest funds were allocated to local initiatives for receiving immigrants, mainly on a local scale, and operating in a precarious manner (Bastenier, 1992). At that time, there was no active policy on either immigrants' living conditions or cultural aspects. And these bodies usually had little power and, for example, functioned as advisory boards.

The law of 17 February 1970 gave the same rights to all immigrant workers as to Belgian workers: to vote and to stand as a candidate for the work councils and other consultative bodies within the enterprise. Moreover, the logistical and financial support provided by the unions allowed the foreigners to build up their own political and cultural organizations. A collective approach by nationality led to a much better organization of the various foreign communities. In 1971, a joint front of the various foreign organizations was formed and led to the constitution of the so-called CLOTI (Comité de liaison des organisations des travailleurs immigrés).

If the economic democracy looked set to become a reality at that time, the immigrants did not have the right to vote and thus they had little access to social housing for example. In the province of Brabant, only 2.6 per cent of the social housing was occupied by migrant families in 1970.[19] Some local consultative bodies regarding immigrants were not only created thanks to the willingness of the local authorities but also following initiatives from immigrants and their associations (Panciera, 1978). As Nizet observed, the majority of public services had a lower sensitivity to the action needed to change the social context in which the immigrant was living (Nizet, 1971). The forms of organization required in this sense drew minor attention from the public authorities. Insufficient budgets and the prevalence of voluntary helpers were the main features of the immigration services, incapable to respond to the scale of the task. All of the above rather confirmed the immigrant place as a marginal one in the society of that time.

Thus in 1972, in Mons, a medium-sized city in Walloon Region, an advisory committee of foreigners called IDEA was created within a public economic body. The status of foreigners in which must more clearly be defined the

Plate 11.1 Trade unions played an important role in the formulation of policies relating to immigration and the migrant workers. Here is a European meeting of young immigrant workers and unionists during the 1960s (source: Collection Salvatore Acquisto).

31 OCTOBRE 1971 — N° 105
Paraît deux fois
par mois

BULLETIN

ÉDITÉ PAR LA CONFÉDÉRATION DES SYNDICATS CHRÉTIENS
135, rue de la Loi, BRUXELLES 4

**L'IMMIGRATION
AU SERVICE DU CAPITALISME
ET DE LA BOURGEOISIE ?**

Nous nous trouvons à un tournant de l'histoire de l'émigration. Les migrants répondent de moins en moins à l'image stéréotypée du pauvre homme à la valise mal ficelée, pour devenir de plus en plus le tissu de base de la vie économique européenne.

Un élément très important pour interpréter correctement la situation des immigrés en vue d'une intégration respectueuse est la connaissance des phénomènes historiques qui ont conditionné leur départ. Ainsi par exemple l'émigration des Italiens a toujours été justifiée par la classe dirigeante italienne — depuis l'unification de l'Italie en 1861 — par l'existence d'une surpopulation chronique, phénomène contre lequel on ne saurait rien faire et qu'il faut subir comme une force impersonnelle : on ne parle guère de l'émigration comme résultat d'une absence de réformes.

Plate 11.2 Bulletin of the Christian Trade Union (CSC), 31 October 1971. The title of the article is rather provocative: immigration au service du capitalism et de la bourgeoisie?

conditions of admission and residence of immigrants for the purpose of employment, and a draft naturalization law aroused lively debate. Thus the committee worked up to the end of the 1970s, at which point this sort of body appeared to be useless and even out of date because its advisory function with no real power of decision had a limited period to get into its stride. Furthermore, for the more active militants, a larger political participation implied a right to vote and to stand in a local assembly with a deliberative power, such as the local council.[20] This step was not got over. The local election of 1982 was therefore, for these immigrant militant groups, an opportunity to claim greater political participation. But in itself the participation process initiated early on the 1970s was paradoxical because it was needed for immigrants to comply with the administrative and institutional structure and a conception of participation that militants wanted to call into question. In other words, the formula wasn't efficient.

Participating in municipal elections: the right to vote and to stand as a candidate

Belgian citizenship law has just emerged from a long period of intense tension. During the period between 1984 and 2000, various reforms were adopted that aimed to make the acquisition of nationality easier. While most of these reforms did not break the coherence between citizenship legislation and migration policy, the changes that came into force on 1 March 2000 were perceived to relax access to Belgian citizenship so much that it neutralized, or even damaged the effects the legislators have tried to achieve by other legislation.

Within the EU, the most pronounced example of compulsory poll attendance is that of Belgium. According to election law, abstaining voters are subject to progressive fines, which become higher with the number of elections missed.[21] "They start from €25–50 for the first time and can rise to €50–125 for the second abstention".[22] Exempted are Belgian citizens abroad and EU and third-country nationals in local elections. Residency remains the central concept that defines access to electoral rights by Belgian citizens living on the national territory.

Electoral rights for EU citizens and for other foreign residents became a major subject of debate in Belgium during the 1990s (Bousetta *et al.*). The main arguments used in favour of extending voting rights to resident non-nationals were mostly the following: no taxation without representation, equal treatment over time, greater political participation of the whole society. On the contrary, the opponents argued that the priority was to prevent ethnic parties, the domino effect, and to encourage naturalization instead. After the Maastricht Treaty in 1993, a directive established the right of EU citizens residing in a member state (of which they are not nationals) to vote and to stand as a candidate in municipal elections (Jacobs, 1999, p. 649). Meanwhile, at the Essen Summit in 1994, Belgium sought and obtained the agreement of other member states to refuse the right to vote and to be eligible for municipal elections to citizens of other member states residing in a Belgian municipality (Jacobs, 1999, p. 651). This demand concerned municipalities in Brussels in which 20 percent of the eligible residents did not have the Belgian nationality. This included the condition that it would apply only to those who had lived for less than six years in the municipality concerned. Considering the fears existing among Belgian parties about the side (the Flemish or the French speaking ones) the EU resident would primarily support, it made it impossible to modify the Constitution, and Article 8 more particularly, to allow non-Belgians to vote. In 1998, the European Court of Justice found Belgium guilty of failing to adopt the directive.[23] So that Belgium amended its constitution to allow resident EU and third-country nationals to vote only after this ruling of 1998. In 2000, EU citizens exercised for the first time their recently acquired rights of local political participation, either as a voter or a candidate. But third country nationals participated in Belgian local elections for the first time in 2006. The low degree of registration of potential voters was one of the most significant results. As underlined by de Rool, "EU citizens were rather reluctant to face the bureaucratic Red tape and the compulsory vote, once they have been registered, is an additional deterring factor".[24]

After the October 2000 election, several Belgians of immigrant non-EU origin became aldermen for the first time,[25] the sign of a changing pattern of the political participation of immigrant origin citizens in the Brussels Capital Region (Jacobs *et al.*, 2002). Studying the electoral success of Turkish, and more significantly Moroccan politicians, and the poor involvement of EU-citizens during these elections, they outlined a phenomenon of preferential voting for immigrant (non-EU origin) candidates, one which was already observed in the regional elections of 1995 and 1999 (Jacobs *et al.*, 2002).

To be able to participate, they had to register as voters in advance. For Belgians voting is compulsory. Non-EU citizens, however, were not allowed to vote in the local elections. A special clause in the constitution stipulated that the electoral laws could only be modified in order to enfranchise third country nationals after the year 2001. The electoral law was modified in 2004, following a heated political debate, which brought the government close to a disruptive conflict. The next Belgian local elections were to be held in 2006 and was to be the first election providing for the participation of third country nationals, albeit only as voters and not as candidates.

Conclusion

Immigration remains an important and contentious issue in the EU and it is certainly the case in Belgium, with a major transformation in migration processes; from a historical situation in which these were dominantly shaped and restrained by being state-centred, to one in which they are increasingly defined and governed by market forces, and the inability of states to enforce their jurisdiction over labour mobility. In the 1960s and 1970s, internal migration was defined almost exclusively in North–South terms in Belgium, with Italy, Spain, Morocco and Turkey namely, being the main countries of emigration. Some 40 years later, the pattern has shifted to one of a centre–periphery relationship, with British and Finnish construction workers, joining Polish and Hungarian workers in the growth centres of Europe, being defined as posting-workers. Confronted with ever increasing public hostility to immigration and immigrants in the continent, and the rise of far-right anti-immigrant parties, West European states are, with great difficulty, trying to manage this issue, addressing new policies that recognize an objective economic and demographic demand for new immigration in future decades.

The legal concept of citizenship of the EU was formally introduced into the EC Treaty in 1993 by the Treaty of Maastricht. EU citizenship comprises a limited bundle of legal rights that citizens can exercise vis-à-vis other member states and the institutions of the EU and, less often, vis-à-vis their own member state. Many EU citizenship rights are focused on mobile EU citizens, who have exercised rights of free movement and reside in a member state other than the one of which they are nationals, e.g. as workers, students or retired persons. The legal status of EU citizenship is derived from member state citizenship. Only the nationals of the member states are EU citizens. The member states have largely unfettered power to determine the scope of their own nationality law, and therefore also are the citizens of the EU. However, through the common citizenship of the Union and its core right of free movement, each member state's citizenship policies impact on the other member states.

In the case of Belgium, electoral rights for EU citizens and for other foreign residents have been became a major subject of debate during the 1990s. In 2000, EU citizens exercised for the first time their recently acquired rights of local political participation, either as a voter or a candidate, while third country nationals participated in Belgian local elections for the first time in 2006. None-theless nationality remains an essential instrument for any discussion on parti-cipation, especially political, since the vast majority of political rights are associated with nationality.

Notes

1 Bousetta, H., Gsir, S. and Jacobs, D. (2005). *Active Civic Participation of Immigrants in Belgium, Country Report prepared for the European research project POLITIS*, Oldenburg, online, available at: www.uni-oldenburg.de/politis-europe.
2 Ibid., p. 5.
3 Martens, A. (1975). *Les immigrés: Flux et reflux d'une main-d'œuvre d'appoint. La politique belge de l'immigration de 1945 à 1970*, Éditions Vie Ouvrière – Presses uni-versitaire de Louvain, 1976.
4 Grimmeau, J-P. (1992). Vagues d'immigration et localisation des étrangers en Belgique, in Anne Morelli (ed.), *Histoire des Etrangers et de l'immigration en Belgique, de la préhistoire à nos jours*, Brussels: Editions Vie ouvrière, pp. 105–118.
5 Beyers, L. (2005). Italians in Belgium since the 1970s: a unique process of changing positions and identities, *Studi Emigrazione*, 160: 762.
6 Idem.
7 Convention concerning Migrations in Abusive Conditions and the Promotion of Equality of Opportunity and Treatment of Migrant Workers (Entry into force: 9 December 1978).
8 Martinello, M. (1992). *Leadership et pouvoir dans les communautés d'origine immi-grée: L'exemple d'une communauté ethnique en Belgique*, Paris: L'Harmattan.
9 Taken by Bousetta, H. *et al.*, op. cit., p. 17.
10 Idem.
11 Idem.
12 See namely Rea, A. (2001). *Jeunes immigrés dans la cité. Citoyenneté locale et poli-tique publique*, Brussels: Labor, collection La Noria.
13 Jacobs, D., Martiniello, M. and Rea, A. (2002). Changing patterns of political parti-cipation of citizens of immigrant origin in the Brussels Capital Region: the October 2000 elections", *Journal of International Migration and Integration/Revue de l'intégration et de la migration internationale*, 3 (2: 201–221).
14 Quoted in Bousetta *et al.*, op. cit., p. 17.
15 Idem.
16 Taken from Jacob, D., Delwit, P. and Delmotte, F. (2009). Political participation and electoral impact of EU citizens in the Brussels Capital Region: the October 2006 local election", in G. De Rool, *Brussels and Europe: Acta of the International Colloquium on Brussels and Europe, held in the Albert Borschette Conference Centre in Brussels, on 18 and 19 December 2009*, Brussels, ASP, p. 306.
17 Idem.
18 Blaise, P. and Martens, A. (1992). Des immigrés à intégrer – Choix politiques et modalités institutionnelles, *Courrier Hebdomadaire du CRISP*, Brussels, 1358–1359.
19 Intercommunale de développement économique (IDEA), Commission des immigrés, pv- de la réunion du 3 avril 1974. Author's documentation.
20 Intercommunale de développement économique (IDEA) (1974). Commission des immigrés, pv-de la réunion du 3 avril 1974. Author's documentation.
21 Malkopoulou, A. (2009). *Lost Voters: Participation in EU elections and the Case for Compulsory Voting*, CEPS Working Document 317: 8. Online, available at: www.ceps.eu/files/book/1886.pdf.
22 Idem.

23 Lafleur, J.-M. (2013). *Access to the Electoral Rights: Belgium, EUDO Citizenship Observatory*, EUI, Florence, June. Online, available at: http://eudo-citizenship.eu/admin/?p=file&appl=countryProfiles&f=134-Belgium-FRACIT.pdf. Case C 323/97 Commission versus Belgium [1998] ECRI-4281.
24 De Groof, R. (2009). *Brussels and Europe. A General Outline*, VUB press/UPA, Brussel, 2009, p. 27.
25 Jacobs, D., Martiniello, M. and Rea, A. (2002). op. cit., p. 1.

References

Bastenier, A. (1992). *L'Etat belge face à l'immigration: les politiques sociales jusqu'en 1980*, Sybidi paper 10, Louvain-la-Neuve, pp. 47–48.

Beyers, L. (2005). "Italians" in Belgium since the 1970s: a unique process of changing positions and identities, *Studi Emigrazione*, 160: 762.

Blaise, P. and Martens, A. (1992). Des immigrés à intégrer – Choix politiques et modalités institutionnelles, *Courrier Hebdomadaire du CRISP*, Brussels, 1358–1359.

Bousetta, H., Gsir, S. and and Jacobs, D. (2005). *Active Civic Participation of Immigrants in Belgium. Country Report prepared for the European research project POLITIS*, Oldenburg, online, available at: www.uni-oldenburg.de/politis-europe.

Coenen, M. T. and Lewin, R. (eds) (1997). *La Belgique et ses immigrés: Les politiques manquées*, Brussels: De Boeck Université p. 22.

Grimmeau, J.P. (1992). Vagues d'immigration et localisation des étrangers en Belgique. In Anne Morelli (ed.). *Histoire des Etrangers et de l'immigration en Belgique, de la préhistoire à nos jours*, Brussels: Editions Vie ouvrière, pp. 105–118.

Jacobs, D. (1998). Nieuwkomers in de Politiek, Het Parlementaire Debat Omtrent Kiesrecht voor Vreemdelingen in Nederland en België, diss. Utrecht: Academia Press, 1998.

Jacobs, D. (1999). The debate over enfranchisement of foreign residents in Belgium, *Journal of Ethnic and Migration Studies*, 25: 649–663.

Jacobs, D., Martiniello, M. and Rea, A. (2002). Changing patterns of political participation of citizens of immigrant origin in the Brussels Capital Region: the October 2000 elections, *Journal of International Migration and Integration/Revue de l'intégration et de la migration internationale*, 3 (2): 201–221.

Martens, A. (1976). *Les immigrés: Flux et reflux d'une main-d'œuvre d'appoint: La politique belge de l'immigration de 1945 à 1970*, Éditions Vie Ouvrière – Presses universitaire de Louvain.

Martinello, M. (1992). *Leadership et pouvoir dans les communautés d'origine immigrée: L'exemple d'une communauté ethnique en Belgique*, Paris: CIEMI L'Harmattan.

Nizet, J. (1971). *La Politique et le Fonctionnement des Services Sociaux pour Immigrés*, mémoire en sociologie, UCL Institut des sciences politiques et sociales, February.

Panciera, S. (1978). *Immigration, force sociale, mouvement politique: Les conseils communaux consultatifs des immigrés en Belgique*, Paris (thèse pour le doctorat du 3ème cycle), IV tomes.

Rea, A. (2001). Jeunes immigrés dans la cité: Citoyenneté locale et politique publique, Brussels, Labor, collection La Noria.

Tilly, P. (1996). *Les Italiens de Mons-Borinage, Une longue histoire*, Brussels: EVO.

Tilly, P. (2008). Il Belgio e il problema della libertà di circolazione dei lavoratori in Europa dal dopoguerra ai primi anni '70. In A. Varsori and L. Mechi, *Lionello Levi Sandri e la politica sociale in Europa*, Franco Angeli, Milano, pp.151–194.

Tricot, A. (1979). Les immigrés et la question du logement à Bruxelles, Brussels: IEV, p. 48.

12 Living on the edge

Migration, citizenship and the renegotiation of social contracts in European border regions

Harlan Koff and Gloria Naranjo Giraldo

Introduction

The field of border studies focuses heavily on the "the social construction of border regions". Scholars generally focus on the role of local authorities and civil society in the promotion of cross-border cooperation. Thus far, the field of migration studies has been slow to recognize this trend. Most studies on migration and borders concentrate on controls, human rights, organized crime, etc. Often these studies discuss the interaction of the EU and national authorities in migration affairs, and borders are simply "the place where politics happens" (Foucher, 1986). Studies on migration and citizenship focus heavily on nation-states and tension with supranational actors.

These trends in contemporary scholarship on borders and migration in Europe reflect political realities on the continent in these fields. The EU is currently promoting two processes that affect both territorial governance and how citizens relate to these territories. First, the evolution of the EU has led to significant development in the field of cross-border cooperation. The emergence of Interreg programmes and the elimination of interior border controls since the signing of the Schengen Accords has fostered a new governance landscape in Europe, generally acknowledged by the term "multi-level governance", which describes the interaction of local, national and European authorities in decision-making, especially in cross-border contexts. This process has extended to include cross-border cooperation between localities at the EU's external borders as well.

Conversely, European responses to migration have reinforced border controls. The emergence of Frontex, the EU border control agency, the construction of walls in certain parts of the EU's external borders and the externalization of these borders through cooperation agreements with third party states have reinforced Europe's commitment to migration control. Scholars in this field such as Hansen and Weil (2001) have noted that these political efforts have reinforced the division between "European" and "non-European" distinctions in terms of citizenship.

Thus, it seems that these two processes lack coherence. On one hand, the EU is fostering cross-border cooperation, but it is simultaneously reinforcing these borders in terms of population movements. For this reason, border areas are the places where the incoherence between these policies is most evident. This has been noted by scholars such as Brunet-Jailly, Alscher, Koff, etc. in terms related to governance, human security, human rights, etc.

One aspect of this political negotiation that has not been highlighted in the border and migration literatures is citizenship. If border regions simultaneously represent political divides and zones of cooperation, the residents of these areas are active participants in these simultaneous processes. For this reason, this chapter examines how the convergence of different levels of citizenship affects territories and their residents at the EU's external borders. The chapter reflects on empirical research conducted in Spain–Morocco (specifically Melilla–Nador) and Italy–Albania (particularly Bari–Durres). It approaches the study of migration, cross-border cooperation and citizenship through the lens of "the social contract" defined as the implicit agreement that binds residents of cross-border regions to each other and polities. The study examines how cross-border cooperation in these border communities has affected notions of citizenship in these regions and how these ideas impact local responses to immigration. Specific attention is paid to the coherence of policies in the fields of cross-border cooperation and immigration. The premise for the chapter is that social contracts are perpetually renegotiated by residents of cross-border regions and thus, citizenship has been de-territorialized in that economic, social, and political rights reflect developments in transnational integration.

Citizenship, borders and migration in the academic literature

The literature on borders and migration has addressed the question of citizenship to varying degrees. However, these literatures rarely speak to each other. This is surprizing considering that both of these literatures discuss mutations of flows and markets that affect nation-states. Having said this, these literatures deal with the issue of citizenship in different ways. This section of the chapter addresses these trends.

Citizenship in cross-border regions

The recent boom in borderland studies has transferred attention from the international arena to the national and local levels, creating a sphere of micro-scaled spatial study. Recent studies have focused not only on the impact of international phenomena on border communities, but they have also examined the impact of local actors in these regions on national and supranational polities. In general, the literature aims to explain the "social construction" of border regions and how integration occurs in cross-border communities.

The first strand of this literature analyses institutional relationships through the lens of "multi-level governance". This framework, originally proposed by Gary Marks and Liesbet Hooghe (2001), argues that successful policy implementation, especially in the arenas of regional and social development is dependent on the activities of local government. The authors describe two types of multi-level governance. Type 1 analyses the standing relationship between agencies of general purpose jurisdiction. Conversely, Type 2 multi-level governance is understood as the interaction of public and private local, national, and supranational actors in specific policy arenas.

More recent empirical studies of EU regional policies have focused on both types of multi-level governance. Institutional studies, such as those conducted by Perkmann, Aykaç, Benington and Harvey, etc., have examined Type 1 governance through discussions of EU programmes, such as Interreg initiatives, in cross-border regions. Perkmann has noted that over 70 border communities (both cities and regions) have entered into some sort of formal organizational agreement with counterparts on the other side of national divides (Perkmann, 2003, p. 155). He, like others (i.e. James Anderson), has also raised doubts about the effectiveness of these programmes. While many observers argue that cross-border co-operation provides both an avenue for political emancipation from central authorities and more efficient policy implementation, Perkmann correctly notes that no comparative empirical evidence exists to prove these claims. In fact, some European studies (see Duprez *et al.*, 1996) demonstrate that cross-border policy-making does not always create expected outcomes.

The second strand of the emerging borderlands literature applies the "borderless world" approach, as it examines market-based integration. Many authors have contended that we will soon live in a world where borders will have minimal importance, should they exist at all, due to economic globalization and regional integration. The foremost proponents of "borderless" politics are not scholars of border communities themselves, but social theorists and scholars of international geopolitics in the Americas. Prominent supporters of this argument include Ohmae, Sassen, Jacobson, Bauböck and Pastor. These scholars argue that socio-economic activities are no longer constrained by state borders and that transnational networks of citizenship, information, intellectual exchange, social mobilization, etc. have created competition to the nation-state. Moreover, political economists, such as Rogowski, Frieden, etc. contend that economic competition has been transformed in the post-Fordist era. Whereas previous cleavages divided states or economic classes, these authors argue that contemporary divisions are based on geographic characteristics (i.e. rural versus urban) or economic sectors (i.e. traditional industry versus high technology), thus decentralizing economic relationships. They conclude that the emergence of this new organization of the global economic system has further eroded the ability of the nation-state to control the activities of non-state actors. The more that borders themselves have "withered away", the more significant border regions have become in domestic and international politics. David Newman correctly argues that: "For some, the notion of a 'borderless' and 'deterritorialized' world has become a buzzword for globalization" (Newman, 2006, p. 1).

Finally, the third strand of literature on border integration examines political identities as the de-territorialization of the nation-state has led to the emergence of new ideologies and movements based on ethnicity, language, place of belonging, etc. Leading scholars in this field, such as Michael Keating, have demonstrated that the nature of local political organization and culture has significantly affected how border politics function. Studies of nationalist movements (such as Northern Ireland), minority groups (such as Gypsies in Eastern Europe), and stateless nations (such as the Québecois or Basques) have examined the connections between these political communities and the global political arena. In his study of pluri-nation states, Keating has demonstrated that these movements are not necessarily integrated into the institutional architecture of their respective countries (Keating, 2001). Thus, territorial boundaries are not fundamental for the construction of identity, which decreases the demarcating influence of borders within ethnic debates. For example, some groups, such as the Scots or Corsicans, correspond to an existing territory and they benefit from special representative structures. Others, such as Basques, Gypsies, etc. adhere to de-territorialized identities that cross state borders.

All three strands of this literature focus on the interactions of institutions, markets and identities in cross-border regions. Obviously, these arenas mark the different spheres of citizenship (economic, political and social citizenship) identified by T. H. Marshall (1964). But what exactly constitutes "cross-border integration"? Is the simple presence of cross-border communities enough? What forms of cooperation or intensity dictate true "integration"? This chapter argues that "social contracts" may provide a lens through which we can understand this phenomenon. This is also valid for the literature on migration studies.

Citizenship and migration

Scholars of immigration often focus on evolving concepts of citizenship. During the 1990s, immigration studies introduced ever broader concepts of citizenship, justice and integration. Specifically, interest grew in how international non-governmental organizations and human rights norms have positively influenced and expanded liberal notions of citizenship at the domestic level. Examples of such models included: "transnational citizenship" (Baubock, 1997), "multicultural citizenship" (Kymlicka, 1989), "differentiated citizenship" (Young, 1989), "neo-Republican citizenship" (Van Gunsteren, 1996), "cultural citizenship" (Turner, 1993), "citizenship across borders" (Jacobson, 1996), and "post-national membership" (Soysal, 1994).

All of these debates focused on the normative content of integration and citizenship in advanced industrial states. Moreover, the context in which these theories were developed varied greatly. "Transnational citizenship" studies examined networks of migrants, with particular focus on the ethnic mobilization that connected home and receiving countries (see Williams, 1999; Brooks and Fox, 2002, etc.). Yasemin Soysal's ground-breaking study (1994) of "post-national membership" included the analysis of welfare regimes. Koff's (2005, 2008) studies of integration have approached this issue from the perspective of social capital, defined as the creation of political community.

In general, these studies examined citizenship through the relationship between rights and their extension to migrants. This strand of the literature represents "post-national" studies of citizenship (Joppke, 1998). Conversely, there has been a similar emphasis in the literature on migration of "national" studies, which reaffirm the relationship between migration and territorial policies (advanced industrial states and the EU). This is especially evident in supranational research on migration in Europe. For example, the study of the evolution of EU policies in the field of immigration is highly developed. Early studies from the 1990s, mainly followed forms of analysis found in EU policy-making debates in other arenas, which pitted realist approaches (based on nation-state power) versus neo-functionalism (based on the emergence of non-nation-state actors). For example, some authors, such as Spencer (1994), Marie (1994), Miller and Walzer (1995), Ucarer and Puchala (1997) correctly focused on the merger of the immigration issue with questions of security in EU states, especially following the adoption of the Schengen Accords, which abolished most of the EU's internal border controls. They noted that immigration policies were tied to the deepening of European integration in the economic sphere. Other studies (i.e. Collinson, 1993; Papademetriou *et al.*, 1999; Geddes, 1994; Ireland, 1994) from the realist school have argued that EU policies resulted from both formal and informal inter-state negotiations that took place in the Council of the EU, and EU policies followed the interests of the EU's largest and most powerful members. In all of these studies, the distinct focus of debates remained centred on how policy was made in the EU rather than the role of migrants within this process.

The politics of citizenship and migration on the other hand does include discussions of migrant mobilization. Usually, these relationships are framed in zero-sum terms, as models based on barriers generally frame the question of immigration in terms of conflict between "haves" and "have-nots:" those who have jobs versus those who do not; those who have decent housing and those who do not; those who enjoy the rights of citizens, such as voting, education, and health care, and those who do not; those who have access to social spaces and those who remain without. It naturally follows that notions of integration are often viewed in terms of a social "struggle" fought by the disenfranchised attempting to re-negotiate a social contract (see Lapeyronnie, 2006). In fact, many of the first scholars of integration at the local level framed their studies in such neo-Marxist terms (i.e. Rex, 1998; Gilroy, 1991).

While these scholars recognize the symbolic importance of walls, their zero-sum framework is too simplistic in its approach. This is one of the largest deficiencies of recent integration studies based on historical institutionalism (see Garbaye, 2005). These contributions focus on migrant efforts to "integrate" through the creation of autonomous political movements. While such movements are important, as autonomy can be considered a true measure of citizenship (see Rawls, 1971), such approaches have their limits because they ignore the economic and social spheres. One could argue that studies of immigrant entrepreneurship (i.e. Valdez, 2011) are also studies of migrant autonomy, but they are rarely framed in these citizenship terms.

Maria Teresa Capechi (Africa Insieme, 1993) correctly refers to the constant rebuilding of the walls that surrounded old city-states during periods of expansion as the goal towards which industrialized societies should strive. Whether referring to the European city-states that she cites or traditional immigrant societies, such as the United States, Canada, Great Britain, France, etc., when immigrants have successfully integrated into the host society, they have contributed to social and economic prosperity, which led to long-term, widespread benefits that far outweighed any immediate costs. Conversely, when tensions have arisen between immigrants and host citizens, the resulting social dislocation, expressed as increased crime, political protest, strikes, riots, etc., has had severe consequences at both the micro and macro levels. For these reasons, this chapter proposes a focus on social contracts. Citizenship rights and responsibilities have become subject to negotiation as indicated in the literature on migration but they have also become less hierarchical, as the literature on border communities indicates. Christian Joppke (1998) accurately contends that we have seen a deterritorialization of citizenship combined with a dilution of rights. For this reason, the notion of social contracts has become quite relevant to contemporary discussions of borders and migration.

Conceptual approach: why contract theory?

The social contract is almost as old as philosophy itself. Coincidentally, so is migration. Despite the fact that migration and borders are so relevant to our conceptualization of citizenship, the literatures presented above do not explicitly focus on social contracts as a means to negotiating citizenship (even though they do refer to elements of such contracts implicitly). This chapter argues that such an approach merits attention.

In general one can identify three characteristics of social contracts that are useful for migration and border studies. First, they link individuals to society through moral codes. The social contract, being an invisible and inherent agreement has a strong normative value. Therefore it links the political, economic and social spheres of citizenship to a single normative approach. Second, because the contract links individuals to society, it includes elements of both system-driven aspects of citizenship and actor-driven aspects. The contract explains both the barriers that block and mechanisms that facilitate access to citizenship and it addresses the roles that both native and migrant actors play in negotiating the terms of integration. Third, the social contract does not represent a zero-sum notion of competition in politics. The perpetual negotiation and renegotiation of social contracts includes an inherent sense of complex competition that does not have to be zero sum in nature.

Social contract theory also relates to important issues relevant to border politics. The first great contract theorist, Thomas Hobbes (1982) focused on security issues. Border security has become a major question in contemporary border politics. Scholars such as Peter Andreas (2000), Emmanuel Brunet-Jailly (2007) and Daniel Sabet (2013) have all acknowledged the prioritized place that security holds in cross-border debates.

Hobbes obviously justified his vision of *Leviathan* by addressing threats to human well-being. It can be said that this view of a social contract where individuals cede autonomy to a government charged with protecting them is valid today. Scholars in border studies, such as Brunet-Jailly have discussed the meaning of border walls in contemporary societies. The walls that divide Israel from the Palestinian authority, the United States and Mexico, and Greek and Turkish communities hold both a policy and symbolic value. On one hand, these barriers are meant to protect the citizens of border communities from cross-border crime. On the other hand, these walls have also "securitized borders". Intra-regional integration has led to inter-regional division. Migration scholars, such as Hansen and Weil (2001) have noted this in their study of EU migration policies. Cross-border mobility, which once was seen and an asset for border communities, has been transformed into a security threat in public discourse. In border studies, these border walls represent what Michel Foucher once called "areas of fracture". Local cross-border communities in Europe, the Middle East, and the Americas have been divided in the name of "national" or even "regional" security.

Of course, should the citizens of these communities accept the restrictions placed upon them then the state owes them the promised protection that Leviathan is supposed to bring. It is here where many border scholars have noted that the system has broken down. Many scholars, such as Cornelius (2004), Alscher (2005), Ramirez and Cadena (2006), etc. have contended that cross-border security has broken down because of the securitization of these communities. Observers such as Herzog (1999) have contended that cross-border communities have suffered from blocked exchanges that securitization has caused, which in turn, has created social vulnerability and risk. In this case, one questions if the social contract remains valid.

Of course, not all social contracts are security based. John Locke (1980) for instance based his vision of the social contract on the protection of private property and the rights of men. For Locke, the state of nature was not insecure but property was unprotected due to a lack of impartial laws. The state's role is to protect property and the natural rights of men through the definition and implementation of impartial laws. These laws are to be based on the consent of governed individuals and they can be revoked whenever they no longer enjoy this consent.

Locke's approach to the social contract is also relevant to developments in contemporary border communities. Scholars such as Ohmae (1990), Alegría (2009), Newman (2006), etc. have formulated border theories around a conception of border areas as territories of flows of goods and services. For many, the defining characteristics of these regions are the economic flows that create "transit territories". This transit nature is similar to Locke's state of nature due to the difficulty of protecting economic rights in these areas. The nature of social contracts in cross-border communities is heavily affected by transnational commerce.

Finally, social contracts in cross-border regions include cultural elements that have been highlighted in the current literature. Similar to Rousseau's (2003) contractual notion of a "general will", which has more meaning than the simple aggregation of individual wills, current border studies often discuss the formation of cross-border identities, Scholars, such as Bonilla *et. al.* (1998), Gilles *et al.* (2013), etc. have examined the mechanisms that have led to the establishment of cross-border identities (languages, shared histories, etc.). Others, such as Scott (2007), have focused on how cross-border identity has been utilized by political actors as a resource for political mobilization. Rousseau's vision of social contract also includes a vision of the state of nature as being characterized by equality, freedom and happiness. This equality is demolished by the invention of private property and the emergence of individual interests. This contractual vision also has a place in contemporary border studies because of the mobilization of local cross-border communities in the struggle for human security and the protection of migrants' rights. A clear example of this is found along the US–Mexico border, where there has been much mobilization against the emergence of maquiladora economies. Similarly, residents of Lampedusa in Italy have assisted migrants with shelter, food and basic services. In short, this vision of the social contract includes the participation of civil society.

For the purposes of this chapter, these visions of the social contract will not be viewed as competing approaches but they are seen to be complementary. The empirical case studies will show that elements from all three visions are necessary for good governance in cross-border communities. Thus, the problem with border governance in Europe and the world in general, is that it is not balanced as some communities are characterized more strongly by one vision of the contract over others. The empirical cases illustrate this point. On one hand, Melilla–Nador represents an unbalanced case where the securitization of the border dominates border policies, thus creating social tension. Conversely, Bari–Durres is a border case where a balanced approach to cross-border citizenship has been implemented and despite policy problems that continue to prevail, the border area is generally characterized by social cohesion.

Migration control and border politics at the EU's external borders: Melilla–Nador and Bari–Durres

When the so-called Arab Spring erupted in 2012, it caused important population movements amid social turmoil. Once again, Mediterranean migrations were thrust into the limelight in European political agendas as some leaders, such as then French president Nicolas Sarkozy and then Italian prime minister Silvio Berlusconi predicted invasions of migrants that needed to be controlled, in some cases (Sarkozy) even questioning the relevance of the Schengen Accords.

In many ways, such debates have been a recurrent theme in European politics. Since the beginning of the 1990s, the EU has focused significant attention to controlling migration in the Mediterranean Basin, and Spain and Italy, amongst other countries, were seen to represent Europe's "soft underbelly". Since the 2002 Seville Council meeting, the EU has further strengthened its efforts to control its external borders. The approved strategies entailed the following:

A   *Harmonizing measures to combat illegal migration*: including the creation of a common visa identification system; acceleration of the conclusion of readmission agreements with specific countries identified by the council; approval for elements of a programme on expulsion and repatriation policies, including the optimization of accelerated repatriations to Afghanistan; and formal approval for reinforcing the framework for the suppression of assistance for illegal migration.

B   *Progressive operationalization of coordinated and integrated administration of external borders*: including joint operations at external borders and the creation of government liaison officials for immigration; drafting a common model of risk analysis; drafting common training procedures for border police together with consolidation of European norms concerning borders; and drafting a study by the Commission on the administration of external borders.

C   *Integration of immigration policy in the relations of the Union with third countries*: including a provision that states that

> a clause be included concerning the common administration of migratory flows and regarding obligatory readmission in the case of illegal immigration in all future agreements of co-operation, association or the equivalent that the European Union or the European Community signs with any country,
>
> (Guardia, 2002)

> and a systematic evaluation of relations with third countries that do not collaborate in the fight against illegal immigration.

Since 2002, the EU has further developed these objectives. Most notably, the so-called Hague Program, announced in November 2004, created a new five–year (2005–2010) multi-annual project in the field of justice and security, setting the following priorities for the Commission:

a   development of a common European asylum system with a common asylum procedure and a uniform status for those granted asylum;
b   definition of measures for foreigners to work legally in the EU;
c   reinforcement of partnerships with third countries to tackle illegal immigration better;
d   establishment of a common policy to expel and return illegal immigrants to their countries of origin;
e   use of biometrics and information systems;
f   establishment of a European framework to guarantee the successful integration of migrants into host societies.

Scholars of EU migration policies (see Lavanex, 2004; Geddes, 1995; Guiraudon and Lahav, 2007, etc.) have documented the externalization of EU migration controls. Aside from the establishment of Frontex, the common European border enforcement agency, the EU has funded technical assistance in third countries and integrated migration into regional security strategies. While the term "externalization" is not present in any texts/communications/projects produced by the European Commission, these texts utilize terminology such as "external dimension" of migration, "global approaches" or "neighbourhood policies".

In 2005 the EC established a Global Approach to Migration, whose priorities for action will now focus on Africa and the Mediterranean with the main objectives of "reducing illegal migration flows and the loss of human lives and assuring the return of illegal immigrants in safe conditions" (EC, 2005, p. 9). This approach also provides that any partnership between the EU and Africa will now systematically include aspects related to the management of legal migration, the fight against illegal migration and, the promotion of the link between migration and development.

The link between migration and development has been articulated through two sets of measures: (1) the outsourcing of border controls, through the sharing of responsibilities in the fight against illegal immigration (short–medium-term goal), (2) the promotion of co-development, understood as development partnerships with the aim of restricting incentives for unwanted migration (long-term objective). The first Euro-African Intergovernmental Conference on Migration (Rabat, 2006) conducted through the initiative of Spain, with the collaboration of Morocco and France led to a declaration stating the need to achieve a concerted management of migration in Africa, through the implementation of development projects. This conference was closely followed by another in Tripoli (November 2006), which resulted in a joint statement discussing "strategies to reduce poverty" and the "co-development of African countries" as key points to reduce flows of migrants and refugees (Conférence ministérielle, 2006b, p. 5). The proposed solutions include the promotion of foreign debt investment, cooperation processes and regional economic integration in Africa through the signing of Economic Partnership Agreements between the two regions. It is also worth mentioning the axes of the Rabat Action Plan through which multilateral and bilateral political and financial instruments have been set up to promote cooperation with Africa on migration issues on: migration management, bilateral readmission agreements, joint development agreements signed with allocation of specific budgets.

Of course, these two policy strategies need to be balanced in order to assure a complementary relationship between migration controls and development programmes. This partnership is highly salient for the EU's external border regions. On one hand, these communities are the places where EU border controls are enforced and where security is maintained. Conversely, local populations share historical ties to neighbour communities and these areas have been characterized by flows of goods, services and people, sometimes for centuries. This chapter discusses how these priorities are negotiated in two EU border communities.

Melilla–Nador

Melilla–Nador is a peculiar border because it is the external border of the EU but it is not recognized by Morocco. Melilla was the head of the Spanish protectorate in Morocco. The city has a population of 80,800 (INE, 2012) and it receives annual funding from Spain of €265 million. This border is said to be one of the most unequal in the world, even more than the US–Mexico border, which receives prominent attention in the borderlands literature. The region is noted for the fence that has been constructed, since 1999, around the Spanish outpost.

However, the day to day life of residents in this cross-border community does not reflect this reality. Instead, the area is characterized by historical economic, social and cultural relations. While the border is formally imposed, there is much informal exchange, as the area is characterized by "by the use and tradition of the 'the undeclared' ".

Traditionally, Morocco has paid little attention to the province of Nador. Consequently, both Melilla and Nador need as permeable a border as possible. Because Morocco does not recognize Melilla, no formal trade exists. However Spain has defined the economic activity in this area as "unusual trade", which is quite extensive and visible.

A dual scheme (legal and illegal) organizes business in such a way that it divides the local and tourist populations on one hand, and illegal, lawless or informal economic activity, linked to the redistribution of goods outside the cities on the other (Planet, 2002, p. 269). These informal trade dynamics are so important that they exceed the total amount of legal exports from Spain to Morocco (Soddu, 2002, p. 38)

Often this trade is conducted by women who have passports from Nador that permit them to enter Melilla legally. They carry heavy goods on their backs. They usually make three, four or five trips per day and they receive 4–5 euros per trip. There is no formal contract involved so this commerce is strictly informal, which leads to paradoxes in the local economy. This commerce moves goods worth up to €1,500 million per year.[1] However, behind this trade there is great poverty in Nador because this merchandize goes to the big cities of Morocco so the local population receives only a fraction of the profits from these sales. However, it is significant that, directly and indirectly, at least 400,000 people make a living from the cross-border smuggling of goods, in "irregular" activities that are tolerated by both countries (Cembrero, 2006, p. 234).

From a cultural point of view, this border region is also characterized by important dynamics. To date, 45 per cent of the population of Melilla is composed of Spanish Muslims. This has become an important part of local politics. Recently, a social and political leader of the United Left who was a member of the European Parliament converted to Islam, thus, highlighting the growing importance of religion as a mobilizing force.

Similarly, religion is visible in local politics in Nador. Specifically, the city is witnessing some signs of Islamic radicalism and this is influencing Melilla. More than the four cultures generally recognized in the region, four religions are promoted and this is very restricting but important. Identity is taking refuge in religion through this process. The "Rif Berber" is losing ground to the "Arab Muslim" in terms of the promotion of political identity (Interview MPDL1-Melilla, 2013). This of course, promotes differentiation that has been also been fostered through EU border policies that separate Melilla and Nador. Thus, local religious politics also affect the local legitimation of the securitization of the border.

This border has, in fact, always been a focal point for migration to Europe. In the 1980s immigration flows were dominated by the native population of Morocco (mainly due to family reunification and cross-border work). In the 2000s, a diversification of migrants began to occur as Algerians and sub-Saharan Africans began to arrive. Currently, local flows are mixed between Moroccans seeking entrance to other parts of Spain, and other migrants, notably sub-Saharan Africans and Pakistanis who have been placed in temporary detention centres.

The Moroccan migration flow represents historical migration. Almost all of these migrants are cross-border workers active in three sectors: domestic work, hotels and construction. Like the cross-border commerce described above, most of this labour is informal. Another group of this population are what could be called "passers-by". This represents a floating migrant population of about 30,000 to 40,000 people crossing the border every day in a kind of "circular labour migration" (Ribas-Mateos, 2005, p. 236). Finally, there is a group of between 10,000 and 15,000 irregular residents who have settled in Melilla since many years ago (Interview Prodein, 2013).

In the case of sub-Saharan migration it is said that this is a transit population but many people have stayed for up to five years in temporary detention centres. Between 1991 and 1994 between 300 and 400 sub-Saharan Africans entered Melilla. Sub-Saharan immigration increased every year since 1997 when policies were hardened. Currently there may be 2,000 people who enter Melilla illegally each year. The temporary detention centres house between 650–700 migrants. Most residents remain there for at least two years (Interview, PSOE-Melilla, Ex-Delegado de Gobierno, 2013).

In fact, the Melilla of today is very different from Melilla in in the 1980s when immigration began. If anything, attitudes against migrants have hardened, making integration programmes difficult to implement. Migration strategies are officially governed by Spanish national authorities. Local officials have relatively little input. Thus, most migration programmes are focused on border control and anti-smuggling/trafficking measures. This approach was made famous in 1996 when then Spanish President Aznar deported 106 migrants from Melilla and publicly declared: "we had a problem and we resolved it" (Martín Rojo and Van Dijk, 1998). Some 18 years have passed and Juan José Imbroda, another member of the Partido Popular, and current president of the Ciudad Autónoma de Melilla, has made a similar proposal: to create an "immediate zone of refusal along the border" as a possible "solution" to the recurring massive attempts to traverse this border fence during 2012 and 2013 (*El Faro de Melilla*, 26 April 2013).

Local NGOs have worked to guarantee minimum standards of human security in the area but their impact has been limited by structural factors related to the local context of Melilla, where the city's geopolitical role as an external border of the EU has dominated migration debates. Several members of NGOs interviewed for this study stated that the Autonomous City of Melilla has increasingly focused on establishing "high security" as its main priority. This trend reflects a decrease in the amount of local autonomy expressed in political decision-making processes while increasing the influence of the Spanish state, the Ministry of Interior and the government office in local migration affairs.

In this context, local NGOs active in migration politics can be divided into two groups: those providing *humanitarian assistance* and those focusing on *political advocacy*. In the first group, one finds those NGOs that are currently operating assistance programmes for the migrant populations in the temporary centres for immigrants, such as the Red Cross, ACCEM, Melilla Acoge and Caritas, among others. These NGOs provide education to youths, empowerment programmes to women, legal assistance, cultural activities and they address health needs as they arise.

In the second group, special reference is made to those NGOs that focus their work around the public denunciation of violations of human rights of immigrants detained in the temporary migration centres as well as those that monitor border crossings and count the number of migrants from sub-Saharan Africa that jump the fence surrounding Melilla (according to these NGOs between 1,000 and 2,000 people allegedly are "waiting to move to Europe" in the mountain area of Nador Province known as the "Monte Gurugú"). These organizations include PRODEIN, MPDL, APDHA-Melilla, Periodismo Humano, Frontra Sur (Blogspot), Quelaya Ecologistas, Caminando Fronteras.

Despite the classification of local NGOs into these two groups, it is important to note that some collaboration does exist between these different types of organizations. For example, advocacy NGOs from time to time conduct training, awareness and participation programmes, with humanitarian NGOs also performing these services in addition to their usual humanitarian assistance. It is also important to note that local NGOs are "forced" at times to collaborate due to the structural factors mentioned above: because Melilla is an external border of the EU, many local organizations are part of international and national networks, programmes and campaigns in defence of the human rights of immigrants. Significant movements that have emerged over the last 15 years have promoted: "intercultural citizenship" (la Red Acoge), "inclusive citizenship" (APDHA), "security, development and human rights" (MPDL). The "Human Rights at the Southern Border" report, which has been presented by the Human Rights Association of Andalusia for more than a decade, is a benchmark of great importance in Spain and North Africa in addition to Europe.

There are two problems with these actions, however. First, they only focus on migrants living in the detention centres. It must be noted that monitoring the human security conditions and rights of the Moroccan population irregularly settled in Melilla (mainly in Districts V and VI) remains less prominent in local debates. A representative of a local NGO stated in an interview:

> Here irregular migrants are completely exposed. At least those living in the detention centers can count on specific services: the can eat, they can sleep, they can live, they can return ... but not the Moroccans, not the irregular migrants.
>
> (Interview MPDL2-Melilla, 2013)

Already, the approach to managing migration in this area does not account for larger questions regarding the political economy or history of the region and the role of human rights in its evolution. Migration strategies are even more restrictive considering that debates squarely focus on those migrants living in detention centres, which represent about 5 per cent of the total irregular migrant population in Melilla. The other 95 per cent are completely marginalized as they do not receive any official support, nor do many NGOs focus their attention on them as the informality in which they live is considered to be part of the local landscape.

Second, these initiatives led by NGOs are assistential in nature. They provide basic services to migrants that have been detained but there is little work to facilitate for migrants the transition from marginalized population to local citizens through long-term integration programmes. Migrants remain clients of these strategies rather than participants. This hurts, in fact, access to citizenship in local debates. Consequently, one can argue that migration strategies in Melilla–Nador have established a dynamic that has not facilitated the re-negotiation of social contracts and this has perpetuated marginalization and exclusion. The limits of this approach are even more evident when placed in a comparative perspective.

Bari–Durres

Like Melilla–Nador, migration between Bari and Durres began in the late 1980s and it increased dramatically in the 1990s. During this period, migration from Albania represented a real human emergency. Between 10,000 and 20,000 clandestine Albanian migrants were intercepted by the Italian coastguard in the province of Bari every year in the early–mid-1990s. The high point of these flows was 1996 when 21,000 clandestine migrants were apprehended along local shores. During this decade, over 4,000 migrants died from drowning in the waters between Bari and Durres.

Throughout this period, the Italian state reacted to migration in a similar way to Spain. A temporary detention centre was established near Bari's airport and local officials were left alone to face integration problems. It must be noted, however, that unlike the reaction in Melilla, the inhabitants of Puglia (the region in which Bari is located) reacted proactively in the face of these migration flows. They provided migrants with food, and clothing and sometimes, they even opened their homes to them. For these reasons, Bari's newspaper led a campaign in 1998 to nominate the region of Puglia for the Nobel Peace Prize.

During this period, Bari was viewed to be a transit city. Like Melilla, the migrants who arrived there often moved on to other parts of Italy or Europe. Moreover, immigration was linked with organized crime as Italian and Albanian criminal groups cooperated in a multinational business that included human trafficking, the importation of illegal cigarettes to Italy, the smuggling of arms and stolen cars into the Balkans and drugs (see Miletitch, 1998).

This phenomenon facilitated a reaction towards the securitization of migration strategies in the area. Bari was formally recognized as a "frontier of Europe", which permitted the EU to invest in border control strategies. The Italian coastguard received financial and technical contributions from the EU to increase their patrols in the Adriatic Basin. By 2000, Italian officials were boarding 3,500 vessels per year, they had detained over 17,000 clandestine migrants and they had arrested 282 traffickers (see Koff, 2005). Clandestine migration was pushed to the South as smuggling routes around Bari were disrupted. In 1999, 243.54 people per 1,000 residents were arrested for contraband in the province of Bari. By 2003, this figure had decreased to 2.42 people per 1,000 residents (see Koff, 2007).

It must be noted, however, the clandestine migration around Bari followed similar patterns to that which is occurring in Melilla. As Albania stabilized politically and improved economically, it transformed from a sending state to a transit country itself. Migrants passing through Albania to Bari included Sri Lankans, Chinese, Moldovans, Kosovars, etc. Like Melilla, this created a bifurcation of migration flows between asylum seekers that were directed towards detention centres and Albanian migrants working in the local informal economy.

This is where the similarity ends between these research cases. The response to migration in Bari–Durres has been significantly more comprehensive than that found in Melilla–Nador. First, civil society cooperation has been significant in the local fight for migrants' rights. During the 1990s, international associations, such as the Red Cross, were active in Durres attempting to provide would-be migrants with the tools to survive their journey across the Adriatic. These organizations also informed their counterparts in Italy of flows so that preparations could be made to receive migrants when they arrived. In Bari, numerous associations were established during this period to provide clandestine migrants with provisions and services. In some case, local NGOs even attempted to facilitate employment for migrants, especially in the domestic or agricultural sectors.

What is interesting about this case, however, is the links that local officials established between migration and cross-border cooperation. In the early 1990s, Bari was a city with very high unemployment and a class of political elites that had been discredited by the *tangentopoli* corruption scandal. In Durres, similar problems existed due to the fall of communism in that country.

In both cities, a new class of political elites emerged, notably from the business sector and civil society, and they created an alliance aimed at opening new economic opportunities in the region. Unlike the cross-border cooperation in Melilla–Nador, which occurred only in the informal sector, cross-border integration between Bari and Durres was aimed at overcoming informality. In Durres, taxes were a real problem following the fall of communism as the Albanian state had no legitimate tax system in place. Similarly, over two-thirds of the economy in Bari was considered informal during this period (see Viesti, 1998). Through a series of programmes that included local government officials on both sides of the Adriatic Sea as well as business organizations and unions, informality (which nonetheless remains an issue in this area) decreased significantly in Bari and Durres. Specific players in this strategy included the Chambers of Commerce from both Bari and Durres and the *Fiera del Levante* trade organization. Moreover, through EU investments, such as the Corridor 8 or Interreg Adriatic programmes, trade between these two port cities has increased significantly, which has provided both cities with important economic platforms and infrastructure on which to plan their future development. Presently, more than two million tons of merchandize pass between these ports, which represent 85 per cent of all imports and exports to/ from Albania (Koff, 2009). In both cities, unemployment rates have decreased to approximately 12 per cent.

This had a positive impact on migration in the area. Between the security measures aimed at combatting organized crime and the improved economic regulation of labour markets, migration became less precarious in nature. While migrants still work informally in rural areas surrounding Bari and Durres, they have entered the regular urban labour market in small and medium size enterprises in both cities (see Koff, 2008). In Bari, an interesting phenomenon has occurred as migrant unemployment rates actually decreased below the overall rates for the city (see Koff, 2008).

Finally, the role of civil society and Bari's local government in local integration strategies must be mentioned. In the 1990s, the city of Bari had a "migrant integration office" that was little more than an information desk. Similarly, a "migrants' council" had been established by representatives of the Communist Refoundation Party but the council never met and it did not participate in native integration debates.

Local associations and representatives maintained high levels of activity during the beginning part of this century to improve both services for migrants and their role in local politics. Specifically, the city of Bari has improved its school services for migrants and in accordance with the Metropoli di Bari project, intercultural integration has become a characteristic of local education. Also, the migrants' council has been activated by the present city government so it provides migrants with a voice in local politics that they did not have before. Consequently, avenues for the integration of migrants have opened as the city of Bari has increased its participation in cross-border cooperation projects with the city of Durres. These projects have opened avenues to migrants for improved political activity, regular economic activities and continued social integration. This seems to indicate that changing cross-border social contracts can have positive effects on migrant integration.

Conclusion

This chapter has argued that the migration and border studies literatures could benefit from more explicit discussions of social contracts. It then discussed this proposal within the framework of reflections on contemporary migration politics in Melilla–Nador and Bari–Durres. In the case of Melilla-Nador, migrants remain as excluded today as they were in 1990. The chapter contends that this has occurred because of the lack of a social contract guaranteeing citizenship to all residents in the region. On one hand, a formal barrier to the renegotiation of this contract is the refusal of the Moroccan government to recognize Melilla. However, this difficulty is compounded by the fact that the EU has securitized the border separating these two cities, which has divided the formal and informal spheres of citizenship. The considerations presented above indicate that the formal contract between local residents and political authorities do not match the dynamics of cross-border exchange that exist in these communities. In fact, migration strategies in the area are based strictly on the notion of control/protection. However, cross-border trade exists informally, outside the sphere of state regulation. Moreover, the seeming radicalization of Islam in the area suggests that a collective general will support cross-border integration and free movement is eroding. This contract is unbalanced because it focuses entirely on protection (Hobbes, 1982) while ignoring the economic (Locke, 1980) and cultural (Rousseau, 2003) aspects of social contracts. As a result, the bases on which the local migration system functions are more present in the informal than in the formal realm of politics, which is a dangerous perspective because this can lead to a "chaotic state of nature" characterized by a lack of legitimate governance.

Conversely, the case of Bari–Durres presents a migration governance strategy that is based on the renegotiation of cross-border social contracts. In the early 1990s, both cities were facing political and economic crises. Socially, migration was regulated more by organized crime than the state. This created a situation of both public and human insecurity. While the protection aspects of the social contract were reinforced through EU investments in policing efforts (Hobbes, 1982), these initiatives were reinforced by local cross-border) economic planning (Locke, 1980) and social cooperation between civil society groups (Rousseau, 2003). Cross-border cooperation led to increased trade between the cities' ports and improved economic relations amongst small and medium sized companies, especially in the field of manufacturing. This has attenuated the problem of informality in the region and it has led to a less precarious situation for migrant workers and the local population in general. Also, cross-border civil society cooperation has led to improved social protection for migrants, and NGOs in Bari have championed increased political representation and participation in local migration debates. While specific problems still exist in relation to migration in the area (the treatment of migrants in detention centres, etc.) there has been a general trend toward the improvement of citizenship and human security in this cross-border community. In this sense, the renegotiation of the social contract across national borders has proven an effective tool through which migration has been governed. While the EU recognizes the need to link development and migration strategies at the macro level, it has not yet identified mechanisms for the implementation of these programmes. The arguments presented here indicate that at least one mechanism already exists and should the EU more forcefully promote cross-border political, socio-economic and cultural cooperation in relation with the promotion of migration flows, then it could more effectively support economic growth in these regions and govern migration intelligently. Coercion control strategies at the union's external borders are not only inefficient and ineffective, but they are counterproductive to the well-being of the communities where they are being implemented.

Note

1 In November 2005, Emilio Carreira, Minister of Economy and Finance of Ceuta, estimated that the money generated by the border trade (Ceuta and Melilla) represents €1 billion annually. Driss Benhima, the director of the Agency of Northern Morocco, estimated in 2003, that the figure reached €1.3 billion. Moreover, Abderrazzak el Mossadeq, who was Minister of Economics and Director of Customs, suggested the figure of €1.5 billion, the same amount provided by the American Chamber of Commerce in Casablanca (Ferrer Gallardo, 2008, p. 138).

References

Africa Insieme (1993). Oltre le vechie mura: una città piu grande. Unpublished acts of a conference held in Livorno 26 March 1993.

Alarcon, R. (2005). Mexican migration flows in Tijuana-San Diego in a context of economic uncertainty. In Kiy, R. and Woodruff, C. (eds). *The Ties that Bind Us*. La Jolla: Center for US–Mexico Studies: 99–122.

Alegría, T. (2009). *Metropólis transfronteriza*. Tijuana: Colegio de la Frontera Norte.

Alscher, S. (2005). Knocking at the doors of "Fortress Europe": migration and border control in Southern Spain and Eastern Poland. *CCIS Working Paper*. 126: 1–28.

Amendola, G. (1985). Segni e Evidenze. In Mendola, G., Barbanente, A., Borri, D., Ferrara, F. and Nuzzolese, V., *Segni & Evidenze*. Bari: Edizioni Dedalo.

Ancona, G. (1990). *Migrazioni mediterranee e mercato del lavoro*. Bari: Cacucci.

Anderson, J. (2001). Theorizing state borders: "politics/economics" and democracy in capitalism. *CIBR Working Papers in Border Studies*. CIBR/WP01–1: 1–34.

Andreas, P. (2000). *Border Games: Policing the US Mexico Divide*. Ithaca: Cornell University Press.

Aykaç, A. (1994). *Transborder Regionalisation: an Analysis of Transborder Cooperation Structures in Western Europe within the Context of European Integration and Decentralisation towards Regional and Local Governments*. Sindelfingen: Libertas.

Aziza, M. (2011). Une frontiere europeenne en terre marocaine. Analyse des relations transfrontalieres entre Nador et Melilla. In Ribas Mateos, N. (ed.). *El Río Bravo Mediterráneo. Las regiones fronterizas en la época de la globalización*. Barcelona: Edicions Bellaterra: 307–319.

Baldwin-Edwards, M. and Arango, J. (1999). *Immigrants and the Informal Economy in Southern Europe*. London: Frank Cass.

Bauböck, R. (1997). *Citizenship and National Identities in the European Union.* Cambridge: Harvard Law School.

Benington, J. and Harvey, J. (1998). Transnational local authority networking within the European Union: passing fashion or new paradigm? In Marsh, D. (ed.). *Comparing Policy Networks.* Buckingham: Open University Press: 149–671.

Blatter, J. (2001). De-bordering the world of states: toward a multilevel system in Europe and a multipolity system in North America: insights from border regions. *European Journal of International Relations* 7: 175–209.

Bonilla, F., Melendez, E., Morales, R. and Torres, M. (eds) (1998). *Borderless Borders: US Latinos, Latin Americans, and the Paradox of Interdependence.* Philadelphia: Temple University Press.

Brooks, D. and Fox, J. (eds) (2002). *Cross-Border Dialogues.* La Jolla: Center for US–Mexican Studies, UCSD.

Brunet-Jailly, E. (2007). *Borderlands.* Ottawa: University of Ottawa Press.

Caraballo, L. (2007). Mecanismos imprescindibles para la integración laboral en la zona de integración fronteriza Táchira-Norte de Santander. *Aldea Mundo* 12 (24): 51–64.

Ceballos, M. (2011). La política migratoria de Ecuador hacia Colombia. Entre la integración y la "contención". *Regions and Cohesion* 1 (2): 45–77.

Cembrero, I. (2006). *Vecinos alejados: Los secretos de la crisis entre España y Marruecos.* Barcelona: Galaxia Gutenberg/Círculo de Lectores.

Collinson, S. (1993). *Europe and International Migration.* London: Pinter Publishers.

Conférence ministérielle (2006b) *Déclaration adoptée lors de la Conférence ministérielle euro-africaine sur les migrations et le développement.* Tripoli, 22–23 November.

Cornelius, W. (2004). Controlling "unwanted" immigration: lessons from the United States, 1993–2004. *CCIS Working Paper.* 92: 775–794.

Decenas de inmigrantes asaltan la valla y al menos 50 lo consiguen (2013). El Faro de Melilla, 26, April. El Faro Digital.es.

Duprez, D., Michèle Leclerc, O. and Michel, P, (1996). *Vivre ensemble les quartiers "sensibles" à l'épreuve de la vie quotidienne.* Lille: IFRESI-CNAF.

España en cifras (2012). Instituto Nacional de Estadística. Catálogo de publicaciones de la Administración General del Estado. Online, available at: http://publicacionesoficiales.boe.es.

Ferrer Gallardo, X. (2008). Acrobacias fronterizas en Ceuta y Melilla: Explorando la gestión de los perímetros terrestres de la Unión Europea en el continente africano. *Anàl. Geogr.* 51: 129–149.

Foucher, M. (1986). *L'Invention des Frontières.* Paris: Documentiation Française.

Frieden, J. (2006). *Global Capitalism: Its Rise and Fall in the Twentieth Century.* New York: W. W. Norton.

Garbaye, R. (2005). Getting Into Local Power. London: Wiley-Blackwell.

Geddes, A. (1995). Immigrant and ethnic minorities and the EU's "democratic deficit". *Journal of Common Market Studies* 33 (2): 197–217.

Gilles, P., Koff, H., Maganda, C. and Schulz, C. (eds) (2013). *Theorizing Borders through Analyses of Power Relationships.* Brussels: PIE–Peter Lang.

Gilroy, P. (1991). *There Ain't No Black in the Union Jack.* Chicago: University of Chicago Press.

Guardia, T. (2002). *New Strategies in the Fight against Trafficking in Human Beings during the Spanish Presidency of 2002.* Spain: Ministry of the Interior Spain.

Guiraudon, V. and Lahav, G. (2007). *Immigration Policy in Europe.* London: Routledge.

Hansen, R. and Weil, P. (2001). *Toward a European Nationality.* New York: Palgrave Macmillan.

Herzog, L. (ed.) (1999). *Shared Space: Re-Thinking the US–Mexico Border Environment.* La Jolla, CA: Center for US–Mexican Studies, UCSD.

Hobbes, T. (1982). *Leviathan.* London: Penguin Books.

Ireland, P. (1994). *The Policy Challenge of Ethnic Diversity.* Cambridge, MA: Harvard University Press.

Jacobson, D. (1996). *Rights across Borders: Immigration and the Decline of Citizenship.* Baltimore: Johns Hopkins University Press.

Joppke, C. (ed.) (1998). *Challenge to the Nation-State.* Oxford: Oxford University Press.

Keating, M. (2001). *Plurinational Democracy: Stateless Nations in a Post-Sovereignty Era.* Oxford: Oxford University Press.

Koff, H. (2005). Migrant participation in local European democracies: understanding social capital through social movement analysis. *Migraciones Internacionales* 9, 3 (2): 5–28.

Koff, H. (2008a). El poder político y la política fronteriza en Europa: la utilidad de comparar las fronteras internas y externas de la UE. *Estudios Políticos* 32: 195–226.

Koff, H. (2008b). *Fortress Europe or a Europe of Fortresses? The Integration of Migrants in Western Europe.* Brussels: PIE–Peter Lang.

Kymlicka, W. (1989). *Liberalism, Community and Culture.* Oxford: Oxford University Press.

Lapeyronnie, D. (2006). Révolte primitive dans les banlieues françaises. *Déviance et Société* 30 (4): 431–448.

Lavanex, S. (2004). EU external governance in "wider Europe" *Journal of European Public Policy* 11 (4): 680–700.

Locke, J. (1980). *Second Treatise of Government.* Indianapolis: Hackett Pub. Co.

Marie, C-V. (1994). From the campaign against illegal migration to the campaign against illegal work. *ANNALS, APSS* 534: 118–132.

Marks, G. and Hooghe, L. (2001). *Multi-Level Governance and European Integration.* Boulder, CO: Rowman & Littlefield.

Martín Rojo, L. and Van Dijk, T. (1998). "Había un problema y se ha resuelto". Legitimación de la Expulsión de Inmigrantes "Ilegales" en el Discurso Parlamentario Español. In Martín Rojo, L. and Whittaker, R. (eds). *Poder-Decir, o el poder de los discursos.* Madrid: Arrecife: 169–234.

Miletitch, N. (1998). *Trafics et Crimes dans les Balkans* Paris: Presses Universitaires de France.

Miller, D. and Walzer, M. (1995). *Pluralism, Justice and Equality.* Oxford: Oxford University Press.

Newman, D. (2006). The lines that continue to separate us: borders in our "borderless" world. *Progress in Human Geography* 30 (2): 143–161.

Ohmae, K. (1990). *The Borderless World.* New York: Harper Collins.

Papademetriou, D. and Meyers, D. (eds) (2001). *Caught in the Middle: Border Communities in the Era of Globalization.* Washington, DC: Carnegie Endowment for International Peace.

Pastor, R. A. (2002). A regional development policy for North America: adapting the European Union model. In Chambers, E. J. and Smith, P. H. (eds). *NAFTA in the New Millennium.* La Jolla: Center for US–Mexican Studies: 397–424.

Perkmann, M. and Sum, N.-L. (eds) (2002). *Globalization, Regionalization and Cross-Border Regions,* London: Palgrave.

Planet, A. I. (2002). La frontière comme ressource: le cas de Ceuta et Melilla. In Cesari, J. *La Méditerranée des réseaux: Marchands, entrepreneurs et migrants entre l'Europe et le Maghreb.* Paris: Maisonneuve et Larose Française: 267–281.

Planet, A. I. (2004). Melilla y Ceuta como regiones de destino migratorio. In López, B. (ed.). *Atlas de la inmigración marroquí en España*. Madrid: Taller de Estudios Internacionales Mediterráneos: 386–388.

Ramirez, Socorro and Cadena, J. M. (2006). *Colombia y Venezuela: Retos de la Convivencia*. Bogota: Universidad Nacional de Colombia.

Rawls, J. (1971). *A Theory of Justice*. Cambridge, MA: Harvard University Press.

Rex, J. (1988). *The Ghetto and the Underclass*. Aldershot, England: Avebury.

Ribas-Mateos, N. (ed.) (2005). *The Mediterranean in the Age of Globalization. Migration, Welfare and Borders*. New Brunswick, NJ: Transaction Publishers.

Rogowski, R. (1989). *Commerce and Coalitions*. Princeton, NJ: Princeton University Press.

Rousseau, J. J. (2003). *On the Social Contract*. New York: Dover Publications.

Sabet, D. (2013). Border burden. public security in Mexican border communities and the challenge of polycentricity. In Gilles, P., Koff, H., Maganda, C. and Schulz, C. (eds). *Theorizing Borders through Analyses of Power Relationships*. Brussels: PIE–Peter Lang: 79–103.

Sandell, R. (2006). ¿Saltaron o les empujaron? El aumento de la inmigración subsahariana. *Demografía y población*: 1–13.

Sassen, S. (1999). *Guests and Aliens*. New York: The New Press.

Scott, J. (2007). Cross-border regionalization in an enlarging EU. In Koff, H (ed.) *Deceiving (Dis)Appearances: Analyzing Current Developments in European and North American Border Regions*. Brussels: PIE–Peter Lang.

Soddu, P. (2002). *Inmigración extracomunitaria en Europa: el caso de Ceuta y Melilla*. Ceuta: Archivo de Ceuta.

Soddu, P. (2006). Ceuta y Melilla: gestión fronteriza, derechos humanos y seguridad. *Med 2006, Balance*. Granada: Euro Arab Management School.

Soysal, Y. (1994). *Limits of Citizenship*. Chicago: University of Chicago Press.

Spencer, S. (ed.) (1994). *Immigration as an Economic Asset: the German Experience*. Oakhill, England: Trentham Books.

Turner, B. S. (ed.) (1993). *Citizenship and Social Theory*. London: Sage Publications.

Ucarer, E. M. and Puchala, D. J. (1997). *Immigration into Western Societies*. London: Pinter.

Valcárcel Lezcano, D. (coord.) (1987). *Ceuta y Melilla en las relaciones de España y Marruecos*. Cuadernos de Estrategia 191. España: Instituto Español de Estudios Estratégicos y Defensa.

Valdez, Z. (2011). *The New Entrepreneurs*. Stanford: Stanford University Press.

Van Gunsteren, H. (1996). Neo-republican Citizenship in the Practice of Education. *Government and Opposition* 31 (1): 77–99.

Viesti, G. (1998). *Bari: Economia di Una Città*. Rome: Laterza.

Williams, H. (1999) Mobile capital and transborder labor right mobilization. *Politics and Society*. 27: 139–166.

Young, I. M. (1989). *Justice and the Politics of Difference*. Princeton, NJ: Princeton University Press.

13 Who am I?

Italian and foreign youth in search of their national identity

Debora Mantovani

Italy's new face

Italy has long been known as a country of emigration. However, during the last three decades, it has progressively shifted from being an emigration country to an immigration destination.

The 1981 population and housing census is a milestone in Italian migratory history, as for the first time net migration[1] expressed a positive trend (Istat, 1987): Italy suddenly found itself to be a country of immigration. This reversal trend was a novel experience, since the number of people entering Italy was due not only to post-colonial migrations and the return of emigrants (or their descendants), but also to the unexpected arrival of non-Italian citizens.

Nowadays,[2] Italy "hosts" almost 5 million foreigners with a legal permit of stay, which means that 8.1 per cent of the entire population is non-Italian. Since the 1981 census the number of foreign citizens has grown steadily, especially after the turn of the century. Immigration to Italy has often been noted for the speed with which it has developed and its heterogeneous composition (Istat, 2008): foreign residents have more than tripled over the last ten years and belong to 192 different nationalities. There are no more doubts: today, in 2014, Italy is a country of immigration.

Tangible and immediately recognizable symbols of Italy's new face are well-represented by at least two public figures: Cécile Kyenge and Mario Balotelli. The former is a Congolese woman who arrived in Italy at the age of 19 and earned an advance degree in ophthalmology; in 1994 she married an Italian and legally became an Italian citizen.[3] She was granted an almost celebrity-like status in 2013 when she was appointed minister for integration, becoming Italy's first black cabinet minister. Balotelli is an Italian football player who was born in Italy to Ghanaian immigrants. His parents gave him up to an Italian foster family, the Balotellis, who took him under their care. As a consequence, in accordance with Italian law, he achieved Italian citizenship when he turned 18.

Despite being less famous, another public figure deserves to be mentioned: Stephan Kareem El Shaarawy. Like Balotelli, he is a football player in a prestigious Italian football club. El Shaarawy is a good example of a mixed couple's son.[4] Brought up by an Egyptian father and an Italian mother, he was born Italian.[5]

These three cases are representative of a migratory process at its final stage. Indeed, settlement by foreign families, inter-ethnic marriages, children born in Italy to foreign couples and children of mixed couples embody a stable form of immigration (Böhning, 1967; Castles and Miller, 1993). This statement is also corroborated by official statistics. At present, nearly one in six (15.0 per cent) children born in Italy is "second generation": native-born children of foreign-born parents.[6] Just ten years ago they numbered only 6.2 per cent. More than one million, or over one-fifth (22.7 per cent) of the total foreign population, is under 18 years of age; and in 2011, 8.8 per cent of all marriages were inter-ethnic, up from 3.7 per cent in 1995 (Istat, 2011; 2012).

As a result, the long-term consequences of foreigners settling in Italy have recently become a crucial issue for politicians and scholars alike. However, even if it feels like a new topic for Italians, such a debate has already developed in countries that experienced immigration much earlier. Since the late nineteenth century, theoretical speculation has flourished around the idea of assimilation, especially prevalent in the United States, where society had to face new challenges linked to immigration and the academic community addressed the question "Who and what is an American?". Now, a century later, Italian scholars are asking the same thing: "Who and what is an Italian?"

National identity

National identity may be a useful topic to address the above question and some official statements issued to the press by the aforementioned personalities may help in finding a reply. "I'm Italian, I feel Italian. I'll forever play with Italy's national team. I've never considered the possibility of playing for Ghana's national team, not even when they summoned me", declared Balotelli; "I've never thought of playing for Egypt's national team, because I'm Italian. I'm proud of my Egyptian roots, but Italy is my home", acknowledged El Shaarawy. And Minister Kyenge, even if she was belatedly socialized to Italian culture, stated: "I am proud to be Italian".

The sense of an exclusive belonging to Italy, pride in being Italian and a feeling of Italian identity seem mostly to typify these "new Italians". Apparently, their statements – affirming a comprehensive national identification with the native group – might fit into the "classical assimilation theory", which had been the main interpretative framework for decades. According to this approach, minority groups, over time and across generations, are expected to become gradually indistinguishable from the native population through a "natural", inevitable and desirable process of re-socialization to the norms, beliefs, values, behaviours and characteristics of the mainstream culture and institutions of the receiving country.[7]

However, there are at least three good reasons to reject such a theory. First, even if the term "assimilation" has never fallen into disrepute in Italy, the ethnocentric bias embedded in this classical approach is reason enough to avoid its implications (Glazer, 1993). Second, it has been demonstrated that assimilation is not an inevitable outcome, nor necessarily a "straight-line" process, but it can follow a "bumpy" path at different speeds (Gans, 1992). Third, even if assimilation takes place, it is just one of many possible integration paths. In fact, Portes and Zhou's (1993) "segmented assimilation theory" recognizes two additional (and more likely) outcomes of migratory processes: "downward assimilation" into the oppositional culture of the streets/ghettos and inclusion in the "rainbow underclass";[8] "selective acculturation", which combines the retention of core elements of the values and norms of the immigrant community with social mobility.[9]

Even if assimilation has recently regained credibility as the most probable outcome (Alba and Nee, 1997, 2003; Brubaker, 2001),[10] a deeper analysis of new Italians' national identification reveals a much more complex scenario. An example is given by El Shaarawy's Italian identity combined with his pride for his Egyptian roots, which suggests that multiple identities may co-exist and that identity is not necessarily made up of mutually exclusive categories (Hutnik, 1991; Stryker and Burke, 2000; Phinney *et al.*, 2001). Immigrant children – chiefly if native-born – play an undoubtedly key role in the assimilation process, since – unlike their parents – they may rely on some advantages, such as: complete linguistic assimilation; strong socialization with native peers due to both the attendance of the same schools and the time spent together in social or extra-curricular contexts; educational qualifications achieved in the same schooling system, which allows for competition with natives for the same jobs. Nevertheless, their personal and direct experiences within the receiving society do not automatically imply a rejection or a lack of appreciation for their roots. A plain and "unhyphenated" identification with the majority group has, by now, become out-of-date and has been replaced with hybrid, multiple and cosmopolitan identities.

It would be a mistake to extend the Italian self-identification expressed by the cases cited above to all of foreign youth. In fact, their strong sense of belonging to Italy might depend on both their unusual position of success within the host society and their role of institutional/athletic representation of Italy around the world. Most foreign youth will never enjoy such popularity nor experience the affection of Italian supporters during a political speech or a football match.[11] Moreover, such celebrities' Italian identity might be reinforced by their achievement of Italian citizenship: a tool of civil, political and social inclusion (Marshall, 1964). In contrast, all children born to foreign parents – regardless of their birthplace – may not enjoy that kind of legal privilege, since Italian citizenship is hard to achieve (Hansen and Weil, 2001; Andall, 2002; Colombo *et al.*, 2009a).

Beyond that, identity building, especially in reference to foreign youth, is a composite issue. In general, different outlooks about this topic converge in considering identity as a multidimensional, dynamic concept. Members of a society do not have just one single identity, since everybody simultaneously owns and plays different roles, which evolve over the course of time. Adolescents are in the midst of a difficult process of constructing their personal and social identity,[12] thus foreign adolescents are doubly in the midst of a "shocking" identity-building process, since they inhabit two different cultural worlds. Hence, foreign youths' self-identification process is often characterized in terms of a "clash" between competing allegiances and attachments. As a result, foreign adolescents wear multiple and hybrid identities and may switch between them as their reference group varies (family, native peers, school, community of origin, wider society) (Rumbaut, 1997; Kasinitz *et al.*, 2002; Suàrez-Orozco, 2004).

Sociological and psychological research suggests that – when immigrants may choose freely – the self-identity of foreigners is a well-balanced mix of traditional and current values, behaviours and beliefs rather than a full assimilation to the mainstream society (Berry, 1980, 1997; Sam, 1995; Van de Vijver *et al.*, 1999; Zagefka and Brown, 2002; Berry and Sabatier, 2010). These two theoretical approaches – despite some differences – consider foreigners' self-identity a helpful aspect in investigating the process of integration in the receiving country.

Data and method

Until recently, Italian sociological literature has paid little attention to the issue of foreign youths' national identification. This is partially due to a lack of numbers, since children of immigrants have only recently become a visible and statistically significant phenomenon. Nevertheless, the dearth of Italian studies on this specific theme also relates to the marginal interest amongst our scholars, at least in the field of quantitative research. Previous Italian surveys on foreign youth have been largely dedicated to other topics, in particular school integration and educational achievement (Casacchia *et al.*, 2008, 2009; Mantovani, 2008; Dalla Zuanna *et al.*, 2009). Further cognitive efforts have been made by qualitative researchers (Bosisio *et al.*, 2005; Ricucci, 2005; Colombo *et al.*, 2009b; Caneva, 2011).

In order to investigate the national self-identity of the children of immigrants, the data used in this chapter are drawn from a survey conducted in 15 upper secondary schools in Bologna (a province in Northeastern Italy).[13] Data were collected during the 2006/2007 school year through a questionnaire administered to 3,020 students, including 663 foreigners[14] and 126 children of mixed couples.[15] The sample's diverse composition allows one to understand if there are actual differences in students' attitudes toward identity according to their national origin.

Table 13.1 shows respondents' chief socio-demographic characteristics and reveals that Italians and children of mixed couples are slightly younger than foreigners. This age difference is due to the fact that it is more common for foreign children to be held back at school. The Italian educational system usually enrols new foreign students in a class that does not correspond to their age. Putting them back a year or two is considered a useful strategy in helping them to acquire language skills: the older they are when they first arrive in Italy, the greater the odds of being enrolled in a lower year at school. Moreover, foreigners – especially those who were born abroad – have a higher probability of failing at school, due to their weaker knowledge of Italian (Mantovani, 2011). Despite such differences, the great majority of respondents (87 per cent) are between the ages of 15 and 17. This range is key when looking at national identity, since in this period adolescents' self-identity evolves and teenagers reinforce their sense of national belonging (Barrett, 2002).

Italians and children of mixed couples are also rather similar with regard to their socio-economic background, since their parents are more likely to have spent at least 13 years in the educational system and belong to the highest social class (service class or bourgeoisie). On the contrary, foreigners are over-represented within less educated and, above all, working class families, since adult immigrants often have jobs disdained by autochthonous people (Abella *et al.*, 1995; Ambrosini, 2001).

Table 13.1 Italians and children of immigrants by gender, age, parents' level of education, social class, length of stay in Italy, geographic area of origin, family composition and language spoken at home (percentage values)

	Italians	*Foreigners*	*Children of mixed couples*
Gender			
Male	54.3	43.4	54.8
Female	45.7	56.6	45.2
Mean age	16.0	16.9	16.1
Parents' level of education			
Low (up to a vocational qualification)	45.0	51.7	36.6
High (at least a diploma)	55.0	48.3	63.4
Parents' social class			
Working class	29.5	56.4	26.4
Petite bourgeoisie	31.4	25.2	35.2
Service class/bourgeoisie	39.1	18.4	38.4
Length of stay in Italy (years)	n/a	7.3	n/a
Geographic area of origin			
Italy	100.0	n/a	n/a
European Union (EU-15)	n/a	0.9	42.9
Eastern Europe	n/a	34.4	11.1
Africa	n/a	33.6	15.9
Asia	n/a	24.9	8.7
South America	n/a	6.2	21.4
Family composition			
Nuclear family	79.8	70.9	76.2
Single-parent or blended families	20.2	29.1	23.8
Language spoken at home			
Language of origin	–	69.5	0.0
Language of origin and Italian	–	16.0	–
Italian	100.0	14.5	100.0
(*N* min/*N* max)	(2,208/2,231)	(642/663)	(123/126)

Note
n/a = not applicable.

Young foreigners are also differentiated with regards to another crucial variable in determining their integration in the host society: the amount of time they have been living in Italy, here operationalized as a continuous variable.

The geographic area of origin reflects the heterogeneous composition of immigration in Italy quite well. Eastern Europeans and Africans are predominant among foreigners, whereas the share hailing from the EU[16] is numerically irrelevant. More than two in five children of mixed couples, on the other hand, have just one parent born in an EU country.

Family composition and language spoken at home are two additional factors usually related to national identity. The former distinguishes between traditional nuclear families – both parents and their children – and other families, such as: single-parent families (one parent has the primary in raising the child/children) and blended families (including children from a previous marriage of one spouse or both). The proportion of single-parent or blended families is slightly higher among foreigners. In fact, foreign families have a higher risk of being broken, since they risk not only divorce or death of a parent, but also the effects of migration, when just one parent decides to emigrate with his/her children.

Language spoken at home is a variable applicable only to foreigners, since – as one might expect – Italians speak only Italian at home, and – quite unexpectedly – the same is true for children of mixed couples.

Who am I?

To collect information on national identity, an open-ended question was asked: "How do you identify yourself, that is, what do you call yourself?" This question is drawn from Portes and Rumbaut's survey (2001), which assumes that identification begins with the cognitive act of self-classification, which reflects the desire to belong to one or more groups (Lam and Smith, 2009).

The four most common categories used in sociological research in order to examine the identity in which foreigners recognize themselves are: a foreign national-origin identity, which emphasizes the strength of an exclusive tie with the country of origin (e.g. Moroccan); a hyphenated identity, which combines a sense of belonging to both the place of origin and the receiving society (e.g. Italian-Moldavian); a plain, unhyphenated national identity, which implies an exhaustive identification with the host society (e.g. Italian); a pan-national identity,[17] which unites multiple minorities with one single label (e.g. Hispanic, Latino, Asian) (Rumbaut, 1997; Portes and Rumbaut, 2001; Song, 2010).

This classification has been widely applied in American sociological surveys and represents a useful starting point to examine the question of identity in Italy as well. Nonetheless, one should bear in mind that migratory flows in Italy differ enormously from those in the United States with reference to many aspects: type and number of national origins, socioeconomic backgrounds, geographic patterns of settlement, time spent in the receiving country. Furthermore, Italy and the United States show diverse economical, institutional and social structural conditions, which may influence identity outcomes.

A preliminary review of respondents' answers reveals a vast assortment of self-identification outcomes: 93 and 42 different responses respectively, among foreigners and children of mixed-couples. Despite this wide range of responses, the great majority (96.4 per cent and 79.5 per cent) may be associated with the traditional four categories. However, interesting differences emerge between these two groups. Foreigners identify primarily in their foreign national origins (46.6 per cent) and, to a lesser degree, choose a hyphenated Italian identification (19.2 per cent) or a pan-national identity (19.2 per cent); only a small minority recognizes itself as plain Italian (11.4 per cent). On the contrary, over two-thirds of children of mixed couples identify themselves as Italians (42.6 per cent), fewer than one in ten opts for the foreign national origin (7.4 per cent) or a pan-national identity (11.5 per cent), and equal proportions choose either a hyphenated Italian identification (18.0 per cent) or an Italian local identity (19.7 per cent). The latter element is rather relevant, since it adds a new category (Table 13.2 A columns).

A similarly detailed classification is also required to catalogue Italians. As one might expect, the majority chooses Italian national identity, but a noteworthy one-third adopts an Italian local dimension (e.g. region, city or town) and 6.3 per cent chooses an unusual hyphenated identity combining national and local dimensions.[18] Moreover, Italians' self-identity is also composed by a not negligible minority identifying in a pan-national category, which embraces two sub-groups: "world citizen" and "European".

A pan-national category is chosen more often by foreigners and children of mixed couples; these results are consistent with American surveys (Portes and Rumbaut, 2001; Song, 2010). Nevertheless, when used abroad the word "pan-national" embraces types such as Hispanic, Asian, Latino; in Italy the same

Table 13.2 Self-identity among Italians and children of immigrants (percentage values)

	Italians		Foreigners		Children of mixed couples	
	A	B	A	B	A	B
Foreign national origin	0.2	0.2	46.6	46.6	7.4	7.4
Hyphenated Italian	0.7	0.7	19.2	19.2	18.0	18.0
Pan-national	5.9	5.9	19.2	19.2	11.5	11.5
Plain Italian	53.2	91.7	11.4	13.5	42.6	63.1
Italian local dimension[a]	32.2		1.9		19.7	
Italian and Italian local dimension[a]	6.3		0.2		0.8	
National origin and pan-national[b]	–		1.4		–	
Italian/local dimension and pan-national[b]	1.4		0.2		–	
Total	100	100	100	100	100	100
(*N*)	(2,181)	(2,150)	(641)	(631)	(122)	(122)

Notes
a Categories reclassified in "Plain Italian".
b Categories excluded in B columns.

label includes other cosmopolitan and ultra-national categories, which reflect those used by Italians: world citizen and European.[19] Only a small minority of foreign youngsters self-identifies in other pan-national categories, but these percentages are irrelevant.

A plausible explanation for the different composition of the pan-national category[20] may be found in the diversity of foreigners' national origins.[21] In this sample more than one-third of foreign youths come from Eastern Europe, hence that may clarify the high proportion of European self-labelling. Nonetheless, if more than half of Eastern Europeans define themselves as Europeans when they choose a pan-national identity, respondents hailing from other geographical areas do not opt for a "continental" label (such as African or Asian) but rather prefer a cosmopolitan dimension (world citizen) (Table 13.3).

An additional explanation concerning the absence of the American-like pan-national identity categories might depend on the lack of such expressions in the Italian language. The US census form has always explicitly registered people's ethnicity – i.e. distinguished among Hispanic, Latino and Spanish origins – and race (white, black/African American, Chinese). These labels are in daily use as part of the vernacular – regardless of social class, status or country of origin differences – and that may influence the identity choice made by minorities, since those labels are imposed on them by others (Omi and Winant, 1994). On the contrary, in Italy such terms are not common, since the host society usually labels foreigners using their own country of origin and, consequently, foreigners themselves identify more in their national origins.[22]

This preliminary identity review requires to be reclassified. From both a semantic and a statistical point of view, it seems useful to combine the "Italian local dimension" and the "Italian and Italian local dimension" categories together with the "plain Italian" class, since all of them refer to a feeling of belonging to the place of current living. After such a reclassification, it appears that: Italians almost exclusively identify themselves as Italians (91.7 per cent); almost half of all foreigners choose their national origin, but the other half is quite equally distributed among hyphenated Italian (19.2 per cent) and pan-national identities (19.2 per cent) and – to a lesser extent – Italian labels (13.5 per cent); children of mixed couples are in between, since most of them identify

Table 13.3 Foreigners' geographic area of origin and self-reported pan-national identity (absolute values)

	European	World citizen	Arab	African	South American	Total
Eastern Europeans	30	23	–	–	–	53
Africans	3	33	4	1	–	41
Asians	2	14	–	–	–	16
South Americans	–	8	–	–	3	11
Total	35	78	4	1	3	121

as Italians (63.1 per cent) – but to a lesser extent than Italians – and, at the same time, a high proportion of them chooses a hyphenated Italian identification (18.0 per cent) (Table 13.2 B columns).

Data suggest that national identity is quite different between Italians and foreigners. The former place themselves at the extremity of a hypothetical continuum, whereas the latter do not just lay at the opposite extreme though being situated at a great distance. In fact, to some extent, foreigners tend to approach Italians displaying a complex identity aspect exemplified not just by hybrid (hyphenated Italian) or cosmopolitan (pan-national) identities, but by a plain Italian label as well. In the middle children of mixed couples are placed, becoming more similar to Italians after such reclassification.

Foreigners' national self-identity: what matters?

It has been demonstrated that children of immigrants – especially if both parents are foreign born – are characterized by multifaceted national identities. At this point, the question to be asked is: "Does foreign youth's self-identity vary significantly according to other variables?"[23]

In order to answer this question, the relationships between some key socio-demographic and cultural variables (shown in Table 13.1) and self-identity were explored.

As far as gender is concerned, results from past studies are quite discordant. Lam and Smith's (2009) survey on the self-identity of African and Caribbean adolescents in Britain revealed that females are more likely than males to retain their country-of-origin identity. Warikoo's study (2005) on Indo-Caribbean teenagers in New York demonstrated that both males and females develop multiple identities, but the latter – due to a stricter parental control and positive media images – are more interested in Indian culture (movies, clothes and Hinduism) and thus identify more with Indian traditions. Rumbaut (1994) found that males were more likely to identify in unhyphenated terms, using either "American" or country-of-origin labels, whereas females were more likely to adopt a hyphenated identity. Waters (1996), on the other hand, found that West Indian girls tend to be more bicultural than males, and Portes and Rumbaut's (2001) longitudinal study stressed how the relationship between gender and self-identity may change over time and a return – like a "boomerang" – to the identity of origin is a distinct possibility (Rumbaut, 1997).

In this study, the percentage distribution of males and females in the different national identity categories is quite similar and, consequently, does not reveal any relationship, as also stressed by an index of association (Cramér's V),[24] which is not statistically significant (Table 13.4). Such a result is consistent with the idea that national identities in late adolescence become less affected by individual demographic features (Portes and Rumbaut, 2001). In fact, another socio-demographic variable, such as age, appears rather non influential on national identity, but that might also depend on its low variability among interviewees.

Table 13.4 Foreigners' self-reported national identity by main socio-demographic and cultural variables (percentage values and Cramer's V)

	National origin	Hyphenated Italian	Plain Italian	Pan-national	(N)	Cramer's V^a
Gender						
Male	46	20	14	20	(279)	0.068
Female	40	19	14	17	(352)	
Mean age[b]	17.0	16.6	16.5	17.0	(631)	
Parents' level of education						
Low (up to a vocational qualification)	52	18	13	17	(314)	0.095
High (at least a diploma)	43	21	14	22	(297)	
Parents' social class						
Working class	51	18	11	20	(351)	0.109
Petite bourgeoisie	48	22	17	13	(157)	
Service class/ bourgeoisie	37	19	17	27	(113)	
Length of stay in Italy (years)[c]	6.1	8.6	10.2	6.8	(631)	
Geographic area of origin						
European Union (EU-15)	33	17	33	17	(6)	0.111**
Eastern Europe	40	19	16	25	(215)	
Africa	47	19	15	19	(212)	
Asia	57	22	10	11	(158)	
South America	53	12	7	28	(40)	
Family composition						
Nuclear family	48	20	13	19	(448)	0.041
Single-parent/blended families	45	19	15	21	(183)	
Language spoken at home						
Language of origin	54	20	8	18	(436)	0.210***
Language of origin and Italian	35	21	22	22	(102)	
Italian	28	18	32	22	(93)	
Total	47	19	14	20	(631)	

Notes

a *** $\alpha < 0.001$; ** $\alpha < 0.05$.

b All differences between means are not statistically significant.

c All differences between means are statistically significant (value for t test varies from $\alpha < 0.001$ and $\alpha < 0.05$, except the difference between the mean length of stay in Italy associated to foreigners identifying as follows: national origin and pan-national; plain Italian and hyphenated Italian; plain Italian and pan-national.

Family socio-economic status plays an ambivalent role: on the one hand, parents' level of education is negligible in determining foreign youths' identity; on the other, a statistically significant relationship is observable between social class and identity. More precisely, foreigners belonging to the service class and bourgeoisie are less likely to keep hold of their national origin identity and have a higher propensity for identifying in a pan-national category.[25] In other words, foreign youths in Italy, who may rely on economic and financial resources, are more likely to consider themselves as Europeans or world citizens. Such findings contrast somewhat with popular thought, since upper-middle class families are often considered more capable of passing down pride for their origins to their offspring. In fact, having parents who succeed (professionally and economically) in the receiving country is considered a good reason to feel pride in the national identity of origin (Rumbaut, 1994). On the contrary, foreign youths hailing from upper classes in this study have wider perspectives: their country of origin and Italy may be too small for them to comprehend. The former might be too far away – geographically and culturally – just indirectly known for being an eligible place in which to identify. The latter is just a crossing point, since they know their parents are able to support their educational and/or occupational careers outside Italian borders.

An uncontested key-role in determining foreign youths' national identity is held by the "length of stay" in the receiving country. The longer foreigners have resided in Italy, the weaker their tendency to identify with their country of origin. In other words, length of stay in Italy is associated with a plain Italian identity, which mostly characterizes native-born youths. This finding is entirely consistent with main international and national surveys, since the time spent in the receiving country is one of the most powerful factors promoting the educational and social integration of foreigners in the host society (Rumbaut, 1994; Boyd and Grieco, 1998; Portes and Rumbaut, 2001; Casacchia *et al.*, 2008; Mantovani, 2008; Dalla Zuanna *et al.*, 2009).

The language spoken at home is another crucial variable in explaining the level of integration in the living country and one that is positively associated with Italian identity too.[26] In fact, being fluent in Italian helps one to succeed in the host society, since the lack of a foreign accent may hide one's origin and hinder discriminating attitudes (Allasino *et al.*, 2004). Furthermore, a good knowledge of the Italian language facilitates relationships with other people and promotes a successful educational career (Casacchia *et al.*, 2008; Mantovani, 2008; Dalla Zuanna *et al.*, 2009). If foreign youths are used to speaking Italian at home, it might suggest a weaker attachment to their roots, which is also possible thanks to the empathy of their parents who have, themselves, acquired local cultural traits. Table 13.4 clearly shows how language may be associated with foreigners' national identity: if they speak their language of origin at home, the tie to their national origin identity is stronger, whereas it weakens in favour of a plain Italian identity among Italian or bilingual speakers.

Geographic area of origin is another variable deserving attention, not only because it is connected statistically to national identity, but also because countries of origin are associated with different lifestyles, attitudes, aspirations and expectations. In fact, as already stated, immigration to Italy has been renowned for its heterogeneous composition and it would be a mistake to analyse foreigners as a homogeneous group. Nonetheless, it is rather difficult to break down foreign youths' national identity by country of origin; sub-samples would not include a sufficient number of cases to ensure representativeness for most nationalities. In order to get around this obstacle, the single country of origin has been replaced with the geographic area of origin. This solution is not exempt from other theoretical implications, since it cannot be assumed that all Eastern Europeans/Asians/Africans/South Americans are similar. However, it is possible to assume that respondents hailing from the same geographic area are much more similar to each other than to people coming from other areas. Moreover, different countries are not equally represented within each geographic area; it is possible to detect few main national origins: 82 per cent of Eastern Europeans are from just four different countries (26 per cent Romania, 22 per cent Albania, 20 per cent Moldova and 14 per cent Ukraine); 83 per cent of Africans are from the Maghreb area (68 per cent Morocco, 10 per cent Tunisia, 5 per cent Egypt); 85 per cent of Asians come from three countries (34 per cent Philippines, 32 per cent China and 19 per cent Pakistan); and 71 per cent of Central and South Americans are from three countries (35 per cent Peru, 18 per cent Cuba and 18 per cent Dominican Republic).[27]

Data shows that Asians and South Americans are more likely to retain a close link with their country of origin, as shown by the high percentage of those identifying in their national origins; South Americans, along with Eastern Europeans, are also more likely to give themselves a pan-national identity, whereas no association is observable between Africans and national identity. No geographic area of origin is significantly associated with plain Italian identity. The only exception is given by youths from the EU, who are few in number and so of little consequence to this study.

The last variable examined is family composition, which does not show any statistically significant relationship with national identity. Such a result is consistent with Portes and Rumbaut's (2001) survey, which emphasizes that family composition tends to become less meaningful in late adolescence.

Foreign youths' self-identity: an in-depth analysis

At this point, it may be interesting to analyse if, and to what extent, "identity markers" (McCrone and Bechhofer, 2008) may depict foreign youths' national identity. In other words, the aim of this paragraph is to capture – if it exists – the association between a specific national identity expressed by foreign youths and a set of independent variables examined simultaneously. To do so, a multinomial logistic regression was performed: the dependent variable (national identity) is categorical with more than two discrete outcomes (foreign national origin, hyphenated Italian, pan-national identity and plain Italian). The foreign national origin was chosen as the reference category as it was both meaningful and the most widespread among foreign youths.

Model 1 in Table 13.5 brings together the different variables discussed up to now, with the exception of age (foreign youths' age within each single category of each variable is essentially a constant; moreover, mean age comparisons are always not statistically significant).

In general, results confirm that, *ceteris paribus*, national identity is closely tied to length of stay in Italy, language spoken at home and, to a lesser extent, geographic area of origin. On the other hand, parents' social class seems to be inconsequential regarding identity choice when all predictors are examined contextually. More precisely, the propensity to label themselves as hyphenated Italians instead of identifying in the country of origin (model 1, column A) is higher among foreign youths speaking both language of origin and Italian at home rather than among pure foreign language speakers. Model 1, column A does not show any other parameter to be statistically significant. A different outcome emerges from model 1, column B: the longer foreigners have been residing in Italy, the higher their propensity to identify as plain Italians instead of using a foreign national label. In this case, Italian speakers also show a higher propensity to identify as plain Italians.

These variables play the same role in model 1, column C, where the propensity to choose a pan-national category is examined. In this case, the length of stay in Italy and the language spoken at home (any non-foreign language) exhibit a positive effect on the propensity to identify oneself in a pan-national category. In addition, coming from an Eastern European country also heightens the probability of selecting a pan-national identity.

Before concluding this analysis, it might be interesting to investigate whether national identity is also affected by an important variable influencing foreigners' lifestyles and integration in the host society: friendships. During adolescence, belonging to a group of friends is very important. Friends are the third socializing agent after family and school, hence they are a key determinant when studying the definition of the self and personality. Friendships may acquire a crucial importance for foreign youths, especially if their friends are Italians, that is, people who know the place in which they live and its social rules very well. Furthermore, sociological literature emphasizes that the greater the friendships are between foreign youths and natives, the higher the probability of developing a positive attitude towards the host society and the lower the risk of encountering prejudices (Allport, 1954; Pettigrew, 1988).

Some data collected refer to the friends with whom interviewees spend their time and distinguish between nationally homogeneous (all foreigners or all Italians) and nationally heterogeneous (both foreigners and Italians) groups of friends.

Models 2 shows that friendship groups' national composition is crucial in determining foreigners' national identity. This model underlines that – *ceteris paribus* – being part of a group comprising Italians amplifies the propensity to identify in non-national origin categories.

Moreover, after the inclusion of friendships, parameters associated with the other variables included in the model do not reveal any significant changes in terms of both estimation and statistical significance. Such results reveal how

Table 13.5 Multinomial logistic regression analyses (model 1 and model 2) for variables describing foreigners' patterns of national identity (N=522)

	Hyphenated Italian: National origin (A)		Plain Italian: National origin (B)		Pan-national: National origin (C)	
	Model 1 β̂	Model 2 β̂	Model 1 β̂	Model 2 β̂	Model 1 β̂	Model 2 β̂
Intercept	-1.204***	-1.557***	-1.916***	-2.068***	-3.890***	-4.595***
Gender						
Female (male)	-0.203	-0.129	0.000	0.059	0.371	0.435
Parents' level of education						
High (low)	0.231	0.178	0.247	0.206	0.000	0.046
Parents' social class						
Petite bourgeoisie (working class)	-0.506	-0.540	0.028	0.009	0.145	0.057
Service class/ bourgeoisie (working class)	0.172	0.140	0.267	0.241	0.239	0.210
Length of stay in Italy	0.043	0.037	0.093***	0.089***	0.164***	0.160***
Geographic area of origin						
Eastern Europe (Africa)	0.331	0.322	0.507	0.497	1.040**	0.993**
Asia (Africa)	-0.511	-0.422	0.185	0.236	-0.105	0.143
South America (Africa)	0.285	0.210	-0.357	-0.400	-0.238	-0.389
Family composition						
Single-parent or blended families (nuclear family)	-0.217	-0.291	-0.395	-0.346	-0.375	-0.514
Language spoken at home						
Language of origin and Italian (language of origin)	0.927*	0.820**	0.332	0.259	2.017***	1.865***
Italian (language of origin)	0.469	0.381	0.653*	0.599	1.640***	1.564***
Friendships						
All Italians (all foreigners)		1.016***		0.635**		1.655***
Italians and foreigners (all foreigners)		0.266		0.047		0.591

Cox and Snell = 0.188 (model 1); 0.223 (model 2)
Nagelkerke = 0.204 (model 1); 0.242 (model 2)

Notes
*** $\alpha<0.01$.
** $\alpha<0.05$.
* $\alpha<0.10$.
Reference category in brackets.

friendship is an additional variable in defining foreign youths' national identity and, more generally, is important for social integration in the host society, especially if their friends are native Italians.

This outcome suggests that foreigners' national identity is a complex and composite issue. The main socio-demographic variables, however important, may only be partially useful in examining this sociologically relevant topic. Other factors might contribute to promoting a sense of belonging to the receiving society and stimulating a self-identity tied to the host country. It would be useful, for example, to investigate other characteristics of friendship groups: number of friends, type of activities conducted together, frequency in attending the group, personal perception of the importance of friends. Friendships seem to play a key-role in the definition of foreign youths' national identity.

Conclusion

The purpose of this chapter was to investigate the integration of foreign youths residing in Italy with specific emphasis on a topic largely neglected by Italian sociologists: national identity.

The sample was made up of youths in mid-adolescence, when self-identity evolves and feelings of belonging to a wider national identity develop. The main limits of this study refer to its sample size and the heterogeneity of the foreign population, which place limits on exploring country of origin's role in the construction of self-identity, the identity of mixed couples' children and their potential greater proximity to Italians than to foreigners.

Despite these restrictions, findings reveal that Italians, foreigners and children of mixed couples' self-identity is rather composite. Italians mainly identify as plain Italians, but a consistent proportion also chooses an Italian local dimension (region or town) or combines national and local dimensions. A high proportion of children of mixed couples prefers Italian or local identities, but many of them also choose either a hyphenated or a pan-national category. On the contrary, almost half of foreigners identify in their country of origin, but nearly one-fifth of them also define themselves as hyphenated Italians, and another one-fifth selects a pan-national category.

Even if variability characterizes all the groups examined, Italians are more likely to resemble each other because they select a territorial dimension embedded within Italian borders; foreigners are the most heterogeneous group; children of mixed couples are in the middle.

The effort to discover which factors are most closely associated with foreign youths' self-identity reveals that the longer they reside in the host country and the more developed is their tendency to speak Italian at home, the lower the chances of their identifying with their country of origin. In terms of segmented assimilation theory, it might be argued that an assimilation outcome – identifiable with professing a plain Italian identity – is more common among native-born children and youths living in families that have acquired some cultural traits of the receiving country (language), whereas a selective acculturation outcome – combining traditions of the country of origin with values of the receiving country, and recognizable in hyphenated identities – is more widespread among youths who are used to speaking both Italian and their language of origin at home. Geographic area of origin seems to be relevant only with reference to pan-national identity: the propensity to choose this category is higher among Eastern Europeans, who mostly identify as Europeans or world citizens. In addition, pan-national identities emerging in this study display different categories than those used by foreigners in the United States.

Perhaps the most important finding connected to foreigners' national identity is the role played by friendship groups. Friendship is an important component in adolescents' life and personality development, and may be able to influence foreign youths' identity. The propensity of foreigners to abandon their country-of-origin identity increases if they associate with Italian peers. This socializing agency seems to accelerate foreign youths' integration/assimilation in the host society, promoting their sense of belonging to the receiving country. As a consequence, friendship deserves a more in-depth analysis in order to better understand foreign youths' integration in host societies.

Notes

1 Net migration is the net flow of migrants during a certain period, that is, the number of immigrants minus the number of emigrants, including both citizens and noncitizens.
2 As of 1 January 2013 (online, available at: www.demo.istat.it).
3 The spouse of an Italian citizen can apply for Italian citizenship via naturalization.
4 In this chapter, unions between an Italian and a foreign born partner are called "mixed couples".
5 Italian citizenship is acquired through birth from at least one Italian parent, regardless of place of birth.
6 Italian citizenship legislation is based on *ius sanguinis* (right of blood): children born to two foreign parents in Italy are also considered to be foreigners. Second generations may acquire Italian citizenship only if they have resided in Italy legally and continuously from birth to adulthood. Applicant may apply for citizenship at the age of 18.
7 In the past, the idea of a straight-line and uniform path toward assimilation had been subscribed to by most scholars, even though it is possible to detect different interpretations of this concept and assessments concerning the key steps in the process. In fact, some considered assimilation as a relatively simple, individual and unidirectional process (Mayo-Smith, 1894a, 1894b; Simons, 1901a, 1901b, 1901c, 1901d, 1902), while others in the United States thought it was a social and reciprocal process made of several steps necessary to become an "American" (Park, 1914; Park and Burgess, 1969); some interpreted prejudice and discrimination as the main barriers to the "Anglo-conformity" process (Gordon, 1964), whereas a few others distinguished between cultural (nurture) and racial (nature) obstacles (Warner and Srole, 1945).
8 Thomas and Znaniecki (1918) already documented a higher propensity to deviant behaviour among immigrant children, and later some authors explained such a path referring to the "second generation revolt" (Piore, 1979) or the "second generation decline" (Gans, 1992).
9 This outcome was completely rejected by the classical assimilation theory, since it considered assimilation as a necessary condition for upward social mobility (Gans, 2007).

10 The "new assimilation theory" claims that – after removing the original ethnocentric bias – assimilation is still a valid hypothesis over the long term. The other outcomes are not rejected, but they are empirically marginal or phase-specific.

11 Nevertheless, popularity does not automatically offer protection from episodes of intolerance, which may hinder identification with the receiving society and strengthen solidarity within the native group (Epstein, 1978).

12 Psychological and sociological literature provides different perspectives on the identity concept and draws a distinction between personal and social identity. The former refers to an identity that promotes individual distinctiveness and hence an identification based on "either–or" dichotomies; the latter pertains to an identity that helps in experiencing a sense of belonging to a larger and more differentiated group following a "both–and" criterion (Elster, 1987; Tajfel, 1981; Stryker and Burke, 2000).

13 Bologna offers an interesting opportunity to explore the integration of non-Italian youth, since immigrants are not equally distributed in Italy and are highly concentrated in northern regions, where they find more and better job opportunities (Mantovani, 2008).

14 In this chapter, children whose parents were both born abroad are called "foreigners".

15 In sociological literature an agreement as regards classification of children of mixed couples does not exist. Portes and Zhou (1993), Portes and Rumbaut (2001; 2006) consider them comparable to children of two foreign parents, whereas others (OECD, 2006; Cebolla Boado, 2007; Szulkin and Jonsson, 2007) classify them along with native-children. According to Italian survey (Casacchia *et al.*, 2008), in this chapter children of mixed couples are examined as a separate category.

16 In this category, countries becoming part of the EU after 2004 are excluded, since many immigrants in Italy come from those states (especially Romanians, who joined the EU in 2007).

17 The original label is "panethnic identity".

18 This data corroborates the evidence emerging from a debate dedicated to young Italians' self-identification (Diamanti, 1997, 1999).

19 Only 14 children of mixed couples self-identified as "pan-national" (against 129 Italians and 123 foreigners), and caution is recommended in reading these data.

20 Once more, caution is necessary in interpreting these results due to the small numbers.

21 For native-born children, parents' area of origin has been considered.

22 Not even the Italian census form provides pre-arranged categories to differentiate foreign people from one another. The form simply requires one to indicate country of birth and citizenship.

23 Analyses addressing the same question with reference to children of mixed couples were performed but are not shown, since this subsample suffers from a low number of cases. Moreover, results do not reveal any statistically significant relationships between socio-demographic variables and self-identity, except for parents' social class.

24 Cramér's V varies between 0 (corresponding to no association between the variables) and 1 (complete association).

25 These considerations stem from the comparison of the distribution by national identity within each social class with the (marginal) distribution by national identity of the entire sample (total).

26 The knowledge of the language spoken in the host society is strongly correlated to the length of stay in the host country (Portes and Hao, 2002; Alba, 2004).

27 Foreigners coming from the EU (EU-15) are the least numerous subsample: only six interviewees. This category is not examined.

References

Abella, M. I., Park, Y. and Böhning, W. R. (1995). *Adjustments to Labour Shortages and Foreign Workers in the Republic of Korea*. Geneva: International Migration Papers (1).

Alba, R. (2004). *Language Assimilation Today: Bilingualism Persists more than in the Past, but English Still Dominates*. Albany, NY: Lewis Mumford Center for Comparative Urban and Regional Research.

Alba, R. and Nee, V. (1997). Rethinking assimilation theory for a new era of immigration. *International Migration Review*. 31 (4): 826–874.

Alba, R. and Nee, V. (2003). *Remaking the American Mainstream: Assimilation and Contemporary Immigration*. Cambridge: Harvard University Press.

Allasino, E., Reyneri, E., Venturini, A. and Zincone, G. (2004). *La discriminazione dei lavoratori immigrati nel mercato del lavoro in Italia*. Geneva: International Migration Papers (67-I).

Allport, W. G. (1954). *The Nature of Prejudice*. Cambridge: Addison-Wesley.

Ambrosini, M. (2001). *La fatica di integrarsi. Immigrazione e mercato in Italia*. Bologna: Il Mulino.

Andall, J. (2002). Second generation attitude? African-Italians in Milan. *Journal of Ethnic and Migration Studies*. 28 (3): 389–407.

Barrett, M. (2002). *Children's Views of Britain and Britishness in 2001: Some Initial Findings from the Developmental Psychology Section Centenary Project*. Paper presented to the Annual Conference of the Developmental Psychology, University of Sussex, 5–8 September.

Berry, J. W. (1980). Acculturation as varieties of adaptation. In Padilla, P. M. (ed.). *Acculturation: Theory, Models and Some Findings*. Boulder: Westview.

Berry, J.W. (1997). Immigration, acculturation and adaptation. *Applied Psychology: An International Review*. 46 (1): 5–68.

Berry, J. W. and Sabatier, C. (2010). Acculturation, discrimination, and adaptation among second generation immigrant youth in Montreal and Paris. *International Journal of Intercultural Relations*. 34 (3): 191–207.

Böhning, W. R. (1967). *International Labour Migration*. London: Macmillan.

Bosisio, R., Colombo, E., Leonini, L. and Rebughini, P. (2005). *Stranieri & italiani: Una ricerca tra adolescenti figli di immigrati nelle scuole superiori*. Working Papers del dipartimento di Studi sociali e politici, Università di Milano.

Boyd, M. and Grieco, E. M. (1998). Triumphant transitions: socioeconomic achievements of the second generation in Canada. *International Migration Review*. 32 (4): 853–876.

Brubaker, R. (2001). The return of assimilation? Changing perspectives on immigration and its sequels in France, Germany and the United States. *Ethnic and Racial Studies*. 24 (4): 531–548.

Caneva, E. (2011). Adolescenza e migrazione: una ricerca sui processi di identificazione e le relazioni sociali dei giovani stranieri. In Barbagli, M. and Schmoll, C. (eds). *Stranieri in Italia. La generazione dopo*. Bologna: Il Mulino.

Casacchia, O., Natale, L., Paterno, A. and Terzera, L. (eds) (2008). *Studiare insieme, crescere insieme? Un'indagine sulle seconde generazioni in dieci regioni italiane*. Milan: Franco Angeli.

Casacchia, O. Natale, L. and Guarneri, A. (eds) (2009). *Tra i banchi di scuola. Alunni stranieri e italiani a Roma e nel Lazio*. Milan: Franco Angeli.

Castles, S. and Miller, M. J. (1993). *The Age of Migration: International Population Movements in the Modern World*. New York: The Guilford Press.

Cebolla Boado, H. (2007). Immigrant concentration in schools: peer pressures in place? *European Sociological Review.* 23 (3): 341–356.

Colombo, E., Domenaschi, L. and Marchetti, C. (2009a). "Prigionieri della burocrazia?" Significati e pratiche della cittadinanza tra i giovani figli di immigrati. *Polis.* 23 (1): 31–55.

Colombo, E., Leonini, L. and Rebughini, P. (2009b). Nuovi italiani. Forme di identificazione tra i figli di immigrati nella scuola superiore. *Sociologia e politiche sociali.* 12 (1): 59–78.

Dalla Zuanna, G., Farina, P. and Strozza, S. (2009). *Nuovi italiani. I giovani immigrati cambieranno il nostro paese?* Bologna: Il Mulino.

Diamanti, I. (1997). L'Italia: un puzzle di piccolo patrie. In Buzzi, C., Cavalli, A. and De Lillo, A. (eds). *Giovani verso il Duemila. Quarto rapporto Iard sulla condizione giovanile in Italia.* Bologna: Il Mulino.

Diamanti, I. (1999). Ha senso discutere ancora di nazione? *Rassegna italiana di sociologia.* 40 (2): 293–321.

Elster, J. (1987). *The Multiple Self.* Cambridge: Cambridge University Press.

Epstein, A. L. (1978). *Ethos and Identity: Three Studies in Ethnicity.* London: Tavistock Publications.

Gans, H. J. (1992). Second generation decline: scenarios for the economic and ethnic futures of the post-1965 American immigrants. *Ethnic and Racial Studies.* 15 (2): 173–192.

Gans, H. J. (2007). *Acculturation, assimilation and mobility: Ethnic and Racial Studies.* 30 (1): 152–164.

Glazer, N. (1993). Is assimilation dead? *Annals of the American Academy of Social and Political Sciences.* (530): 122–136.

Gordon, M. (1964). *Assimilation in American Life.* New York: Oxford University Press.

Hansen, R. and Weil, P. (2001) Introduction: citizenship, immigration and nationality: towards a convergence in Europe? In Hansen, R. and Weil, P. (eds). *Towards a European Nationality.* Basingstoke: Palgrave.

Horowitz, D. L. (1985). *Ethnic Groups in Conflict.* Berkeley: University of California.

Hutnik, N. (1991). *Ethnic Minority Identity: A Social Psychological Perspective.* Oxford: Oxford University Press.

ISTAT (1987). *XXII Censimento generale della popolazione, 25 ottobre 1981.* Rome: Istat (vol. VI, Atti del censimento).

ISTAT (2008). *La popolazione straniera residente in Italia al 1° gennaio 2008.* Rome: Istat.

ISTAT (2011). *Il matrimonio in Italia.* Rome: Istat.

ISTAT (2012). *La popolazione straniera residente in Italia – bilancio demografico.* Rome: Istat.

Kasinitiz, P., Mollenkopf, J. and Waters, M. C. (2002). Becoming American/becoming New Yorkers: immigrant incorporation in a majority minority city. *International Migration Review.* 36 (4): 1020–1037.

Lam, V. and Smith, G. (2009). *African and Caribbean Adolescents in Britain: Ethnic Identity and Britishness.* 32 (7): 1248–1270.

McCrone, D. and Bechhofer, F. (2008). National identity and social inclusion. *Ethnic and Racial Studies.* 31 (7): 1245–1266.

Mantovani, D. (2008). *Seconde generazioni all'appello: Studenti stranieri e istruzione secondaria superiore a Bologna.* Bologna: Istituto Cattaneo.

Mantovani, D. (2011). Ritardo e ripetenza scolastica fra gli studenti stranieri nella provincia di Bologna. In Barbagli, M. and Schmoll, C. (eds). *Stranieri in Italia: La generazione dopo*. Bologna: Il Mulino.

Marshall, T. H. (1964). *Class, Citizenship and Social Development: Essays by T.H. Marshall*. New York: Anchor Books.

Mayo-Smith, R. (1894a). Assimilation of nationalities in the United States. I. *Political Science Quarterly*. 9 (3): 426–444.

Mayo-Smith, R. (1894b). Assimilation of nationalities in the United States. II. *Political Science Quarterly*. 9 (4): 649–670.

OECD (Organization for Economic Cooperation and Development) (2006). *Where Immigrant Students Succeeds: a comparative Review of Performance and Engagement in Pisa 2003*. Paris: OECD.

Omi, M. and Winant, H. (1994). *Racial Formation in the United States: From the 1960s to the 1990s*. 2nd edition. New York and London: Routledge.

Park, R. E. (1914). Racial assimilation in secondary groups with particular reference to the Negro. *American Journal of Sociology*. 19 (5): 606–623.

Park, R. E. and Burgess, W. E. (1969). *Introduction to the Science of Sociology*. 3rd edition. London: University of Chicago.

Pettigrew, T. F. (1988). Reactions toward the new minorities of Western Europe. *Annual Review of Sociology*. 24 (1): 77–103.

Phinney, J. S., Horenczyk, G., Liebkind, K. and Vedder, P. (2001). Ethnic identity, immigration, and well-being: an interactional perspective. *Journal of Social Issues*. 57 (3): 493–510.

Piore, M. (1979). *Birds of Passage: Migrant Labor and Industrial Societies*. Cambridge: Cambridge University Press.

Portes, A., Hao, L. (2002). The price of uniformity: language, family and personality adjustment in the immigrant second generation. *Ethnic and Racial Studies*. 25 (6): 889–912.

Portes, A. and Rumbaut, R. G. (2001). *Legacies: the Story of the Immigrant Second Generation*. Berkeley: University of California Press.

Portes, A. and Rumbaut, R. G. (2006). *Immigrant America: A Portrait*. 3rd edition. Berkeley: University of California Press.

Portes, A. and Zhou, M. (1993). The new second generation: segmented assimilation and its variants. *Annals of the American Academy of Political and Social Science*. 530. Interminority Affairs in the US, Pluralism at the Crossroads: 74–96.

Ricucci, R. (2005). La generazione "1.5" di minori stranieri. Strategie di identità e percorsi di integrazione fra famiglia e tempo libero. *Polis*. 19(2): 233–261.

Rumbaut, R. G. (1994). The crucible within: ethnic identity, self-esteem and segmented assimilation among children of immigrants. *International Migration Review*. 28 (4): 748–794.

Rumbaut, R. G. (1997). Assimilation and its discontents: between rhetoric and reality. *International Migration Review*. 31 (4): 923–960.

Sam, D. L. (1995). Acculturation attitudes among young immigrants as a function of perceived parental attitudes to cultural change. *Journal of Early Adolescence*. 15 (2): 238–258.

Simons, S. E. (1901a). Social assimilation I. *American Journal of Sociology*. 6 (6): 790–822.

Simons, S. E. (1901b). Social assimilation II. *American Journal of Sociology.* 7 (1): 53–79.

Simons, S. E. (1901c). Social assimilation VII. Assimilation in the modern world. *American Journal of Sociology.* 7 (2): 234–248.

Simons, S. E. (1901d). Social assimilation IV. *American Journal of Sociology.* 7 (3): 386–404.

Simons, S. E. (1902). Social assimilation V. *American Journal of Sociology.* 7 (4): 539–556.

Song, S. (2010). Finding one's place: shifting ethnic identities of recent immigrant children from China, Haiti and Mexico in the United States. *Ethnic and Racial Studies.* 33 (6): 1006–1031.

Stryker, S. and Burke, P. J. (2000). The past, present, and future of identity theory. *Social Psychology Quarterly.* 63 (4): 284–297.

Suàrez-Orozco, C. (2004). Formulating identity in a globalized world. In Suárez-Orozco, M. M. and Qin-Hilliard, D. (eds). *Globalization: Culture and Education in the New Millennium.* University of California Press and Ross Institute. Online, available at: www.geocities.ws/iaclaca/globalizedIdentity.pdf.

Szulkin, R. and Jonsson, J. O. (2007). *Ethnic Segregation and Educational Outcomes in Swedish Comprehensive Schools.* Working Paper. Online, available at: www.su.se/sulcis.

Tajfel, H. (1981). *Human Groups and Social Categories.* Cambridge: Cambridge University Press.

Thomas, W. I. and Znaniecki, F. (1918). *The Polish Peasant in Europe and America: A Classic Work in Immigration History.* Chicago: University of Chicago Press.

Van De Vijver, F. J., Helms-Lorenz, M. and Feltzer, M. J. A. (1999). Acculturation and cognitive performance of migrant children in the Netherlands. *International Journal of Psychology.* 34 (3): 149–162.

Warikoo, N. (2005). Gender and ethnic identity among second-generation Indo-Caribbeans. *Ethnic and Racial Studies.* 28 (5): 803–831.

Warner, W. L. and Srole, L. (1945). *The Social Systems of American Ethnic Groups.* New Haven: Yale University Press.

Waters, M. C. (1996). The intersection of gender, race, and ethnicity in identity development of Caribbean American teens. In Ross Leadbeater, B. J. and Niobe, W. (eds). *Urban Girls: Resisting Stereotypes, Creating Identities.* New York: New York University.

Zagefka, H. and Brown, R. (2002). The relationship between acculturation strategies, relative fit and intergroup relations: immigrant–majority relations in Germany. *European Journal of Social Psychology.* 32 (2), pp. 171–188.

Index

Page numbers in *italics* denote tables, those in **bold** denote figures.

For Product Safety Concerns and Information please contact our EU
representative GPSR@taylorandfrancis.com
Taylor & Francis Verlag GmbH, Kaufingerstraße 24, 80331 München, Germany

www.ingramcontent.com/pod-product-compliance
Ingram Content Group UK Ltd.
Pitfield, Milton Keynes, MK11 3LW, UK
UKHW021014180425
457613UK00020B/933